Parke Godwin, William Cullen Bryant

**Prose Writings of William Cullen Bryant**

Parke Godwin, William Cullen Bryant

**Prose Writings of William Cullen Bryant**

ISBN/EAN: 9783744686327

Printed in Europe, USA, Canada, Australia, Japan

Cover: Foto ©Thomas Meinert / pixelio.de

More available books at **www.hansebooks.com**

# PROSE WRITINGS

OF

# WILLIAM CULLEN BRYANT.

EDITED BY

## PARKE GODWIN.

Volume Second.

*TRAVELS, ADDRESSES, AND COMMENTS.*

# CONTENTS.

## I. SKETCHES OF TRAVEL.

## II. OCCASIONAL ADDRESSES.

## III. EDITORIAL COMMENTS AND CRITICISMS.

I.

# SKETCHES OF TRAVEL.

# ILLINOIS FIFTY YEARS AGO.*

HAGERSTOWN, MD., MAY 24, 1832: We left New York on the steamboat New York early in the morning (May 22d), and, as there was nobody on board whom I knew, I passed the time downstairs in reading Camoens. When, however, we arrived at a short distance from New Brunswick, we were all landed and transferred to stage-coaches, which conveyed us through a flat, uninteresting country to Bordentown, on the Delaware, a little below Trenton, where a sight of Joseph Bonaparte's grounds, beautifully planted with trees of various kinds, with a spacious mansion and a towering observatory that overlooks the river, made some amends for the dulness of the previous journey. Embarking on a little boat, with a civil captain, we arrived at Philadelphia about four o'clock in the afternoon, which gave us a short opportunity for looking at the city by daylight. It is better built than ours, or, at least, it is more to my taste, the private dwellings being solid, comfortable-looking edifices, without that tawdriness which you see in New York houses. The streets are remarkably clean, looking as if just swept.

At six o'clock on Wednesday morning we went on board the William Penn for Newcastle, where we arrived about nine o'clock, and proceeded on the railroad to Frenchtown, a

---

* From private letters to Mrs. Bryant.

distance of sixteen miles and a half, which we travelled at the
rate of ten miles an hour.  At Frenchtown the passengers
were put on board the Carrol, which likewise had a very civil
captain, an old, fat, rosy-faced, respectable-looking man; so
that I like what I have seen of the boats on the Delaware and
Chesapeake better than of those on the Hudson.  The com-
manders are, as such men ought to be, efficient, smiling, oblig-
ing men.  We sailed down the Chesapeake, a wide expanse
of water, with flat, low shores, very much indented, and offer-
ing scarcely anything to look at.  We reached Baltimore at
five o'clock.  I went to Barnum's Hotel, where I found John
Mumford,* who insisted upon introducing me to Mr. Flagg,
Secretary of State for New York, and one of the New York
delegates to the Baltimore Convention, which had just finished
its labors by renominating Old Hickory for the Presidency.
Mr. Flagg took me to a room where he made me go through
the ceremony of a particular introduction to about fifteen
gentlemen and ten ladies, and before it was ended I began to
feel, and I dare say to look, very foolish.

This morning I set out again at five o'clock on the Balti-
more Railroad.  There were in the cars with me three Virginia
planters from the lower part of the State, who had come, as I
judged from their conversation, to attend the Baltimore Con-
vention.  They were remarkably intelligent men—slovenly in
their dress, but gentlemanly in their manners, expressing
themselves with uncommon propriety and good sense, and
noticing very particularly as they passed every object worthy
of remark.  They did not seem to be professed politicians, for
they did not talk of politics at all, but well-informed country
gentlemen, and were, take them all together, a specimen from
which I am inclined to judge well of their class.  Two of
them exhibited somewhat of that tendency to metaphysical
speculation which is mentioned as characteristic of the Vir-
ginians.  The railroad is made, for the greater part of the

---

* A New York editor.

way, along the Patapsco, and, after it leaves that, along another little stream running westerly. The work is expensive, being cut through hills, and carried by high causeways through valleys, with stone bridges of solid masonry over the streams. This mode of travelling is agreeable and rapid. The vegetation in this latitude is scarcely more advanced than in the neighborhood of New York. The dog-wood flowers have not fallen, and the azalea, which I saw in flower in New Jersey, is in flower here also. Hagerstown, twenty-five miles west of Fredericktown, is a dirty little town, built in imitation of a city. It stands in a limestone country of irregular surface, rather fertile and pleasant, which is more than I can say for the greater part of Maryland which I have seen.

CUMBERLAND, MD., MAY 25th: Here I am, in the midst of the spurs of the Alleghanies, at a little, ugly town rather pleasantly situated on the banks of the Potomac, near the foot of the Great Alleghany or Back Bone Ridge. Twelve miles beyond Hagerstown I came to Clear Spring, so called from a very large spring in the village, and three or four miles beyond I passed Indian Spring, which is also a large spring in an enclosure under a great tree. Near the spring an emigrating family had halted with their wagon, and had made a fire to cook their breakfast. All along the road I observed frequently fires in the woods or enclosures by the wayside, where women were washing clothes at some spring or brook. Just beyond Clear Spring we crossed the first ridge of the Alleghanies, and, descending on the other side, came to the Potomac, on the banks of which we had a pleasant drive of at least ten miles. After passing a little town called Hancock, we crossed a loftier and wilder ridge, and so on, ridge after ridge, each one giving a magnificent look at hill and dale, till we descended to the Potomac again at Cumberland, having travelled sixty-seven miles. A woman, living in the mountains, being in the stage with us, pointed out, in a lonely hollow on a stream, the spot where the Cottrels murdered an Englishman some years since for the sake of his money. "The Cottrels," said she, " were working *hare* on this *pike*, and they came on with the Englishman a little ways on pretence of chatting with him, and as if in friendship. They got him near *whar* yon drift-wood *lays*, and *thar* they killed him in a thicket." The place where this woman lives, on the wildest part of the road, between two of the highest ridges I have passed, with a ragged forest on each side, is called Belgrove. The village consists of log-houses—that is, houses of hewn logs.

OFF MARIETTA: We breakfasted at Frostburg, on the Alleghanies, at a tavern where there was a grate as large as a kitchen-chimney, roaring with a great fire of bituminous coal, which is found in these parts in abundance. A severe frost had fallen the night previous, and the leaves of several kinds of trees had turned black, as if scorched. We dined at Smithfield, on the Youghiogheny, on corned beef roasted, pickled eggs, and boiled potatoes, with gravy poured over them on the dish. Saturday night brought us to Union, in Pennsylvania, situated in the midst of a most beautiful and rich country of undulating surface. The buildings are mostly mean and ugly, and the whole village, as all I have seen since I left home, is arranged without taste. The next day the weather was fine, though cold, and I rode to Wheeling, in Virginia. At eight o'clock I took the steamboat for Cincinnati, expecting to arrive in two days.

CINCINNATI, MAY 31st: The shores of the Ohio have nothing to distinguish them from those of a river of the Atlantic States except the continuity of the forests with which they are covered, and the richness and various forms of the foliage. The appearance of the woods is more like that of the Berkshire woods than those of any other part of the country I have seen. They consist of oak, sugar-maple, hickory, buckeye, which is a kind of horse-chestnut, the tulip-tree, the buttonwood, and sometimes the cotton-wood, which appears to be a gigantic poplar, and other trees common at the eastward, except evergreens, of which there are none. Springing from a kindly soil, they grow to a colossal size, and, standing at a greater distance from each other than in our forests, and being covered with a dense foliage, the outline of each tree is perceptible to the eye, so that you may almost count them by the view you have of their summits. With us you know they appear blended into one mass. It is possible that somewhat of the effect I have mentioned may be occasioned by the atmosphere. At a little past sunset it was very striking; each tree-top and each projecting branch, with its load of foliage, stood forth in strong and distinct relief, surrounded by deep shadows. The aspect of the shore where I have seen it did not remind me at all of the Highlands. The round, wooded hills which overlook the greater part of the way, sometimes approaching close to the water, and at others receding so as to leave a border of rich alluvial land, resembled, to my eye, the hills of Stockbridge, Lenox, and some other parts of Berkshire.

Cincinnati is surrounded by hills, and they are all covered with wood. They recede north from the river in a kind of semicircle, in which lies the town, and on the southern side of the river are hills also, so that it appears to be placed in a sylvan amphitheatre, through the most of which flows the Ohio, always quiet and placid, one of our noblest and longest streams, and justifying, in the placidity and evenness of its current and the beauty of its shores, the French appellation of *La Belle Rivière.* Cincinnati contains thirty thousand inhabitants. Some of the private houses are very handsome and costly, and the public edifices equal the average of those in New York. Many new buildings are going up, and among others a spacious theatre. The market is well supplied, especially with strawberries, of which I have seen tubsful. The inhabitants appear to be very industrious and busy, but they have a sallow look in comparison with the people of the mountains of Maryland, and the hills of Fayette County, in Pennsylvania.

STEAMER WATER WITCH, ON THE MISSISSIPPI, JUNE 3: As the boat in which I came to Louisville would not set out for St. Louis for a day or two, I transferred my luggage immediately to the Water Witch; but before she sailed I had time to look up several acquaintances. The town is built almost entirely of brick, and has the appearance of a place of much business—more than Cincinnati, although it contains but twelve or thirteen thousand inhabitants. Just below the town are the falls, the only rapids by which the smooth course of the Ohio is broken from Pittsburg to the Mississippi, a distance of nearly twelve hundred miles. They are avoided by means of a canal, though steamboats of the ordinary size which navigate the Ohio pass, but the large steamboats plying between Louisville and New Orleans stop below the falls.

We left Louisville at three o'clock P. M., and, the river being high, the captain announced his intention of going over the falls, the roaring of which we could hear from where we lay. The falls are divided by a little, low, narrow island, on the north side of which is what is called the Illinois *shoot*, and on the south side the Kentucky *shoot*, a corruption of the French word *chute*. We took the Illinois shoot, and, when we arrived among the broken waters, it was evident, from the circumspection of the captain, the frequent turns we were obliged to make, and the slackening of the speed of the boat, that the channel was very narrow. In one place the narrowness of the channel among the craggy rocks produced a great inequality in the surface of the stream, so that the waves were like those of the sea. In passing over it, the boat reeled and swung to and fro, turning up first one side of its keel and then the other, obliging the passengers to seize hold of something to keep them upright, and frightening the inmates of the ladies' cabin. It was over in a moment, however. A little below the falls the captain stopped the boat to let us look at the Homer, a magnificent steamboat intended for the New Orleans trade, just built at New Albany, on the Indiana side. It is as great a thing in its way as a seventy-four. On the lower deck is an immensely powerful engine, with, I think, eleven parallel boilers. Here also is the kitchen and other offices. Below this is a spacious hold, which appeared to be full of barrels of flour. On the second deck or story is the cabin, which had on each side twenty-five state-rooms, each as large as Fanny's bedroom in the *new house*, and each containing ten berths, with all the accommodations of a ship's apartment. The cabin is spacious and well carpeted, and each state-room has a good-sized window of two sashes. In one of them I saw a bedstead. The upper deck, or third story, is reached by a covered staircase directly from the lower deck, and is intended for what are called *deck* or *steerage* passengers. It contains berths for two hundred and twenty persons.

Last night a little before sunset we stopped on the Kentucky side to take in wood. I went into a Kentuckian's garden and gathered roses. His house was a large, ugly, unpainted frame house, with an underpinning like that of a New England barn—that is, consisting of here and there a log and a large stone, with wide spaces between. His peas were poled with dry young canes. About this time we passed the Wabash, which is the boundary between Indiana and Illinois. Its waters are more transparent than those of the Ohio, which are somewhat turbid, and the difference is distinguishable for some distance below their junction. We passed the mouths of the Cumberland and of the Tennessee in the night. This morning at half-past seven we came to where the Ohio empties into the Mississippi. The muddy current of the Father of Waters, covered with flakes of foam, rushes rapidly by the clearer stream of the Ohio, damming it up and causing it to spread into a broad expanse for a considerable distance above its mouth. Yet the Mississippi is not wider, apparently, than the Ohio. Its banks are low and covered with cottonwood, and a peculiar species of willow, or with thick brakes of cane, the same of which fishing-poles are made. Its current is so rapid that we are obliged to creep along the shore at the rate of about four miles an hour.

MISSISSIPPI RIVER, SIXTY MILES BELOW ST. LOUIS, JUNE 4th: Yesterday the day was most beautiful—an agreeable change from the weather of the day previous, which was

very hot and sultry.  I took occasion to go on shore in the
State of Missouri while the captain was taking in wood, and
examined some of the plants and trees of the country.  The
shores for the whole distance were low and unhealthy.  The
banks are continually dropping into the river, which is full of
large, wooded islands, and very irregular in its course.  I have
seen no prairies thus far, as the Mississippi everywhere rolls
through stately woods, in the midst of which you see, once in
five or ten miles, perhaps, a log-cabin.

Yet the whole scene appeared beautiful to me.  The sun-
shine, whether it was fancy or reality, seemed richer and more
golden than it is wont to be in our climate, and the magnifi-
cent forests, covered with huge vines of various kinds, seemed
worthy to flourish under so glowing a sun.  This morning
we stopped to get wood at a little town called Chester, just
below the mouth of the Kaskaskia, on the Illinois side, where
we learned that all the State was in alarm about the Indians,
who had made an incursion to the east of the Illinois River
and murdered several families.  You have probably seen that
previous to this there had been an engagement between the
Indians and a detachment of the whites, in which the latter
were defeated with the loss of fifteen persons.  I shall be
obliged to relinquish my projected route to Chicago, which
is said to be unsafe, in consequence of the neighborhood of
the savages.  In St. Louis, where the steamboat is carrying
us as fast as it can, which is slowly enough, we also learn
there has been a commotion of another nature.  An inmate
of a low house, called Indian Margaret, being part Indian,
stabbed a white man about a fortnight since in a quarrel, and
he died of the wound.  The inhabitants were so exasperated
that they rose *en masse* and attacked all the low houses in the
place, tore down two, set fire to a third, and burned the beds
and other furniture in all of them.  A black man called Abra-
ham, who was the owner of fourteen of these places, having
made a fortune in this way, was seized, a barrel of tar was
emptied upon him, and he was then slipped into a feather bed.

The people, among whom were some of the most respectable inhabitants of the place, began the work early in the morning and kept it up until sunset, while the magistrates stook looking on. Abraham made his escape to Canada, and Indian Margaret is in prison.

ST. LOUIS, JUNE 5th : We arrived here this morning at three o'clock. St. Louis is beautifully situated on a hill overlooking the river. Two handsome houses a little out of town are erected on old Indian mounds, on which the forest-trees have been thinned out. On Saturday evening we passed Cape Girardeau, a rather neat-looking French settlement, fifty miles from the mouth of the Ohio, on a green bluff—and a little while since we came to the old settlement of St. Genevieve, where we stopped to take in freight. I went on shore and talked to the men and women, who are very dark complexioned—some as dark as Indians, but with a decided French physiognomy. Most of them could speak broken English, but preferred to converse in their own tongue. The shores of the Missouri side now begin to rise into precipices, some of which are highly picturesque. It is, however, a cold, gray day, and natural objects by no means have the beauty which they borrowed yesterday from the state of the atmosphere.

There is much talk in St. Louis concerning the Indians. The families lately murdered lived on Rock River, to the west of the Illinois River. There were three families, consisting of fifteen persons in all. Their bodies were left to be devoured by hogs and dogs. A man has been killed in Buffalo Grove, near Galena, and it is supposed that an Indian agent has been murdered by the savages.

JACKSONVILLE, JUNE 12th: I left St. Louis on the 6th inst. at eleven o'clock in the morning, and proceeded up the Mississippi. I think I omitted in my last to say anything of the scenery on the river between St. Genevieve and St. Louis. The eastern bank still continues to be low, but the western is steep and rocky. The rocks sometimes rise into lofty precipices which impend over the river and are worn by some cause into fantastic figures, presenting in some places the appearance of the arches, pillars, and cornices of a ruined city. Near a place called Selma I saw where one of these precipices was made into a tower, for the purpose of converting the lead of the neighboring mines into shot. A small wooden building projects over the verge of a very high perpendicular cliff, and the melted lead falls from the floor of this building into a vat at the foot of the precipice filled with water.

I saw nothing remarkable on the Mississippi until we arrived within a few miles of its junction with the Missouri. I then perceived that the steamboat had emerged from the thick, muddy water, in which it had been moving, into a clear, transparent current. We were near the eastern bank, and this was the current of the Mississippi. On the other side of us we could discern the line which separated it from the turbid waters of the Missouri. We at length arrived at the meeting of these two great streams. The Missouri comes in through several channels between islands covered with lofty trees, and where the two currents encounter each other there is a violent agitation of the waters, which rise into a ridge of short, chopping waves, as if they were contending with each other. The currents flow down side by side unmingled for the distance of twelve miles or more, until at length the Missouri prevails, and gives its own character and appearance to the whole body of water.

At a place called Lower Alton, a few miles above the mouth of the Missouri, we stopped to repair one of the boilers, and I climbed up a steep grassy eminence on the shore, which commanded a very extensive view of the river and surrounding country. Everything lay in deep forest. I could see the woods beyond the Missouri, but the course of that stream was hidden by the gigantic trees with which it is bordered. On every side was solitude, vast, dark, and impenetrable.

When I awoke the next morning we were in the Illinois, a gentle stream about as large as the Connecticut, with waters like the Ohio, somewhat turbid. The Mississippi has generally on one side a steep bank of soft earth ten or twelve feet in height which the current is continually wearing away, and which is constantly dropping in fragments into the water, while on the other side it has a sandy beach. But the Illinois has most commonly a shore which presents no appearance of being eaten by the current, but which slopes as regularly to the water as if it had been smoothed by the spade. As we proceeded up the river, bluffs began to make their appearance on the west side. They consisted of steep walls of rock, the tops of which were crowned with a succession of little round eminences covered with coarse grass and thinly scattered trees, having quite a pastoral aspect, though the country does not appear to be inhabited. We stopped to take in wood on the west shore, and I proceeded a few rods through the forest to take my first look at a natural prairie. It was one of the wet or alluvial prairies. The soil was black, and rather moist and soft, and as level as if the surface had been adjusted by some instrument of art. To the north and south along the river it stretches to an extent of which I can not judge, but to the east it was bounded at the distance of about five miles by a chain of rounded eminences, their sides principally covered with grass and their summits with wood, forming the commencement of the uplands on which the dry prairies are situated. The prairie itself was covered with coarse, rank grass four or five feet in height, intermingled with a few flowers. Here and there stood a tall and lonely tree in the midst of a wilderness of verdure.

We arrived at Jacksonville about eleven o'clock. I supped at the tavern at a long table covered with loads of meat, and standing in a room in which was a bed. I was afterward shown into an upper apartment in which were seven huge double beds, some holding two brawny, hard-breathing fellows, and some only one. I had a bed to myself, in which I contrived to pass the time until four o'clock in the morning, when I got up, and, having nothing else to do, took a look at Jacksonville. It is a horribly ugly village, composed of little shops and dwellings, stuck close together around a dirty square, in the middle of which stands the ugliest of possible brick court-houses, with a spire and weather-cock on its top. The surrounding country is a bare, green plain, with gentle undulations of surface, unenlivened by a single tree save what you see at a distance in the edge of the prairie, in the centre of which the village stands. This plain is partly enclosed and cultivated, and partly open and grazed by herds of cattle and horses. The vegetation of the unenclosed parts has a kind of wild aspect, being composed of the original prairie plants, which are of strong and rank growth, and some of which produce gaudy flowers. This is not, however, the flowering season. About a fortnight since they were red with the blossoms of the violet, wood-sorrel, and the phlox (*Divaricata lychnidia*) of our gardens. They will soon be yellow with syngenesious plants.

JUNE 12: I have been to look at my brother's farm. There is a log-cabin on it, built by a squatter, an ingenious fellow, I warrant him, and built without a single board or sawed material of any sort. The floors and doors are made of split oak, and the bedstead, which still remains, is composed of sticks framed into the wall in one corner of the room and bottomed with split oak, the pieces being about the size of staves. The chimney is built of sticks, plastered with mud inside. There are two apartments, the kitchen and the parlor, although most of the houses have but one room. The kitchen is without any floor but the bare ground, and between that and the parlor there is a passage on the ground, roofed over but open on the sides, large enough to drive a wagon through.

JUNE 13th: To-day I am to set out with brother John on horseback on a tour up the Illinois. I carry my "plunder" in a pair of saddle-bags, with an umbrella lashed to the crupper, and for my fare on the road I shall take what Providence pleases to send. I have told you little about the natural productions of the soil and other peculiarities of the country. The forests are of a very large growth, and contain a greater variety of trees than are common to the eastward. The soil of the open country is fat and fertile, and the growth of all the vegetable tribes is rapid and strong to a degree unknown in your country. There is not a stone, a pebble, or bit of gravel in all these prairies. A plough lasts a man his lifetime, a hoe never wears out, and the horses go unshod. Wild plums grow in large thickets, loaded with a profusion of fruit said to be of excellent flavor. The earth in the woods is covered with May-apples not yet ripe, and in the enclosed prairies with large, fine strawberries, now in their perfection. Wild gooseberries with smooth fruit are produced in abundance. The prairie and the forest have each a different set of animals. The prairie-hen, as you walk out, starts up and whirs away from under you, but the spotted prairie-squirrel hurries through the grass, and the prairie-hawk balances himself in the air for a long time over the same spot. While observing him we heard a kind of humming noise in the grass, which one of the company said proceeded from a rattlesnake. We dismounted, and found, in fact, that it was made by a prairie-rattlesnake, which lay coiled around a tuft of herbage, and which we soon despatched. The Indians call this small variety of the rattlesnake the Massasauger. Horses are frequently bitten by it, and come to the doors of their owners with their heads horribly swollen, but they are recovered by the application of hartshorn. A little farther on one of the party raised the cry of wolf, and, looking, we saw a prairie-wolf in the path before us, a prick-eared animal of a reddish-gray color, standing and gazing at us with great composure. As we approached, he trotted off into the grass, with his nose near the ground, not deigning to hasten his pace for our shouts, and shortly afterward we saw two others running in a different direction. The prairie-wolf is not so formidable an animal as the name of wolf would seem to denote; he is quite as great a coward as robber, but he is exceedingly mischievous. He never takes full-grown sheep unless he goes with a strong troop of his friends, but seizes young lambs, carries off sucking-pigs, robs the hen-roost, de-

vours sweet corn in the gardens, and plunders the watermelon
patch.   A heard of prairie-wolves will enter a field of melons
and quarrel about the division of the spoils as fiercely and
noisily as so many politicians.   It is their way to gnaw a hole
immediately into the first melon they lay hold of.   If it hap-
pens to be ripe, the inside is devoured at once; if not, it is
dropped and another is sought out, and a quarrel is picked
with the discoverer of a ripe one, and loud and shrill is the
barking, and fierce the growling and snapping which is heard
on these occasions.   It is surprising, I am told, with what
dexterity a wolf will make the most of a melon, absorbing
every remnant of the pulp, and hollowing it out as clean as it
could be scraped with a spoon.   This is when the allowance
of melons is scarce, but when they are abundant he is as care-
less and wasteful as a government agent.

I believe this to be the most salubrious, and I am sure it is
the most fertile, country I ever saw; at the same time I do
not think it beautiful.   Some of the views, however, from the
highest parts of the prairies are what, I have no doubt, some
would call beautiful in the highest degree, the green heights
and hollows and plains blend so softly and gently with one
another.

JACKSONVILLE, JUNE 19th : I set out, as I wrote you I should
do, from this place on Wednesday, the 13th of this month, on a
little excursion toward the north.   John accompanied me.
The first day brought us to Springfield, the capital of Sanga-
mon County, where the land office for this district is kept, and
where I was desirous of making some inquiries as to the land
in market.   Springfield is thirty-five miles east of Jacksonville,
situated just on the edge of a large prairie, on ground some-
what more uneven than Jacksonville, but the houses are not
so good, a considerable proportion of them being log-cabins,
and the whole town having an appearance of dirt and discom-
fort.   The night we spent at a filthy tavern, and the next
morning resumed our journey, turning toward the north.
The general aspect of Sangamon County is like that of Morgan,

except that the prairies are more extensive and more level. We passed over large tracts covered with hazel bushes, among which grew the red lily and the painted cup, a large scarlet flower. We then crossed a region thickly scattered with large trees, principally of black or white oak, at the extremity of which we descended to the bottom-lands of the Sangamon, covered with tall, coarse grass. About seven miles north of Springfield we forded the Sangamon, which rolls its transparent waters through a colonnade of huge button-wood trees and black maples, a variety of the sugar-maple. The immediate edge of the river was muddy, but the bottom was of solid rock, and the water was up to our saddle-skirts. We then mounted to the upland by a ravine, and, proceeding through another tract of scattered oaks, came out again on the open prairie. Having crossed a prairie of seven or eight miles in width, we came to a little patch of strawberries in the grass a little way from the edge of the woodland, where we alighted to gather them. My horse, in attempting to graze, twitched the bridle out of my hand, and, accidentally setting his foot on the rein, became very much frightened. I endeavored to catch him, but could not. He reared and plunged, shook off the saddle-bags which contained my clothing and some other articles, kicked the bags to pieces, and, getting into the wood by which we came, galloped furiously out of sight toward Springfield. I now thought my expedition at an end, and had the comfortable prospect of returning on foot or of adopting the method called "to ride and tie." I picked up the saddle-bags and their contents, and, giving them to John, I took charge of the umbrellas, which had also fallen off, and walked back for two miles under a hot sun, when I was met by a man riding a horse, which I was very glad to discover was the one that had escaped. A foot-passenger, who was coming on from Springfield, had stopped him after he had galloped about four miles, and had taken advantage of the circumstance to treat himself to a ride. I then went back to the strawberries and finished them.

As it was now three o'clock, we went to a neighboring house to get something to eat for ourselves and our horses. An old scarlet-faced Virginian gave our horses some corn, and his tall, prim-looking wife set a table for us with a rasher of bacon, a radish, bread and milk in pewter tumblers. They were Methodists, and appeared to live in a comfortable way, there being two rooms in their house, and in one of them only one bed. A little farther on we forded Salt Creek, a beautiful stream, perfectly clear, and flowing over pebbles and gravel—a rare sight in this country. A small prairie intervenes between this and Sugar Creek, which we also forded, but with better success than two travellers who came after us, who, attempting to cross it in another place, were obliged to swim their horses, and one of them was thrown into the water. At evening we stopped at a log-cabin on the edge of a prairie, the width of which we were told was fifteen miles, and on which there was not a house. The man had nothing for our horses but "a smart chance of pasture," as he called it, in a little spot of ground enclosed from the prairie, and which appeared, when we saw it the next morning, to be closely grazed to the very roots of the herbage. The dwelling was of the most wretched description. It consisted of but one room, about half of which was taken up with beds and cribs, on one of which lay a man sick with a fever, and on another sprawled two or three children, besides several who were asleep on the floor, and all of whom were brown with dirt. In a cavernous fireplace blazed a huge fire, built against an enormous back-log reduced to a glowing coal, and before it the hostess and her daughter were busy cooking a supper for several travellers, who were sitting under a kind of piazza or standing about in the yard. As it was a great deal too hot in the house, and a little too cool and damp in the night air, we endeavored to make the balance even by warming ourselves in the house and cooling ourselves out of doors alternately. About ten o'clock the sweaty hostess gave us our supper, consisting of warm cakes, bacon, coffee, and lettuce, with bacon-grease poured over it. About eleven, preparations were made for repose; the dirty children were picked up from the floor, and a feather bed was pulled out of a corner and spread before the great fire for John and myself, but on our intimating that we did not sleep on feathers, we had a place assigned to us near the door, where we stretched ourselves on our saddle-blankets for the night. The rest of the floor was taken up by the other travellers, with the exception of a small passage left for the sick man to get to the door. The floor of the piazza was also occupied with men wrapped in their blankets. The heat of the fire, the stifling atmosphere, the groans and tossings of the sick man, who got up once in fifteen minutes to take medicine or go to the door, the whimperings of the children, and the offensive odors of the place, prevented us from sleeping, and by four o'clock the next morning we had caught and saddled our horses and were on our journey.

We crossed the fifteen-mile prairie, and nearly three miles beyond came to the Mackinaw, a fine, clear stream (watering Tazewell County), which we forded, and about half a mile beyond came to a house where live a Quaker family of the name of Wilson. Here we got a nice breakfast, which we enjoyed with great relish, and some corn for our horses.

Seven or eight miles farther brought us to Pleasant Grove, a fine tract of country, and ten miles from Wilson's we came to a Mr. Shurtliff's, where we had been advised to stop for the purpose of making some inquiries about the country. Shurtliff lives near the north end of Pleasant Grove, and within four miles of the northern limit of the lands in market. The soil is fertile and well watered, the streams being rather more rapid than in Jacksonville, and the region more than usually healthy. It is within eight miles of Pekin, on the Illinois River, so that it is within convenient distance of a market; there is plenty of stone within a few miles, and saw-mills have been erected on some of the streams. I am strongly inclined to purchase a quarter-section in this place. We were now within two days'

ride of Dixon's, where the American army is to be stationed;
but, being already much fatigued with our journey, the weather
being hot, and our horses, though young and strong, so very
lazy and obstinate as to give us constant employment in whip-
ping them to keep them on a gentle trot on the smoothest
road, we concluded to proceed no farther. The next morn-
ing, therefore, we set out on our return. I should have men-
tioned that every few miles on our way we fell in with bod-
ies of Illinois militia proceeding to the American camp, or
saw where they had encamped for the night. They generally
stationed themselves near a stream or a spring on the edge of
a wood, and turned their horses to graze on the prairie. Their
way was marked by trees barked or girdled, and the road
through the uninhabited country was as much beaten and as
dusty as the highways on New York Island. Some of the
settlers complained that they made war upon the pigs and
chickens. They were a hard-looking set of men, unkempt
and unshaved, wearing shirts of dark calico, and sometimes
calico capotes.*

In returning, we crossed the large prairie, already men-
tioned, by a newer way and more direct road to Jackson-
ville. In this direction the prairie was at least twenty-five
miles across. In all this distance we found but one inhabited
house, and one place, about a quarter of a mile from it, at
which to water our horses. This house was stationed on the
edge of a small wood on an eminence in the midst of the
prairie. An old woman was spinning at the door, and a young
woman and boy had just left, with some fire, to do the fam-
ily washing at the watering-place I have just mentioned. Two
or three miles farther on we came to another house on the
edge of another grove, which appeared to have been built
about two years, and which, with the surrounding enclosures,
had been abandoned, as I afterward learned, on account of

---

* One of these militia companies had for its captain a raw youth, in whose quaint
and pleasant talk Mr. Bryant was much interested. He learned some years after-
ward that the name of the youth was Abraham Lincoln.

sickness and the want of water. We frequently passed the holes of the prairie-wolf, but saw none of the animals. The green-headed prairie - fly came around our horses whenever we passed a marshy spot of ground, and fastened upon them with the greediness of wolves, almost maddening them. A little before sunset we came to a wood of thinly scattered oaks, which marks the approach to a river in this country, and, descending a steep bluff, came to the moist and rich bottom-lands of the Sangamon. Next we passed through a thick wood of gigantic old elms, sycamores, mulberries, etc., and crossed the Sangamon in a ferry-boat. We had our horses refreshed at the ferry-house, and, proceeding three miles farther, roused up a Kentuckian of the name of Armstrong, who we understood had some corn. The man and his wife made no scruple in getting up to accommodate us. Every house on a great road in this country is a public house, and nobody hesitates to entertain the traveller or accept his money. The woman, who said she was Dutch (High Dutch, probably), bestirred herself to get our supper. We told her we wanted nothing but bread and milk, on which she lamented that she had neither buttermilk nor sour milk ; but was answered that we were Yankees, and liked sweet milk best. She baked some cakes of corn-bread and set them before us, with a pitcher of milk and two tumblers. In answer to John, who said something of the custom of the Yankees to eat the bread cut into the milk, she said that she could give us spoons if we were in *yearnest ;* but we answered they were quite unnecessary. On my saying that I had lived among the Dutch in New York and elsewhere, she remarked that she reckoned that was the reason why I did not talk like a Yankee. I replied that no doubt living among the Dutch had improved my English. We were early on the way next morning, and about ten o'clock came to Cox's Grove, a place about twenty-five miles from Jacksonville. In looking for a place to feed our horses, I asked for corn at the cabin of an old settler named Wilson, when I saw a fat, dusky-looking woman, barefoot, with six children as dirty as pigs and shaggy as bears. She was cleansing one of them and cracking certain unfortunate insects between her thumb-nails. I was very glad when she told me she had no corn nor oats. At the next house we found corn, and, seeing a little boy of two years old running about with a clean face, I told John that we should get a clean breakfast. I was right. The young man, whose name was Short, had a tall young wife in a clean cotton gown, and shoes and stockings. She baked us some cakes, fried some bacon, and made a cup of coffee, which, being put on a clean table-cloth, and recommended by a good appetite, was swallowed with some eagerness. Yet the poor woman had no tea-spoons in the house, and but one spoon for every purpose, and this was pewter and had but half the handle. With this implement she dipped up the brown sugar and stirred it in our cups before handing them to us. Short was also from Kentucky, or Kaintucky, as they call it, as indeed was every man whom I saw on my journey, except the Virginian, the Quaker family, who were from Pennsylvania, and Shurtliff, who is from Massachusetts, but who has a Kentucky wife. I forgot to tell you that at Armstrong's we were accommodated for the night after the Kentucky fashion—with a sheet under our persons and a blanket of cotton and wool over them. About nine in the evening we reached Wiswall's, very glad to repose from a journey which had been performed in exceedingly hot weather, on horses which required constant flogging to keep them awake, and during which we had not slept at the rate of more than three hours a night. What I have thought and felt amid these boundless wastes and awful solitudes I shall reserve for the only form of expression in which it can be properly uttered.*

---

* See "The Prairies," Poetical Works, vol. i, p. 228.

# A TOUR IN THE OLD SOUTH.

RICHMOND, VIRGINIA, MARCH 2, 1843: I arrived at this place last night from Washington, where I had observed little worth describing. The statue of our first President, by Greenough, was, of course, one of the things which I took an early opportunity of looking at, and, although the bad light in which it is placed prevents the spectator from properly appreciating the features, I could not help seeing with satisfaction that no position, however unfavorable, could impair the majesty of that noble work, or, at all events, destroy its grand general effect.

As we proceeded southward in Virginia, the snow gradually became thinner and finally disappeared altogether. It was impossible to mistake the region in which we were. Broad inclosures were around us, with signs of extensive and superficial cultivation; large dwellings were seen at a distance from each other, and each, with its group of smaller buildings, looking as solitary and chilly as French chateaus; and now and then we saw a gang of negroes at work in the fields, though oftener we passed miles without the sight of a living creature. At six in the afternoon we arrived at Richmond. A beautiful city is Richmond, seated on the hills that overlook the James River. The dwellings have a pleasant appearance, often standing by themselves in the midst of gardens. In front of several I saw large magnolias, their dark, glazed leaves glittering in the March sunshine. The river, as yellow as the Tiber, its waters now stained with the earth of the upper country, runs by the upper part of the town in noisy rapids, embracing several islands, shaded with the plane-tree, the hackberry, and the elm, and prolific, in spring and summer, of wild-flowers.  I went upon one of these islands, by means of a foot-bridge, and was pointed to another, the resort of a quoit-club comprising some of the most distinguished men of Richmond, among whom in his lifetime was Judge Marshall, who sometimes joined in this athletic sport.  We descended one of the hills on which the town is built, and went up another to the east, where stands an ancient house of religious worship, the oldest Episcopal Church in the State.  It is in the midst of a burying-ground, where sleep some of the founders of the colony, whose old graves are greenly overgrown with the trailing and matted periwinkle.  In this church Patrick Henry, at the commencement of the American Revolution, made that celebrated speech which so vehemently moved all who heard him, ending with the sentence: " Give me liberty or give me death."  We looked in at one of the windows; it is a low, plain room, with small, square pews, and a sounding-board over the little pulpit.  From the hill on which this church stands you have a beautiful view of the surrounding country, a gently undulating surface, closed in by hills on the west; and the James River is seen wandering through it, by distant plantations, and between borders of trees.  A place was pointed out to us, a little way down the river, which bears the name of Powhatan; and here, I was told, a flat rock is still shown as the one on which Captain Smith was placed by his captors, in order to be put to death, when the intercession of Pocahontas saved his life.

I went with an acquaintance to see the inspection and sale of tobacco.  Huge, upright columns of dried leaves, firmly packed and of a greenish hue, stood in rows, under the roof of a broad, low building, open on all sides; these were the hogsheads of tobacco, stripped of the staves.  The inspector, a portly man, with a Bourbon face, his white hair gathered in a tie behind, went very quietly and expeditiously through his task of determining the quality, after which the vast bulks were disposed of, in a very short time, with sur-prisingly little noise, to the tobacco merchants. Tobacco to the value of three millions of dollars annually is sent by the planters to Richmond, and thence distributed to different na-tions, whose merchants frequent this mart. In the sales it is always sure to bring cash, which, to those who detest the weed, is a little difficult to understand. Afterward I went to a tobacco factory, the sight of which amused me, though the narcotic fumes made me cough. In one room a black man was taking apart the small bundles of leaves of which a hogs-head of tobacco is composed, and carefully separating leaf from leaf; others were assorting the leaves according to the quality, and others again were arranging the leaves in layers and sprinkling each layer with the extract of licorice. In an-other room were about eighty negroes—boys they are called, from the age of twelve years up to manhood—who received the leaves thus prepared, rolled them into long, even rolls, and then cut them into plugs of about four inches in length, which were afterward passed through a press, and thus became ready for market. As we entered the room we heard a murmur of psalmody running through the sable assembly, which now and then swelled into a strain of very tolerable music.

"Verse sweetens toil,"

says the stanza which Dr. Johnson was so fond of quoting, and really it is so good that I will transcribe the whole of it:

> "Verse sweetens toil, however rude the sound—
> All at her work the village maiden sings,
> Nor, while she turns the giddy wheel around,
> Revolves the sad vicissitudes of things."

Verse, it seems, can sweeten the toil of slaves in a tobacco factory. "We encourage their singing as much as we can," said the brother of the proprietor, himself a diligent mastica-

tor of the weed, who attended us, and politely explained to us
the process of making plug tobacco; "we encourage it as
much as we can, for the boys work better while singing.
Sometimes they will sing all day long with great spirit; at
other times you will not hear a single note. They must sing
wholly of their own accord; it is of no use to bid them do it."
"What is remarkable," he continued, "their tunes are all
psalm-tunes, and the words are from hymn-books; their taste
is exclusively for sacred music; they will sing nothing else.
Almost all these persons are church-members; we have not
a dozen about the factory who are not so. Most of them are
of the Baptist persuasion; a few are Methodists." I saw in
the course of the day the Baptist Church in which these peo-
ple worship, a low, plain, but spacious brick building, the
same in which the sages of Virginia, a generation of great
men, debated the provisions of the Constitution. It has a
congregation of twenty-seven hundred persons, and the best
choir, I heard somebody say, in all Richmond. Near it is the
Monumental Church, erected on the site of the Richmond
Theatre after the terrible fire which carried mourning into so
many families.

In passing through an old part of Main Street, I was shown
an ancient stone cottage of rude architecture and humble
dimensions, which was once the best hotel in Richmond.
Here, I was told, there are those in Richmond who remember
dining with General Washington, Judge Marshall, and their
contemporaries. I could not help comparing it with the
palace-like building put up at Richmond within two or three
years past, named the Exchange Hotel, with its spacious
parlors, its long dining-rooms, its airy dormitories, and its
ample halls and passages, echoing to the steps of busy waiters,
and guests coming and departing. I paid a visit to the capi-
tol, nobly situated on an eminence which overlooks the city,
and is planted with trees. The statue of Washington, exe-
cuted by Houdon for the State of Virginia, in 1788, is here.
It is of the size of life, representing General Washington in

the costume of his day, and in an ordinary standing posture. It gratifies curiosity, but raises no particular moral emotion. Compared with the statue by Greenough, it presents a good example of the difference between the work of a mere sculptor —skilful indeed, but still a mere sculptor—and the work of a man of genius.

CHARLESTON, MARCH 6th : I left Richmond, on the afternoon of a keen March day, in the railway train for Petersburg, where we arrived after dark, and, therefore, could form no judgment of the appearance of the town. Here we were transferred to another train of cars. About two o'clock in the morning we reached Blakely, on the Roanoke, where we were made to get out of the cars, and were marched in long procession for about a quarter of a mile down to the river. A negro walked before us to light our way, bearing a blazing pine torch, which scattered sparks like a steam-engine, and a crowd of negroes followed us, bearing our baggage. We went down a steep path to the Roanoke, where we found a little old steamboat ready for us, and in about fifteen minutes were struggling upward against the muddy and rapid current. In little more than an hour we had proceeded two miles and a half up the river, and were landed at a place called Weldon. Here we took the cars for Wilmington, in North Carolina, and shabby vehicles they were, denoting our arrival in a milder climate by being extremely uncomfortable for cold weather. As morning dawned we saw ourselves in the midst of the pine forests of North Carolina. Vast tracts of level sand—overgrown with the long-leaved pine, a tall, stately tree, with sparse and thick twigs, ending in long brushes of leaves, murmuring in the strong, cold wind—extended everywhere around us. At great distances from each other we passed log-houses, and sometimes a dwelling of more pretensions, with a piazza, and here and there fields in which cotton or maize had been planted last year, or an orchard with a few small mossy trees. The pools beside the roads were covered with ice just formed, and the negroes, who like a good fire at almost any season of the year, and who find an abundant supply of the finest fuel in these forests, had made blazing fires of the resinous wood of the pine wherever they were at work. The tracts of sandy soil, we perceived, were interspersed with marshes, crowded with cypress-trees, and verdant at their borders with a growth of evergreens, such as the swamp-bay, the gallberry, the holly, and various kinds of evergreen creepers, which are unknown to our northern climate, and which became more frequent as we proceeded. We passed through extensive forests of pine, which had been *boxed*, as it is called, for the collection of turpentine. Every tree had been scored by the axe upon one of its sides, some of them as high as the arm could reach, down to the roots, and the broad wound was covered with the turpentine, which seems to saturate every fibre of the long-leaved pine. Sometimes we saw large flakes or crusts of the turpentine, of a light yellow color, which had fallen, and lay beside the tree on the ground. The collection of turpentine is a work of destruction ; it strips acre after acre of these noble trees, and, if it goes on, the time is not far distant when the long-leaved pine will become nearly extinct in this region, which is so sterile as hardly to be fitted for producing anything else. We saw large tracts covered with the standing trunks of trees already killed by it ; and other tracts beside them had been freshly attacked by the spoiler. I am told that the tree which grows up when the long-leaved pine is destroyed is the loblolly pine, or, as it is sometimes called, the short-leaved pine, a tree of very inferior quality and in little esteem.

About half-past two in the afternoon we came to Wilmington, a little town built upon the white sands of Cape Fear, some of the houses standing where not a blade of grass or other plant can grow. A few evergreen oaks in places pleasantly overhang the water. Here we took the steamer for Charleston, and the next morning, at eight o'clock, we found ourselves entering the harbor ; Sullivan's Island, with Fort Moultrie, breathing recollections of the Revolution, on

our right; James Island on our left; in front, the stately dwell-
ings of the town, and, on the land side, the horizon bounded
all around by an apparent belt of evergreens—the live-oak,
the water-oak, the palmetto, the pine, and, planted about the
dwellings, the magnolia and the wild orange—giving to the
scene a summer aspect. The city of Charleston strikes the
visitor from the North most agreeably. He perceives at
once that he is in a different climate. The spacious houses
are surrounded with broad piazzas, often a piazza to each
story, for the sake of shade and coolness, and each house
generally stands by itself in a garden planted with trees and
shrubs, many of which preserve their verdure through the
winter. We saw early flowers already opening; the peach-
and plum-tree were in full bloom; and the wild orange, as
they call the cherry-laurel, was just putting forth its blossoms.
The buildings—some with stuccoed walls, some built of large
dark-red bricks, and some of wood—are not kept fresh with
paint like ours, but are allowed to become weather-stained by
the humid climate, like those of the European towns. The
streets are broad and quiet, unpaved in some parts, but in
none, as with us, offensive both to sight and smell. The
public buildings are numerous for the size of the city, and
well-built in general, with sufficient space about them to give
them a noble aspect, and all the advantage which they could
derive from their architecture. The inhabitants, judging from
what I have seen of them, which is not much, I confess, do
not appear undeserving of the character which has been given
them—of possessing the most polished and agreeable manners
of all Americans.

BARNWELL DISTRICT, SOUTH CAROLINA, MARCH 29th:
Since I last wrote I have passed three weeks in the interior
of South Carolina; visited Columbia, the capital of the State,
a pretty town; roamed over a considerable part of Barnwell
district, with some part of the neighboring one of Orange-
burg; enjoyed the hospitality of the planters—very agree-
able and intelligent men; been out on a raccoon hunt; been

present at a corn-shucking; listened to negro ballads, negro jokes, and the banjo; witnessed negro dances; seen two alligators at least, and eaten bushels of hominy.

Whoever comes out on the railroad to this district, a distance of seventy miles or more, if he were to judge only by what he sees in his passage, might naturally take South Carolina for a vast pine-forest, with here and there a clearing made by some enterprising settler, and would wonder where the cotton which clothes so many millions of the human race is produced. The railway keeps on a tract of sterile sand, overgrown with pines, passing here and there along the edge of a morass, or crossing a stream of yellow water. A lonely log-house under these old trees is "a sight for sore eyes"; and only two or three plantations, properly so called, meet the eye in the whole distance. The cultivated and more productive lands lie apart from this tract, near streams, and interspersed with more frequent ponds and marshes. Here you find plantations comprising several thousands of acres, a considerable part of which always lies in forest; cotton- and corn-fields of vast extent, and a negro village on every plantation, at a respectful distance from the habitation of the proprietor. Evergreen trees of the oak family and others, which I mentioned in my last letter, are generally planted about the mansions. Some of them are surrounded with dreary clearings, full of the standing trunks of dead pines; others are pleasantly situated on the edge of woods, intersected by winding paths. A ramble or a ride—a ride at a hard gallop it should be—in these pine woods, on a fine March day, when the weather has all the spirit of our March days without its severity, is one of the most delightful recreations in the world. The paths are upon a white sand, which, when not frequently travelled, is very firm under foot; on all sides you are surrounded by noble stems of trees, towering to an immense height, from whose summits, far above you, the wind is drawing deep and grand harmonies; and often your way is beside a marsh, verdant with magnolias, where the yellow jasmine, now in flower, fills the air with fragrance, and the bamboo-brier, an evergreen creeper, twines itself with various other plants, which never shed their leaves in winter. These woods abound in game, which, you will believe me when I say, I had rather start than shoot: flocks of turtle-doves; rabbits rising and scudding before you; bevies of quails—partridges they call them here—chirping almost under your horse's feet; wild ducks swimming in the pools; and wild turkeys, which are frequently shot by the practiced sportsman.

But you must hear of the corn-shucking. The one at which I was present was given on purpose that I might witness the humors of the Carolina negroes. A huge fire of *light-wood* was made near the corn-house. Light-wood is the wood of the long-leaved pine, and is so called, not because it is light, for it is almost the heaviest wood in the world, but because it gives more light than any other fuel. In clearing land, the pines are girdled and suffered to stand; the outer portion of the wood decays and falls off; the inner part, which is saturated with turpentine, remains upright for years, and constitutes the planter's provision of fuel. When a supply is wanted, one of these dead trunks is felled by the axe. The abundance of light-wood is one of the boasts of South Carolina. Wherever you are, if you happen to be chilly, you may have a fire extempore; a bit of light-wood and a coal give you a bright blaze and a strong heat in an instant. The negroes make fires of it in the fields where they work; and, when the mornings are wet and chilly, in the pens where they are milking the cows. At a plantation where I passed a frosty night, I saw fires in a small enclosure, and was told by the lady of the house that she had ordered them to be made to warm the cattle. The light-wood fire was made, and the negroes dropped in from the neighboring plantations, singing as they came. The driver of the plantation, a colored man, brought out baskets of corn in the husk, and piled it in a heap; and the negroes began to strip the husks from the ears, singing with great

glee as they worked, keeping time to the music, and now and
then throwing in a joke and an extravagant burst of laughter.
The songs were generally of a comic character; but one of
them was set to a singularly wild and plaintive air, which
some of our musicians would do well to reduce to notation.
These are the words :

> " Johnny come down de hollow.
>             Oh hollow !
> Johnny come down de hollow.
>             Oh hollow !
> De nigger-trader got me.
>             Oh hollow !
> De speculator bought me.
>             Oh hollow !
> I'm sold for silver dollars.
>             Oh hollow !
> Boys, go catch de pony.
>             Oh hollow !
> Bring him round the corner.
>             Oh hollow !
> I'm goin' away to Georgia.
>             Oh hollow !
> Boys, good-by forever !
>             Oh hollow ! "

The song of " Jenny gone Away " was also given, and
another, called the monkey-song, probably of African origin,
in which the principal singer personated a monkey, with all
sorts of odd gesticulations, and the other negroes bore part
in the chorus, " Dan, Dan, who's de Dandy?"  One of the
songs commonly sung on these occasions represents the vari-
ous animals of the woods as belonging to some profession or
trade.   For example :

> " De cooter is de boatman."

The cooter means the terrapin, and a very expert boatman
he is.

> " De cooter is de boatman.
>     John John Crow.
>   De red-bird de soger.
>     John John Crow.
>   De mocking-bird de lawyer.
>     John John Crow.
>   De alligator sawyer.
>     John John Crow."

The alligator's back is furnished with a toothed ridge, like the edge of a saw, which explains the last line.

When the work of the evening was over, the negroes adjourned to a spacious kitchen. One of them took his place as musician, whistling, and beating time with two sticks upon the floor. Several of the men came forward and executed various dances, capering, prancing, and drumming with heel and toe upon the floor, with astonishing agility and perseverance, though all of them had performed their daily tasks and had worked all the evening, and some had walked from four to seven miles to attend the corn-shucking. From the dances a transition was made to a mock military parade, a sort of burlesque of our militia trainings, in which the words of command and the evolutions were extremely ludicrous. It became necessary for the commander to make a speech, and, confessing his incapacity for public speaking, he called upon a huge black man named Toby to address the company in his stead. Toby, a man of powerful frame, six feet high, his face ornamented with a beard of fashionable cut, had hitherto stood leaning against the wall, looking upon the frolic with an air of superiority. He consented, came forward, demanded a bit of paper to hold in his hand, and harangued the soldiery. It was evident that Toby had listened to stump speeches in his day. He spoke of " de majority of Sous Carolina," " de interests of de State," " de honor of ole Ba'nwell district," and these phrases he connected by various expletives, and sounds of which we could make nothing. At length he began to falter, when the captain, with admirable presence of mind, came to his relief, and interrupted and closed the harangue with a hurrah from the company. Toby was allowed by all the spectators, black and white, to have made an excellent speech.

The blacks of this region are a cheerful, careless, dirty race, not hard-worked, and in many respects indulgently treated. It is, of course, the desire of the master that his slaves shall work hard; on the other hand, the determination of the slave is to lead as easy a life as he can. The master has power of punishment on his side; the slave, on his, an invincible indolence, and a thousand expedients learned by long practice. The result is a compromise, in which each party yields something, and a good-natured though imperfect and slovenly obedience on one side is purchased by good treatment on the other. I have been told by planters that the slave brought from Africa is much more serviceable, though more high-spirited and dangerous, than the slave born in this country and early trained to his condition.

PICOLATA, EAST FLORIDA, APRIL 7th: As I landed at this place, a few hours since, I stepped into the midst of summer. Yesterday morning, when I left Savannah, people were complaining that the winter was not over. The temperature, which at this time of the year is usually warm and genial, continued to be what they called chilly, though I found it agreeable enough, and the showy trees, called the *Pride of India*, which are planted all over the city, and are generally in bloom at this season, were still leafless. Here I find everything green, fresh, and fragrant, trees and shrubs in full foliage, and wild roses in flower. The dark waters of the St. John's, one of the noblest streams of the country, in depth and width like the St. Lawrence, draining almost the whole extent of the peninsula, are flowing under my window. On the opposite shore are forests of tall trees, bright in the new verdure of the season. A hunter who has ranged them the whole day has just arrived in a canoe, bringing with him a deer which he has killed. I have this moment returned from a ramble with my host through a hammock, he looking for his cows, and I, unsuccessfully, for a thicket of orange-trees. He is something of a florist, and gathered for me, as we went, some of the forest-plants which were in bloom. "We have flowers here," said he, " every month in the year."

I have used the word hammock, which here, in Florida, has a peculiar meaning. A hammock is a spot covered with a growth of trees which require a richer soil than the pine, such as the oak, the mulberry, the gum-tree, the hickory, etc. The greater part of east Florida consists of pine barrens—a sandy level, producing the long-leaved pine and the dwarf palmetto, a low plant, with fan-like leaves, and roots of a prodigious size. The hammock is a kind of oasis, a verdant and luxuriant island in the midst of these sterile sands which make about nine tenths of the soil of east Florida. In the hammocks grow the wild lime, the native orange, both sour and bitter-sweet, and the various vines and gigantic creepers of the country. The hammocks are chosen for plantations; here the cane is cultivated, and groves of the sweet orange planted. But I shall say more of Florida hereafter, when I have seen more of it. Meantime, let me speak of my journey hither.

I left Charleston on the 30th of March, in one of the steamers which ply between that city and Savannah. These steamers are among the very best that float—quiet, commodious, clean, fresh as if just built, and furnished with civil and ready-handed waiters. We passed along the narrow and winding channels which divide the broad islands of South Carolina from the mainland—islands famed for the rice culture, and particularly for the excellent cotton with long fibers, named the sea-island cotton. Our fellow-passengers were mostly planters of these islands, and their families—persons of remarkably courteous, frank, and agreeable manners. The shores on either side had little of the picturesque to show us. Extensive marshes waving with coarse water-grass, sometimes a canebrake, sometimes a pine grove or a clump of cabbage-leaved palmettoes; here and there a pleasant bank bordered with live-oaks streaming with moss, and at wide intervals the distant habitation of a planter—these were the elements of the scenery. The next morning early we were passing up the Savannah River, and the city was in sight, standing among its trees on a high bank of the stream.

Savannah is beautifully laid out; its broad streets are thickly planted with the Pride of India, and its frequent open squares shaded with trees of various kinds. Oglethorpe seems to have understood how a city should be built in a warm climate, and the people of the place are fond of reminding the stranger that the original plan of the founder has never been departed from. The town, so charmingly embowered, reminded me of New Haven, though the variety of trees is greater. South of the town extends an uninclosed space, near a pleasant grove of pines, in the shade of which the members of a quoit-club practice their athletic sport. Here on a Saturday afternoon—for that is their stated time of assembling—I was introduced to some of the most distinguished citizens of Savannah, and witnessed the skill with which they threw the discus. No apprentices were they in the art; there was no striking far from the stake, no sending the discus rolling over the green; they heaped the quoits as snugly around the stakes as if the amusement had been their profession. In the same neighborhood, just without the town, lies the public cemetery, surrounded by an ancient wall, built before the Revolution, which in some places shows the marks of shot fired against it in the skirmishes of that period. I entered it, hoping to find some monuments of those who founded the city a hundred and ten years ago, but the inscriptions are of comparatively recent date. Most of them commemorate the death of persons born in Europe or the Northern States. I was told that the remains of the early inhabitants lie in the brick tombs, of which there are many, without any inscription whatever. At a little distance, near a forest, lies the burial-place of the black population. A few trees, trailing with long moss, rise above hundreds of nameless graves, overgrown with weeds; but here and there are scattered memorials of the dead, some of a very humble kind, with a few of marble, and half a dozen spacious brick tombs like those in the cemetery of the whites. Some of them are erected by masters and mistresses to the memory of favorite slaves. One of them commemorates the death of a young woman who perished in the catastrophe of the steamer Pulaski, of whom it is recorded that, during the whole time that she was in the service of her mistress, which was many years, she never committed a theft nor uttered a falsehood. A brick monument, in the shape of a little tomb, with a marble slab inserted in front, has this inscription:

" In memory of Henrietta Gatlin, the infant stranger, born in East Florida, aged 1 year 3 months."

A graveyard is hardly the place to be merry in, but I could not help smiling at some of the inscriptions. A fair upright marble slab commemorates the death of York Fleming, a cooper, who was killed by the explosion of a powder-magazine while tightening the hoops of a keg of powder. It closes with this curious sentence:

" This stone was erected by the members of the Axe Company, Coopers and Committee of the 2nd African Church of Savannah for the purpose of having a Herse for benevolent purposes, of which he was the first sexton."

A poor fellow, who went to the other world by water, has a wooden slab to mark his grave, inscribed with these words:

" Sacred to the memory of Robert Spencer who came to his Death by A Boat, July 9th, 1840, aged 21 years.

   Reader as you am now so once I
   And as I am now so Mus you be Shortly.
        Amen."

Another monument, after giving the name of the dead, has this sentence:

" Go home Mother dry up your weeping tears. Gods will be done."

Another, erected to Sarah Morel, aged six months, has this ejaculation : " Sweet withered lilly farewell."

One of the monuments is erected to Andrew Bryan, a black preacher, of the Baptist persuasion. A long inscription states that he was once imprisoned " for preaching the Gospel, and, without ceremony, severely whipped "; and that, while undergoing the punishment, " he told his persecutors that he not only rejoiced to be whipped, but was willing to suffer death for the cause of Christ." He died in 1812, at the age of ninety-six; his funeral, the inscription takes care to state, was attended by a large concourse of people, and adds :

"An address was delivered at his death by the Rev. Mr. Johnson, Dr. Kollock, Thomas Williams, and Henry Cunningham."

While in Savannah I paid a visit to Bonaventure, formerly a country-seat of Governor Tatnall, but now abandoned. A pleasant drive of a mile or two, through a budding forest, took us to the place, which is now itself almost grown up into forest. Cedar and other shrubs hide the old terraces of the garden, which is finely situated on the high bank of a river. Trees of various kinds have also nearly filled the space between the noble avenues of live-oaks which were planted around the mansion. But these oaks—I never saw finer trees— certainly I never saw so many majestic and venerable trees together. I looked far down the immense arches that over-shadowed the broad passages, as high as the nave of a Gothic cathedral, apparently as old, and stretching to a greater distance. The huge boughs were clothed with gray moss, yards in length, which clung to them like mist, or hung in still festoons on every side, and gave them the appearance of the vault of a vast vapory cavern. The cawing of the crow and the scream of the jay, however, reminded us that we were in the forest. Of the mansion there are no remains ; but in the thicket of magnolias and other trees, among rose-bushes and creeping plants, we found a burial-place, with monuments of some persons to whom the seat had belonged.

I left, with a feeling of regret, the agreeable society of Savannah. The steamboat took us to St. Mary's, through passages between the sea-islands and the mainland, similar to those by which we had arrived at Savannah. In the course of the day we passed a channel in which we saw several huge alligators basking on the bank. The grim creatures slid slowly into the water at our approach. We passed St. Mary's in the night, and in the morning we were in the main ocean, approaching the St. John's, where we saw a row of pelicans standing, like creatures who had nothing to do, on the sand. We entered the majestic river, the vast current of which is dark with the infusion of the swamp turf from which it is drained. We passed Jacksonville, a little town of great activity, which has sprung up on the sandy bank within two or three years. Beyond, we swept by the mouth of the Black Creek, the water of which, probably from the color of the mud which forms the bed of its channel, has to the eye an ebony blackness, and reflects objects with all the distinctness of the kind of looking-glass called a black mirror. A few hours brought us to Picolata, lately a military station, but now a place with only two houses.

St. Augustine, East Florida, April 2d: When we left Picolata, on the 8th of April, we found ourselves journeying through a vast forest. A road of eighteen miles in length, over the level sands, brings you to this place. Tall pines, a thin growth, stood wherever we turned our eyes, and the ground was covered with the dwarf palmetto, and the whortleberry, which is here an evergreen. Yet there were not wanting sights to interest us, even in this dreary and sterile region. As we passed a clearing, in which we saw a young white woman and a boy dropping corn, and some negroes covering it with their hoes, we beheld a large flock of white cranes, which rose in the air and hovered over the forest, and wheeled and wheeled again, their spotless plumage glistening in the sun like new-fallen snow. We crossed the track of a recent hurricane, which had broken off the huge pines midway from the ground and whirled the summits to a distance from their trunks. From time to time we forded little streams of a deep-red color, flowing from the swamps, tinged, as we were told, with the roots of the red bay, a species of magnolia. As the horses waded into the transparent crimson, we thought of the butcheries committed by the Indians on that road, and could almost fancy that the water was still colored with the blood they had shed. The driver of our wagon told us many narratives of these murders, and pointed out the places where they were committed. He showed us where the father of this young woman was shot dead in his wagon as he was going from St. Augustine to his plantation, and the boy whom he had seen was wounded and scalped by them, and left for dead. In another place he showed us the spot where a party of play-ers, on their way to St. Augustine, were surprised and killed. The Indians took possession of the stage-dresses, one of them arraying himself in the garb of Othello, another in that of Richard the Third, and another taking the costume of Falstaff. I think it was Wild Cat's gang who engaged in this affair, and I was told that, after the capture of this chief and some of his warriors, they recounted the circumstances with great glee. At another place we passed a small thicket, in which several armed Indians, as they afterward related, lay concealed while an officer of the United States army rode several times around it, without any suspicion of their presence. The same men committed, immediately afterward, several murders and rob-beries on the road.

At length we emerged upon a shrubby plain, and soon came in sight of this oldest city of the United States, seated among its trees on a sandy swell of land, where it has stood for three hundred years. I was struck with its ancient and homely aspect, even at a distance, and could not help likening it to pictures which I had seen of Dutch towns, though it wanted a windmill or two to make the resemblance perfect. We drove into a green square, in the midst of which was a monument erected to commemorate the Spanish constitution of 1812, and

thence through the narrow streets of the city to our hotel. I
have called the streets narrow. In few places are they wide
enough to allow two carriages to pass abreast. I was told that
they were not originally intended for carriages, and that in
the time when the town belonged to Spain many of them
were floored with an artificial stone, composed of shells and
mortar, which in this climate takes and keeps the hardness of
rock, and that no other vehicle than a hand-barrow was al-
lowed to pass over them. In some places you see remnants of
this ancient pavement, but for the most part it has been ground
into dust under the wheels of the carts and carriages intro-
duced by the new inhabitants. The old houses, built of a kind
of stone which is seemingly a pure concretion of small shells,
overhang the streets with their wooden balconies, and the gar-
dens between the houses are fenced on the side of the street
with high walls of stone. Peeping over these walls you see
branches of the pomegranate and of the orange-tree, now fra-
grant with flowers, and, rising yet higher, the leaning boughs
of the fig, with its broad, luxuriant leaves. Occasionally you
pass the ruins of houses—walls of stone, with arches and stair-
cases of the same material, which once belonged to stately
dwellings. You meet in the streets with men of swarthy com-
plexions and foreign physiognomy, and you hear them speak-
ing to each other in a strange language. You are told that
these are the remains of those who inhabited the country
under the Spanish dominion, and that the dialect you have
heard is that of the island of Minorca. "Twelve years ago,"
said an acquaintance of mine, "when I first visited St. Augus-
tine, it was a fine old Spanish town. A large proportion of
the houses, which you now see roofed like barns, were then
flat-roofed; they were all of shell-rock, and these modern
wooden buildings were not yet erected. That old fort, which
they are now repairing, to fit it for receiving a garrison, was a
sort of ruin, for the outworks had partly fallen, and it stood
unoccupied by the military, a venerable monument of the
Spanish dominion. But the orange-groves were the ornament

and wealth of St. Augustine, and their produce maintained the inhabitants in comfort. Orange-trees, of the size and height of the pear-tree, often rising higher than the roofs of the houses, embowered the town in perpetual verdure. They stood so close in the groves that they excluded the sun, and the atmosphere was at all times aromatic with their leaves and fruit, and in spring the fragrance of the flowers was almost oppressive." These groves have now lost their beauty. A few years since a severe frost killed the trees to the ground, and, when they sprouted again from the roots, a new enemy made its appearance—an insect of the *coccus* family, with a kind of shell on its back, which enables it to withstand all the common applications for destroying insects, and the ravages of which are shown by the leaves becoming black and sere and the twigs perishing. In October last a gale drove in the spray from the ocean, stripping the trees, except in sheltered situations, of their leaves, and destroying the upper branches. The trunks are now putting out new sprouts and new leaves, but there is no hope of fruit for this year at least.

The old fort of St. Mark, now called Fort Marion, a foolish change of name, is a noble work, frowning over the Matanzas, which flows between St. Augustine and the island of St. Anastasia, and it is worth making a long journey to see. No record remains of its original construction, but it is supposed to have been erected about a hundred and fifty years since, and the shell-rock of which it is built is dark with time. We saw where it had been struck with cannon-balls, which, instead of splitting the rock, became imbedded and clogged among the loosened fragments of shell. This rock is, therefore, one of the best materials for a fortification in the world. We were taken into the ancient prisons of the fort—dungeons, one of which was dimly lighted by a grated window, and another entirely without light; and by the flame of a torch we were shown the half-obliterated inscriptions scrawled on the walls long ago by prisoners. But in another corner of the fort we were taken to look at two secret cells, which were discovered a few years since, in consequence of the sinking of the earth over a narrow apartment between them. These cells are deep under ground, vaulted overhead, and without windows. In one of them a wooden machine was found, which some supposed might have been a rack, and in the other a quantity of human bones. The doors of these cells had been walled up and concealed with stucco before the fort passed into the hands of the Americans. " If the Inquisition," said the gentle- man who accompanied us, " was established in Florida as it was in the other American colonies of Spain, these were its secret chambers."

Yesterday was Palm Sunday, and in the morning I at- tended the services in the Catholic Church. One of the cere- monies was that of pronouncing the benediction over a large pile of leaves of the cabbage-palm, or palmetto, gathered in the woods. After the blessing had been pronounced, the priest called upon the congregation to come and receive them. The men came forward first, in the order of their age, and then the women ; and, as the congregation consisted mostly of the de- scendants of Minorcans, Greeks, and Spaniards, I had a good opportunity of observing their personal appearance. The younger portion of the congregation had, in general, expressive countenances. Their forms, it appeared to me, were generally slighter than those of our people ; and, if the cheeks of the young women were dark, they had regular features and brill- iant eyes, and finely formed hands. There is spirit, also, in this class, for one of them has since been pointed out to me in the streets as having drawn a dirk upon a young officer who presumed upon some improper freedoms of behavior. The services were closed by a plain and sensible discourse in Eng- lish, from the priest, Mr. Rampon, a worthy and useful French ecclesiastic, on the obligation of temperance ; for the temper- ance reform has penetrated even hither, and cold water is all the rage. I went again, the other evening, into the same church, and heard a person declaiming, in a language which, at first, I took be Minorcan, for I could make nothing else of it. After listening for a few minutes, I found that it was a Frenchman preaching in Spanish, with a French mode of pronunciation which was odd enough. I asked one of the old Spanish inhabitants how he was edified by this discourse, and he acknowledged that he understood about an eighth part of it.

St. Augustine, April 24th: You cannot be in St. Augustine a day without hearing some of its inhabitants speak of its agreeable climate. During the sixteen days of my residence here the weather has certainly been as delightful as I could imagine. We have the temperature of early June, as June is known in New York. The mornings are sometimes a little sultry, but after two or three hours a fresh breeze comes in from the sea, sweeping through the broad piazzas and breathing in at the windows. At this season it comes laden with the fragrance of the flowers of the Pride of India, and sometimes of the orange-tree, and sometimes brings the scent of roses, now in full bloom. The nights are gratefully cool, and I have been told, by a person who has lived here many years, that there are very few nights in the summer when you can sleep without a blanket. An acquaintance of mine, an invalid, who has tried various climates and has kept up a kind of running fight with death for many years, retreating from country to country as he pursued, declares to me that the winter climate of St. Augustine is to be preferred to that of any part of Europe, even that of Sicily, and that it is better than the climate of the West Indies. He finds it genial and equable, at the same time that it is not enfeebling. The summer heats are prevented from being intense by the sea-breeze, of which I have spoken. I have looked over the work of Dr. Forry on the climate of the United States, and have been surprised to see the uniformity of climate which he ascribes to Key West. As appears by the observations he has collected, the seasons at that place glide into each other by the softest gradations, and the heat never, even in midsummer, reaches that extreme which is felt in higher latitudes of the American continent. The climate of Florida is in fact an insular climate; the Atlantic on the east and the Gulf of Mexico on the west temper the airs that blow over it, making them cooler in summer and warmer in winter. I do not wonder, therefore, that it is so much the resort of invalids; it would be more so if the softness of its atmosphere and the beauty and serenity of its seasons were generally known. Nor should it be supposed that accommodations for persons in delicate health are wanting ; they are in fact becoming better with every year, as the demand for them increases. Among the acquaintances whom I have made here, I remember many who, having come hither for the benefit of their health, are detained for life by the amenity of the climate. " It seems to me," said an intelligent gentleman of this class, the other day, "as if I could not exist out of Florida. When I go to the North I feel most sensibly the severe extremes of the weather; the climate of Charleston itself appears harsh to me." Here at St. Augustine we have occasional frosts in the winter, but at Tampa Bay, on the western shore of the peninsula, no farther from this place than from New York to Albany, the dew is never congealed on the grass, nor is a snowflake ever seen floating in the air. Those who have passed the winter in that place speak with a kind of rapture of the benignity of the climate. In that country grow the cocoa and the banana, and other productions of the West Indies. Persons who have explored Florida to the south of this during the past winter, speak of having refreshed themselves with melons in January, growing where they had been self-sown, and of having seen the sugar-cane, where it had been planted by the Indians, towering, uncropped, almost to the height of the forest-trees.

The other day I went out with a friend to a sugar plantation in the neighborhood of St. Augustine. As we rode into the enclosure we breathed the fragrance of young orange-trees in flower, the glossy leaves of which, green at all seasons, were trembling in the wind. A troop of negro children were at play at a little distance from the cabins, and one of them ran

along with us to show us a grove of sour oranges, which we
were looking for.   He pointed us to a copse in the middle of
a field, to which we proceeded.   The trees, which were of con-
siderable size, were full of flowers, and the golden fruit was
thick on the branches, and lay scattered on the ground below.
I gathered a few of the oranges, and found them almost as
acid as the lemon.   We stopped to look at the buildings in
which the sugar was manufactured.   In one of them was the
mill where the cane was crushed with iron rollers; in another
stood the huge caldrons, one after another, in which the juice
was boiled down to the  proper  consistence; in another were
barrels of sugar, of syrup—a favorite article of consumption
in this city — of molasses, and a kind of spirits resembling
Jamaica rum, distilled from the refuse of the molasses.   The
proprietor was absent, but three negroes, well-clad young men,
of a very respectable appearance and intelligent physiognomy,
one of whom was a distiller, were occupied about the build-
ings, and showed them to us.   Near by in the open air lay a
pile of sugar-cane, of the ribbon variety, striped with red and
white, which had been plucked up by the roots and reserved
for planting.   The negroes of St. Augustine are good-looking
specimens of the race, and have the appearance of being very
well treated.   You rarely see a negro in ragged clothing, and
the colored children, though slaves, are often dressed with
great neatness.   In the colored people whom I saw in the
Catholic Church I remarked a more agreeable, open, and gen-
tle physiognomy than I have been accustomed to see in that
class.   The Spanish race blends more kindly with the African
than does the English, and produces handsomer men and
women.

I have been to see the quarries of *coquina*, or shell-rock,
on the island of St. Anastasia, which lies between St. Augus-
tine and the main ocean.   We landed on the island, and, after
a walk of some distance on a sandy road through the thick
shrubs, we arrived at some huts built of a frame-work of poles,
thatched with the radiated leaves of the dwarf palmetto, which

had a very picturesque appearance. Here we found a circular hollow in the earth, the place of an old excavation, now shaded with red-cedars, and the palmetto-royal bristling with long, pointed leaves, which bent over and embowered it, and at the bottom was a spring within a square curb of stone, where we refreshed ourselves with a draught of cold water. The quarries were at a little distance from this. The rock lies in the ridges, a little below the surface, forming a stratum of no great depth. The blocks are cut out with crowbars thrust into the rock. It is of a delicate cream-color, and is composed of mere shells and fragments of shells, apparently cemented by the fresh water percolating through them and depositing calcareous matter brought from the shells above. Whenever there is any mixture of sand with the shells, rock is not formed. Of this material the old fort of St. Mark and the greater part of the city are built. It is said to become harder when exposed to the air and the rain, but to disintegrate when frequently moistened with sea-water. Large blocks were lying on the shore ready to be conveyed to the fort, which is undergoing repairs. It is some consolation to know that this fine old work will undergo as little change in the original plan as is consistent with the modern improvements in fortification. Lieutenant Benham, who has charge of the repairs, has strong antiquarian tastes, and will preserve as much as possible of its original aspect. It must lose its battlements, however, its fine mural crown. Battlements are now obsolete, except when they are of no use, as on the roofs of churches and Gothic cottages.

In another part of the same island, which we visited afterward, is a dwelling-house situated amid orange-groves. Closely planted rows of the sour orange, the native tree of the country, intersect and shelter orchards of the sweet orange, the lemon, and the lime. The trees were all young, having been planted since the great frost of 1835, and many of them still show the ravages of the gale of last October, which stripped them of their leaves. "Come this way," said a friend who accompanied me. He forced a passage through a tall hedge of the sour orange, and we found ourselves in a little fragrant enclosure, in the midst of which was a tomb, formed of the artificial stone of which I have heretofore spoken. It was the resting-place of the former proprietor, who sleeps in this little circle of perpetual verdure. It bore no inscription. Not far from this spot I was shown the root of an ancient palm-tree, the species that produces the date, which formerly towered over the island, and served as a sea-mark to vessels approaching the shore. Some of the accounts of St. Augustine speak of dates as among its fruits; but I believe that only the male tree of the date-palm has been introduced into the country. On our return to the city, in crossing the Matanzas Sound, so named, probably, from some sanguinary battle with the aborigines on its shores, we passed two Minorcans in a boat, taking home fuel from the island. These people are a mild, harmless race, of civil manners and abstemious habits. Mingled with them are many Greek families, with names that denote their origin, such as Geopoli, Cercopoli, etc., and with a cast of features equally expressive of their descent. The Minorcan language, the dialect of Mahon, *el Mahones*, as they call it, is spoken by more than half of the inhabitants who remained here when the country was ceded to the United States, and all of them, I believe, speak Spanish besides. Their children, however, are growing up in disuse of these languages, and in another generation the last traces of the majestic speech of Castile will have been effaced from a country which the Spaniards held for more than two hundred years.

Some old customs which the Minorcans brought with them from their native country are still kept up. On the evening before Easter Sunday, about eleven o'clock, I heard the sound of a serenade in the streets. Going out, I found a party of young men, with instruments of music, grouped about the window of one of the dwellings, singing a hymn in honor of the Virgin in the Mahonese dialect. They began, as I was told, with tapping on the shutter. An answering knock within had told them that their visit was welcome, and they immediately opened the serenade. If no reply had been heard, they would have passed on to another dwelling. I give the hymn as it was kindly taken down for me in writing by a native of St. Augustine. I presume this is the first time that it has been put in print, but I fear the copy has several corruptions, occasioned by the unskilfulness of the copyist. The letter *e* which I have put in italics represents the guttural French *e*, or perhaps more nearly the sound of *u* in the word but. The *sh* of our language is represented by *sc* followed by an *i* or an *e*; the *g*, both hard and soft, has the same sound as in our language.

Disciar*e*m lu dol,
Cantar*e*m anb' alagria,
Y n'arem a dá
Las pascuas a Maria.
    O Maria !

Sant Gabriel,
Qui portaba la anbasciada ;
Des nostro rey del cel
Estarau vos prefiada.
Ya omiliada,
Tu o vais aqui serventa,
Fia del Deu contenta,
Para fe lo que el vol.
    Disciar*e*m lu dol, etc.

Y a milla nit,
Pariguero vos regina ;
A un Deu infinit,
Dintra una establina.
Y a millo dia,
Que los Angles van cantant
Pau y abondant
De la gloria de Deu sol.
    Disciar*e*m lu dol, etc.

Y a Libalam,
Allá la terra santa,
Nus nat Jesus,
Anb' alagria tanta.
Infant petit
Que tot lu mon salvaria ;
Y ningu y bastaria,
Nu mes un Deu tot sol.
    Disciar*e*m lu dol, etc.

Cuant d'Orien lus
Tres reys la stralla veran,
Deu omnipotent,
Adorá lo vingaran.
Un present inferan,
De mil *e*ncens y or,
A lu beneit Señó,
Que conesce cual se vol.
    Disciar*e*m lu dol, etc.

Tot fu gayant
Para cumplí lu prumas ;
Y lu Esperit sant
De un angel fau gramas.
Gran foc ences,

Que crama lu curagia ;
Deu nos da lenguagia,
Para fe lo que Deu vol.
 Disciarem lu dol, etc.

Cuant trespasá
De quest mon nostra Señora,
Al cel s'empugiá
Sun fil la matescia ora.
O emperadora,
Que del cel sou eligida !
Lu rosa florida,

Mé resplanden que un sol.
 Disciarem lu dol, etc.

Y el tercer giorn
Que Jesus resuntá
Deu y Aboroma,
Que la mort triumfá.
De alli se ballá
Para perldrá Lucife,
An tot a seu peudá,
Que de nostro ser el sol.
 Disciarem lu dol, etc.

After this hymn, the following stanzas, soliciting the customary gift of cakes or eggs, are sung:

Ce set sois que vam cantant,
 Regina celastial !
Dunus pau y alagria,
 Y bonas festas tingau.
Yo vos dou sus bonas festas,
 Danaus dinés de sus nous ;
Sempre tarem lus mans llestas
 Para recibí un grapat de ous.

Y el giorn de pascua florida
 Alagramos y giuntament ;

As qui es mort par darnos vida
 Ya viú gloriosament.

Aquesta casa está empedrada,
 Bien halla que la empedró ;
Sun amo de aquesta casa
 Baldria duná un do.
Furmagiada, o empanada,
 Cucutta o flaó ;
Cual se vol cosa me grada,
 Sol que no me digas que no.

The shutters are then opened by the people within, and a supply of cheese-cakes, or other pastry, or eggs, is dropped into a bag carried by one of the party, who acknowledge the gift in the following lines, and then depart :

Aquesta casa está empedrada,
 Empedrada de cuatro vens ;

Sun amo de aquesta casa,
 *E*s omo de compliment.*

If nothing is given, the last line reads thus:

 No es omo de compliment.

---

* Thus in the Spanish :

Aquesta casa está empedrada,
 Empedrada de cuatro vientos ;

El amo de aquesta casa
Es hombre de cortesia.

# THE EARLY NORTHWEST.

STEAMER OREGON, LAKE HURON, OFF THUNDER BAY, JULY 24, 1846 : Buffalo continues to extend on every side, but the late additions to the city do not much improve its beauty. Its nucleus of well-built streets does not seem to have grown much broader within the last five years, but the suburbs are rapidly spreading—small wooden houses, scattered or in clusters, built hastily for emigrants along unpaved and powdery streets. I saw, however, on a little excursion which I made into the surrounding country, that pleasant little neighborhoods are rising up at no great distance, with their neat houses, their young trees, and their new shrubbery.

On Tuesday evening, at seven o'clock, we took passage in the steamer Oregon for Chicago, and soon lost sight of the roofs and spires of Buffalo. The next morning found us with the southern shore of Lake Erie in sight—a long line of woods, with here and there a cluster of habitations on the shore. " That village where you see the light-house," said one of the passengers who came from the hills of Maine, " is Grand River, and from that place to Cleveland, which is thirty miles distant, you have the most beautiful country under the sun— perfectly beautiful, sir ; not a hill the whole way, and the finest farms that were ever seen ; you can buy a good farm there for two thousand dollars." In two or three hours afterward we were at Cleveland, and I hastened on shore. It is situated beyond a steep bank of the lake, nearly as elevated as the shore at Brooklyn, which we call Brooklyn Heights. As I stood on the edge of this bank and looked over the broad lake below me, stretching beyond the sight and quivering in the summer wind, I was reminded of the lines of Southey:

> ——"Along the bending line of shore
> Such hue is thrown as when the peacock's neck
> Assumes its proudest tint of amethyst,
> Embathed in emerald glory."

But it was not only along the line of the shore that these hues prevailed; the whole lake glowed with soft amethystine and emerald tinges, in irregular masses, like the shades of watered silk. Cleveland stands in that beautiful country without a hill, of which my fellow-passenger spoke—a thriving village yet to grow into a proud city of the lake country. It is built upon broad dusty ways, in which not a pebble is seen in the fat dark earth of the lake shore, and which are shaded with locust-trees, the variety called seed-locust, with crowded twigs and clustered foliage—a tree chosen, doubtless, for its rapid growth, as the best means of getting up a shade at the shortest notice. Here and there were gardens filled with young fruit-trees; among the largest and hardiest in appearance was the peach-tree, which here spreads broad and sturdy branches, escapes the diseases that make it a short-lived tree in the Atlantic States, and produces fruit of great size and richness. One of my fellow-passengers could hardly find adequate expressions to signify his high sense of the deliciousness of the Cleveland peaches.

I made my way to a street of shops; it had a busy appearance, more so than usual, I was told, for a company of circus-riders, whose tents I had seen from a distance on the lake, was in town, and this had attracted a throng of people from the country. I saw a fruit-stall tended by a man who had the coarsest red hair I think I ever saw, and of whom I bought two or three enormous "bough-apples," as he called them.

He apologized for the price he demanded. " The farmers,"
said he, "know that just now there is a call for their early
fruit, while the circus people are in town, and they make me
pay a 'igh price for it." I told him I perceived he was no
Yankee. " I am a Londoner," he replied ; " and I left London
twelve years ago to slave and be a poor man in Ohio." He
acknowledged, however, that he had two or three times got
together some property, " but the Lord," he said, " laid his
hand on it."

On returning to the steamer, I found a party of country
people, mostly young persons, of both sexes, thin and lank fig-
ures, by no means equal, as productions of the country, to their
bough-apples. They passed through the fine spacious cabin
on the upper deck, extending between the state-rooms the
whole length of the steamer. At length they came to a large
mirror, which stood at the stern, and seemed by its reflection
to double the length of the cabin. They walked on, as if they
would extend their promenade into the mirror, when suddenly
observing the reflection of their own persons advancing, and
thinking it another party, they politely made way to let it
pass. The party in the mirror at the same moment turned to
the same side, which first showed them the mistake they had
made. The passengers had some mirth at their expense, but I
must do our visitors the justice to say that they joined in the
laugh with a very good grace.

The same evening, at twelve o'clock, we were at Detroit.
" You must lock your state-rooms in the night," said one of
the persons employed about the vessel, " for Detroit is full of
thieves." We followed the advice, slept soundly, and saw
nothing of the thieves, nor of Detroit either, for the steamboat
was again on her passage through Lake St. Clair at three this
morning, and when I awoke we were moving over the flats,
as they are called, at the upper end of the lake. The steamer
was threading her way in a fog between large patches of
sedge of a pea-green color. We had waited several hours at
Detroit, because this passage is not safe at night, and steam-

ers of a larger size are sometimes grounded here in the day-time.

JULY 25th: Soon after passing the flats and entering the river St. Clair, the steamer stopped to take in wood on the Canadian side. Here I went on shore. All that we could see of the country was a road along the bank, a row of cottages at a considerable distance from each other along the road, a narrow belt of cleared fields behind them, and beyond the fields the original forest, standing like a long lofty wall, with its crowded stems of enormous size and immense height, rooted in the strong soil—ashes and maples and elms, the largest of their species. Scattered in the foreground were numbers of leaf-less elms, so huge that the settlers, as if in despair of bringing them to the ground by the axe, had girdled them and left them to decay and fall at their leisure. We went up to one of the houses, before which stood several of the family, attracted to the door by the sight of our steamer. Among them was an intelligent-looking man, originally from the State of New York, who gave quick and shrewd answers to our inquiries. He told us of an Indian settlement about twenty miles farther up the St. Clair. Here dwell a remnant of the Chippewa tribe, collected by the Canadian government, which has built for them comfortable log-houses with chimneys, furnished them with horses and neat cattle, and utensils of agriculture, erected a house of worship, and given them a missionary. " The design of planting them here," said the settler, " was to encourage them to cultivate the soil." " And what has been the success of the plan?" I asked. " It has met with no success at all," he answered. " The worst thing that the government could do for these people is to give them everything as it has done, and leave them under no necessity to provide for them-selves. They chop over a little land, an acre or two to a fam-ily ; their squaws plant a little corn and a few beans, and this is the extent of their agriculture. They pass their time in hunting and fishing, or in idleness. They find deer and bears in the woods behind them, and fish in the St. Clair before their

doors ; and they squander their yearly pensions.  In one re-
spect they are just like white men : they will not work if they
can live without it."  " What fish do they find in the St.
Clair ? "  " Various sorts.  Trout and white-fish are the finest,
but they are not so abundant at this season.  Sturgeon and
pike are just now in season, and the pike are excellent."  One
of us happening to observe that the river might easily be
crossed by swimming, the settler answered : " Not so easily
as you might think.  The river is as cold as a well, and the
swimmer would soon be chilled through, and perhaps taken
with the cramp.  It is this coldness of the water which makes
the fish so fine at this season."

We now proceeded up the river, and in about two hours
came to a neat little village on the British side, with a wind-
mill, a little church, and two or three little cottages, prettily
screened by young trees.  Immediately beyond this was the
beginning of the Chippewa settlement of which we had been
told.  Log-houses, at the distance of nearly a quarter of a mile
from each other, stood in a long row beside the river, with
scattered trees about them, the largest of the forest, some
girdled and leafless, some untouched and green, the smallest
trees between having been cut away.  Here and there an In-
dian woman, in a blue dress and bareheaded, was walking
along the road ; cows and horses were grazing near the houses;
patches of maize were seen, tended in a slovenly manner and
by no means clear of bushes, but nobody was at work in the
fields.  Two females came down to the bank, with paddles,
and put off into the river in a birch-bark canoe, the ends of
which were carved in the peculiar Indian fashion.  A little be-
yond stood a group of boys and girls on the water's edge, the
boys in shirts and leggings, silently watching the steamer as it
shot by them.  Still farther on a group of children of both
sexes, seven in number, came running, with shrill cries, down
the bank.  It was then about twelve o'clock, and the weather
was extremely sultry.  The boys in an instant threw off their
shirts and leggings, and plunged into the water with shouts,

but the girls were in before them, for they wore only a kind of petticoat, which they did not take off, but cast themselves into the river at once and slid through the clear water like seals. This little Indian colony on the edge of the forest extends for several miles along the river, where its banks are highest and best adapted to the purpose of settlement.  It ends at last just below the village which bears the name of Fort Saranac, in the neighborhood of which I was shown an odd-looking wooden building, and was told that this was the house of worship provided for the Indians by the government.

At Fort Huron, a village on the American side, opposite Fort Saranac, we stopped to land passengers.  Three Indians made their appearance on the shore, one of whom, a very large man, wore a kind of turban, and a white blanket made into a sort of frock, with bars of black in several places— altogether a striking costume.  One of this party, a well-dressed young man, stopped to speak with somebody in the crowd on the wharf, but the giant in the turban, with his companion, strode rapidly by, apparently not deigning to look at us, and disappeared in the village.  He was scarcely out of sight when I perceived a boat approaching the shore with a curiously mottled sail.  As it came nearer I saw that it was a quilt of patchwork taken from a bed.  In the bottom of the boat lay a barrel, apparently of flour; a stout young fellow pulled a pair of oars, and a slender-waisted damsel, neatly dressed, sat in the stern, plying a paddle with a dexterity which she might have learned from the Chippewa ladies, and guiding the course of the boat, which passed with great speed over the water.

We were soon upon the broad waters of Lake Huron, and when the evening closed upon us we were already out of sight of land.  The next morning I was awakened by the sound of rain on the hurricane deck.  A cool east wind was blowing. I opened the outer door of my state-room and snuffed the air, which was strongly impregnated with the odor of burnt leaves or grass, proceeding, doubtless, from the burning of woods or prairies somewhere on the shores of the lake. For mile after mile, for hour after hour, as we flew through the mist, the same odor was perceptible: the atmosphere of the lake was full of it. " Will it rain all day? " I asked of a fellow-passenger, a Salem man, in a white cravat. " The clouds are thin," he answered; "the sun will soon burn them off." In fact, the sun soon melted away the clouds, and before ten o'clock I was shown, to the north of us, the dim shore of the Great Manitoulin Island, with the faintly descried opening called the West Strait, through which a throng of speculators in copper mines are this summer constantly passing to the Sault St. Marie. On the other side was the sandy isle of Bois Blanc, the name of which is commonly corrupted into Bob Low Island, thickly covered with pines, and showing a tall lighthouse on the point nearest us. Beyond another point lay like a cloud the island of Mackinaw. I had seen it once before, but now the hazy atmosphere magnified it into a lofty mountain; its limestone cliffs, impending over the water, seemed larger; the white fort—white as snow—built from the quarries of the island, looked more commanding, and the rocky crest above it seemed almost to rise to the clouds. There was a good deal of illusion in all this, as we were convinced as we came nearer; but Mackinaw, with its rocks rising from the most transparent waters that the earth pours out from her springs, is a stately object in any condition of the atmosphere. The captain of our steamer allowed us but a moment at Mackinaw; a moment to gaze into the clear waters, and count the fish as they played about without fear twenty or thirty feet below our steamer, as plainly seen as if they lay in the air; a moment to look at the fort on the heights, dazzling the eyes with its new whiteness; a moment to observe the habitations of this ancient village, some of which show you roofs and walls of red-cedar bark confined by horizontal strips of wood, a kind of architecture between the wigwam and the settler's cabin. A few baskets of fish were lifted on board, in which I saw trout of enormous size—trout a yard in length, and white-fish smaller, but held, perhaps, in higher esteem, and we turned our course to the straits which lead into Lake Michigan. But we hope to see more of Mackinaw on our return.

JULY 31st: The odor of burnt leaves continued to accompany us, and from the western shore of the lake, thickly covered with wood, we saw large columns of smoke, several miles apart, rising into the hazy sky. The steamer turned toward the eastern shore, and about an hour before sunset stopped to take in wood at the upper Maneto Island, where we landed and strolled into the forest. Part of the island is high, but this, where we went on shore, consists of hillocks and hollows of sand, like the waves of the lake in one of its storms, and looking as if successive storms had swept them up from the bottom. They were covered with an enormous growth of trees which must have stood for centuries. We admired the astonishing transparency of the water on this shore, the clean sands, without any intermixture of mud, the pebbles of almost chalky whiteness, and the stones in the edge of the lake, to which adhered no slime, nor green moss, nor aquatic weed. In the light-green depths, far down, but distinctly seen, shoals of fish, some of them of large size, came quietly playing about the huge hull of our steamer. On the shore were two log-houses inhabited by woodmen, one of whom drew a pail of water, for the refreshment of some of the passengers, from a well dug in the sand by his door. "It is not so good as the lake water," said I, for I saw it was not so clear. "It is colder, though," answered the man; "but I must say that there is no purer or sweeter water in the world than that of our lake."

Next morning we were coasting the western shore of Lake Michigan, a high bank presenting a long line of forest. This was broken by the little town of Sheboygan, with its lighthouse among the shrubs of the bank, its cluster of houses just built, among which were two hotels, and its single schooner lying at the mouth of a river. You probably never heard of

Sheboygan before; it has just sprung up in the forests of Wisconsin; the leaves have hardly withered on the trees that were felled to make room for its houses; but it will make a noise in the world yet. "It is the prettiest place on the lake," said a passenger, whom we left there, with three chubby and healthy children, a lady who had already lived long enough at Sheboygan to be proud of it. Farther on we came to Milwaukee, which is rapidly becoming one of the great cities of the West. It lies within a semicircle of green pastoral declivities sprinkled with scattered trees, where the future streets are to be built. We landed at a kind of wharf, formed by a long platform of planks laid on piles, under which the water flows, and extending to some distance into the lake, and along which a car, running on a railway, took the passengers and their baggage, and a part of the freight of the steamer, to the shore. "Will you go up to town, sir?" was the question with which I was saluted by the drivers of a throng of vehicles of all sorts as soon as I reached the land. They were ranged along a firm sandy beach between the lake and the river of Milwaukee. On one side the light-green waters of the lake, of crystalline clearness, came rolling in before the wind, and on the other the dark thick waters of the river lay still and stagnant in the sun. We did not go up to the town, but we could see that it was compactly built, and in one quarter nobly. A year or two since, that quarter had been destroyed by fire, and on the spot several large and lofty warehouses had been erected, with an hotel of the largest class. They were of a fine light-brown color, and, when I learned that they were of brick, I inquired of a by-stander if that was the natural color of the material. "They are of Milwaukee brick," he answered, "and neither painted nor stained; and are better brick, besides, than are made at the eastward." Milwaukee is said to contain, at present, about ten thousand inhabitants. Here the belt of forest that borders the lake stretches back for several miles to the prairies of Wisconsin. "The Germans," said a passenger, "are already in the woods hacking at the trees, and will soon open the country to the prairies."

We made a short stop at Racine, prettily situated on the bank among the scattered trees of an oak opening, and another at Southport, a rival town eleven miles farther south. It is surprising how many persons travel as way-passengers from place to place on the shores of these lakes. Five years ago the number was very few; now they comprise, at least, half the number on board a steamboat plying between Buffalo and Chicago. When all who travel from Chicago to Buffalo shall cross the peninsula of Michigan by the more expeditious route of the railway, the Chicago and Buffalo line of steamers, which its owners claim to be the finest line in the world, will still be crowded with people taken up or to be set down at some of the intermediate towns.

When we awoke the next morning our steamer was at Chicago. Any one who had seen this place, as I had done five years ago, when it contained less than five thousand people, would find some difficulty in recognizing it now, when its population is more than fifteen thousand. It has its long rows of warehouses and shops, its bustling streets; its huge steamers, and crowds of lake-craft, lying at the wharves; its villas embowered with trees; and its suburbs, consisting of the cottages of German and Irish laborers, stretching northward along the lake and westward into the prairies, and widening every day. The slovenly and raw appearance of a new settlement begins in many parts to disappear. The Germans have already a garden in a little grove for their holidays, as in their towns in the old country, and the Roman Catholics have just finished a college for the education of those who are to proselyte the West. The day was extremely hot, and at sunset we took a short drive along the little belt of firm sand which forms the border of the lake. Light-green waves came to the shore in long lines, with a crest of foam, like a miniature surf, rolling in from that inland ocean, and, as they dashed against the legs of the horses and the wheels of our carriage, the air that played over them was exceedingly refreshing. . . .

SAULT ST. MARIE, AUGUST 13th: It was a hot August morning as the steamer Wisconsin, an unwieldy bulk, dipping and bobbing upon the small waves, and trembling at every stroke of the engine, swept out into the lake on our return from Chicago. The southwest wind during the warmer portion of the summer months is a sort of sirocco in Illinois. It blows with considerable strength, but, passing over an immense extent of heated plains, it brings no coolness. It was such an air that accompanied us on our way north from Chicago ; and, as the passengers huddled into the shady places outside of the state-rooms on the upper deck, I thought of the flocks of quails I had seen gasping in the shadow of the rail-fences on the prairies. People here expose themselves to a draught of air with much less scruple than they do in the Atlantic States. "We do not take cold by it," they said to me when I saw them sitting in a current of wind, after perspiring freely. If they do not take cold, it is odds but they take something else—a fever, perhaps, or what is called a bilious attack. The vicissitudes of climate at Chicago and its neighborhood are more sudden and extreme than with us, but the inhabitants say that they are not often the cause of catarrhs, as in the Atlantic States. Whatever may be the cause, I have met with no person since I came to the West who appeared to have a catarrh. From this region, perhaps, will hereafter proceed singers with the clearest pipes.

Some forty miles beyond Chicago we stopped for half an hour at Little Fort, one of those flourishing little towns which are springing up on the lake shore to besiege future Congresses for money to build their harbors. This settlement has started up in the woods within the last three or four years, and its cluster of roofs, two of the broadest of which cover respectable-looking hotels, already makes a considerable figure when viewed from the lake. We passed to the shore over a long platform of planks framed upon two rows of posts or piles planted in the sandy shallows. "We make a port in this manner on any part of the western shore of the lake," said a passenger, "and convenient ports they are, except in very high winds. On the eastern shore, the coast of Michigan, they have not this advantage; the ice and the northwest winds would rend such a wharf as this in pieces. On this side, too, the water of the lake, except when an east wind blows, is smoother than on the Michigan coast, and the steamers therefore keep under the shelter of this bank."

At Southport, still farther north, in the new State of Wisconsin, we procured a kind of omnibus and were driven over the town, which, for a new settlement, is uncommonly pretty. We crossed a narrow inlet of the lake, a *creek* in the proper sense of the term, a winding channel, with water in the midst, and a rough growth of water-flags and sedges on the sides. Among them grew the wild rice, its bending spikes, heavy with grain, almost ready for the harvest. "In the northern marshes of Wisconsin," said one of our party, "I have seen the Indian women gathering this grain. Two of them take their places in a canoe; one of them, seated in the stern, pushes it with her paddle through the shallows of standing water, while the other, sitting forward, bends the heads of the rice-plant over the sides of the canoe, strikes them with a little stick, and causes the grain to fall within it. In this way are collected large quantities, which serve as the winter food of the Menomonies and some other tribes." The grain of the wild rice, I was told, is of a dark color, but palatable as food. The gentleman who gave me this account had made several attempts to procure it, in a fit state to be sown, for Judge Buel, of Albany, who was desirous of trying its cultivation on the grassy shallows of our Eastern rivers. He was not successful at first, because, as soon as the grain is collected, it is kiln-dried by the Indians, which destroys the vegetative principle. At length, however, he obtained and sent on a small quantity of the fresh rice, but it reached Judge Buel only a short time before his death, and the experiment probably has not been made.

On one side of the creek was a sloping bank of some height, where tall old forest-trees were growing. Among these stood three houses, just built, and the space between them and the water was formed into gardens with regular terraces faced with turf. Another turn of our vehicle brought us into a public square, where the oaks of the original forest were left standing, a miniature of the *Champs Elysées*, surrounding which, among the trees, stand many neat houses, some of them built of a drab-colored brick. Back of the town we had a glimpse of a prairie approaching within half a mile of the river. We were next driven through a street of shops, and thence to our steamer. The streets of Southport are beds of sand, and one of the passengers, who professed to speak from some experience, described the place as haunted by myriads of fleas.

It was not till about one o'clock of the second night after leaving Chicago that we landed again at Mackinaw, and, after an infinite deal of trouble in getting our luggage together, and keeping it together, we were driven to the Mission House, a plain, comfortable old wooden house, built thirty or forty years since by a missionary society, and now turned into a hotel. Beside the road, close to the water's edge, stood several wigwams of the Pottawattamies, pyramids of poles wrapped around with rush matting, each containing a family asleep. The place was crowded with people on their way to the mining regions of Lake Superior, or returning from it, and we were obliged to content ourselves with narrow accommodations for the night. At half-past seven the next morning we departed for the Sault St. Marie in the little steamer General Scott. The wind was blowing fresh, and a score of persons who had intended to visit the Sault were withheld by the fear of sea-sickness, so that half a dozen of us had the steamer to ourselves. In three or four hours we found ourselves gliding out of the lake, through smooth water, between two low points of land covered with firs and pines, into the west strait. We passed Drummond's Island, and then coasted St. Joseph's Island, on the woody shore of which I was shown a solitary house. There I was told lives a long-nosed Englishman, a half-pay officer, with two wives, sisters, each the mother of a numerous offspring. This English polygamist has been more successful in seeking solitude than in avoiding notoriety. The very loneliness of his habitation on the shore causes it to be remarked, and there is not a passenger who makes the voyage to the Sault to whom his house is not pointed out and his story related. It was hinted to me that he had a third wife in Toronto, but I have my private doubts of this part of the story, and suspect that it was thrown in to increase my wonder.

Beyond the island of St. Joseph we passed several islets of rock, with fir-trees growing from the clefts. Here, in summer, I was told, the Indians often set up their wigwams, and subsist by fishing. There were none in sight as we passed, but we frequently saw on either shore the skeletons of the Chippewa habitations. These consist, not like those of the Pottawattamies, of a circle of sticks placed in the form of a cone, but of slender poles bent into circles, so as to make an almost regular hemisphere, over which, while it serves as a dwelling, birch-bark and mats of bulrushes are thrown. On the western side of the passage, opposite St. Joseph's Island, stretches the long coast of Sugar Island, luxuriant with an extensive forest of the sugar-maple, where the Indians manufacture maple-sugar in the spring. I inquired concerning their agriculture. " They plant no corn nor squashes," said a passenger, who had resided for some time at the Sault; " they will not ripen in this climate; but they plant potatoes in the sugar-bush, and dig them when the spring opens. They have no other agriculture; they plant no beans, as I believe the Indians do elsewhere." A violent squall of wind and rain fell upon the water just as we entered that broad part of the passage which bears the name of Muddy Lake. In ordinary weather the waters here are perfectly pure and translucent, but now their agitation brought up the loose earth from the shallow bottom, and made them as turbid as the Missouri, with the exception of a narrow channel in the midst, where the current runs deep. Rocky hills now began to show themselves to the east of us; we passed the sheet of water known by the name of Lake George, and came to a little river which appeared to have its source at the foot of a precipitous ridge on the British side. It is called Garden River, and a little beyond it, on the same side, lies Garden Village, inhabited by the Indians. It was deserted, the Indians having gone to attend a great assemblage of their race, held on one of the Manitoulin islands, where they are to receive their annual payments from the British government. Here were log-houses, and skeletons of wigwams, from which the coverings had been taken. An Indian, when he travels, takes with him his family and his furniture, the matting for his wigwam, his implements for hunting and fishing, his dogs and cats, and finds a home wherever he finds poles for a dwelling. A tornado had recently passed over the Garden Village. The numerous girdled trees which stood on its little clearing had been twisted off midway or near the ground by the wind, and the roofs had, in some instances, been lifted from the cabins. At length, after a winding voyage of sixty miles, between wild banks of forest, in some places smoking with fires, in some looking as if never violated either by fire or steel, with huge carcasses of trees mouldering on the ground, and venerable trees standing over them, bearded with streaming moss, we came in sight of the white rapids of the Sault St. Marie. We passed the humble cabins of the half-breeds on either shore, with here and there a round wigwam near the water; we glided by a white chimney standing behind a screen of fir-trees, which, we were told, had belonged to the dwelling of Tanner, who himself set fire to his house the other day, before murdering Mr. Schoolcraft, and in a few minutes were at the wharf of this remotest settlement of the Northwest.

FALLS OF ST. MARIE, AUGUST 15th: A crowd had assembled on the wharf of the American village at the Sault St. Marie, popularly called the *Soo*, to witness our landing; men of all ages and complexions, in hats and caps of every form and fashion, with beards of every length and color, among which I discovered two or three pairs of mustaches. It was a party of copper-mine speculators, just flitting from Copper Harbor and Eagle River, mixed with a few Indian and half-breed inhabitants of the place. Among them I saw a face or two quite familiar in Wall Street. I had a conversation with an intelligent geologist, who had just returned from an examination of the copper mines of Lake Superior. He had pitched his tent in the fields near the village, choosing to pass the night in this manner, as he had done for several weeks past, rather than in a crowded inn. In regard to the mines, he told me that the external tokens—the surface indications, as he called them—were more favorable than those of any copper mines in the world. They are still, however, mere surface indications; the veins had not been worked to that depth which was necessary to determine their value with any certainty. The mixture of silver with the copper he regarded as not giving any additional value to the mines, inasmuch as it is only occasional and rare. Sometimes, he told me, a mass of metal would be discovered of the size of a man's fist, or smaller, composed of copper and silver, both metals closely united, yet both perfectly pure, and unalloyed with each other. The masses of virgin copper found in beds of gravel are, however, the most remarkable feature of these mines. One of them, which has been discovered this summer, but which has not been raised, is estimated to weigh twenty tons. I saw in the propeller Independence, by which this party from the copper mines was brought down to the Sault, one of these masses, weighing seventeen hundred and fifty pounds, with the appearance of having once been fluid with heat. It was so pure that it might have been cut in pieces by cold steel and stamped at once into coin.

Two or three years ago this settlement of the Sault St. Marie was but a military post of the United States, in the midst of a village of Indians and half-breeds. There were, perhaps, a dozen white residents in the place, including the family of the Baptist missionary and the agent of the American Fur Company, which had removed its station hither from Mackinaw, and built its warehouse on this river. But, since the world has begun to talk of the copper mines of Lake Superior, settlers flock into the place; carpenters are busy in putting up houses with all haste on the government lands, and large warehouses have been built upon piles driven into the shallows of the St. Marie. Five years hence, the primitive character of the place will be altogether lost, and it will have become a bustling Yankee town, resembling the other new settlements of the West.

Here the navigation from lake to lake is interrupted by the falls or rapids of the river St. Marie, from which the place receives its name. The crystalline waters of Lake Superior, on their way through the channel of this river to Lake Huron, rush and foam and roar, for about three quarters of a mile, over rocks and large stones. Close to the rapids, with birchen canoes moored in little inlets, is a village of the Indians, consisting of log-cabins and round wigwams, on a shrubby level, reserved to them by the government. The morning after our arrival we went through this village in search of a canoe and a couple of Indians, to make the descent of the rapids, which is one of the first things that a visitor to the Sault must think of. In the first wigwam that we entered were three men and two women as drunk as they could well be. The squaws were speechless and motionless—too far gone, as it seemed, to raise either hand or foot; the men, though apparently unable to rise, were noisy, and one of them, who called himself a half-breed and spoke a few words of English, seemed disposed to quarrel. Before the next door was a woman busy in washing, who spoke a little English. "The old man out there," she said, in answer to our questions, " can paddle canoe, but he is very drunk; he cannot do it to-day." "Is there nobody else," we asked, "who will take us down the falls?" "I don't know; the Indians all drunk to-day." "Why is that? why are they all drunk to-day?" "Oh! the whiskey," answered the woman, giving us to understand that when an Indian could get whiskey he got drunk as a matter of course. By this time the man had come up, and, after addressing us with the customary "*bon jour*," manifested a curiosity to know the nature of our errand. The woman explained it to him in English. "Oh! messieurs, je vous servirai," said he, for he spoke Canadian French; "I go, I go." We told him that we doubted whether he was quite sober enough. "Oh! messieurs, je suis parfaitement capable—first rate, first rate." We shook him off as soon as we could, but not till after he had time to propose that we should wait till the next day, and to utter the maxim, "Whiskey, good—too much whiskey, no good."

In a log-cabin, which some half-breeds were engaged in building, we found two men who were easily persuaded to leave their work and pilot us over the rapids. They took one of the canoes which lay in a little inlet close at hand, and, entering it, pushed it with their long poles up the stream in the edge of the rapids. Arriving at the head of the rapids, they took in our party, which consisted of five, and we began the descent. At each end of the canoe sat a half-breed, with a paddle, to guide it while the current drew us rapidly down among the agitated waters. It was surprising with what dexterity they kept us in the smoothest part of the water, seeming to know the way down as well as if it had been a beaten path in the fields. At one time we would seem to be directly approaching a rock against which the waves were dashing, at another to be descending into a hollow of the waters in which our canoe would be inevitably filled, but a single stroke of the paddle given by the man at the prow put us safely by the seeming danger. So rapid was the descent that almost as soon as we descried the apparent peril it was passed. In less than ten minutes, as it seemed to me, we had left the roar of the rapids behind us, and were gliding over the smooth water at their foot.

In the afternoon we engaged a half-breed and his brother to take us over to the Canadian shore. His wife, a slender young woman with a lively physiognomy, not easily to be distinguished from a French woman of her class, accompanied us in the canoe with her little boy. The birch-bark canoe of the savage seems to me one of the most beautiful and perfect things of the kind constructed by human art. We were in one of the finest that float on St. Marie River, and when I looked at its delicate ribs, mere shavings of white cedar, yet firm enough for the purpose, the thin, broad laths of the same wood with which these are enclosed, and the broad sheets of birch-bark, impervious to water, which sheathed the outside, all firmly sewed together by the tough, slender roots of the fir-tree, and when I considered its extreme lightness and the grace of its form, I could not but wonder at the ingenuity of those who had invented so beautiful a combination of ship-building and basket-work. "It cost me twenty dollars," said the half-breed, "and I would not take thirty for it." We were ferried over the waves where they dance at the foot of the rapids. At this place large quantities of white-fish, one of the most delicate kinds known on our continent, are caught by the Indians, in their season, with scoop-nets. The whites are about to interfere with this occupation of the Indians, and I saw the other day a seine of prodigious length constructing, with which it is intended to sweep nearly half the river at once. "They will take a hundred barrels a day," said an inhabitant of the place.

On the British side the rapids divide themselves into half a dozen noisy brooks, which roar around little islands, and 'in the boiling pools of which the speckled trout is caught with the rod and line. We landed at the warehouses of the Hudson Bay Company, where the goods intended for the Indian trade are deposited, and the furs brought from the Northwest are collected. They are surrounded by a massive stockade, within which lives the agent of the company, the walks are gravelled and well-kept, and the whole bears the marks of British solidity and precision. A quantity of furs had been brought in the day before, but they were locked up in the warehouse, and all was now quiet and silent. The agent was absent; a half-breed nurse stood at the door with his child, and a Scotch servant, apparently with nothing to do, was lounging in the court enclosed by the stockade; in short, there was less bustle about this centre of one of the most powerful trading companies in the world than about one of our farm-houses. Crossing the bay, at the bottom of which these buildings stand, we landed at a Canadian village of half-breeds. Here were one or two wigwams and a score of log-cabins, some of which we entered. In one of them we were received with great appearance of deference by a woman of decidedly Indian features, but light-complexioned, barefoot, with blue embroidered leggings falling over her ankles and sweeping the floor, the only peculiarity of Indian costume about her. The house was as clean as scouring could make it, and her two little children, with little French physiognomies, were fairer than many children of the European race. These people are descended from the French *voyageurs* and settlers on one side; they speak Canadian French more or less, but generally employ the Chippewa language in their intercourse with each other.

Near at hand was a burial-ground, with graves of the Indians and half-breeds. Some of the graves were covered with a low roof of cedar-bark, others with a wooden box; over others was placed a little house like a dog-kennel, except that it had no door; others were covered with little log-cabins. One of these was of such a size that a small Indian family would have found it amply large for their accommodation. It is a practice among the savages to protect the graves of the dead from the wolves by stakes driven into the ground and meeting at the top like the rafters of a roof; and, perhaps, when the Indian or half-breed exchanged his wigwam for a log-cabin, his respect for the dead led him to make the same improvement in the architecture of their narrow houses. At the head of most of these monuments stood wooden crosses, for the population here is principally Roman Catholic, some of them inscribed with the names of the dead, not always accurately spelled. Not far from the church stands a building, regarded by the half-breeds as a wonder of architecture, the stone house, *la maison de pierre*, as they call it, a large mansion built of stone by a former agent of the Northwest or Hudson Bay Company, who lived here in a kind of grand manorial style, with his servants and horses and hounds, and gave hospitable dinners in those days when it was the fashion for the host to do his best to drink his guests under the table. The old splendor of the place has departed, its gardens are overgrown with grass, the barn has been blown down, the kitchen in which so many grand dinners were cooked consumed by fire, and the mansion, with its broken and patched windows, is now occupied by a Scotch farmer of the name of Wilson.

We climbed a ridge of hills back of the house to the church of the Episcopal Mission, built a few years ago as a place of worship for the Chippewas, who have since been removed by the government. It stands remote from any habitation, with three or four Indian graves near it, and we found it filled with hay. The view from its door is uncommonly beautiful, the broad St. Marie lying below, with its bordering villages and woody valley, its white rapids and its rocky islands, picturesque with the pointed summits of the fir-tree. To the northwest the sight followed the river to the horizon, where it issued from Lake Superior, and I was told that in clear weather one might discover, from the spot on which I stood, the promontory of Gros Cap, which guards the outlet of that mighty lake. The country around was smoking in a dozen places with fires in the woods. When I returned I asked who kindled them. "It is old Tanner," said one, "the man who murdered Schoolcraft." There is great fear here of Tanner,

who is thought to be lurking yet in the neighborhood. I was
going the other day to look at a view of the place from an
eminence, reached by a road passing through a swamp, full of
larches and firs. "Are you not afraid of Tanner?" I was
asked. Mrs. Schoolcraft, since the assassination of her hus-
band, has come to live in the fort, which consists of barracks
protected by a high stockade. It is rumored that Tanner has
been seen skulking about within a day or two, and yesterday
a place was discovered which is supposed to have served for
his retreat. It was a hollow, thickly surrounded by shrubs,
which some person had evidently made his habitation for a
considerable time. There is a dispute whether this man is
insane or not, but there is no dispute as to his malignity. He
has threatened to take the life of Mr. Bingham, the venerable
Baptist missionary at this place, and, as long as it is not cer-
tain that he has left the neighborhood, a feeling of insecurity
prevails. Nevertheless, as I know no reason why this man
should take it into his head to shoot me, I go whither I list,
without the fear of Tanner before my eyes.

MACKINAW, AUGUST 19th: We were detained two days
longer than we expected at the Sault St. Marie by the fail-
ure of the steamer General Scott to depart at the proper
time. If we could have found a steamer going up Lake Su-
perior, we should most certainly have quieted our impatience
at this delay by embarking on board of her. But the only
steamer in the river St. Marie above the falls, which is a sort
of arm or harbor of Lake Superior, was the Julia Palmer, and
she was lying aground in the pebbles and sand of the shore.
She had just been dragged over the portage which passes
round the falls, where a broad path, with hillocks flattened, and
trunks hewn off close to the surface, gave tokens of the vast
bulk that had been moved over it. The moment she touched
the water she stuck fast, and the engineer was obliged to go
to Cleveland for additional machinery to move her forward.
He had just arrived with the proper apparatus, and the
steamer had begun to work its way slowly into the deep water;

but some days must yet elapse before she can float, and after that the engine must be put together.

Had the Julia Palmer been ready to proceed up the lake, I should have seized the occasion to be present at an immense assemblage of Indians on Madeleine Island. This island lies far in the lake, near its remoter extremity. On one of its capes, called La Pointe, is a missionary station and an Indian village, and here the savages are gathering in vast numbers to receive their annual payments from the United States. "There were already two thousand of them at La Pointe when I left the place," said an intelligent gentleman who had just returned from the lake, "and they were starving. If an Indian family has a stock of provisions on hand sufficient for a month, it is sure to eat it up in a week, and the Indians at La Pointe had already consumed all they had provided, and were living on what they could shoot in the woods, or get by fishing in the lake." I inquired of him the probable number of Indians the occasion would bring together. "Seven thousand," he answered. "Among them are some of the wildest tribes on the continent, whose habits have been least changed by the neighborhood of the white man. A new tribe will come in who never before would have any transactions with the government. They are called the Pillagers, a fierce and warlike race, proud of their independence, and, next to the Blackfeet and the Comanches, the most ferocious and formidable tribe within the territory of the United States. They inhabit the country about Red River and the head-waters of the Mississippi." I was further told that some of the Indian traders had expressed their determination to disregard the law, set up their tents at La Pointe, and sell spirits to the savages. "If they do, knives will be drawn," was the common saying at the Sault; and at the fort I learned that a requisition had arrived from La Pointe for twenty men to enforce the law and prevent disorder. "We cannot send half the number," said the officer who commanded at the fort; "we have but twelve men in all; the rest of the garrison have been

ordered to the Mexican frontier, and it is necessary that some.
body should remain to guard the public property." The call
for troops has since been transferred to the garrison at Macki-
naw, from which they will be sent. I learned afterward, from
an intelligent lady of the half-caste at the Sault, that letters
had arrived from which it appeared that more than four thou-
sand Indians were already assembled at La Pointe, and that
their stock of provisions was exhausted. "They expected,"
said the lady, "to be paid off on the 15th of August, but the
government has changed the time to nearly a month later.
This is unfortunate for the Indians, for now is the time of their
harvest, the season for gathering wild rice in the marshes, and
they must, in consequence, not only suffer with hunger now,
but in the winter also."

In a stroll which we made through the Indian village, situ-
ated close to the rapids, we fell in with a half-breed, a sensible-
looking man, living in a log-cabin, whose boys, the offspring of
a squaw of the pure Indian race, were practicing with their
bows and arrows. "You do not go to La Pointe?" we asked.
"It is too far to go for a blanket," was his answer; he spoke
tolerable English. This man seemed to have inherited from
the white side of his ancestry somewhat of the love of a con-
stant habitation, for a genuine Indian has no particular dislike
to a distant journey. He takes his habitation with him, and is
at home wherever there is game and fish, and poles with which
to construct his lodge. In a further conversation with the
half-breed, he spoke of the Sault as a delightful abode, and ex-
patiated on the pleasures of the place. "It is the greatest
place in the world for fun," said he; "we dance all winter;
our women are all good dancers; our little girls can dance sin-
gle and double jigs as good as anybody in the States. That
little girl there," pointing to a long-haired girl at the door,
"will dance as good as anybody." The fusion of the two
races in this neighborhood is remarkable, the mixed breed
running by gradual shades into the aboriginal on the one hand,
and into the white on the other—children with a tinge of the

copper hue in the families of white men, and children scarcely less fair sometimes seen in the wigwams. Some of the half-caste ladies at the Falls of St. Marie, who have been educated in the Atlantic States, are persons of graceful and dignified manners and agreeable conversation.

I attended worship at the fort on Sunday. The services were conducted by the chaplain, who is of the Methodist persuasion and a missionary at the place, assisted by the Baptist missionary. I looked about me for some evidence of the success of their labors, but among the worshippers I saw not one male of Indian descent. Of the females, half a dozen, perhaps, were of the half-caste; and, as two of these walked away from the church, I perceived that they wore a fringed clothing for the ankles, as if they took a certain pride in this badge of their Indian extraction. In the afternoon we drove down the west bank of the river to attend religious service at an Indian village, called the Little Rapids, about two miles and a half from the Sault. Here the Methodists have built a mission-house, maintain a missionary, and instruct a fragment of the Chippewa tribe. We found the missionary, Mr. Speight, a Kentuckian, who has wandered to this northern region, quite ill, and there was consequently no service. We walked through the village, which is prettily situated on a swift and deep channel of the St. Marie, where the green waters rush between the main-land and a wooded island. It stands on rich meadows of the river, with a path running before it, parallel with the bank, along the velvet sward, and backed at no great distance by the thick original forest, which not far below closes upon the river on both sides. The inhabitants at the doors and windows of their log-cabins had a demure and subdued aspect; they were dressed in their clean Sunday clothes, and the peace and quiet of the place formed a strong contrast to the debaucheries we had witnessed at the village by the falls. We fell in with an Indian, a quiet little man, of very decent appearance, who answered our questions with great civility. We asked to whom be-

longed the meadows lying back of the cabins, on which we
saw patches of rye, oats, and potatoes. "Oh! they belong to
the mission; the Indians work them." "Are they good peo-
ple, these Indians?" "Oh, yes, good people." "Do they
never drink too much whiskey?" "Well, I guess they drink
too much whiskey sometimes." There was a single wigwam
in the village, apparently a supplement to one of the log-
cabins. We looked in and saw two Indian looms, from which
two unfinished mats were depending. Mrs. Speight, the wife
of the missionary, told us that, a few days before, the village
had been full of these lodges; that the Indians delighted in
them greatly, and always put them up during the mosquito
season; "for a mosquito," said the good lady, "will never
enter a wigwam;" and that lately, the mosquitoes having
disappeared, and the nights having grown cooler, they had
taken down all but the one we saw. We passed a few minutes
in the house of the missionary, to which Mrs. Speight kindly
invited us. She gave a rather favorable account of the Indians
under her husband's charge, but manifestly an honest one, and
without any wish to extenuate the defects of their character.
"There are many excellent persons among them," she said;
"they are a kind, simple, honest people, and some of them are
eminently pious." "Do they follow any regular industry?"
"Many of them are as regularly industrious as the whites, ris-
ing early and continuing at their work in the fields all day.
They are not so attentive as we could wish to the education
of their children. It is difficult to make them send their
children regularly to school; they think they confer a favor
in allowing us to instruct them, and, if they happen to take a
little offence, their children are kept at home. The great evil
against which we have to guard is the love of strong drink.
When this is offered to an Indian, it seems as if it was not in
his nature to resist the temptation. I have known whole con-
gregations of Indians—good Indians—ruined and brought to
nothing by the opportunity of obtaining whiskey as often as
they pleased." We inquired whether the numbers of the

people at the mission were diminishing. She could not speak with much certainty as to this point, having been only a year and a half at the mission, but she thought there was a gradual decrease. "The families of the Indians," she said, in answer to one of my questions, "are small. In one family at the village are six children, and it is the talk of all the Indians, far and near, as something extraordinary. Generally the number is much smaller, and more than half the children die in infancy. Their means would not allow them to rear many children, even if the number of births was greater." Such appears to be the destiny of the red race while in the presence of the white—decay and gradual extinction, even under circumstances apparently the most favorable to its preservation.

On Monday we left the Falls of St. Marie, in the steamer General Scott, on our return to Mackinaw. There were about forty passengers on board—men in search of copper-mines and men in search of health, and travellers from curiosity, Virginians, New Yorkers, wanderers from Illinois, Indiana, Massachusetts, and I believe several other States. On reaching Mackinaw in the evening, our party took quarters in the Mansion House, the obliging host of which stretched his means to the utmost for our accommodation. Mackinaw is at the present moment crowded with strangers, attracted by the cool, healthful climate and the extreme beauty of the place. We were packed for the night almost as closely as the Pottawattamies, whose lodges were on the beach before us. Parlors and garrets were turned into sleeping-rooms; beds were made on the floors and in the passages, and double-bedded rooms were made to receive four beds. It is no difficult feat to sleep at Mackinaw, even in an August night, and we soon forgot, in a refreshing slumber, the narrowness of our quarters.

STEAMER ST. LOUIS, LAKE HURON, AUGUST 20th: Yesterday evening we left the beautiful island of Mackinaw, after a visit of two days delightfully passed. We had climbed its cliffs, rambled on its shores, threaded the walks among its thickets, driven out on the roads that wind through its woods —roads paved by nature with limestone pebbles, a sort of natural macadamization, and the time of our departure seemed to arrive several days too soon. The fort which crowns the heights near the shore commands an extensive prospect, but a still wider one is to be seen from the old fort—Fort Holmes, as it is called—among whose ruined intrenchments the half-breed boys and girls now gather gooseberries. It stands on the very crest of the island, overlooking all the rest. The air, when we ascended it, was loaded with the smoke of burning forests, but from this spot, in clear weather, I was told a magnificent view might be had of the Straits of Mackinaw, the wooded islands, and the shores and capes of the great main-land—places known to history for the past two centuries. For when you are at Mackinaw you are at no new settlement.

In looking for samples of Indian embroidery with porcu-pine quills, we found ourselves one day in the warehouse of the American Fur Company at Mackinaw. Here on the shelves were piles of blankets, white and blue, red scarfs, and white boots; snow-shoes were hanging on the walls, and wolf-traps, rifles, and hatchets were slung to the ceiling—an assort-ment of goods destined for the Indians and half-breeds of the Northwest. The person who attended at the counter spoke English with a foreign accent. I asked him how long he had been in the northwestern country. "To say the truth," he answered, "I have been here sixty years and some days." "You were born here, then?" "I am a native of Mackinaw, French by the mother's side; my father was an Englishman." "Was the place as considerable sixty years ago as it now is?" "More so. There was more trade here, and quite as many inhabitants. All the houses, or nearly all, were then built; two or three only have been put up since." I could easily imagine that Mackinaw must have been a place of conse-quence when here was the centre of the fur trade, now re-moved farther up the country. I was shown the large house in which the heads of the companies of *voyageurs* engaged in the trade were lodged, and the barracks, a long, low building, in which the *voyageurs* themselves, seven hundred in number, made their quarters from the end of June to the beginning of October, when they went out again on their journeys. This interval of three months was a merry time with those light-hearted Frenchmen. When a boat made its appearance approaching Mackinaw, they fell to conjecturing to what company of *voyageurs* it belonged ; as the dispute grew warm the conjectures became bets, till finally, unable to restrain their impatience, the boldest of them dashed into the waters, swam out to the boat, and, climbing on board, shook hands with their brethren, amid the shouts of those who stood on the beach. They talk, on the New England coast, of Chebacco boats, built after a peculiar pattern, and called after Chebacco, an ancient settlement of seafaring men, who have foolishly changed the old Indian name of their place to Ipswich. The Mackinaw navigators have also given their name to a boat of peculiar form, sharp at both ends, swollen at the sides, and flat-bottomed, an excellent sea-boat, it is said, as it must be to live in the wild storms that surprise the mariner on Lake Superior.

We took yesterday a drive to the western shore. The road twined through a wood of overarching beeches and maples, interspersed with the white-cedar and fir. The driver stopped before a cliff sprouting with beeches and cedars, with a small cavity at the foot. This he told us was the Skull Cave. It is only remarkable on account of human bones having been found in it. Farther on a white paling gleamed through the trees ; it enclosed the solitary burial-ground of the garrison, with half a dozen graves. "There are few buried here," said a gentleman of our party ; "the soldiers who come to Mackinaw sick get well soon." The road we travelled was cut through the woods by Captain Scott, who commanded at the fort a few years since. He is the marksman whose aim was so sure that the Western people say of

him that a raccoon on a tree once offered to come down
and surrender without giving him the trouble to fire. We
passed a farm surrounded with beautiful groves. In one of
its meadows was fought the battle between Colonel Croghan
and the British officer Holmes in the war of 1813. Three
luxuriant beeches stand on the edge of the woods, north of the
meadow; one of them is the monument of Holmes; he lies
buried at its root. Another quarter of a mile led us to a little
bay on the solitary shore of the lake looking to the northwest.
It is called the British Landing, because the British troops
landed here in the late war to take possession of the island. We
wandered about awhile, and then sat down upon the embank-
ment of pebbles which the waves of the lake, heaving for cen-
turies, have heaped around the shore of the island—pebbles
so clean that they would no more soil a lady's white muslin
gown than if they had been of newly polished alabaster. The
water at our feet was as transparent as the air around us. On
the main-land opposite stood a church with its spire, and sev-
eral roofs were visible, with a background of woods behind
them. "There," said one of our party, "is the old Mission
Church. It was built by the Catholics in 1680, and has been
a place of worship ever since. The name of the spot is Point
St. Ignace, and there lives an Indian of the full caste, who was
sent to Rome and educated to be a priest, but he preferred the
life of a layman, and there he lives on that wild shore, with a
library in his lodge, a learned savage, occupied with reading
and study." You may well suppose that I felt a strong de-
sire to see Point St. Ignace, its venerable Mission Church, its
Indian village, so long under the care of Catholic pastors, and
its learned savage who talks Italian; but the time of my de-
parture was already fixed. My companions were pointing
out on that shore the mouth of Carp River—which comes
down through the forest roaring over rocks, and in any of the
pools of which you have only to throw a line, with any sort
of bait, to be sure of a trout—when the driver of our vehicle
called out, "Your boat is coming." We looked, and saw the

St. Louis steamer, not one of the largest, but one of the finest boats on the line between Buffalo and Chicago, making rapidly for the island, with a train of black smoke hanging in the air behind her. We hastened to return through the woods, and in an hour and a half we were in our clean and comfortable quarters in this well-ordered little steamer.

But I should mention that before leaving Mackinaw we did not fail to visit the principal curiosities of the place, the Sugar Loaf Rock—a remarkable rock in the middle of the island, of a sharp conical form, rising above the trees by which it is surrounded, and lifting the stunted birches on its shoulders higher than they, like a tall fellow holding up a little boy to overlook a crowd of men—and the Arched Rock on the shore. The atmosphere was thick with smoke, and through the opening spanned by the arch of the rock I saw the long waves, rolled up by a fresh wind, come one after another out of the obscurity and break with roaring on the beach. The path along the brow of the precipice and among the evergreens, by which this rock is reached, is singularly wild, but another, which leads to it along the shore, is no less picturesque—passing under impending cliffs and overshadowing cedars, and between huge blocks and pinnacles of rock. I spoke in one of my former letters of the manifest fate of Mackinaw, which is to be a watering-place. I cannot see how it is to escape this destiny. People already begin to repair to it, for health and refreshment, from the southern borders of Lake Michigan. Its climate during the summer months is delightful; there is no air more pure and elastic, and the winds of the south and the southwest, which are so hot on the prairies, arrive here tempered to a grateful coolness by the waters over which they have swept. The nights are always, in the hottest season, agreeably cool, and the health of the place is proverbial. The world has not many islands so beautiful as Mackinaw, as you may judge from the description I have already given of parts of it. The surface is singularly irregular, with summits of rock and pleasant hollows, open glades of pasturage, and shady nooks. To some, the savage visitors—who occasionally set up their lodges on its beach, as well as on that of the surrounding islands, and paddle their canoes in its waters—will be an additional attraction. I cannot but think with a kind of regret on the time, which I suppose is near at hand, when its wild and lonely woods will be intersected with highways, and filled with cottages and boarding-houses.

# GLIMPSES OF EUROPE.*

FIRST IMPRESSIONS OF FRANCE.—PARIS, AUGUST 9, 1834:
Since we first landed in France, every step of our journey has
reminded us that we were in an old country. Everything we
saw spoke of the past, of an antiquity without limit; every-
where our eyes rested on the handiwork of those who had
been dead for ages, and we were in the midst of customs
which they had bequeathed to their descendants. The
churches were so vast, so solid, so venerable, and time-eaten;
the dwellings so gray, and of such antique architecture, and
in the large towns, like Rouen, rose so high, and overhung
with such quaint projections the narrow and cavernous streets;
the thatched cots were so mossy and so green with grass!
The very hills about them looked scarcely as old, for there
was youth in their vegetation—their shrubs and flowers. The
countrywomen wore such high caps, such long waists, and
such short petticoats!—the fashion of bonnets is an innova-
tion of yesterday, which they regard with scorn. We passed
females riding on donkeys, the Old Testament beast of bur-

---

* Mr. Bryant made no less than six voyages to Europe, of all of which he gave
running accounts in letters to his journal, which were subsequently gathered in vol-
umes, entitled "Letters of a Traveller" (G. P. Putnam & Son, 1869), "Letters
from Spain" (G. P. Putnam & Son, 1869), and "Letters from the East" (G. P. Put-
nam & Son, 1869). The interest of these have largely passed away, owing to lapses
of time, yet a few extracts from them may not be unacceptable to the general
reader.

den, with panniers on each side, as was the custom hundreds
of years since. We saw ancient dames sitting at their doors
with distaffs, twisting the thread by twirling the spindle be-
tween the thumb and finger, as they did in the days of Homer.
A flock of sheep was grazing on the side of a hill; they were
attended by a shepherd and a brace of prick-eared dogs,
which kept them from straying, as was done thousands of
years ago. Speckled birds were hopping by the sides of the
road: it was the magpie, the bird of ancient fable. Flocks of
what I at first took for the crow of our country were stalking
in the fields, or sailing in the air over the old elms: it was the
rook, the bird made as classical by Addison as his cousin the
raven by the Latin poets.

Then there were the old chateaus on the hills, built with
an appearance of military strength, their towers and battle-
ments telling of feudal times. The groves by which they
were surrounded were for the most part clipped into regular
walls, and pierced with regularly arched passages, leading in
various directions, and the trees compelled by the shears to
take the shape of obelisks and pyramids, or other fantastic fig-
ures, according to the taste of the middle ages. As we drew
nearer to Paris, we saw the plant which Noah first commit-
ted to the earth after the deluge—you know what that was, I
hope—trained on low stakes, and growing thickly and luxuri-
antly on the slopes by the side of the highway. Here, too,
was the tree which was the subject of the first Christian mira-
cle—the fig—its branches heavy with the bursting fruit just
beginning to ripen for the market.

But when we entered Paris, and passed the Barrière d'Étoile
with its lofty triumphal arch; when we swept through the
arch of Neuilly, and came in front of the Hôtel des Invalides,
where the aged or maimed soldiers, the living monuments of
so many battles, were walking or sitting under the elms of its
broad esplanade; when we saw the colossal statues of states-
men and warriors frowning from their pedestals on the bridges
which bestride the muddy and narrow channel of the Seine;

when we came in sight of the gray pinnacles of the Tuileries, and the Gothic towers of Notre Dame, and the Roman ones of St. Sulpice, and the dome of the Pantheon, under which lie the remains of so many of the great men of France, and the dark column of Place Vendôme, wrought with figures in relief, and the obelisk brought from Egypt to ornament the Place Louis Quatorze—the associations with antiquity which the country presents, from being general, became particular and historical. They were recollections of power and magnificence and extended empire; of valor and skill ·in war which had held the world in fear; of dynasties that had risen and passed away; of battles and victories which had left no other fruits than their monuments.

A DAY IN FLORENCE.—SEPTEMBER 27, 1834: I have now been in this city a fortnight, and have established myself in a suite of apartments lately occupied, as the landlord told me, in hopes, I presume, of getting a higher rent, by a Russian prince. The Arno flows, or rather stands still, under my windows, for the water is low, and near the western wall of the city is frugally dammed up to preserve it for the public baths. Beyond, this stream, so renowned in history and poetry, is at this season but a feeble rill, almost lost among the pebbles of its bed, and scarcely sufficing to give drink to the pheasants and hares of the Grand Duke's *cascine* on its banks. Opposite my lodgings, at the south end of the *Ponte alla Carraia*, is a little oratory, before the door of which every good Catholic who passes takes off his hat with a gesture of homage : and at this moment a swarthy, weasel-faced man, with a tin box in his hand, is gathering contributions to pay for the services of the chapel, rattling his coin to attract the attention of the pedestrians, and calling out to those who seem disposed to pass without paying. To the north and west the peaks of the Apennines are in full sight, rising over the spires of the city and the groves of the *cascine*. Every evening I see them through the soft, delicately colored haze of an Italian sunset, looking as if they had caught something of the transparency of the sky, and appearing like mountains of fairy-land, instead of the bleak and barren ridges of rock which they really are. The weather since my arrival in Tuscany has been continually se-rene, the sky wholly cloudless, and the temperature uniform —oppressively warm in the streets at noon, delightful at morn-ing and evening, with a long, beautiful, golden twilight, occa-sioned by the reflection of light from the orange-colored haze which invests the atmosphere. Every night I am reminded that I am in the land of song, for until two o'clock in the morning I hear "all manner of tunes" chanted by people in the streets in all manner of voices.

But let me give you the history of a fine day in October, passed at the window of my lodgings on the Lung' Arno, close to the bridge *Alla Carraja.* Waked by the jangling of all the bells in Florence, and by the noise of carriages departing, loaded with travellers, for Rome and other places in the south of Italy, I rise, dress myself, and take my place at the window. I see crowds of men and women from the country, the former in brown velvet jackets, and the latter in broad-brimmed straw hats, driving donkeys loaded with panniers, or trundling hand-carts before them, heaped with grapes, figs, and all the fruits of the orchard, the garden, and the field. They have hardly passed when large flocks of sheep and goats make their appearance, attended by shepherds and their families, driven by the approach of winter from the Apennines, and seeking the pastures of the Maremma, a rich, but, in the sum-mer, an unhealthy tract on the coast. The men and boys are dressed in knee-breeches, the women in bodices, and both sexes wear capotes with pointed hoods, and felt hats with coni-cal crowns; they carry long staves in their hands, and their arms are loaded with kids and lambs too young to keep pace with their mothers. After the long procession of sheep and goats and dogs, and men and women and children, come horses loaded with cloths and poles for tents, kitchen utensils, and the rest of the younglings of the flock. A little after sun-rise I see well-fed donkeys, in coverings of red cloth, driven over the bridge, to be milked for invalids. Maid-servants, bareheaded, with huge, high-carved combs in their hair; waiters of coffee-houses carrying the morning cup of coffee or chocolate to their customers; bakers' boys with a dozen loaves on a board balanced on their heads; milkmen with rush baskets filled with flasks of milk—are crossing the streets in all directions. A little later the bell of the small chapel opposite my window rings furiously for a quarter of an hour, and then I hear mass chanted in a deep, strong, nasal tone. As the day advances, the English, in white hats and white pantaloons, come out of their lodgings, accompanied sometimes by their hale and square-built spouses, and saunter stiffly along the Arno, or take their way to the public galleries and museums. Their massive, clean, and brightly polished carriages also begin to rattle through the streets, setting out on excursions to some part of the environs of Florence—to Fiesole, to the Pratolino, to the Bello Sguardo, to the Poggio Imperiale. Sights of a different kind now present themselves. Sometimes it is a troop of stout Franciscan friars, in sandals and brown robes, each carrying his staff and wearing a brown broad-brimmed hat with a hemispherical crown. Sometimes it is a band of young theological students, in purple cassocks with red collars and cuffs, let out on a holiday, attended by their clerical instructors, to ramble in the *cascine.* There is a priest coming over the bridge, a man of venerable age and great reputation for sanctity; the common people crowd around him to kiss his hand, and obtain a kind word from him as he passes. But what is that procession of men in black gowns, black gaiters, and black masks, moving swiftly along, and bearing on their shoulders a litter covered with black cloth? These are the Brethren of Mercy, who have assembled at the sound of the cathedral bell, and are conveying some sick or wounded person to the hospital. As the day begins to decline, the numbers of carriages in the streets, filled with gayly-dressed people attended by servants in livery, increases. The Grand Duke's equipage, an elegant carriage

drawn by six horses, with coachmen, footmen, and outriders in
drab-colored livery, comes from the Pitti Palace and crosses
the Arno, either by the bridge close to my lodgings, or by
that called *Alla Santa Trinità*, which is in full sight from the
windows.  The Florentine nobility, with their families, and
the English residents, now throng to the *cascine*, to drive at a
slow pace through its thickly-planted walks of elms, oaks, and
ilexes.  As the sun is sinking I perceive the quay, on the
other side of the Arno, filled with a moving crowd of well-
dressed people, walking to and fro, and enjoying the beauty of
the evening.  Travellers now arrive from all quarters, in ca-
briolets, in calashes, in the shabby *vettura*, and in the elegant
private carriage drawn by post-horses, and driven by postil-
ions in the tightest possible deer-skin breeches, the smallest
red coats, and the hugest jack-boots.  The streets about the
doors of the hotels resound with the cracking of whips and
the stamping of horses, and are encumbered with carriages,
heaps of baggage, porters, postilions, couriers, and travellers.
Night at length arrives—the time of spectacles and funerals.
The carriages rattle toward the opera-houses.  Trains of
people, sometimes in white robes and sometimes in black,
carrying blazing torches and a cross elevated on a high
pole before a coffin, pass through the streets chanting the ser-
vice for the dead.  The Brethren of Mercy may also be seen
engaged in their office.  The rapidity of their pace, the flare
of their torches, the gleam of their eyes through their masks,
and their sable garb, give them a kind of supernatural appear-
ance.  I return to bed, and fall asleep amid the shouts of
people returning from the opera, singing, as they go, snatches
of the music with which they had been entertained during the
evening.

PISA AND THE PISANS.—DECEMBER, 1834: Pisa offers a
greater contrast to Florence than I had imagined could exist
between two Italian cities.  This is the very seat of idleness
and slumber, while Florence, from being the residence of the
Court, and from the vast number of foreigners who throng to

it, presents during several months of the year an appearance of great bustle and animation. Four thousand English, an American friend tells me, visit Florence every winter, to say nothing of the occasional residents from France, Germany, and Russia. The number of visitors from the latter country is every year increasing, and the echoes of the Florence gallery have been taught to repeat the strange accents of the Sclavonic tongue. But in Pisa all is stagnation and repose ; even the presence of the sovereign, who really passes a part of the winter here, is unable to give a momentary liveliness to the place. It is nearly as large as Florence, with not one third of the population. The number of strangers is few ; most of them are invalids, and the rest are the quietest people in the world. The rattle of carriages is rarely heard in the streets, in some of which there reigns a stillness so complete that you might imagine them deserted. Pisa has a delightful winter climate, though Madame de Staël has left on record a condemnation of it, having passed here a season of unusually bad weather. Orange- and lemon-trees grow in the open air, and are now loaded with ripe fruit. The fields in the environs are green with grass nourished by abundant rains, and are spotted with daisies in blossom. Crops of flax and various kinds of pulse are showing themselves above the ground, a circumstance sufficient to show that the cultivators expect nothing like what we call winter.

We have now been more than three months in Pisa, where we have obtained very comfortable and pleasant lodgings, looking immediately on the Arno. I had letters to two of the professors of the university here, both of whom received me with great civility. One of them, Biancini, professor of anatomy, whose anatomical preparations have great fame in the United States, and who has been employed to make them for the Medical School in Charleston, and I believe one or two other institutions in our country, was so ill that he could do nothing for me. The other, Rossini, author of several romances and poems, has been very attentive and given me an opportunity of seeing a little of Pisan society. He took me to several *conversazioni*, where the ladies and gentlemen amuse themselves with playing cards and divers other games. The Pisan ladies are not handsome, though some of them have rather a fine presence. In latitude of person they exceed the ladies of our own country by about one third; indeed, both sexes are considerably stouter than with us. I am sorry to say the practice of cicisbeism is very common. Most of the ladies among the nobility who are in opulent circumstances keep their *cavalier servente* in the same house with their good-natured husband. Often the person acting in this capacity is a young man of plebeian extraction, whom you will remark as the constant attendant of some elderly lady, driving out with her in her carriage, sitting with her at her box at the opera, and carrying about her shawl and tippet at a ball. All this, however, is scandal—though, upon second thought, it is no scandal here; yet, as it is scandal in America, I beg you will let it go no further. I would not have you mention either, from me, that the Tuscan nobility are poor and horribly in debt, and that, though they contrive to dress richly when abroad, to keep carriages and maintain a few servants in livery, they live in all other respects with great parsimony. With a few exceptions, they give no entertainments. Here, in Pisa, at the houses of Franceschini, the gonfalonier of the city, of the Countess Mastiani, and one or two others, *conversazioni* are held, and now and then a ball given; the rest of the nobility are simply content with morning calls and with seeing each other at the theatres or on the Lung' Arno, where they promenade a little before sunset. The present winter has been uncommonly gay in Pisa. The Grand Duke is passing the winter here, which he does once in three years; of course, balls have been given at the palace, and several in return have been given to the Court. The most brilliant of these was one at the Countess Mastiani's, at which were present many persons from Florence and Leghorn, and several belonging to the Court at Lucca.

All the Pisan nobility attended, and some of the richest commoners; and between the two classes there was a studied rivalry in splendor of dress. We took F——, who is as tall as her mother, to the ball; the creature was half beside herself at the honor of figuring in a waltz at the same time that the Grand Duke was dancing with an Italian lady. Before we left Florence we had been presented at Court. Both there and here the Grand Duke's balls have been crowded with English—the omnipresent English—the universal English nation—better entitled to that epithet than the Yankees, for the whole continent of Europe is overrun with them. They are generally much the same conceited, dissatisfied beings here that we find them in America.

The carnival began a week or two since, and last Sunday the streets were full of carriages, and people in masks, passing up and down and playing all sorts of fooleries. The Lung' Arno, on the north side of the river, a noble street, stretching in a semicircle from one end of the city to the other, is the principal scene of this diversion. Our lodgings are situated near the centre of the concavity of this semicircle, so that we have a good view of what is going on in it from one extremity to the other. Crowds of men and women from the country came to witness the frolic, the women wearing white handkerchiefs on their heads, pinned over combs, with huge flat, gilt pendants in their ears, resting on their shoulders, and broad crosses of a similar fashion hanging from the neck over the bosom. The maskers appeared to be mostly of the fair sex. J—— was at the open window—for the mildness of the climate is such that an open window in February is no great inconvenience—laughing with all her might at the strange figures below.

A DESOLATE REGION.—APRIL 15, 1835: Toward the end of March I went from Pisa to Volterra. This, you know, is a very ancient city, one of the strongholds of Etruria when Rome was in its cradle; and, in more modern times, in the age of Italian republics, large enough to form an independent community of considerable importance. It is now a decayed town, containing about four thousand inhabitants, some of whom are families of the poor and proud nobility common enough over all Italy, who are said to quarrel with each other more fiercely in Volterra than almost anywhere else. It is the old feud of the Montagues and the Capulets on a humbler scale, and the disputes of the Volterra nobility are the more violent and implacable for being hereditary. Poor creatures! too proud to engage in business, too indolent for literature, excluded from political employments by the nature of the government, there is nothing left for them but to starve, intrigue, and quarrel. You may judge how miserably poor they are when you are told that they cannot afford even to cultivate the favorite art of modern Italy—the art best suited to the genius of a soft and effeminate people. There is, I was told, but one piano-forte in the whole town, and that is owned by a Florentine lady who has recently come to reside here.

For several miles before reaching Volterra our attention was fixed by the extraordinary aspect of the country through which we were passing. The road gradually ascended, and we found ourselves among deep ravines and steep, high, broken banks, principally of clay, barren, and in most places wholly bare of herbage—a scene of complete desolation were it not for a cottage here and there perched upon the heights, a few sheep, attended by a boy and a dog, grazing on the brink of one of the precipices, or a solitary patch of bright green wheat in some spot where the rains had not yet carried away the vegetable mould. Imagine to yourself an elevated country like the highlands of Pennsylvania, or the western part of Massachusetts; imagine vast beds of loam and clay in place of the ledges of rock, and then fancy the whole region to be torn by water-spouts and torrents into gulleys too profound to be passed, with sharp ridges between—stripped of its trees and its grass—and you will have some idea of the country near Volterra. I could not help fancying, while I looked at it, that as the earth grew old, the ribs of rock which once upheld the mountains had become changed into the bare heaps of earth which I saw about me, that time and the elements had destroyed the cohesion of the particles of which they were formed, and that now the rains were sweeping them down to the Mediterranean, to fill its bed and cause its waters to encroach upon the land—it was impossible for me to prevent the apprehension from passing through my mind that such might be the fate of other quarters of the globe in ages yet to come; that their rocks must crumble and their mountains be levelled until the waters shall again cover the face of the earth, unless new mountains shall be thrown up by eruptions of internal fire. They told me in Volterra that this frightful region had once been productive and under cultivation, but that after a plague, which, four or five hundred years since, had depopulated the country, it was abandoned and neglected, and the rains had reduced it to its present state.

In the midst of this desolate tract, which is, however, here and there interspersed with fertile spots, rises the mountain on which Volterra is situated, where the inhabitants breathe a pure and keen atmosphere, almost perpetually cool, and only die of pleurisies and apoplexies; while below, on the banks of the Cecina, which in full sight winds its way to the sea, they die of fevers. One of the ravines of which I have spoken—the *balza* they call it at Volterra—has ploughed a deep chasm on the north side of this mountain, and is every year rapidly approaching the city on its summit. I stood on its edge and looked down a bank of soft red earth five hundred feet in height. A few rods in front of me I saw where a road had crossed the spot in which the gulf now yawned; the tracks of the last year's carriages were seen reaching to the edge on both sides. The ruins of a convent were close at hand, the inmates of which, two or three years since, had been removed by the government to the town for safety. These will soon be undermined by the advancing chasm, together with a fine piece of old Etruscan wall, once enclosing the city, built of enormous uncemented parallelograms of stone, and looking as if

it might be the work of the giants who lived before the flood ;
a neighboring church will next fall into the gulf, which finally,
if means be not taken to prevent its progress, will reach and
sap the present walls of the city, swallowing up what time has
so long spared. " A few hundred crowns," said an inhabitant
of Volterra to me, " would stop all this mischief. A wall at
the bottom of the chasm, and a heap of branches of trees or
other rubbish, to check the fall of the earth, are all that would
be necessary." I asked why these means were not used.
" Because," he replied, " those to whom the charge of these
matters belongs will not take the trouble. Somebody must
devise a plan for the purpose, and somebody must take upon
himself the labor of seeing it executed. They find it easier
to put it off."

The antiquities of Volterra consist of an Etruscan burial-
ground, in which the tombs still remain ; pieces of the old and
incredibly massive Etruscan wall, including a far larger circuit
than the present city ; two Etruscan gates of immemorial an-
tiquity, older, doubtless, than anything at Rome, built of enor-
mous stones, one of them serving even yet as an entrance to
the town ; and a multitude of cinerary vessels, mostly of ala-
baster, sculptured with numerous figures in *alto relievo.* These
figures are sometimes allegorical representations, and some-
times embody the fables of the Greek mythology. Among
them are some in the most perfect style of Grecian art, the
subjects of which are taken from the poems of Homer ; groups
representing the besiegers of Troy and its defenders, or Ulys-
ses with his companions and his ships. I gazed with exceed-
ing delight on these works of forgotten artists, who had the
verses of Homer by heart—works just drawn from the tombs
where they had been buried for thousands of years, and look-
ing as if fresh from the chisel.

We had letters to the commandant of the fortress, an
ancient-looking stronghold, built by the Medici family, over
which we were conducted by his adjutant, a courteous gen-
tleman with a red nose, who walked as if keeping time to

military music. From the summit of the tower we had an extensive and most remarkable prospect. It was the 19th day of March, and below us the sides of the mountain, scooped into irregular dells, were covered with fruit-trees just breaking into leaf and flower. Beyond stretched the region of barren-ness I have already described, to the west of which lay the green pastures of the Maremma, the air of which, in summer, is deadly, and still farther west were spread the waters of the Mediterranean, out of which were seen rising the mountains of Corsica. To the north and northeast were the Apennines, capped with snow, embosoming the fertile lower valley of the Arno, with the cities of Pisa and Leghorn in sight. To the south we traced the windings of the Cecina, and saw ascend-ing into the air the smoke of a hot-water lake, agitated per-petually with the escape of gas, which we were told was vis-ited by Dante, and from which he drew images for his descrip-tion of Hell. Some Frenchman has now converted it into a borax manufactory, the natural heat of the water serving to extract the salt. The fortress is used as a prison for persons guilty of offences against the state. On the top of the tower we passed four prisoners of state, well-dressed young men, who appeared to have been entertaining themselves with mu-sic, having guitars and other instruments in their hands. They saluted the adjutant as he went by them, who, in return, took off his hat. They had been condemned for a conspiracy against the government.

The commandant gave us a hospitable reception. In show-ing us the fortress he congratulated us that we had no occa-sion for such engines of government in America. We went to his house in the evening, where we saw his wife, a handsome young lady, whom he had lately brought from Florence, the very lady of the piano-forte whom I have already mentioned, and the mother of two young children, whose ruddy cheeks and chubby figures did credit to the wholesome air of Vol-terra. The commandant made tea for us in tumblers, and the lady gave us music. The tea was so strong a decoction that

I seemed to hear the music all night, and had no need of being waked from sleep when our *vetturino*, at an early hour the next morning, came to take us on our journey to Sienna.

IN AND ABOUT NAPLES.—JUNE, 1835: I have said the more of Volterra because it lies rather out of the usual course of ordinary travellers. After a day passed in this place we proceeded to Sienna, where we stayed three days; to Rome, where we stayed five weeks; and to Naples, where we stayed three. Of course we visited all the ruins of Rome, including the grandest, the Coliseum, went down into the Catacombs, carrying a wax-light part of the way, and seeing everything else which travellers must see, not forgetting St. Peter's, my first thought on entering which was that it was as fine as a ballroom or a cabin in a new steamboat, and it was only after several visits that my mind was opened to the grandeur and majesty of its proportions. Of course, also, we made excursions to Tivoli and Terni and Pozzuoli and Pompeii and Herculaneum and Vesuvius. That last was an adventure worth telling of. We set out at midnight on account of the heat, though it was no later than the 17th of May. For four miles or more before arriving at the cone of loose cinders which surrounds the crater, we rode on asses and ponies up a rugged winding road, attended by a dozen torch-bearers and guides. Two American gentlemen accompanied us. It was quite a grand affair: there was the darkness, the flare of the torches, the rocks of ancient lava, the black craggy trains of the lava of last year, the hollow path, the flapping of the branches of the wild fig-trees in our faces as we passed, and the half-savage looks and strange gibberish of the guides. We stopped to rest at the Hermitage, a house surrounded by vineyards just on the edge of the streams of lava poured forth in the last eruption, and occupied by a friar of some sort or other. Half an hour's farther riding brought us to the cone, and we climbed up its almost perpendicular sides with extreme toil, wading in the volcanic gravel mixed with craggy fragments of lava. My wife and daughter were fairly dragged up by the guides. Of course we were out of breath when we arrived at the summit, just as the sun was rising. We now stood on the edge of a vast hollow, within which extended a black crust of irregular surface intersected with fissures which sent up an acrid vapor and insupportable heat. Our station was on the north side of the crater, where the surface for a considerable distance was tolerably level. South of this little plain sank a deep black valley, at the farther side of which was a profound opening, sending up continually huge volumes of reddish-looking smoke, which rolled over each other down the mountain, in a direction opposite to that in which we stood. The edges of the crater, except where we came upon it, were high, sharp, steep, and broken, as if the summit of the mountain had suddenly fallen into the gulf below. Nothing could be more beautiful than the green and yellow hues on the western edge; it looked for all the world like a bank of green grass and buttercups. One of the party asked what were the flowers which made so gay an appearance. I told him they were only flowers of sulphur, which was the literal fact, for it was the sublimated sulphur, deposited on the crags of lava, which gave them this brilliant coloring. Our cicerone told us alarming stories of the occasional sinking of the crust of the crater on which we stood —how the frightful opening which sent forth the smoke shifted from one side to the other, and mountains swelled up within the crater at one time, and were suddenly engulfed at another—and talked of the symptoms of an approaching eruption—whether from a desire to impart information, or because he wanted to go home for his breakfast, I could not judge. I will not undertake to describe what has been described so often—the glorious prospect beheld from the summit of the volcano; the bright blue Mediterranean with its dark shores of rocky mountains; the ancient Parthenope, burial-place of Virgil, sitting proudly on the slope of her hills; Pompeii, Herculaneum, Baiæ; the towering islands of Capri, Procida, and Ischia, the heights gilded and the waters shining in the morning sun. We shot to the bottom of the cone in ten minutes;

my wife and daughter gave their boots, which were reduced to a most rueful plight, to the guides, who pocketed them with thanks; we arrived at Naples about ten in the morning, and deliberately went to bed. I have only room to tell you further that Naples is populous, lively, as noisy as New York, and inexpressibly dirty; that whoever visits either that place or Rome must pay his account in being eaten up alive by fleas; that the farther you go south from Tuscany the greater cheats you find the people; and that half at least of the pleasure you take in looking at objects of curiosity is counterbalanced by being plagued by swarms of beggars, ragamuffins, and rogues of all sorts, who come upon you at every turn and keep a perpetual din in your ears. The scenery of the Bay of Naples is among the most stupendously picturesque I ever looked at, but the lazzaroni, I confess, disappointed me. They looked altogether too decent, too comfortable, too well clad; they were not half so naked nor half so queer as I had been taught to expect. I had seen quite as shabby-looking men and women in other parts of Italy. We were, however, much amused with Naples, and our stay there was rendered more agreeable by the pleasant situation of our apartment, looking on the bay and the beautiful public walk called the Chiaja.

THE SHETLAND ISLANDS.—JULY 19, 1849: From Wick, a considerable fishing town in Caithness, on the northern coast of Scotland, a steamer, named the Queen, departs once a week, in the summer months, for Kirkwall, in the Orkneys, and Lerwick, in Shetland. We went on board of her about ten o'clock on the 14th of July. The herring fishery had just begun, and the artificial port of Wick, constructed with massive walls of stone, was crowded with fishing vessels which had returned that morning from the labors of the night; for in the herring fishery it is only in the night that the nets are spread and drawn. Many of the vessels had landed their cargo; in others the fishermen were busily disengaging the herrings from the black nets and throwing them in eahps; and now and then a boat, later than the rest, was entering from the sea.   The green heights all around the bay were covered with groups of women, sitting or walking, dressed for the most part in caps and white, short gowns, waiting for the arrival of the boats manned by their husbands and brothers, or belong- ing to the families of those who had come to seek occupation as fishermen.   I had seen two or three of the principal streets of Wick that morning swarming with strapping fellows, in blue highland bonnets, with blue jackets and pantaloons, and coarse blue flannel shirts.   A shopkeeper, standing at his door, instructed me who they were.   " They are men of the Celtic race," he said.   The term Celtic has grown to be quite fashion- able, I find, when applied to the Highlanders.   " They came from the Hebrides and other parts of western Scotland to get employment in the herring fishery.   These people have trav- elled perhaps three hundred miles, most of them on foot, to be employed six or seven weeks, for which they will receive about six pounds wages.   Those whom you see are not the best of their class; the more enterprising and industrious have boats of their own, and carry on the fishery on their own ac- count."

We found the Queen a strong steamboat, with a good cabin and convenient state-rooms, but dirty, and smelling of fish from stem to stern.   It has seemed to me that the farther north I went the more dirt I found.   Our captain was an old Aberdeen seaman, with a stoop in his shoulders, and looked as if he was continually watching for land, an occupation for which the foggy climate of these latitudes gives him full scope. We left Wick between eleven and twelve o'clock in the fore- noon, and glided over a calm sea, with a cloudless sky above us, and a thin haze on the surface of the waters.   The haze thickened to a fog, which grew more and more dense, and finally closed overhead.   After about three hours' sail, the cap- tain began to grow uneasy, and was seen walking about on the bridge between the wheel-houses, anxiously peering into the mist, on the lookout for the coast of the Orkneys.   At length he gave up the search and stopped the engine. The passengers amused themselves with fishing. Several coal-fish, a large fish of slender shape, were caught, and one fine cod was hauled up by a gentleman who united in his person, as he gave me to understand, the two capacities of portrait-painter and preacher of the Gospel, and who held that the universal Church of Christendom had gone sadly astray from the true primitive doctrine in regard to the time when the millennium is to take place.

The fog cleared away in the evening; our steamer was again in motion; we landed at Kirkwall in the middle of the night; and when I went on deck the next morning we were smoothly passing the shores of Fair Isle—high and steep rocks impending over the waters, with a covering of green turf. Before they were out of sight we saw the Shetland coast, the dark rock of Sumburgh Head, and behind it, half shrouded in mist, the promontory of Fitfiel Head—Fitful Head, as it is called by Scott in his novel of " The Pirate." Beyond, to the east, black, rocky promontories came in sight, one after the other, beetling over the sea. At ten o'clock we were passing through a channel, between the islands, leading to Lerwick, the capital of Shetland, on the principal island, bearing the name of Mainland. Fields, yellow with flowers, among which stood here and there a cottage, sloped softly down to the water, and beyond them rose the bare declivities and summits of the hills, dark with heath, with here and there still darker spots of an almost inky hue, where peat had been cut for fuel. Not a tree, not a shrub was to be seen, and the greater part of the soil appeared never to have been reduced to cultivation.

About one o'clock we cast anchor before Lerwick, a fishing village, built on the shore of Bressay Sound, which here forms one of the finest harbors in the world. It has two passages to the sea, so that, when the wind blows a storm on one side of the islands, the Shetlander in his boat passes out in the other direction, and finds himself in comparatively smooth water.

It was Sunday, and the man who landed us at the quay, and took our baggage to our lodging, said as he left us: "It's the Sabbath, and I'll no tak' my pay now, but I'll call the morrow. My name is Jim Sinclair, pilot, and if ye'll be wanting to go anywhere, I'll be glad to tak' ye in my boat." In a few minutes we were snugly established at our lodgings.

The little town of Lerwick consists of two-story houses, built mostly of unhewn stone, rough-cast, with steep roofs, and a chimney at each end. They are arranged along a winding street parallel with the shore, and along narrow lanes running upward to the top of the hill. The main-street is flagged with smooth stones, like the streets in Venice, for no vehicle runs on wheels in the Shetland Islands. We went up Queen's Lane, and soon found the building occupied by the Free Church of Scotland until a temple of fairer proportions, on which the masons are now at work, on the top of the hill, shall be completed for their reception. It was crowded with attentive worshippers, one of whom obligingly came forward and found a seat for us. The minister, Mr. Frazer, had begun the evening service, and was at prayer. When I entered he was speaking of "our father the devil"; but the prayer was followed by an earnest, practical discourse, though somewhat crude in the composition, and reminding me of an expression I once heard used by a distinguished Scotchman, who complained that the clergy of his country, in composing their sermons, too often "mak' rough wark of it."

I looked about among these descendants of the Norwegians, but could not see anything singular in their physiognomy; and, but for the harsh accent of the preacher, I might almost have thought myself in the midst of a country congregation in the United States. They are mostly of a light complexion, with an appearance of health and strength, though of a sparer make than the people of the more southern British isles. After the service was over we returned to our lodgings, by a way which led to the top of the hill, and made the circuit of the little town. The paths leading into the interior of the island were full of people returning homeward; the women in their best attire, a few in silks, with wind-tanned faces. We saw them disappearing, one after another, in the hollows, or over the dark, bare hill-tops. With a population of less than three thousand souls, Lerwick has four places of worship—a church of the Establishment, a Free church, a church for the Seceders, and one for the Methodists. The road we took commanded a fine view of the harbor, surrounded and sheltered by hills. Within it lay a numerous group of idle fishing-vessels, with one great steamer in the midst; and, more formidable in appearance, a Dutch man-of-war, sent to protect the Dutch fisheries, with the flag of Holland flying at the mast-head. Above the town, on tall poles, were floating the flags of four or five different nations, to mark the habitation of their consuls. On the side opposite to the harbor lay the small fresh-water lake of Cleikimin, with the remains of a Pictish castle in the midst—one of those circular buildings of unhewn, uncemented stone, skilfully laid, forming apartments and galleries of such small dimensions as to lead Sir Walter Scott to infer that the Picts were a people of a stature considerably below the ordinary standard of the human race. A deep Sabbath silence reigned over the scene, except the sound of the wind, which here never ceases to blow from one quarter or another, as it swept the herbage and beat against the stone walls surrounding the fields. The ground under our feet was thick with daisies and the blossoms of the crow-foot and other flowers; for in the brief summer of these islands nature, which has no groves to embellish, makes amends by pranking the ground, particularly in the uncultivated parts, with a great profusion and variety of flowers.

The next morning we were rowed, by two of Jim Sinclair's boys, to the island of Bressay, and one of them acted as our guide to the remarkable precipice called the Noup of the Noss. We ascended its smooth slopes and pastures, and passed through one or two hamlets, where we observed the construction of the dwellings of the Zetland peasantry. They are built of unhewn stone, with roofs of turf held down by ropes of straw neatly twisted; the floors are of earth; the cow, pony, and pig live under the same roof with the family, and the manure pond, a receptacle for refuse and filth, is close to the door. A little higher up we came upon the uncultivated grounds, abandoned to heath, and only used to supply fuel by the cutting of peat. Here and there women were busy piling the square pieces of peat in stacks, that they might dry in the wind. "We carry home these pits in a basket on our showlders, when they are dry," said one of them to me; but those who can afford to keep a pony, make him do this work for them. In the hollows of this part of the island we saw several fresh-water ponds, which were enlarged with dikes and made to turn grist-mills. We peeped into one or two of these mills, little stone buildings, in which we could hardly stand upright, enclosing two small stones turned by a perpendicular shaft, in which are half a dozen cogs; the paddles are fixed below, and these, struck by the water, turn the upper stone.

A steep descent brought us to the little strait, bordered with rocks, which divides Brassey from the island called the Noss. A strong south wind was driving in the billows from the sea with noise and foam, but they were broken and checked by a bar of rocks in the middle of the strait, and we crossed to the north of it in smooth water. The ferryman told us that when the wind was northerly he crossed to the south of the bar. As we climbed the hill of the Noss the mist began to drift thinly around us from the sea, and flocks of sea-birds rose screaming from the ground at our approach. At length we stood upon the brink of a precipice of fearful height, from which we had a full view of the still higher precipices of the neighboring summit. A wall of rock was before us six hundred feet in height, descending almost perpendicularly to the sea, which roared and foamed at its base among huge masses of rock, and plunged into great caverns, hollowed out by the beating of the surges for centuries. Midway on the rock, and above the reach of the spray, were thousands of sea-birds, sitting in ranks on the numerous shelves, or alighting, or taking wing, and screaming as they flew. A cloud of them were constantly in the air in front of the rock and over our heads. Here they make their nests and rear their young, but not entirely safe from the pursuit of the Zetlander, who causes himself to be let down by a rope from the summit and plunders their nests. The face of the rock, above the portion which is the haunt of the birds, was fairly tapestried with herbage and flowers which the perpetual moisture of the atmosphere keeps always fresh—daisies nodding in the wind, and the crimson phlox, seeming to set the cliffs on flame; yellow buttercups, and a variety of other plants in bloom, of which I do not know the name.

Magnificent as this spectacle was, we were not satisfied without climbing to the summit. As we passed upward, we saw where the rabbits had made their burrows in the elastic peat-like soil close to the very edge of the precipice. We now found ourselves involved in the cold streams of mist which the strong sea-wind was drifting over us; they were in fact the lower skirts of the clouds. At times they would clear away and give us a prospect of the green island summits around us, with their bold headlands, the winding straits between, and the black rocks standing out in the sea. When we arrived at the summit we could hardly stand against the wind, but it was almost more difficult to muster courage to look down that dizzy depth over which the Zetlanders suspend themselves with ropes, in quest of the eggs of the sea-fowl. My friend captured a young gull on the summit of the Noup. The bird had risen at his approach, and essayed to fly toward the sea, but the strength of the wind drove him back to the land. He rose again, but could not sustain a long flight, and, coming to the ground again, was caught, after a spirited chase, amid a wild clamor of the sea-fowl over our heads.

Not far from the Noup is the Holm, or, as it is sometimes called, the Cradle, or Basket, of the Noss. It is a perpendicular mass of rock, two or three hundred feet high, with a broad, flat summit, richly covered with grass, and is separated from the island by a narrow chasm, through which the sea flows. Two strong ropes are stretched from the main island to the top of the Holm, and on these is slung the cradle or basket, a sort of open box made of deal-boards, in which the shepherds pass with their sheep to the top of the Holm. We found the cradle strongly secured by lock and key to the stakes on the side of the Noss, in order, no doubt, to prevent any person from crossing for his own amusement.

As we descended the smooth pastures of the Noss, we fell in with a herd of ponies, of a size somewhat larger than is common on the islands. I asked our guide, a lad of fourteen years of age, what was the average price of a sheltie. His answer deserves to be written in letters of gold : " It's jist as they're bug an' smal'."

From the ferryman, at the strait below, I got more specific information. They vary in price from three to ten pounds, but the latter sum is only paid for the finest of these animals, in the respects of shape and color. It is not a little remarkable that the same causes which, in Shetland, have made the horse the smallest of ponies, have almost equally reduced the size of the cow. The sheep, also—a pretty creature, I might call it—from the fine wool of which the Shetland women knot the thin webs known by the name of Shetland shawls, is much smaller than any breed I have ever seen. Whether the cause be the perpetual chilliness of the atmosphere or the insufficiency of nourishment—for, though the long Zetland winters are temperate, and snow never lies long on the ground, there is scarce any growth of herbage in that season—I will not undertake to say, but the people of the islands ascribe it to the insufficiency of nourishment. It is, at all events, remarkable that the traditions of the country should ascribe to the Picts, the early inhabitants of Shetland, the same dwarfish stature, and that the numerous remains of their habitations which still exist should seem to confirm the tradition. The race which at present possesses the Shetlands is, however, of what the

French call "an advantageous stature," and well limbed. If it be the want of a proper and genial warmth which prevents the due growth of the domestic animals, it is a want to which the Zetlanders are not subject. Their hills afford the man apparently an inexhaustible supply of peat, which costs the poorest man nothing but the trouble of cutting it and bringing it home; and their cottages, I was told, are always well warmed in winter.

In crossing the narrow strait which separates the Noss from Bressay, I observed on the Bressay side, overlooking the water, a round hillock, of very regular shape, in which the green turf was intermixed with stones. "That," said the ferryman, "is what we call a Pictish castle. I mind when it was opened; it was full of rooms, so that ye could go over every part of it." I climbed the hillock, and found, by inspecting several openings which had been made by the peasantry to take away the stones, that below the turf it was a regular work of Pictish masonry, but the spiral galleries, which these openings revealed, had been completely choked up in taking away the materials of which they were built. Although plenty of stone may be found everywhere in the islands, there seems to be a disposition to plunder these remarkable remains for the sake of building cottages, or making those enclosures for their cabbages which the islanders call *crubs.* They have been pulling down the Pictish castle, on the little island in the fresh-water loch called Cleikimin, near Lerwick, described with such minuteness by Scott in his journal, till very few traces of its original construction are left. If the enclosing of lands for pasturage and cultivation proceeds as it has begun, these curious monuments of a race which has long perished will disappear.

Now that we were out of hearing of the cries of the seabirds, we were regaled with more agreeable sounds. We had set out, as we climbed the island of Bressay, amid a perfect chorus of larks, answering each other in the sky, and sometimes apparently from the clouds; and now we heard them again overhead, pouring out their sweet notes so fast and so ceaselessly that it seemed as if the little creatures imagined they had more to utter than they had time to utter it in. In no part of the British Islands have I seen the larks so numerous or so merry as in the Shetlands.

We waited awhile, at the wharf by the minister's house in Bressay, for Jim Sinclair, who at length appeared in his boat to convey us to Lerwick. "He is a noisy fellow," said our good landlady, and truly we found him voluble enough, but quite amusing. As he rowed us to town he gave us a sample of his historical knowledge, talking of Sir Walter Raleigh and the settlement of North America, and told us that his greatest pleasure was to read historical books in the long winter nights. His children, he said, could all read and write. We dined on a leg of Shetland mutton, with a tart made "of the only fruit of the island," as a Scotchman called it, the stalks of the rhubarb plant, and went on board of our steamer about six o'clock in the afternoon. It was matter of some regret to us that we were obliged to leave Shetland so soon. Two or three days more might have been pleasantly passed among its grand precipices, its winding straits, its remains of a remote and rude antiquity, its little horses, little cows, and little sheep, its sea-fowl, its larks, its flowers, and its hardy and active people. There was an amusing novelty also in going to bed, as we did, by daylight, for at this season of the year the daylight is never out of the sky, and the flush of early sunset only passes along the horizon from the northwest to the northeast, where it brightens into sunrise.

The Zetlanders, I was told by a Scotch clergyman who had lived among them forty years, are naturally shrewd and quick of apprehension; "as to their morals," he added, "if ye stay among them any time ye'll be able to judge for yourself." So, on the point of morals, I am in the dark. More attention, I hear, is paid to the education of their children than formerly, and all have the opportunity of learning to read and write in the parochial schools. Their agriculture is still very rude;

they are very unwilling to adopt the instruments of husbandry used in England, but, on the whole, they are making some progress. A Shetland gentleman, who, as he remarked to me, had "had the advantage of seeing some other countries" besides his own, complained that the peasantry were spending too much of their earnings for tea, tobacco, and spirits. Last winter a terrible famine came upon the islands; their fisheries had been unproductive, and the potato crop had been cut off by the blight. The communication with Scotland by steamboat had ceased, as it always does in winter, and it was long before the sufferings of the Shetlanders were known in Great Britain; but, as soon as the intelligence was received, contributions were made and the poor creatures were relieved.

Their climate, inhospitable as it seems, is healthy, and they live to a good old age. A native of the island, a baronet, who has a great white house on a bare field in sight of Lerwick, and was a passenger on board the steamer in which we made our passage to the island, remarked that, if it was not the healthiest climate in the world, the extremely dirty habits of the peasantry would engender disease, which, however, was not the case. "It is, probably, the effect of the saline particles in the air," he added. His opinion seemed to be that the dirt was salted by the sea-winds, and preserved from further decomposition. I was somewhat amused in hearing him boast of the climate of Shetland in winter. "Have you never observed," said he, turning to the old Scotch clergyman of whom I have already spoken, "how much larger the proportion of sunny days is in our islands than at the south?" "I have never observed it," was the dry answer of the minister.

The people of Shetland speak a kind of Scottish, but not with the Scottish accent. Four hundred years ago, when the islands were transferred from Norway to the British crown, their language was Norse, but that tongue, although some of its words have been preserved in the present dialect, has become extinct. "I have heard," said an intelligent Shetlander to me, "that there are yet, perhaps, half a dozen persons in one of our remotest neighborhoods who are able to speak it, but I never met with one who could."

In returning from Lerwick to the Orkneys we had a sample of the weather which is often encountered in these latitudes. The wind blew a gale in the night, and our steamer was tossed about on the waves like an egg-shell, much to the discomfort of the passengers. We had on board a cargo of ponies, the smallest of which were from the Shetlands, some of them not much larger than sheep, and nearly as shaggy; the others, of larger size, had been brought from the Faro Isles. In the morning, when the gale had blown itself to rest, I went on deck and saw one of the Faro Island ponies, which had given out during the night, stretched dead upon the deck. I inquired if the body was to be committed to the deep. " It is to be skinned first," was the answer.

We stopped at Kirkwall, in the Orkneys, long enough to allow us to look at the old cathedral of St. Magnus, built early in the twelfth century—a venerable pile, in perfect preservation, and the finest specimen of the architecture once called Saxon, then Norman, and lately Romanesque, that I have ever seen. The round arch is everywhere used, except in two or three windows of later addition. The nave is narrow, and the central groined arches are lofty ; so that an idea of vast extent is given, though the cathedral is small compared with the great minsters in England. The work of completing certain parts of the building, which were left unfinished, is now going on at the expense of the government. All the old flooring, and the pews, which made it a parish church, have been taken away, and the original proportions and symmetry of the building are seen as they ought to be. The general effect of the building is wonderfully grand and solemn.

THE CITY OF BURGOS.—OCTOBER 14, 1857 : The first aspect of Burgos, the ancient city of the Cid and the chief city of Old Castile, is imposing. As the traveller looks at the castle on its hill, with its surrounding fortifications ; the massive remains of its ancient walls; its vast cathedral, worthy, by

its magnificence, to have exhausted the revenues of an empire;
its public pleasure-grounds, stretching along the banks of its
river, almost out of sight; the colossal effigies of its former
kings, standing at the bend of the stream called the Espolon ;
and its stately gate of Santa Maria, where the statues of the
Cid and other men of the heroic age of Spain frown in their
lofty niches—he naturally thinks of Burgos as the former seat
of power and dominion.

The morning after our arrival Don Luis, a gentleman to
whom I had an introduction, called with a friend of his, Don
Pedro, to take us to the cathedral.   I shall not weary those
who may read this letter with a formal description of the
building, of which there are so many accounts and so many
engravings.   No engraving, however, nor any drawing that I
have seen—and I have seen several by clever English artists
in water-colors—gives any idea of the magnificence and gran-
deur of its interior.   The immense round pillars that support
the dome in the centre of the building rise to a height that
fatigues the eye.   Your sight follows them up, climbing from
one noble statue to another, placed on pedestals that sprout
from their sides as if they were a natural growth, until it reaches
the broad vault, where, amid crowds of statues and the grace-
ful tracery of the galleries, the light of heaven streams in and
floods the nave below.   It is one of the merits of the cathe-
dral of Burgos that, numerous and sumptuous as are the ac-
cessories, they detract nothing from the effect of its grandeur,
and that the most profuse richness of detail harmonizes geni-
ally with the highest majesty of plan.   The sculptures in re-
lief, with which the walls are incrusted ;. the statues, the cano-
pies, the tracery, even the tombs, seem as necessary parts of
the great whole, as forests and precipices are of the mountains
of Switzerland.

As I stood under the great dome and looked at its majestic
supports, I was strongly reminded of the mosques at Constan-
tinople, built in the time of the munificent Saracen dynasties.
It was impossible not to recognize a decided resemblance be-

tween them and this building, so different from the cathedrals of the North. The cathedral of Burgos was evidently designed by a mind impregnated with Saracenic ideas of architecture; its towers, wrought with a lightness and delicacy which makes them look as if woven from rods of flexible stone, are of the northern Gothic; but its dome in the centre, with the enormous round pillars on which it is uplifted, is Oriental. It is wonderful how perfect is the preservation of its purely architectural parts. The sculptures have been, in some instances, defaced in the wars by which Spain has suffered so much; the carvings about the altar have been in some part destroyed, and inadequately restored; but time has respected the stones of the building, and, from the pedestals of the columns up to their capitals, they look almost as fresh from the chisel as they must have looked four centuries ago.

We were taken, as a matter of course, to the chapel called *del Santisimo Cristo*, in which is a figure of Christ on the Cross, of the size of life, with his head bowed in the final agony. It is a clever but somewhat frightful representation of the last sufferings of the Saviour, but the devout of Burgos hold that it exceeds the ordinary perfection of art, and attribute to it the power of working miracles. In a book lying before me, I am informed that, according to the "generally received opinion," it is the work of Nicodemus. "It is of leather," said Don Luis, "and so much like the living body that the flesh yields to your touch, and, when you withdraw your finger, recovers its place." We had passed through most of the chapels, including that magnificent one of the Condestable, in which lie the bones of the founders—one of the Velasco family and his wife—under a broad marble slab, supporting their own colossal statues, exquisitely carved in marble, with coronets on their heads, and ample robes of state, rich with lace and embroidery, flowing to their feet. As we were about leaving the cathedral by the principal entrance, Don Luis took me into the chapel of Santa Tecla, to the north of the great portal. " This," said he, "is the latest built of all the chapels, and it is

easy to see that it is not of the same age with any of the others."
I looked about me, and felt as if I had suddenly fallen from a
world of beauty into a region of utter ugliness. The chapel
in all its parts is rough with endless projections and elaborate
carvings, without meaning or grace, and blazes with gilding;
the general effect is tawdry and ignoble. How any architect,
with the example of the cathedral before him, and the beauti-
ful chapels which open from it, could have designed anything
in so wretched a style, I cannot imagine.

We dined that day at the ordinary, or *mesa redonda*, which
was served at two o'clock, the fashionable hour at Burgos.
With the exception of one or two, who sat at the head of the
table, the men wore their hats while eating. The Spaniards
consider the eating-room in a hotel as much a public place as
the great square, and, consequently, use much the same free-
dom in it. I saw the guests at the table turn their heads and
spit on the floor. They shovelled down the chick-peas and
cabbage with the blades of their knives, which they used with
great dexterity. They were polite, however; not one of them
would allow himself to be helped to any dish until after all the
ladies; at the dessert they offered the ladies the peaches they
had peeled, and they rose and bowed when the ladies left the
room. On going out, we were again met by the hostess, who
hoped that we had dined well; and, being assured that we had,
expressed her pleasure at the information.

The talk at the table was principally of the bull-fight
which was to take place that day at Burgos. I took a turn
after dinner with Don Luis and Don Pedro on the new pub-
lic walk, the *Paseo de la Tinta*, extending along the Arlanza
for the space of a league, and found it almost deserted; only
here and there a solitary stroller, and a few children with their
nurses. From time to time the air was rent with the shouts
of a multitude at no great distance. "It is the clamor of
the spectators of the bull-fight," said Don Pedro; "the pub-
lic walks are forsaken for the *plaza de toros*. I do not know
whether your sight is as good as mine, but do you see that

crowd of people on the hill?" I looked in the direction to which he pointed, and beheld an eminence, nearly half a mile from the broad circular amphitheatre of rough boards erected for the bull-fight, thronged with people. "There," said Don Pedro, " is a proof of the interest which is taken in these spectacles. Those people cannot pay for admission to the amphitheatre, and therefore content themselves with what little they can see of it from that distance. All Burgos is either in the amphitheatre or on the hill."

GRANADA AND THE ALHAMBRA. — DECEMBER, 1857: At length Granada lay before our eyes, on a hill-side, with her ancient towers rising over her roofs and her woods, and towering far above all gleamed the snowy summits of the Sierra Nevada, in which her rivers have their source. We drove into the city through a wretched suburb, and were instantly surrounded by a mob of young beggars, who trotted and shouted beside the diligence, while the people gazed and grinned at us from the doors and windows. Every city in Spain has its particular custom-house, and our baggage had, of course, to undergo an inspection, after which we had it sent to the *Fonda de Minerva*, on the Darro, a tolerable hotel, but miserably sunless and chilly at this season of the year. After having dined in an uncomfortably airy saloon, we went out into the pleasant evening sunshine and walked upon the Alameda, planted with majestic elms that overhang a broad space with their long spreading branches, and form one of the finest public walks in all Spain. The extent and beauty of its public walks are the most remarkable characteristics of Granada. They surround the hill on which stands the Alhambra, and intersect its thick woods; they accompany the Genil a considerable way on its course; they follow the stream of the Darro; they border the town at its different extremities and issues.

I am not about to describe Granada. After what Irving has written of it, I should as soon think of attempting a poem on the wrath of Achilles in competition with Homer. Let me

say of it, however, that its site is as beautiful and striking as
its antiquities.  There is but one Alhambra; there is but one
Granada.  Could it have been the taste of the Moorish sov-
ereigns; could it have been their sense of the beauty of na-
ture which led them to fix their residence in a spot presenting
such glorious combinations of mountain and valley, forest and
stream—a spot where you hear on all sides the sound of fall-
ing waters and the murmur of rivers; where the hill-sides
and water-courses clothe themselves with dense woods; where
majestic mountains stand in sight, capped with snow, while
at their foot, stretching away from the town, lies one of the
fairest and most fertile valleys that the sun ever shone upon?
However this may be, the place was the fitting seat of a great
and splendid dominion.

If in any respect the Alhambra did not correspond with
the idea I had previously formed of it, it was in the minute-
ness of its ornamentation.  I did not expect that the figures
into which the surface of its walls is wrought, and which yet,
in most places, preserve the sharp outline of a stereotype
plate, would prove to be no larger than some engravings in
which they are represented.  Yet this very minuteness, I must
admit, harmonizes perfectly with the general character of the
architecture, which is that of the utmost lightness and delicacy
possible in buildings of stone.  The architecture of the Al-
hambra is that of the harem; it is the architecture of a race
who delighted in voluptuous ease, who wrapped themselves
in soft apparel, and lolled upon divans.  The Alhambra was
the summer palace of the Moorish monarchs—a place of luxu-
rious retreat from the relaxing heats of the season—a place of
shade and running waters, courting the entrance of the winds
under its arches and between its slender pillars, yet spreading
a screen against the sunshine.  To this end the stones of the
quarry were shaped into a bower, with columns as light as the
stems of the orange-trees planted in its courts, and walls in-
crusted with scroll-work and foliage as delicate as the leaves
of the myrtle growing by its fountains.  Yet the most re-

markable parts of the Alhambra are those lofty rooms with circular vaults, from which hang innumerable little points like icicles, with rounded recesses between them. These are as strangely beautiful as a dream, and translate into a visible reality the poetic idea of a sparry cavern formed by genii in the chambers of the rock.

I was glad to see workmen employed in restoring the defaced parts of this palace. The work goes on sluggishly, it is true, but it is a comfort to perceive that the ingenuity of man renews faster than time destroys. I was still more pleased to learn that the clumsy additions with which the Spanish monarchs disfigured the beautiful work of the Moors are to be taken down. On the original flat roofs they built another story, on the sides of which they ostentatiously displayed the arms of Castile, by way of publishing their own bad taste, and this superstructure they covered with a pointed roof of heavy tiles. " All that," said the keeper of the place, when I expressed my disgust at its deformity, "is to come down—everything that you see above the Moorish cornice—and the building is to be left as it was at first." Besides miserably spoiling the general effect, these roofs load the columns below with too great a weight. An earthquake which happened two or three years since made them reel under their burden ; it moved several of them from their upright position, and rendered it necessary to prop others with a framework of wooden posts and braces. When the barbarian additions made by the Spaniards shall be removed, it will be easy, I suppose, to restore the columns to their upright state, and the wooden supports will become unnecessary. At some future time we may hope that the visitor will see this palace, if not in its original splendor, yet cleared at least of what now prevents him from perceiving much of its original beauty and grace.

I was told that visitors are no longer allowed admission to the garden under the walls of the citadel, called the Garden of the Moorish Kings ; but a letter to the Governor of the

Alhambra, with which I had been furnished at Madrid, opened it to our party. Here an enormous vine, said to be of the time of the Moors, twists its half-decayed trunk around a stone pillar. It looks old enough, certainly, to have yielded its clusters to Arab hands, and perhaps will yet yield them to their descendants, when, in the next century, the Arab race, imbued with the civilization of western Europe, and becoming fond of travel and curious in matters of antiquity, shall visit hospitable Spain to contemplate the vestiges of power and splendor left in that land by their fathers. Two lofty cypresses, planted by the Moors on this part of the hill of the Alhambra, yet stand in their full vigor and freshness—a sight scarcely less interesting than the Alhambra itself. These trees have survived wars and sieges, droughts and earthquakes, and flourish in perpetual greenness, while generations and dynasties and empires have passed away, and while even the massive fortresses built by those who planted them are beginning to crumble. Thus they may outlast not only empires, but the monuments of empires.

A general letter of introduction from Archbishop Hughes, of New York, obtained for us access to the relics of Ferdinand and Isabella, in the Royal Chapel of the cathedral, and to the vaults below, in which their remains are laid. The mausoleum of these sovereigns before the altar is one of the most superb things of its kind in the world; their colossal effigies lie crowned and sceptred in their robes of state, and on the sides of their marble couch is sculptured the story of their conquests. I was amused by an odd fancy of one of our companions. "Do you perceive," said he, "that the head of Ferdinand makes scarcely any impression on his pillow, while the head of Isabella sinks deep into hers? The artist no doubt intended to signify that the Queen's head was much better furnished than that of her consort."

An ecclesiastic sent to accompany us, by the Archbishop of Granada, called to an attendant, who brought a light, and, removing a carpet on the floor between the mausoleum and the altar, pulled up a trap-door, below which, leading down to a vault, was a flight of steps. We descended, and here we were introduced to the coffins of Ferdinand and Isabella, immediately under the monument which we had just been admiring. They are large, shapeless leaden boxes, in which the bodies of the royal pair were enclosed at their death, and deposited near to the spot where the priests chant their litanies and offer the sacrifice. The contrast between the outside of this sepulchre and what we now saw was striking; above, in the beautiful chapel, everything was pompous and splendid, but here lay the dead, within a bare dungeon of hewn stone, in dust, darkness, and silence. When we again ascended to the chapel, the ecclesiastic caused the crown and sceptre of Isabella, and the sword of Ferdinand, to be brought forth and shown us, along with one or two other relics, among which was a *dalmatica*, or ecclesiastical mantle, heavily embroidered with thread of gold by the pious hands of Isabella, to be worn by the priests in the ceremonies of the church. The crown, I must say, appeared to me to be rather a rude bauble of its kind, but it had been worn by a great sovereign.

We could not help regretting, every moment of our stay at Granada, that we had not visited it earlier in the season; for now the air, after the first day, was keen and sharp, and the braziers brought into our room were quite insufficient to remove the perpetual comfortless feeling of chilliness. Still more fortunate should we have been if we could have visited Granada in the spring. That is the time to see Granada, and not to see it merely, but to enjoy it with the other senses—to inhale the fragrance of its blossomed orange-trees, and of other flowers just opened; to hear the music of the nightingales, with which its woods are populous; to listen at open windows to the murmur of its mountains and streams, and to feel the soft winds that blow over its luxuriant Vega, and all this in the midst of scenes associated with a thousand romantic memories.

As a town, Granada forms a perfect contrast with the

beauty that surrounds it; it is ugly; the houses for the most part mean, and the streets narrow, winding, and gloomy, in some places without a pavement, and generally, owing to certain habits of the people, nasty. There is a group of beggars for every sunny corner at this season, and I suppose for every shady one in summer. The people of the place are said to have the general character of the Andalusians; that is to say, to be fond of pleasure, mirth, and holidays, and averse to labor; improvident, lively, eloquent, given to exaggeration, and acutely sensible to external impressions. Every afternoon during our stay a swarm of well-dressed people gathered upon the public walk on the other side of the Darro, before our windows, where we saw them slowly pacing the ground, and then turning to pace it over again. A few seated themselves occasionally on the stone benches, in spite of the keen air, which they bore bravely. I had a letter to a gentleman, a native of Granada, an intelligent man, who, under one of the previous administrations, had held a judicial post in Valencia. At his first visit I spoke of calling to pay my respects to him at his house. " Why give yourself that trouble?" he asked; "I will come to see you every evening." And come he did, with the most exact punctuality, and informed me of many things which I desired to know, and manifested much more curiosity in regard to the institutions and condition of our country than is usual among Spaniards.

In looking across from the Alhambra to the Albaicin, which is the old Moorish part of the town, we saw the hill-side above the houses hollowed into caverns. " There live the gypsies," said our guide; " they burrow in the earth like rabbits, and live swinishly enough together; but in some respects they set a good example; the women are faithful to their marriage vow, and the gypsy race is kept unmingled." A practiced eye easily discerns the gypsy, not merely by the darker complexion and by the silken hair of the women, but by the peculiar cast of countenance, which is more than I have been able to do. " There," said our guide one day, pointing to a man who stood by himself in the street, "there is the captain of the gypsies." For my part, I could not have distinguished him from the common race of Andalusians. He was a small, thin man, of sallow complexion, wearing the *majo* dress—a colored handkerchief tied round his head, and over that a black cap; a short, black jacket, an embroidered waistcoat, a bright crimson sash wrapped tightly round his waist, black knee-breeches, and embroidered leathern gaiters.

The women of Granada appeared to me uncommonly handsome, and this beauty I often saw in persons of the humblest condition, employed in the rudest labors. The mixture of races has had a favorable effect in raising the standard of female beauty—casting the features in a more symmetrical mould, and giving them a more prepossessing expression. I had frequent occasion to make this remark since I left the province of New Castile. The physiognomy changes as you pass to the softer climate of the country lying on the sea-coast, where the blending of the different branches of the Caucasian stock has been most miscellaneous and most complete.

# CUBA AND THE CUBANS.

HAVANA, APRIL 10, 1849: The city of Havana has a cheerful appearance, seen from the harbor. Its massive houses, built for the most part of the porous rock of the island, are covered with stucco, generally of a white or cream color, but often stained sky-blue or bright yellow. Above these rise the dark towers and domes of the churches, apparently built of a more durable material, and looking more venerable for the gay color of the dwellings amid which they stand. The extensive fortifications of Cabañas crown the heights on that side of the harbor which lies opposite to the town; and south of the city a green, fertile valley, in which stand scattered palm-trees, stretches toward the pleasant village of Cerro.

I find that it requires a greater effort of resolution to sit down to the writing of a long letter in this soft climate than in the country I have left. I feel a temptation to sit idly, and let the grateful wind from the sea, coming in at the broad windows, flow around me, or read, or talk, as I happen to have a book or a companion. That there is something in a tropical climate which indisposes one to vigorous exertion I can well believe, from what I experience in myself, and what I see around me. The ladies do not seem to take the least exercise, except an occasional drive on the Paseo, or public park; they never walk out, and when they are shopping, which is no less the vocation of their sex here than in other civilized countries, they never descend from their *volantes*, but the goods are brought out by the obsequious shopkeeper, and the lady makes her choice and discusses the price as she sits in her carriage.

Yet the women of Cuba show no tokens of delicate health. Freshness of color does not belong to a latitude so near the equator; but they have plump figures, placid, unwrinkled countenances, a well-developed bust, and eyes the brilliant languor of which is not the languor of illness. The girls, as well as the young men, have rather narrow shoulders, but, as they advance in life, the chest, in the women particularly, seems to expand from year to year, till it attains an amplitude by no means common in our country. I fully believe that this effect and their general health, in spite of the inaction in which they pass their lives, are owing to the free circulation of air through their apartments. For in Cuba the women, as well as the men, may be said to live in the open air. They know nothing of close rooms in all the island, and nothing of foul air, and to this, I have no doubt, quite as much as to the mildness of the temperature, the friendly effect of its climate upon invalids from the north is to be ascribed. Their ceilings are extremely lofty, and the wide windows, extending from the top of the room to the floor, and guarded by long perpendicular bars of iron, are without glass, and, when closed, are generally only closed with blinds, which, while they break the force of the wind when it is too strong, do not exclude the air. Since I have been on the island I may be said to have breakfasted and dined and supped and slept in the open air, in an atmosphere which is never in repose except for a short time in the morning after sunrise. At other times a breeze is always stirring: in the day-time bringing in the air from the ocean, and at night drawing it out again to the sea.

In walking through the streets of the towns in Cuba, I have been entertained by the glimpses I had through the ample windows of what was going on in the parlors. Sometimes a curtain hanging before them allowed me only a sight of the small hands which clasped the bars of the grate, and the dusky faces and dark eyes peeping into the street and scanning the passers by. At other times the whole room was seen, with its furniture, and its female forms sitting in languid postures, courting the breeze as it entered from without. In the evening, as I passed along the narrow sidewalk of the narrow streets, I have been startled at finding myself almost in the midst of a merry party gathered about the window of a brilliantly lighted room, and chattering the soft Spanish of the island in voices that sounded strangely near to me. I have spoken of their languid postures: they love to recline on sofas; their houses are filled with rocking-chairs imported from the United States; they are fond of sitting in chairs tilted against the wall, as we sometimes do at home. Indeed, they go beyond us in this respect; for in Cuba they have invented a kind of chair which, by lowering the back and raising the knees, places the sitter precisely in the posture he would take if he sat in a chair leaning backward against a wall. It is a luxurious attitude, I must own, and I do not wonder that it is a favorite with lazy people, for it relieves one of all the trouble of keeping the body upright.

It is the women who form the large majority of the worshippers in the churches. I landed here in Passion Week, and the next day was Holy Thursday, when not a vehicle on wheels of any sort is allowed to be seen in the streets; and the ladies, contrary to their custom during the rest of the year, are obliged to resort to the churches on foot. Negro servants of both sexes were seen passing to and fro, carrying mats on which their mistresses were to kneel in the morning service. All the white female population, young and old, were dressed in black, with black lace veils. In the afternoon three wooden or waxen images of the size of life, representing Christ in the different stages of his passion, were placed in the spacious Church of St. Catharine, which was so thronged that I found it difficult to enter. Near the door was a figure of the Saviour sinking under the weight of his cross, and the worshippers were kneeling to kiss his feet. Aged negro men and women, half-naked negro children, ladies richly attired, little girls in Parisian dresses, with lustrous black eyes and a profusion of ringlets, cast themselves down before the image and pressed their lips to its feet in a passion of devotion. Mothers led up their little ones, and showed them how to perform this act of adoration. I saw matrons and young women rise from it with their eyes red with tears.

The next day, which was Good Friday, about twilight a long procession came trailing slowly through the streets under my window, bearing an image of the dead Christ lying upon a cloth of gold. It was accompanied by a body of soldiery, holding their muskets reversed, and a band playing plaintive tunes; the crowd uncovered their heads as it passed. On Saturday morning, at ten o'clock, the solemnities of holy week were over; the bells rang a merry peal; hundreds of *volantes* and drays, which had stood ready harnessed, rushed into the streets; the city became suddenly noisy with the rattle of wheels and the tramp of horses; the shops which had been shut for the last two days were opened; and the ladies, in white or light-colored muslins, were proceeding in their *volantes* to purchase at the shops their costumes for the Easter festivities.

I passed the evening on the *Plaza de Armas,* a public square in front of the Governor's house, planted with palms and other trees, paved with broad flags, and bordered with a row of benches. It was crowded with people in their best dresses, the ladies mostly in white, and without bonnets, for the bonnet in this country is only worn while travelling. Chairs had been placed for them in a double row around the edge of the square, and a row of *volantes* surrounded the square, in each of which sat two or more ladies, the ample folds of their muslin dresses flowing out on each side over the steps of the carriage. The Governor's band played various airs, martial and civic, with great beauty of execution. The music continued for two hours, and the throng, with only occasional intervals of conversation, seemed to give themselves up wholly to the enjoyment of listening to it.

It was a bright moonlight night—so bright that one might almost see to read, and the temperature the finest I can conceive, a gentle breeze rustling among the palms overhead. I was surprised at seeing around me so many fair brows and snowy necks. It is the moonlight, said I to myself, or perhaps it is the effect of the white dresses, for the complexions of these ladies seem to differ several shades from those which I saw yesterday at the churches. A female acquaintance has since given me another solution of the matter. "The reason," she said, "of the difference you perceived is this: that during the ceremonies of holy week they take off the *cascarilla* from their faces, and appear in their natural complexions." I asked the meaning of the word *cascarilla*, which I did not remember to have heard before. "It is the favorite cosmetic of the island, and is made of egg-shells finely pulverized. They often fairly plaster their faces with it. I have seen a dark-skinned lady as white almost as marble at a ball. They will sometimes, at a morning call or an evening party, withdraw to repair the *cascarilla* on their faces." I do not vouch for this tale, but tell it "as it was told to me." Perhaps, after all, it was the moonlight which had produced this transformation, though I had noticed something of the same improvement of complexion just before sunset, on the Paseo Isabel, a public park without the city walls, planted with rows of trees, where, every afternoon, the gentry of Havana drive backward and forward in their *volantes*, with each a glittering harness, and a liveried negro bestriding, in large jack-boots, the single horse which draws the vehicle.

The next day the festivities which were to indemnify the people for the austerities of Lent and Passion Week began. The cock-pits were opened during the day, and masked balls were given in the evening at the theatres. You know, probably, that cock-fighting is the principal diversion of the island, having entirely supplanted the national spectacle of bull-baiting. Cuba, in fact, seemed to me a great poultry-yard. I heard the crowing of cocks in all quarters, for the game-cock is the noisiest and most boastful of birds, and is perpetually uttering his notes of defiance. In the villages I saw the veterans of the pit—a strong-legged race, with their combs cropped smooth to the head, the feathers plucked from every part of the body except their wings, and the tail docked like that of a coach-horse—picking up their food in the lanes among the chickens. One old cripple I remember to have seen, in the little town of Guines, stiff with wounds received in combat, who had probably got a furlough for life, and who, while limping among his female companions, maintained a sort of strut in his gait, and now and then stopped to crow defiance to the world. The peasants breed game-cocks and bring them to market; amateurs in the town train them for their private amusement. Dealers in game-cocks are as common as horse-jockeys with us, and every village has its cock-pit.

I went on Monday to the *Valla de Gallos*, situated in that part of Havana which lies without the walls. Here, in a spacious enclosure, were two amphitheatres of benches, roofed, but without walls, with a circular area in the midst. Each was crowded with people, who were looking at a cock-fight, and half of whom seemed vociferating with all their might. I mounted one of the outer benches, and saw one of the birds laid dead by the other in a few minutes. Then was heard the chink of gold and silver pieces, as the betters stepped into the area and paid their wagers; the slain bird was carried out and thrown on the ground, and the victor, taken into the hands of the owner, crowed loudly in celebration of his victory. Two other birds were brought in, and the cries of those who offered wagers were heard on all sides. They ceased at last, and the cocks were put down to begin the combat. They fought warily at first, but at length began to strike in earnest; the blood flowed, and the bystanders were heard to vociferate, "*ahí estdn pelezando!*"*—"*mata! mata! mata!*"† gesticulating at the same time with great violence, and new wagers were laid as the interest of the combat increased. In ten minutes one of the birds was despatched, for the combat never ends till one of them has his death-wound. In the mean time several other combats had begun in smaller pits which lay within the same enclosure, but were not surrounded with circles of benches.

In the evening there was a masked ball in the Tacon Theatre, a spacious building, one of the largest of its kind in the world. The pit, floored over, with the whole depth of the stage open to the back wall of the edifice, furnished a ball-room of immense size. People in grotesque masks, in hoods or fancy dresses, were mingled with a throng clad in the ordinary costume, and Spanish dances were performed to the music of a numerous band. A well-dressed crowd filled the first and second tier of boxes. The Creole smokes everywhere, and seemed astonished when the soldier who stood at the door ordered him to throw away his lighted cigar before entering. Once upon the floor, however, he lighted another cigar, in defiance of the prohibition. The Spanish dances, with their graceful movements, resembling the undulations of the sea in its gentlest moods, are nowhere more gracefully performed than in Cuba, by the young women born on the island. I could not help thinking, however, as I looked on that gay crowd, on the quaint maskers, and the dancers whose flexible limbs seemed swayed to and fro by the breath of the music, that all this was soon to end at the Campo Santo, whither I had been the day before, and I asked myself how many of all this crowd would be huddled uncoffined, when their sports were over, into the foul trenches of the public cemetery.

MATANZAS, APRIL 16th: My expectations of the scenery of the island of Cuba, and of the magnificence of its vegetation, have not been quite fulfilled. At this season the hills about

---

* " Now they are fighting ! "       † " Kill ! kill ! kill ! "

Havana, and the pastures everywhere, have an arid look, a russet hue, like sandy fields with us when scorched by a long drought, or like our meadows in winter. This, however, is the dry season; and when I was told that but two showers of rain have fallen since October, I could only wonder that so much vegetation was left, and that the verbenas and other herbage which clothed the ground should yet retain, as I perceived they did when I saw them nearer, an unextinguished life. I have, therefore, the disadvantage of seeing Cuba not only in the dry season, but near the close of an uncommonly dry season. Next month the rainy season commences, when the whole island, I am told, even the barrenest parts, flushes into a deep verdure, creeping plants climb over all the rocks and ascend the trees, and the mighty palms put out their new foliage.

Shade, however, is the great luxury of a warm climate, and why the people of Cuba do not surround their habitations in the country, in the villages, and in the environs of the large towns, with a dense umbrage of trees, I confess I do not exactly understand. In their rich soil, and in their perpetually genial climate, trees grow with great rapidity, and they have many noble ones, both for size and foliage. The royal palm, with its tall, straight, columnar trunk of a whitish hue, only uplifts a Corinthian capital of leaves, and casts but a narrow shadow; but it mingles finely with other trees, and, planted in avenues, forms a colonnade nobler than any of the porticos to the ancient Egyptian temples. There is no thicker foliage or fresher green than that of the mango, which daily drops its abundant fruit for several months in the year, and the mammea and the sapote, fruit-trees also, are in leaf during the whole of the dry season; even the Indian fig—which clasps and kills the largest trees of the forest, and at last takes their place, a stately tree with a stout trunk of its own—has its unfading leaf of vivid green.

It is impossible to avoid an expression of impatience that these trees have not been formed into groups, embowering

the dwellings, and into groves, through which the beams of
the sun, here so fierce at noonday, could not reach the ground
beneath.    There is, in fact, nothing of ornamental cultivation
in Cuba except of the most formal kind.    Some private gar-
dens there are, carefully kept, but all of the stiffest pattern ;
there is nothing which brings out the larger vegetation of the
region in that grandeur and magnificence which might belong
to it.    In the Quinta del Obispo, or Bishop's Garden, which
is open to the public, you find shade which you find nowhere
else, but the trees are planted in straight alleys, and the water-
roses, a species of water-lily of immense size, fragrant and
pink-colored, grow in a square tank, fed by a straight canal,
with sides of hewn stone.

Let me say, however, that when I asked for trees I was
referred to the hurricanes which have recently ravaged the
island.    One of these swept over Cuba in 1844, uprooting the
palms and the orange groves, and laying prostrate the avenues
of trees on the coffee plantations.    The Paseo Isabel, a public
promenade between the walls of Havana and the streets of
the new town, was formerly over-canopied with lofty and
spreading trees, which this tempest levelled to the ground ; it
has now been planted with rows of young trees, which yield
a meagre shade.    In 1846 came another hurricane, still more
terrific, destroying much of the beauty which the first had
spared.    Of late years, also, such of the orange-trees as were not
uprooted, or have recently been planted, have been attacked
by the insect which a few years since was so destructive to
the same tree in Florida.    The effect upon the tree resembles
that of a blight; the leaves grow sere, and the branches die.
You may imagine, therefore, that I was somewhat disap-
pointed not to find the air, as it is at this season in the south
of Italy, fragrant with the odor of orange and lemon blossoms.
Oranges are scarce, and not so fine, at this moment, in Havana
and Matanzas as in the fruit-shops of New York.    I hear,
however, that there are parts of the island which were spared
by these hurricanes, and that there are others where the rav-

ages of the insect in the orange groves have nearly ceased, as I have been told is also the case in Florida.

Let me mention my excursion to San Antonio. I went thither by railway, in a car built at Newark, drawn by an engine made in New York, and worked by an American engineer. For some distance we passed through fields of the sweet-potato, which here never requires a second planting, and propagates itself perpetually in the soil; patches of maize, low groves of bananas with their dark stems, and of plantains with their green ones, and large tracts producing the pineapple growing in rows like carrots. Then came plantations of the sugar-cane, with its sedge-like blades of pale-green; then extensive tracts of pasturage, with scattered shrubs and tall, dead weeds, the growth of the last summer, and a thin herbage bitten close to the soil. Here and there was an abandoned coffee plantation, where cattle were browzing among the half-perished shrubs and broken rows of trees; and the neglected hedges of the wild pine, *piña raton*, as the Cubans call it, were interrupted with broad gaps. Sometimes we passed the cottages of the *monteros*, or peasants, built often of palm-leaves, the walls formed of the broad sheath of the leaf, fastened to posts of bamboo, and the roof thatched with the long plume-like leaf itself. The door was sometimes hung with a kind of curtain to exclude the sun, which the dusky-complexioned women and children put aside to gaze at us as we passed. These dwellings were often picturesque in their appearance, with a grove of plantains behind, a thicket of bamboo by its side, waving its willow-like sprays in the wind; a pair of mango-trees near, hung with fruit just ripening and reddish blossoms just opening, and a cocoa-tree or two lifting high above the rest its immense feathery leaves and its clusters of green nuts.

We now and then met the *monteros* themselves scudding along on their little horses, in that pace which we call a rack. Their dress was a Panama hat, a shirt worn over a pair of pantaloons, a pair of rough cow-skin shoes, one of which was

armed with a spur, and a sword lashed to the left side by a
belt of cotton cloth.   They are men of manly bearing, of thin
make, but often of a good figure, with well-spread shoulders,
which, however, have a stoop in them, contracted, I suppose,
by riding always with a short stirrup.   Forests, too, we passed.
You doubtless suppose that a forest in a soil and climate like
this must be a dense growth of trees with colossal stems and
leafy summits.   A forest in Cuba—all that I have seen are
such—is a thicket of shrubs and creeping plants, through
which one would suppose that even the wild cats of the country
would find it impossible to make their way.   Above this im-
passable jungle rises here and there the palm, or the gigantic
*ceyba* or cotton-tree, but more often trees of far less beauty,
thinly scattered and with few branches, disposed without sym-
metry, and at this season often leafless.

We reached San Antonio at nine o'clock in the morning,
and went to the inn of La Punta, where we breakfasted on
rice and fresh eggs, and a dish of meat so highly flavored
with garlic that it was impossible to distinguish to what ani-
mal it belonged.   Adjoining the inn was a cock-pit, with cells
for the birds surrounding the enclosure, in which they were
crowing lustily.   Two or three persons seemed to have noth-
ing to do but to tend them; and one, in particular, with a
gray beard, a grave aspect, and a solid gait, went about the
work with a deliberation and solemnity which to me, who had
lately seen the hurried burials at the Campo Santo in Havana,
was highly edifying.   A man was training a game-cock in the
pit; he was giving it lessons in the virtue of perseverance.
He held another cock before it, which he was teaching it to
pursue, and striking it occasionally over the head to provoke
it, with the wing of the bird in his hand, he made it run after
him about the area for half an hour together.

I had heard much of the beauty of the coffee estates of
Cuba, and in the neighborhood of San Antonio are some
which have been reputed very fine ones.   A young man, in
a checked blue and white shirt, worn like a frock over

checked pantaloons, with a spur on one heel, offered to pro-
cure us a *volante*, and we engaged him. He brought us one
with two horses, a negro postilion sitting on one, and the
shafts of the vehicle borne by the other. We set off, passing
through fields guarded by stiff-leaved hedges of the ratoon-
pine, over ways so bad that, if the motion of the *volante* were
not the easiest in the world, we should have taken an unpleas-
ant jolting. The lands of Cuba fit for cultivation are divided
into red and black; we were in the midst of the red lands,
consisting of a fine earth of a deep brick-color, resting on a
bed of soft, porous, chalky limestone. In the dry season the
surface is easily dispersed into dust, and stains your clothes of
a dull red. A drive of four miles, through a country full of
palm and cocoanut trees, brought us to the gate of a coffee
plantation, which our friend in the checked shirt, by whom
we were accompanied, opened for us. We passed up to the
house through what had been an avenue of palms, but was
now two rows of trees at very unequal distances, with here
and there a sickly orange-tree. On each side grew the coffee
shrubs, hung with flowers of snowy white, but unpruned, and
full of dry and leafless twigs. In every direction were ranks
of trees, prized for ornament or for their fruit, and shrubs,
among which were magnificent oleanders loaded with flowers,
planted in such a manner as to break the force of the wind,
and partially to shelter the plants from the too fierce rays of
the sun. The coffee estate is, in fact, a kind of forest, with the
trees and shrubs arranged in straight lines. The *mayoral*, or
steward of the estate, a handsome Cuban, with white teeth, a
pleasant smile, and a distinct utterance of his native language,
received us with great courtesy, and offered us *cigarillos*,
though he never used tobacco; and spirit of cane, though he
never drank. He wore a sword, and carried a large flexible
whip, doubled for convenience, in the hand. He showed us
the coffee plants, the broad platforms with smooth surfaces of
cement and raised borders, where the berries were dried in
the sun, and the mills where the negroes were at work sepa-

rating the kernel from the pulp in which it is enclosed.
"These coffee estates," said he, "are already ruined, and the
planters are abandoning them as fast as they can; in four
years more there will not be a single coffee plantation on the
island. They cannot afford to raise coffee for the price they
get in the market." I inquired the reason. "It is," replied
he, "the extreme dryness of the season when the plant is in
flower. If we have rain at this time of the year, we are sure
of a good crop; if it does not rain, the harvest is small; and
the failure of rain is so common a circumstance that we must
leave the cultivation of coffee to the people of San Domingo
and Brazil." I asked if the plantation could not be converted
into a sugar estate. "Not this," he answered; "it has been
cultivated too long. The land was originally rich, but it is
exhausted"—tired out was the expression he used; "we may
cultivate maize or rice, for the dry culture of rice succeeds
well here, or we may abandon it to grazing. At present we
keep a few negroes here, just to gather the berries which
ripen, without taking any trouble to preserve the plants, or
replace those which die." I could easily believe, from what I
saw on this estate, that there must be a great deal of beauty
of vegetation in a well-kept coffee plantation; but the formal
pattern in which it is disposed, the straight alleys and rows of
trees, the squares and parallelograms, showed me that there
was no beauty of arrangement. We fell in, before we re-
turned to our inn, with the proprietor, a delicate-looking per-
son, with thin white hands, who had been educated at Boston,
and spoke English as if he had never lived anywhere else.
His manners, compared with those of his steward, were ex-
ceedingly frosty and forbidding; and when we told him of the
civility which had been shown us, his looks seemed to say he
wished it had been otherwise.

Returning to our inn, we dined, and, as the sun grew low,
we strolled out to look at the town. It is situated on a clear
little stream, over which several bathing-houses are built, their
posts standing in the midst of the current. Above the town,

it flows between rocky banks, bordered with shrubs, many of them in flower. Below the town, after winding a little way, it enters a cavern yawning in the limestone rock, immediately over which a huge *céyba* rises, and stretches its leafy arms in mid-heaven. Down this opening the river throws itself, and is never seen again. This is not a singular instance in Cuba. The island is full of caverns and openings in the rocks, and I am told that many of the streams find subterranean passages to the sea. There is a well at the inn of La Punta in which a roaring of water is constantly heard. It is the sound of a subterranean stream rushing along a passage in the rocks, and the well is an opening into its roof. In passing through the town, I was struck with the neat attire of those who inhabited the humblest dwellings. At the door of one of the cottages I saw a group of children, of different ages, all quite pretty, with oval faces and glittering black eyes, in clean fresh dresses, which, one would think, could scarcely have been kept a moment without being soiled in that dwelling, with its mud floor. The people of Cuba are sparing in their ablutions; the men do not wash their faces and hands till nearly mid-day, for fear of spasms; and of the women, I am told that many do not wash at all, contenting themselves with rubbing their cheeks and necks with a little *aguardiénte ;* but the passion for clean linen, and, among the men, for clean white pantaloons, is universal. The *montero* himself, on a holiday or any public occasion, will sport a shirt of the finest linen, smoothly ironed and stiffly starched throughout, from the collar downward.

LOS GUINES, APRIL 18th: In the long circuit of railway which leads from Havana to Matanzas I saw nothing remarkably different from what I observed on my excursion to San Antonio. There was the same smooth country, of great apparent fertility, sometimes varied with gentle undulations, and sometimes rising, in the distance, into hills covered with thickets. We swept by dark-green fields planted with the yucca, an esculent root, of which the cassava-bread is made; pale-green fields of the cane ; brown tracts of pasturage, partly formed of abandoned coffee estates, where the palms and scattered fruit-trees were yet standing, and forests of shrubs and twining plants growing for the most part among rocks. Some of these rocky tracts have a peculiar appearance; they consist of rough projections of rock a foot or two in height, of irregular shape and full of holes; they are called *diente de perro*, or dog's-teeth. Here the trees and creepers find openings filled with soil, by which they are nourished. We passed two or three country cemeteries, where that foulest of birds, the turkey-vulture, was seen sitting on the white stuccoed walls, or hovering on his ragged wings in circles over them.

In passing over the neighborhood of the town in which I am now writing, I found myself on the black lands of the island. Here the rich, dark earth of the plain lies on a bed of chalk as white as snow, as was apparent where the earth had been excavated to a little depth, on each side of the railway, to form the causey on which it ran. Streams of clear water, diverted from a river to the left, traversed the plain with a swift current, almost even with the surface of the soil, which they kept in perpetual freshness. As we approached Matanzas we saw more extensive tracts of cane clothing the broad slopes with their dense blades, as if the coarse sedge of a river had been transplanted to the uplands.

At length the bay of Matanzas opened before us—a long tract of water stretching to the northeast, into which several rivers empty themselves. The town lay at the southwestern extremity, sheltered by hills, where the San Juan and the Yumuri pour themselves into the brine. It is a small but prosperous town, with a considerable trade, as was indicated by the vessels at anchor in the harbor.

As we passed along the harbor I remarked an extensive, healthy-looking orchard of plantains growing on one of those tracts which they call *diente de perro*. I could see nothing but the jagged teeth of whitish rock, and the green, swelling stems of the plantain, from ten to fifteen feet in height, and as large as a man's leg, or larger. The stalks of the plantain are juicy and herbaceous, and of so yielding a texture that with a sickle you might entirely sever the largest of them at a single stroke. How such a multitude of succulent plants could find nourishment on what seemed to the eye little else than barren rock I could not imagine.

The day after arriving at Matanzas we made an excursion on horseback to the summit of the hill immediately overlooking the town, called the Cumbre. Light, hardy horses of the country were brought us, with high pommels to the saddles, which are also raised behind in a manner making it difficult to throw the rider from his seat. A negro fitted a spur to my right heel, and, mounting by the short stirrups, I crossed the river Yumuri with my companions, and began to climb the Cumbre. They boast at Matanzas of the perpetual coolness of temperature enjoyed upon the broad summit of this hill, where many of the opulent merchants of the town have their country houses, to which the mosquitoes and the intermittents that infest the town below never come, and where, as one of them told me, you may play at billiards in August without any inconvenient perspiration.

From the Cumbre you behold the entire extent of the harbor. The town lies below you, with its thicket of masts and its dusty *pasco*, where rows of the Cuba pine stand rooted in the red soil. On the opposite shore your eye is attracted to a chasm between high rocks, where the river Canimar comes forth through banks of romantic beauty—so they are described to me—and mingles with the sea. But the view to the west was much finer; there lay the valley of the Yumuri, and a sight of it is worth a voyage to the island. In regard to this, my expectations suffered no disappointment. Before me lay a deep valley, surrounded on all sides by hills and mountains, with the little river Yumuri twining at the bottom. Smooth, round hillocks rose from the side next to me, covered with clusters of palms, and the steeps of the southeastern corner of the valley were clothed with a wood of intense green, where I could almost see the leaves glisten in the sunshine. The broad fields below were waving with cane and maize, and cottages of the *monteros* were scattered among them, each with its tuft of bamboos and its little grove of plantains. In some parts the cliffs almost seemed to impend over the valley; but to the west, in a soft golden haze, rose summit behind summit, and over them all, loftiest and most remote, towered the mountain called the *Pan de Matanzas*.

We stopped for a few moments at a country seat on the top of the Cumbre, where this beautiful view lay ever before the eye. Round it, in a garden, were cultivated the most showy plants of the tropics; but my attention was attracted to a little plantation of damask roses blooming profusely. They were scentless; the climate which supplies the orange blossom with intense odors exhausts the fragrance of the rose. At nightfall—the night falls suddenly in this latitude—we were again at our hotel.

We passed our Sunday on a sugar estate, at the hospitable mansion of a planter from the United States, about fifteen miles from Matanzas. The house stands on an eminence, once embowered in trees which the hurricanes have levelled, overlooking a broad valley, where palms were scattered in every direction; for the estate had formerly been a coffee plantation. In the huge buildings containing the machinery and other apparatus for making sugar, which stood at the foot of the eminence, the power of steam, which had been toiling all the week, was now at rest. As the hour of sunset approached, a smoke was seen rising from its chimney, presently puffs of vapor issued from the engine, its motion began to be heard, and the negroes, men and women, were summoned to begin the work of the week. Some fed the fire under the boiler with coal; others were seen rushing to the mill with their arms full of the stalks of the cane, freshly cut, which they took from a huge pile near the building; others lighted fires, under a row of huge caldrons, with the dry stalks of cane from which the juice had been crushed by the mill. It was a spectacle of activity such as I had not seen in

Cuba. The sound of the engine was heard all night, for the work of grinding the cane, once begun, proceeds day and night, with the exception of Sundays and some other holidays.

I was early next morning at the mill. A current of cane-juice was flowing in a long trunk to a vat in which it was clarified with lime; it was then made to pass successively from one seething caldron to another, as it obtained a thicker consistence by boiling. The negroes, with huge ladles turning on pivots, swept it from caldron to caldron, and finally passed it into a trunk, which conveyed it to shallow tanks in another apartment, where it cooled into sugar. From these another set of workmen scooped it up in moist masses, carried it in buckets up a low flight of stairs, and poured it into rows of hogsheads pierced with holes at the bottom. These are placed over a large tank, into which the moisture dripping from the hogsheads is collected and forms molasses.

This is the method of making the sugar called Muscovado. It is drained a few days, and then the railways take it to Matanzas or to Havana. We visited afterward a plantation in the neighborhood in which clayed sugar is made. Our host furnished us with horses to make the excursion, and we took a winding road, over hill and valley, by plantations and forests, till we stopped at the gate of an extensive pasture-ground. An old negro, whose hut was at hand, opened it for us, and bowed low as we passed. A ride of half a mile farther brought us in sight of the cane-fields of the plantation called Saratoga, belonging to the house of Drake & Company, of Havana, and reputed one of the finest on the island. It had a different aspect from any plantation we had seen. Trees and shrubs there were none, but the canes, except where they had been newly cropped for the mill, clothed the slopes and hollows with their light-green blades, like the herbage of a prairie.

We were kindly received by the administrator of the estate, an intelligent Biscayan, who showed us the whole process of making clayed sugar. It does not differ from that of making the Muscovado, so far as concerns the grinding and boiling. When, however, the sugar is nearly cool, it is poured into iron vessels of conical shape, with the point downward, at which is an opening. The top of the sugar is then covered with a sort of black, thick mud, which they call clay, and which is several times renewed as it becomes dry. The moisture from the clay passes through the sugar, carrying with it the cruder portions, which form molasses. In a few days the draining is complete. We saw the work-people of the Saratoga estate preparing for the market the sugar thus cleansed, if we may apply the word to such a process. With a rude iron blade they cleft the large loaf of sugar just taken from the mould into three parts, called first, second, and third quality, according to their whiteness. These are dried in the sun on separate platforms of wood with a raised edge, the women standing and walking over the fragments with their bare, dirty feet, and beating them smaller with wooden mallets and clubs. The sugar of the first quality is then scraped up and put into boxes; that of the second and third, being moister, is handled a third time and carried into the drying-room, where it is exposed to the heat of a stove, and, when sufficiently dry, is boxed up for market like the other.

. The sight of these processes was not of a nature to make one think with much satisfaction of clayed sugar as an ingredient of food, but the inhabitants of the island are superior to such prejudices, and use it with as little scruple as they who do not know in what manner it is made. In the afternoon we returned to the dwelling of our American host, and, taking the train at *Caobas,* or Mahogany Trees—so called from the former growth of that tree on the spot—we were at Matanzas an hour afterward. The next morning the train brought us . to this little town, situated half way between Matanzas and Havana, but a considerable distance to the south of either.

HAVANA, APRIL 22d: The other day, when we were at Guines, we heard that a negro was to suffer death early the next morning by the *garrote,* an instrument by which the neck of the criminal is broken and life extinguished in an instant. I asked our landlady for what crime the man had been condemned. "He has killed his master," she replied, "an old man, in his bed." "Had he received any provocation?" "Not that I have heard; but another slave is to be put to death by the *garrote* in about a fortnight whose offence had some palliation. His master was a man of harsh temper, and treated his slaves with extreme severity; the negro watched his opportunity, and shot him as he sat at table."

We went to the place of execution a little before eight o'clock, and found the preparations already made. A platform had been erected, on which stood a seat for the prisoner, and back of the seat a post was fixed, with a sort of iron collar for his neck. A screw, with a long transverse handle on the side of the post opposite to the collar, was so contrived that, when it was turned, it would push forward an iron bolt against the back of the neck and crush the spine at once. Sentinels in uniform were walking to and fro, keeping the spectators at a distance from the platform. The heat of the sun was intense, for the sea-breeze had not yet sprung up, but the crowd had begun to assemble. As near to the platform as they could come stood a group of young girls, two of whom were dressed in white, and one was pretty, with no other shade for their dusky faces than their black veils, chatting and laughing and stealing occasional glances at the new-comers. In another quarter were six or eight *monteros* on horseback, in their invariable costume of Panama hats, shirts, and pantaloons, with holsters to their saddles, and most of them with swords lashed to their sides. About half-past eight a numerous crowd made its appearance coming from the town. Among them walked, with a firm step, a large black man, dressed in a long white frock, white pantaloons, and a white cap with a long peak which fell backward on his shoulders. He was the murderer; his hands were tied together by the wrists; in one of them he held a crucifix; the rope by which they were fastened was knotted around his waist, and the end of it was held by another athletic negro, dressed in blue cotton with white facings, who walked behind him. On the left of the criminal walked an officer of justice; on his right an ecclesiastic, slender and stooping, in a black gown and a black cap, the top of which was formed into a sort of coronet, exhorting the criminal, in a loud voice and with many gesticulations, to repent and trust in the mercy of God. When they reached the platform the negro was made to place himself on his knees before it, the priest continuing his exhortations, and now and then clapping him, in an encouraging manner, on the shoulder. I saw the man shake his head once or twice, and then kiss the crucifix. In the mean time a multitude, of all ages and both sexes, took possession of the places from which the spectacle could be best seen. A stone-fence, such as is common in our country, formed of loose stones taken from the surface of the ground, upheld a long row of spectators. A well-dressed couple, a gentleman in white pantaloons, and a lady elegantly attired, with a black lace veil and a parasol, bringing their two children and two colored servants, took their station by my side; the elder child found a place on the top of the fence, and the younger, about four years of age, was lifted in the arms of one of the servants, that it might have the full benefit of the spectacle. The criminal was then raised from the ground, and, going up on the platform, took the seat ready for him. The priest here renewed his exhortations, and at length, turning to the audience, said, in a loud voice: "I believe in God Almighty and in Jesus Christ his only Son, and it grieves me to the heart to have offended them." These words, I suppose, were meant, as the confession of the criminal, to be repeated after the priest, but I heard no response from his lips. Again and again the priest repeated them, the third time with a louder voice than ever; the signal was then given to the executioner. The iron collar was adjusted to the neck of the victim and fastened under the chin. The athletic negro in blue, standing behind the post, took the handle of the screw and turned it deliberately. After a few turns the criminal gave a sudden shrug of the shoulders; another turn of the screw, and a shudder ran over his whole frame, his eyes rolled wildly, his hands, still tied with the rope, were convulsively jerked upward, and then dropped back to their place motionless forever. The priest advanced and turned the peak of the white cap over the face to hide it from the sight of the multitude.

I had never seen, and never intended to see, an execution; but the strangeness of this manner of inflicting death, and the desire to witness the behavior of an assembly of the people of Cuba on such an occasion, had overcome my previous determination. The horror of the spectacle now caused me to regret that I made one of a crowd drawn to look at it by an idle curiosity. The negro in blue next stepped forward and felt the limbs of the dead man one by one, to ascertain whether life were wholly extinct, and then returning to the screw, gave it two or three turns more, as if to make his work sure. In the mean time my attention was attracted by a sound like that of a light buffet and a whimpering voice near me. I looked, and two men were standing by me, with a little white boy at their side, and a black boy of nearly the same age before them, holding his hat in his hand and crying. They were endeavoring to direct his attention to what they considered the wholesome spectacle before him. *"Mira, mira, no te hard daño,"* * said the men, but the boy steadily refused to look in that direction, though he was evidently terrified by some threat of punishment, and his eyes filled with tears. Finding him obstinate, they desisted from their purpose, and I was quite edified to see the little fellow continue to look away from the spectacle which attracted all other eyes but his. The white boy now came forward, touched the hat of the little black, and, good-naturedly saying *"pontelo, pontelo,"* † made him put it on his head. The crowd now began to disperse, and in twenty minutes the place was nearly solitary, except the sentinels pacing backward and forward. Two hours afterward

---

* " Look, look, it will do you no harm."     † " Put it on, put it on."

the sentinels were pacing there yet, and the dead man, in his white dress and iron collar, was still in his seat on the platform.

It is generally the natives of Africa by whom these murders are committed; the negroes born in the country are of a more yielding temper. They have better learned the art of avoiding punishment, and submit to it more patiently when inflicted, having understood from their birth that it is one of the conditions of their existence. The whip is always in sight. " Nothing can be done without it," said an Englishman to me, who had lived eleven years on the island; " you cannot make the negroes work by the mild methods which are used by slave-holders in the United States; the blacks there are far more intelligent, and more easily governed by moral means." Africans, the living witnesses of the present existence of the slave-trade, are seen everywhere; at every step you meet blacks whose cheeks are scarred with parallel slashes, with which they were marked in the African slave-market, and who can not even speak the mutilated Spanish current in the mouths of the Cuban negroes.

One day I stood upon the quay at Matanzas and saw the slaves unloading the large lighters which brought goods from the Spanish ships lying in the harbor—casks of wine, jars of oil, bags of nuts, barrels of flour. The men were naked to the hips, their only garment being a pair of trousers. I admired their ample chests, their massive shoulders, the full and muscular proportions of their arms, and the ease with which they shifted the heavy articles from place to place, or carried them on their heads. " Some of these are Africans?" I said to a gentleman who resided on the island. " They are all Africans," he answered, "Africans to a man; the negro born in Cuba is of a lighter make."

When I was at Guines I went out to look at a sugar estate in the neighborhood, where the mill was turned by water, which a long aqueduct, from one of the streams that traverse the plain, conveyed over arches of stone so broad and massive that I could not help thinking of the aqueducts of Rome. A gang of black women were standing in the *secadero*, or drying-place, among the lumps of clayed sugar, beating them small with mallets; before them walked to and fro the major-domo, with a cutlass by his side and a whip in his hand. I asked him how a planter could increase his stock of slaves. "There is no difficulty," he replied; "slaves are still brought to the island from Africa. The other day five hundred were landed on the sea-shore to the south of this; for you must know, señor, that we are but three or four leagues from the coast." "Was it done openly?" I inquired. "*Publicamente*, señor, *publicamente;* * they were landed on the sugar estate of *El Pastor*, and one hundred and seven more died on the passage from Africa." "Did the government know of it?" He shrugged his shoulders. "Of course the government knows it," said he; "everybody else knows it." The truth is, that the slave-trade is now fully revived, the government conniving at it, making a profit on the slaves imported from Africa, and screening from the pursuit of the English the pirates who bring them. There could scarcely be any arrangement of coast more favorable for smuggling slaves into a country than the islands and long peninsulas and many channels of the southern shore of Cuba. Here the mangrove thickets, sending down roots into the brine from their long branches that stretch over the water, form dense screens on each side of the passages from the main ocean to the inland, and render it easy for the slaver and his boats to lurk undiscovered by the English men-of-war.

During the comparative cessation of the slave-trade a few years since, the negroes, I have been told, were much better treated than before. They rose in value, and when they died it was found not easy to supply their places; they were therefore made much of, and everything was done which it was thought would tend to preserve their health and maintain them in bodily vigor. If the slave-trade should make them

---

* "Publicly, sir, publicly."

cheap again, their lives, of course, will be of less consequence to their owners, and they will be subject again to be overtasked, as it has been said they were before. There is certainly great temptation to wear them out in the sugar mills, which are kept in motion day and night during half the year—namely, through the dry season. "If this was not the healthiest employment in the world," said an overseer to me on one of the sugar estates, "it would kill us all who are engaged in it, both black and white."

Perhaps you may not know that more than half of the island of Cuba has never been reduced to tillage. Immense tracts of the rich black or red mould of the island, accumulated on the coral rock, are yet waiting the hand of the planter to be converted into profitable sugar estates. There is a demand, therefore, for laborers on the part of those who wish to become planters, and this demand is supplied not only from the coast of Africa, but from the American continent and southwestern Asia.

In one of the afternoons of Holy Week I saw amid the crowd on the *Plaza de Armas*, in Havana, several men of low stature, of a deep-olive complexion, beardless, with high cheekbones and straight black hair, dressed in white pantaloons of cotton, and shirts of the same material worn over them. They were Indians, natives of Yucatan, who had been taken prisoners of war by the whites of the country and sold to white men in Cuba, under a pretended contract to serve for a certain number of years. I afterward learned that the dealers in this sort of merchandise were also bringing in the natives of Asia, Chinese they call them here, though I doubt whether they belong to that nation, and disposing of their services to the planters. There are six hundred of these people, I have been told, in this city. Yesterday appeared in the Havana papers an ordinance concerning the "Indians and Asiatics imported into the country under a contract to labor." It directs how much Indian corn, how many plantains, how much jerked-pork and rice, they shall receive daily, and how many lashes the master may inflict for misbehavior. Twelve stripes with the cow-skin he may administer for the smaller offences, and twenty-four for transgressions of more importance; but if any more become necessary, he must apply to a magistrate for permission to lay them on. Such is the manner in which the government of Cuba sanctions the barbarity of making slaves of the free-born men of Yucatan. The ordinance, however, betrays great concern for the salvation of the souls of those whom it thus delivers over to the lash of the slave-driver. It speaks of the Indians from America as Christians already; but, while it allows the slaves imported from Asia to be flogged, it directs that they shall be carefully instructed in the doctrines of our holy religion.

Yet the policy of the government favors emancipation. The laws of Cuba permit any slave to purchase his freedom on paying a price fixed by three persons, one appointed by his master and two by a magistrate. He may also, if he pleases, compel his master to sell him a certain portion of his time, which he may employ to earn the means of purchasing his entire freedom. It is owing to this, I suppose, that the number of free blacks is so large in the island, and it is manifest that if the slave-trade could be checked, and these laws remain unaltered, the negroes would gradually emancipate themselves—all at least who would be worth keeping as servants. The population of Cuba is now about a million and a quarter, rather more than half of whom are colored persons, and one out of every four of the colored population is free. The mulattoes emancipate themselves as a matter of course, and some of them become rich by the occupations they follow. The prejudice of color is by no means so strong here as in the United States. Five or six years since, the negroes were shouting and betting in the cock-pits with the whites; but since the mulatto insurrection, as it is called, in 1843, the law forbids their presence at such amusements. I am told there is little difficulty in smuggling people of mixed blood, by the help of legal forms, into the white race, and, if they are rich, into good society, provided their hair is not frizzled.

You hear something said now and then in the United States concerning the annexation of Cuba to our confederacy; you may be curious, perhaps, to know what they say of it here. A European who had long resided in the island gave me this account : " The Creoles, no doubt, would be very glad to see Cuba annexed to the United States, and many of them ardently desire it. It would relieve them from many great burdens they now bear, open their commerce to the world, rid them of a tyrannical government, and allow them to manage their own affairs in their own way. But Spain derives from the possession of Cuba advantages too great to be relinquished. She extracts from Cuba a revenue of twelve millions of dollars ; her government sends its needy nobility, and all for whom it would provide, to fill lucrative offices in Cuba —the priests, the military officers, the civil authorities, every man who fills a judicial post or holds a clerkship, is from old Spain. The Spanish government dares not give up Cuba if it were inclined. Nor will the people of Cuba make any effort to emancipate themselves by taking up arms. The struggle with the power of Spain would be bloody and uncertain, even if the white population were united ; but the mutual distrust with which the planters and the peasantry regard each other would make the issue of such an enterprise still more doubtful. At present it would not be safe for a Cuban planter to speak publicly of annexation to the United States. He would run the risk of being imprisoned or exiled."

Of course, if Cuba were to be annexed to the United States, the slave-trade with Africa would cease to be carried on as now, though its perfect suppression might be found difficult. Negroes would be imported in large numbers from the United States, and planters would emigrate with them. Institutions of education would be introduced, commerce and religion would both be made free, and the character of the islanders would be elevated by the responsibilities which a free government would throw upon them. The planters, how-ever, would doubtless adopt regulations insuring the per-petuity of slavery; they would unquestionably, as soon as they were allowed to frame ordinances for the island, take away the facilities which the present laws give the slave for effecting his own emancipation.

# A VISIT TO MEXICO.

MEXICO, MARCH 6, 1872: Our voyage from Havana to Vera Cruz was in all respects a holiday. The temperature was most agreeable, the airs the softest that ever blew, the sea like a looking-glass, and the steamer—the British steamer Corsica—comfortable and roomy. In a little more than three days we were anchored in the harbor of Vera Cruz, in the middle of the night. The morning showed us the city, somewhat picturesque in its aspect, with its spires and stuccoed houses, and with its ancient fort on a little isle in front of it. A range of blue mountains lay to the west, and high above these the peak of Orizaba, white with perpetual snow, was seen among the clouds. I was told that the captain of the port desired to speak with me; and, meeting him, was informed that, by direction of the Minister of Finance, he had come with the government boat to take me and my party to town. We landed at a wharf against which the sea was beating with its gentlest ripples, but this is not always its mood. When a strong north wind blows, it rolls up vast waves, beginning at the coast of Louisiana and Florida, and sweeps them into the roadstead before Vera Cruz. The surf is hurled against the sea-wall that protects the city, and the outer streets are drenched with the spray. No vessel can then discharge or receive its cargo, and it often happens that several days elapse before there can be a communication between ship and shore. The harbor at Tampico is no better; indeed, it is said to be worse, and equally exposed to the fury of the northers. In fact, there is no good harbor on the eastern coast of Mexico, and the proper communication between that country and all others that lie to the east of it must be by means of railways and through the United States, unless, indeed, the Mexican government should build artificial harbors for its towns on the coast, an undertaking for which it has no money. Yet, I am told, there is a pretty good harbor at Anton Lizardo, less than twenty miles south of Vera Cruz, but at Anton Lizardo there is no town. Moreover, there is the yellow fever, which broods almost perpetually over the towns on the low coasts. At Vera Cruz they told me that the place was never without it; but they made light of the distemper, as a sort of seasoning process which every stranger residing there for three months must assuredly go through.

But the far greater part of the republic of Mexico consists of high table-lands. "Nine tenths of our country," said a Mexican gentleman to me, "belongs to what we call the *tierra templada*—the region which produces the harvests of the temperate zones." Perhaps this is an excessive estimate, but no one who has the map of that country before him can fail to see that a railway, beginning at our own frontier, might convey the traveller from one cool upland valley to another, till it landed him, almost without a consciousness that he was under a tropical sun, in the capital of the republic. This will yet be the principal means of communication between the two countries.

"You will find Vera Cruz a dirty, miserable place," said the bluff English commander of our steamer, the Corsica; but he did it injustice. The city lies low, and is under the suspicion of being badly drained, but the streets are a great deal cleaner than those of New York, and the black vultures, which are seen hopping about them or sitting by scores on the cupolas of its churches, devour everything above ground that can corrupt in the heat and poison the air. The dwellings and warehouses are necessarily built each of two stories around a square court; they have lofty ceilings, spacious rooms and airy galleries, the sitting-rooms so arranged as to admit the fresh sea-breeze that comes in from the harbor.

Early the next morning we were on the railway which is partly constructed from Vera Cruz to the city of Mexico. It was a somewhat dreary road for the first fifty miles, yet not without its interest. The iron track swept by a circuitous course through vast grazing-grounds of a russet hue, thinly set with low trees, yet leafless for the most part, but now and then blossoming with great strange flowers, bright yellow, or pink, or crimson. Here and there we passed a village of the aborigines, in which the dwellings were mere wigwams, built with four stout posts sustaining a roof thatched with coarse grass or leaves of the aloe. The walls of these cabins were rows of sticks or reeds, set in the ground so thinly as scarce to afford a shelter from the wind. There were a few houses of more pretension, built of sun-dried bricks whitewashed, and roofed with coarse tiles. The brown inhabitants, a race of rather low stature, but square built, loitered in the simplest possible attire about their dwellings, the women, for the most part, sitting on the ground at their doors. It could be seen at once that they were a people of few wants, and that these wants were easily supplied.

About fifty miles from Vera Cruz the country began to wear a different aspect. There were tokens of irrigation, or at least of more frequent rains, in this the dry section; the trees and shrubs were all in leaf, and there were fields green with harvests, and plantations of the banana. As we went on we found ourselves on the border of a stream flowing in a deep ravine, between almost perpendicular banks, hundreds of yards below us. A tall forest rose on each side, the trees sprouting with half a dozen parasitic plants, some of which were in bloom. The castor-bean grew by the track to the size of a tree, and the morning-glory, which here never feels the frost, climbed the trees and tied her blue or crimsoned blossoms to the branches a hundred feet from the ground.

We stopped at the present termination of the railway, seventy miles from Vera Cruz, at a place called Fortin, from which we were taken by a diligence to the city of Orizaba, situated among sugar estates, orange gardens, and coffee plantations. We had heard stories of robberies committed on the road between Vera Cruz and Mexico, and we did not feel quite sure that they were not the mere echo of what had happened some time since; but here at Orizaba the landlord of our hotel told us of a recent incident of the kind. "If you go on," he said, "you will stop for the night at San Agustin de Palmar. Not far from that place, two or three days since, the diligence was stopped, and two passengers, a Mr. Foote and companion, were robbed of fifteen thousand dollars, their trunks, and all the valuables they had with them." It therefore became a question whether it was prudent for us to proceed. We consulted together, and, concluding that the robbers would not be likely to repeat their crime immediately, we determined to go on. We threaded the long valley in which Orizaba lies, passing between banana patches and hedges in which the finest roses were in bloom, and beside little rivulets running by the wayside to water the fields. There are points in Orizaba commanding some of the most beautiful views of mountain scenery that ever met my eyes—summits, crests, ridges, spurs of mountains, interlocking each other, with valleys penetrating far between, the haunt of eternal spring, with the peak of Orizaba overlooking out from the region of eternal winter.

Coming to where the mountains bounded the valley at its western end, our vehicle ascended what are called the Heights of Aculcingo by a zigzag path cut in the rocks, and in one place crossed by a pretty waterfall. These heights are famed for the fine views they afford of the gulfy valleys below and the great mountain buttresses one behind another. But of these we had little more than a glimpse, for the mist gathered round us, and the darkness fell. A man who sat at the left hand of the driver of the diligence lighted a rope of combus-

tibles, which served for a torch to light our way. And this
was soon shown to be necessary, for the road, which since we
left Fortin had been for the most part a good macadamized
highway, became one of the worst on which I ever travelled.
The track was full of inequalities; it lay deep in fine dust,
which concealed them from sight; and we plunged from one
to another with fearful jolts, which almost seemed as if they
would shake the old diligence to fragments.  We drove on in
a cloud of white dust, surrounding us at every step.  I have
never seen our good old mother, the Earth, under a more
ghastly aspect than that which she wore in the light of our
torch.  Everything looked white—the road, the banks, the
fields, as far as we could see on each side—and the vegetation
which bordered our way was of the ugliest and grimmest
that the earth produces: cactuses, with their angular and un-
shapely growth, twelve or fifteen feet in height; the stiff and
pointed leaves of the *maguey*, or aloe; and, grimmer than they,
a kind of palm with branches, and at the end of every branch
a tuft of bayonet-shaped leaves, pointing in every direction
from a common centre, like the hair of a human head standing
on end with horror.  It seemed the very region where one
might expect a robber to spring from the bank of the road,
put his pistol to your breast, and demand your money.

At eleven o'clock in the evening we were at the little town
of San Agustin de Palmar, and, finding that our vehicle was
to set out again at half-past one, we exchanged places with
some passengers who desired to go on immediately, but whose
conveyance would not be ready till five o'clock in the morn-
ing.  The morning found us journeying over a broad, arid,
herbless, treeless plain, encircled by mountains equally bare
of vegetation, and of a pale-brown hue.  We were still
shrouded and almost choked with the dust.  Little whirlwinds
of dust crossed the highway before us and passed off toward
the mountains.  This is the season when the earth is at rest—
the barren season of the year; in the summer, when the rains
fall, these now bare fields are green and fresh with the growing

harvests. The mountains gradually came nearer the highway, and we passed from this highland valley into another, which I was told is of still higher elevation, and so we journeyed on from one region enclosed by high mountains to another, the cool, spring-like airs indicating that we were in the temperate regions of the republic. Vast fields of the *maguey*, the *Agave Americana*, sometimes called the aloe, from which the intoxicating liquor called *pulque* is drawn, now made their appearance—the dark-green plants set in rows at such a distance from each other as allowed the cultivation of maize and other grains between them. Here and there was a field green with irrigation, and soon the spires of Puebla were seen against the evening sky. The roads were full of people of the aboriginal race, returning to their cabins from the town, which we entered a little after sunset.

The next morning, while waiting for the train, I walked, with my friends, the streets of Puebla, which have a cheerful look. Above all the dwellings rises the cathedral with its domes and spires. We entered it, and found the floor covered with worshippers, three fourths of whom were women, murmuring aloud their prayers in a supplicating, half-tremulous tone. The exterior of the edifice is imposing; the ribbed columns of Roman architecture are both tall and massive, and not without a certain simplicity in the detail, which, joined to the somewhat dark color of the marble, gives to the whole a grave aspect well suited to the house of prayer.

At half-past eleven the next morning we took the railway train to convey us over the hundred and fifteen miles lying between Puebla and the capital. The region was much like that over which we had travelled, save that in approaching Mexico we passed by abandoned habitations, the tokens of a dwindled population, and for a space skirted the shallow waters of Lake Tezcoco, which in places covered the ground on its edge with a sediment as white as snow. The train stopped at a rather shabby station in the suburbs of the capital. Our luggage had to undergo an inspection at the custom-house, and shortly after we were installed in pleasant quarters at the Hotel Iturbide, named after the young adventurer who resided for a short time in the building, and who, aspiring to be the Emperor of Mexico, paid for his ambition with his life.

MEXICO, MARCH 8th: One of the first things which we had to do on arriving at the city of Mexico was to conform our dress to the climate. We were now in a cool region nearly eight thousand feet above the level of the sea, and the temperature admonished us to resume our winter under-clothing. The sunshine at this season is perpetual and the weather spring-like. It is only from May to October that the clouds thicken into rain. In the early part of winter spangles of frost are sometimes seen on the ground. On an estate in the neighborhood of the city, and on the pleasant slopes of Tacubaya, amid stately palms and orange-trees loaded with their golden fruit, and roses in bloom, I saw a tree, more than fifteen feet high, wrapped in matting to the very top. " What does that mean?" I asked. " It is some tender tree," was the answer, "from the hot country south of us, which they have covered in that way to protect it from the frost." The summers in this region, I am told, are but little warmer than the winters, the chief difference being that the summer is the rainy season, when the afternoons and evenings are showery, and the fields are in their fullest luxuriance.

The city stands so far above the sea-level that the inhabitants breathe a thin air, which, as the stranger immediately perceives, puts him out of breath in ascending a staircase or declivity. Those who suffer from symptoms of heart-disease find them considerably aggravated here, and the remark is often made that deaths from that disease are more frequent here than in most places. The air is as dry as it is thin. It requires very brisk exercise, even in warm weather, to bring out anything like sensible perspiration. " I suppose," said a medical gentleman with whom I was talking on this subject, " that there are persons here, born in Mexico, who never in their lives experienced anything like sensible perspiration." "It is an insidious climate," said another resident. "You take cold easily; you expose yourself to a draught which is neither considerable nor unpleasant, and the next day you have a severe cold." The disease of the lungs which they call *pulmonia* in Madrid, and which is there so violent and fatal, is almost equally so here, and carries off its victims after a short illness. Yet Mexico is a healthy city, notwithstanding that it is badly drained; indeed, it can scarcely be said that it is drained at all, so slight is all the descent that can be given to the drains. There can be no cellars to the houses, for, on digging two or three feet in the ground, you come to water. Great shallow, plashy lakes cover vast tracts in the neighborhood of the city, and sometimes, in seasons of copious rain, overflow their banks and invade the streets, and ripple against the thresholds of the dwellings. Yet is the air, so they say, never charged with moisture, and Mexico will yet be the frequent resort of those who suffer from any disease of the lungs or throat requiring a dry atmosphere. I doubt, however, whether the climate is particularly favorable to longevity, for I saw few old men, either among the aboriginal inhabitants or those of Spanish descent.

One who takes his idea of this city from photographs and engravings is apt to suppose it a city of small houses; but this is a mistake. It is true that the houses are not often of more than one story, but they are spacious and massively built, with lofty ceilings. They generally enclose a court of ample size, round which, on the second story, runs a gallery supported by sturdy columns or square pillars of heavy masonry. From these galleries the doors open into the rooms where the family live, including the sleeping-rooms, and standing in the galleries or in the roomy antechambers are vases of flowering plants of brilliant bloom, which in this spring-like climate need no other attention than the water which moistens the soil about their roots. I can scarcely imagine a pleasanter abode in a large town than some of these houses belonging to opulent families—houses airy, cheerful, and luxuriously commodious. Yet beside this opulence you see the most squalid poverty; ragged and dirty human beings, who saunter about during the day and lie down at night wherever the night surprises them. In a climate so soft as this, with a soil so genial and productive, people are tempted to be poor. It costs but little labor to obtain the means of living; slight clothing is all that is needed; slight shelter suffices; a few beans, *frijoles*, and two or three *tortillas*, or flap-jacks, wind up the living machine for the day. Where poverty is so easy a condition of life, and its few wants are so cheaply supplied, there must be many poor. "How many are there in the city of Mexico, rich and poor taken together?" I asked of a resident. "Probably somewhat over two hundred thousand," was the answer, "but no man can speak with any certainty. The moment that any person employed by the government appears and begins to take the enumeration, the suspicion is awakened that there is to be a conscription, or that a new tax is to be levied. The people disappear like a brood of young partridges, and keep out of the way till the supposed danger is over."

Side by side with the utter poverty which I have just described there is great luxury. The day after my arrival I was a guest at a private banquet, and, without professing an admiration for luxurious dinners, I may say that I never sat at any in which sumptuousness exceeded it. The blaze of gas-lights, the glitter of plate, the variety and delicacy of the viands, the exquisite wines, the rich attire of the ladies, the number and dexterity of the attendants—were all there in as great perfection as at the tables of the most luxurious of our own merchant-princes, with a dessert of fruits of such various flavors as our climate does not afford. Nor should I leave out of the account the profusion of flowers, both of tropical and temperate climates, which sweetened the atmosphere—all gathered from their beds in the open air.

The day following was Sunday, and as I went to the cathedral I was struck with the number of persons whom I met selling lottery-tickets. Gambling is one of the besetting vices of the Mexicans, and the numerous lotteries give them the opportunity to gamble as they are going to church. I found the floor of the cathedral occupied by a crowd on their knees, mostly women, while priests in their rich vestments were officiating at the principal altar. The building without is not imposing; its front is covered with a jumble of pilasters and capitals and scrolls, and other architectural ornaments; but within it is grave and grand, though in some parts wanting in simplicity.

I have spoken of the vestments of the priests. By the " laws of reform," as they are called, no ecclesiastical costume can be worn in the streets. You might traverse Mexico from Sonora to Yucatan and never meet with any person whom you would recognize as a priest, save when you entered the churches. They are obliged to dress as others do ; they can get up no religious processions: all such are forbidden ; the convents are suppressed ; there is neither monk nor nun in all Mexico; the convent buildings and grounds have been taken by the government; many of the churches have shared the same fate, and the schools, of which at one time the priests had the sole direction, are all secularized and given to the control of laymen. So dissatisfied are the Catholic clergy with these restrictions that, as I am told, they are the most zealous friends of annexation to the United States that are found in all Mexico, in the hope of recovering by it some of their lost privileges.

From the cathedral I followed the street till I came to a chapel belonging to what was called the Church of Jesus. This church and another, both of them large, have been sold by the government, at a low price, to the Protestant worshippers. In the chapel I found about four hundred persons, which were as many as could be seated, in devout attitudes, while in the pulpit a minister in a white surplice was engaged in prayer. The form of the service was partly liturgical, and there were occasional responses. After the prayer a hymn was given out, and sung by the congregation with great apparent fervor. I looked round upon the assembly, which was composed of men in the proportion of three to one of the other sex, and perceived that they were mostly of the aboriginal race. Most of them, however, were neatly dressed, and all were attentive. The minister then preached a sermon; he spoke with animation, and was apparently heard with very great interest. I inquired afterward the meaning of what I had seen. "The person whom you saw in the pulpit," was the answer, "is Father Agnas, a Catholic priest of no little eloquence, who has been converted to the Protestant faith; but the principal head of the Protestant Church here, and the composer of its liturgy, is Father Reilly, who is a citizen of the United States, although reared in Chili. He has engaged with great zeal in the cause of Protestantism, and is aided by several ministers who once belonged to the Church of Rome, and are now as zealous as he in making converts from it. The government favors them, and would doubtless be glad of their success, for the government and the Catholic priesthood bear no good-will to each other. There are now more than a score of these Protestant congregations in the city of Mexico, and more than thirty in the neighboring country. The priesthood are naturally vexed at seeing the Protestants in churches which once were theirs, but the effect upon them is salutary, for it has made them more attentive to their own personal morals."

Those who have read the accounts of Mexico given by travellers will remember that the clergy of this country are generally spoken of as exceedingly loose in their morals. The truth of this was afterward confirmed to me by a gentleman who had resided for some years in Mexico. "I am a Catholic," said he, "brought up as a Catholic in the United States. When I came here I expected to find the clergy of my Church such as they are in the country I left—men of pure lives, and watchful guardians of the morals of their flocks. I was disappointed; I found them immoral in their own lives, and indifferent to the morals of those who were under their spiritual care, I must say that they have not done their duty ; and if the Mexican people are not what they ought to be, the clergy are in a good degree responsible." Afterward I saw Father Reilly, as he is often called here. He assured me that all which I had heard of his success and the displeasure of the clergy was true, and expressed strong hopes of further success. I mentioned to him that by far the greater part of the worshippers whom I saw in the cathedral were women, and that, on the other hand, in his church I found that the men greatly outnumbered the women. He replied that in some of the Protestant congregations the women were most numerous. There is no question that the Catholic clergy in Mexico have been fearfully corrupted by what may be called the monopoly of religious worship which they possessed, by the immense riches of their Church, and the power of persecution which was placed in their hands. They will become better men by the effect of adversity and the formidable rivalry to which they are now subjected.

MEXICO, MARCH 10th: One of the first visits I made to the country surrounding the city of Mexico was to Chapultepec, a rocky mount rising from the midst of a plain west of the town. A grove of cypresses and other trees shades its eastern slope, and hither the kings of Mexico, before the conquest, are said to have resorted for recreation. One of these cypresses yet bears the name of Montezuma's Tree, and even before his time must have seen several generations of the Aztec monarchs. We measured it, and found it thirty-seven feet and four inches in circumference—the largest tree that I ever saw in any part of the world. It is still in full vigor, and will outlast many generations of men yet to come. I looked into its broad extent of branches, hung with gray, thread-like mosses clinging to them like mist, and thought of the dim antiquity which dwelt there, and of the unwritten histories, both sorrowful and pleasant, bound up in the long life of that silent tree.

It was a holiday, and there were several parties of pleasure in these ancient shades. In one part was a family group at a picnic; in another a guitar was tinkling, and two or three couples dancing; in another were a young man and woman withdrawn from the rest—most likely lovers—engaged in such talk as lovers use. I climbed with my companions to the top of the hill, where is a palace which had been fitted up by Maximilian for his own residence, but in which the poor fellow, during his short and most unhappy reign, could be scarcely said to have ever resided. It stands in the midst of a garden, where the air is sweetened all the year with shrubs in bloom. Near it, on the esplanade, the Mexican gentleman who accompanied us pointed out what at first seemed to us a deep well—a circular opening in the ground—walled up with stones apparently hewn. "This," he said, "belongs to the time of the Aztecs. It communicates with a cavern below, having its issue on the west side of the hill, so that it forms an underground passage."

The view from the top of Chapultepec is very fine. The Mexicans are fond of repeating a saying ascribed to Humboldt—that it is the finest view in the world; to which I should not agree, for there are finer in the neighborhood of Orizaba. But it was very striking as I saw it—the great valley of Mexico stretching away on every side, the city with its spires, the green fields artificially watered, the brown pasture-lands, the great glimmering lakes, the rows and groups of trees in full leaf that mark the place of the floating gardens, and finally the circle of mountains enclosing all. Beyond these, in clear weather, the snowy peaks of the two great and now silent volcanoes of Popocatepetl and Iztaccihuatl are seen rising to an immense height. Near at hand, and in full sight, is the building called the Molino del Rey, or King's Mill, around which was fought the bloody battle of that name, just before the entrance of the United States troops into the city in the late war with Mexico. With the narrative of that war before him, one may stand on Chapultepec and trace the progress of the

American armies step by step as they drew near to the capital which was to fall into their hands.

On the slope of Chapultepec we passed the large basin of a copious spring, forty feet in depth, and so clear that the bottom seems almost close to the eye. A rapid stream rushes from it and is received in a stately aqueduct, which carries it off to the city of Mexico on its tall arches, resembling those which cross the Roman Campagna. Looking to the south, you see another and longer aqueduct, which strides across the plain, bringing water from a more distant point. Lower down gushes from the ground another spring, no less copious, which supplies commodious baths, public and private, and then flows on to irrigate the fields, marking its course by tracts of verdure. Leaving these behind us, we followed the road a little distance to the village of Tacubaya, situated on ground somewhat elevated above the plain, and noted for its beautiful country seats, the property of opulent families in the city. We entered and wandered over one of these—the Escandon estate, as it is called, from the name of the family owning it. It was a perfect labyrinth of walks among fruit-trees and flowering shrubs. The walks, twining through the grove, are somewhat neglected, to be sure. Here and there were towering over the palms the fruit-trees. A spacious mansion stood in the midst of an ample flower-garden. " Is not the family there?" I asked. " No," was the answer, " the family is safer in town. The members sometimes come out to visit this place in the daytime and return by daylight, but they never venture to remain here over night. They might be robbed, or perhaps kidnapped, and made to pay a heavy ransom." I looked round on the orange-trees dropping their fruit, and on the neglected walks, where the weeds were beginning to make their appearance, and, beautiful as the place was, I did not much wonder that it was not more carefully tended by those who were able to enjoy its beauty only by snatches, or in constant fear of a visit from banditti. That Tacubaya was not a safe place for those who had anything to lose I had a proof before I got home, for, arriving at the railway-station just before sunset, I entered the cars amid a crowd of people returning to town, and soon after, having occasion to consult my watch, I found that it was missing.

The most unsafe place, however, at present, seems to be the railway between this city and Puebla. The newspapers here give accounts of attacks made by robbers on the trains conveying *pulque*, which is the beverage drawn from the plant called here the *maguey*. These attacks, however, have been generally repulsed. Not so fortunate has been the superintendent and paymaster of the railway which is yet constructing between Puebla and Orizaba, Mr. Quin, whom I saw the day after my arrival, just returned from an adventure with the robbers. They seized him when he happened to be without money, took away his watch, and, after a detention of two hours, bargained with him for his release on the payment of fifty dollars, which he brought them, and they returned him his watch. But the watch he was not to keep, for two days afterward I heard that they found him with sixteen hundred dollars on his person, and took that and the watch also. Soon afterward news came that Mr. Quin was kidnapped a third time. He had no money with him, and, after detaining him a day or two, the robbers allowed him to depart, with the message to his employers that if forty thousand dollars were not immediately sent them they would tear up the iron rails. The money, however, has not been paid, and the railway is yet untouched. The leader of these bandits is one Negrete, who calls himself a general and claims to be a revolutionist, instead of a robber.

MEXICO, MARCH 11th : One of the most interesting things to be seen in Mexico is the school of Tecpan de Santiago, a charitable institution, founded and supported by a Mexican lady, the Señora Baz, wife of an opulent gentleman who has formerly filled the post of Governor of the province of Mexico. We called first at the house of Governor Baz, as he is called, one of the finest mansions in Mexico, fitted up with great taste and attention to comfort.   His lady, a native Mexican of some-what slight but elegant figure and quiet manners, came out and accompanied us in our visit to the school.   Just on the skirts of the city, or perhaps a little outside of them, stands a spa-cious building, once the convent of Tecpan de Santiago, and this has been taken by Señora Baz for the charitable purpose to which she devotes a large income and gives her daily care. In this school five hundred boys—picked up in the city, parent-less, or neglected by their parents, utterly friendless, and, if not taken from the streets, certain to belong to that miserable class called the *leperos*, and to grow up in ignorance and habits of indolence and vice—are clothed, fed, educated, taught a variety of trades and employments, and fitted to become useful members of society.   We passed from room to room, in some of which the lads were studying their lessons, and in others attending to the occupations in which they were to be trained. Here were the future shoemakers of Mexico, busy over their lasts and lapstones; there the tailors learning to sew and cut out and fit garments, and in another place the printers busy at their types.   " The proceedings and ordinances of the Com-mon Council are printed here," said Señor Baz, and we were shown several samples neatly executed.   In one room were the young cabinet-makers, smoothing and polishing slabs of rosewood ; in another, carpenters learning to handle the saw and plane ; in a third, several turning-lathes were humming. The boys were all neatly and comfortably clad in the gar-ments made by their own tailors.   We passed through the prodigiously long halls which serve as dormitories, with their neat beds, numerous enough to lodge a regiment of soldiers, and came last to the kitchen, where ample preparations were making for their meals.

In this school the course of education includes grammar, drawing, and music.   The benevolent founder of the school visits it every day, observes the progress of the pupils, sees that their comfort is not neglected, and that her plan is faith-fully carried out.   Such an inroad as her institution is making into the worthless class of *leperos* must at length reduce their number and increase the proportion of those who live in comfortable houses and follow habits of regular industry. I can hardly imagine a fairer omen of the future peace and prosperity of Mexico than this noble example of one of her daughters, who applies her large fortune, and gives the leisure which her large fortune allows her, to the work of rescuing such numbers of her fellow-creatures from the degradation and misery to which they seemed to be doomed by the circumstances of their birth.

There is yet another department of this school which answers to our House of Refuge, just as the department which I have already described answers to our Children's Aid Society. There are seventy-five boys sent to it from the criminal tribunals for reformation. These young delinquents are all kept by themselves, and never see the other inmates. I fancied that I saw in the faces of some of them a peculiar expression—a premature sharpness and slyness. One of them, and one of the youngest, was asked for what cause he had been sent there. His answer was a little too discreet. He was *charged*, he said, with taking something that belonged to another.

The same day we visited the market which lies beside the canal connecting the lake of Tezcoco with that of Chalco. There the flat-bottomed boats come in loaded with the products of the *chinampas*, or floating gardens, as they are sometimes called, though they are only narrow parallelograms of fertile soil surrounded by canals, from which they are watered and kept constantly green. Over a large space of this market we saw women squatted on the ground in the dust beside their vegetables, their fruits, and their wares, for at this season the sunshine is constant, and the showers are not to fall till May. If any shelter from the sun is wanted, a rude one is formed by a piece of matting supported on poles. No season in Mexico seems to be without its fruits; the banana may be had in perfection all the year round; the orange is now as fine as it can be; the *granadilla*, or fruit of the edible passion-flower, is at this time common in the markets, as well as the *sapote prieto*, or dark-colored sapote, a green fruit, filled with a rich, jetty pulp, like a sort of marmalade. Meantime, the *aguacate*, or what in the English West Indies is called the alligator-pear, is reserved for a later season, and the Manila mango, the finest variety of mango, is just putting forth its clusters of red blossoms ; its fruits are not to be ripe before next summer. Other fruits follow in that order till the year completes its circle.

On our return to our hotel we saw a crowd of people about an open door, and, looking in, we saw the drawing of a lottery, in which the bystanders seemed to be much interested. A hollow cylinder, full of bits of paper indicating the blanks and prizes, was made to revolve a few times ; a little boy then thrust in an awl through an opening among these bits of paper, and on its point drew out either a blank or a prize, and this determined the fate of the ticket of which the number was read just before the cylinder was made to revolve. A large proportion of the earnings of the humbler class in Mexico are thrown away in the purchase of lottery-tickets, and it is not to be wondered at that, where the passion for this sort of gambling is so very common, there should be such extreme poverty.

I have since visited an institution in which, until the era of Mexican independence, orphan children of the emigrants from Biscay to Mexico were educated. It was a magnificent endowment, founded by the opulent Biscayans while the country was under the rule of Spain. A million of dollars was expended in erecting a building of vast dimensions—a perfect palace, enclosing several quadrangles—and half a million dollars set aside for the support of the inmates. It was originally called the Colegio de las Biscayinas ; but the Basques in Mexico might, I suppose, now be counted on the fingers of one's hand, and the Mexican government has taken possession of the institution and named it the National School for Girls. Here seventy-eight orphan girls of all the different races in Mexico are sheltered, reared, educated, and provided with a home till

they marry. Drawing and music are among the accomplish-
ments which they are taught—embroidery, of course. The
inmates were of all ages; some had already reached middle
life, and as spinsters were sure of a shelter till they died of
old age. We were shown over the whole, and could not but
admire the clean and comfortable appearance of everything
in their airy apartments. The long sleeping-rooms, in which
were rows of neat little beds, stretched away like the galleries
of the Louvre in Paris. The matron who showed us these
rooms, and who accompanied us to the great kitchen, where
the dinner of the inmates was simmering, smoked, as she went,
a *cigarillo*, a pinch or two of fine tobacco rolled up in paper so
as to form a little cylinder. It is customary among the elderly
Mexican women and those of middle age to smoke tobacco
in this form, but when I spoke of this to a Mexican lady she
answered: "The practice is going out of vogue; the young
women now do not smoke."

But I have not yet done with the school. All these ample
accommodations are not alone for the orphans who are gratui-
tously provided for. A hundred and forty girls of Mexican
families are received here as boarders and pupils on payment
of ten dollars monthly. Besides these, there is kept in the
building a day-school for little girls of the poorer class, who
amount to an indefinite number, and for whom nothing is
paid.

From the National School for Girls I went to the Found-
ling Hospital, which is here called the *Cuna*, or Cradle. Here
I found myself in a swarm of three hundred of these parent-
less creatures, from grown-up boys and girls down to the babe
of yesterday. Some of them were plump-looking infants,
asleep in their little beds, and there were one or two lying
uneasily and panting with fever. I was surprised at the small
number of boys in the hospital. "How is this?" I asked;
"what is the proportion of boys to girls in this institution?"
"Three fourths are girls," was the answer. "But why should
they send girls to this place rather than boys?" "Simply

because there are more of them. The births settle that mat-
ter. Here in Mexico are born three girls to one boy." I
expressed my astonishment at this, but I was assured that the
statistics of the country showed the fact to be as here stated;
and, indeed, the register of the Foundling Hospital is pretty
good evidence of the vast preponderance of female over male
births in Mexico. A smiling ecclesiastic, with an asthmatic
laugh, conducted us over the building, or rather the two large
private houses so connected as to form one, and caused one of
the inmates, already a woman grown, to play for us on the
piano, which she did very creditably. Fourteen of the girls
then sang in chorus two or three songs with a precision which
showed that they had been carefully trained.

We closed the day, as it is often closed here, with a drive
on the *Paseo* west of the city. On our way we passed through
the Alameda, a fine grove of tall trees intersected with walks
and carriage-roads. Hither on holidays come crowds of the
Mexican people in their best dresses. Here some sit on
benches and listen to music, while others, in couples, move to
the *jarabe*, a peculiar and not ungraceful dance of this country
and of Cuba. Hither resort on these occasions the sellers of
sweetmeats and fruits, and find a ready market for their wares.
The sober shadow cast by those great old trees is then
lighted up through all its extent by the brilliant hues, not
only of the women's dresses, but of the *sarapes*, or light shawls,
with bright-colored stripes, worn by the broad-brimmed Mexi-
cans. The Spanish minister, a most amiable man and a favor-
ite among the Mexicans, sent from Spain, doubtless, to win
their hearts and keep them in good humor, had given me a
seat in his carriage, and we drove to the broad space beyond
the city bounds, about an eighth of a mile in length, where the
carriages were passing backward and forward and by each
other, from one end of the *Paseo* to the other, a favorite amuse-
ment of the Mexicans, and adopted from the Spaniards. The
earth in this dry season requires profuse watering, and on that
day the place had been but slightly sprinkled, so that we were

involved in clouds of dust. After several rounds we drew up on one side of the *Paseo*, where a row of carriages had already ranged themselves, and observed the handsome equipages and gayly dressed women as they passed. Two or three turns more on the *Paseo* completed the entertainment, which seemed to me excessively dull, considering the dust, and with the setting sun I returned to the Hotel Iturbide.

MEXICO, MARCH 11th : In company with my travelling companions, I have been presented to Señor Juarez, the President of the Mexican republic. We went to the palace, a spacious building of massive construction, where in the time of the Spanish dominion the viceroys dwelt in semi-regal state. Mr. Romero, the Minister of Finance, had promised to accompany us, and we called on him at his cabinet in a corner of the building, where we found him, as usual, closely engaged in the business of his department. It is no holiday task to have charge of the exchequer of Mexico, the expenditures of which are greater than the income, and we wondered not that our friend should have the look of one who is greatly overworked and beset by many perplexities. We followed him through spacious antechambers and long halls to the cabinet of the President. The palace, in its present state, is large, including several quadrangles ; but it was considerably larger before the time of Maximilian, who pulled down a considerable part of it, with a view of rebuilding it in a style more conformable to his taste. He had just time to demolish, but defeat and death overtook him before he had time to rebuild.

We reached the cabinet of the President, and found him expecting us. I was struck with his appearance. There stood before me a man of low stature and dark complexion, evidently of the Aztec race, square-built and sturdy in figure, with a mild expression of countenance, yet with something in his aspect which indicated inflexible resolution. He is sixty-six years of age, but time seems to have dealt gently with him ; his hair is not sprinkled with gray, nor his face marked with wrinkles. The image of him which remains in my memory is that of a man not much older than fifty years. I had already seen three of his daughters at an evening party, children of a lady of Italian extraction. They seemed to me to be favorable samples of the blending of the European with the Aztec race.

He received us courteously. We spoke of the signal defeat of the insurgents a few days before by the government forces under General Rocha, the news of which had been received with great rejoicings at the capital. "It is," he said, "the end of the revolt. We shall hear but little more of it. After the first of May, when the rainy season begins, and the insurgents find themselves without shelter, they will come out of their hiding-places in the woods and submit." We talked of the state of the country. "We have," he said, "great advantages of soil and climate, but we want capital for enterprises important to the country, and we want the strong arms of skilled laborers to execute them." He might have added that, more than all, the country wants internal quiet. The revolt by which the republic is now disturbed will certainly be suppressed ; the rebels will submit ; the roads will be again safe from robberies perpetrated in the name of revolution ; but those who have lived for some years in the country do not feel certain that the quiet will last. "We shall have a peaceful condition of things," said one of them to me, "for about two years ; then these fellows who are now running away from Rocha will become uneasy again ; we shall have another *pronunciamiento* and another revolt, and fresh robberies on the highways." I hope this anticipation will not become a reality. It is founded on the restlessness of the mixed race in Mexico, who are about one-fifth part of the inhabitants. The Aztec race, who form the greater part of the population, I was told, are generally mild, docile, and submissive to the government. Hard-working they are not, but nearly all the labor of the fields in Mexico is performed by their hands. It is they who are the handicraftsmen for the most part, and the regular industry of the country, such as it is, is theirs. In the mixed

race, I was told, are found the men who will not work, and
are ready to engage in a revolt against the government, which
gives them an opportunity of living by extorting contribu-
tions from the peaceable part of the population. These fel-
lows will fight on any side indiscriminately, and, when beaten,
enlist in the victorious army.

President Juarez dismissed me with words which I may
cite as a characteristic example of Spanish courtesy. Taking
both my hands in his, he said : " Remember, Señor, that in me
you have a servant and a friend. If at any time you have oc-
casion for my aid, apply to me confidently, and the service you
desire shall be performed."

To understand the nature of the revolt which now seems
to have received its death-blow, it should be remembered that
at the last election of President in Mexico there were three
candidates—Juarez, who now fills that post; Lerdo, now the
principal judge of the highest tribunal in Mexico, and Porfirio
Diaz, who had distinguished himself as an able general in the
war which ended in the overthrow of Maximilian. Juarez
obtained the office ; his rivals complained of unfairness in the
election; Lerdo and his friends submitted, but Porfirio Diaz
took up arms, issued a *pronunciamiento*, and attempted to seize
upon the government by force. He drew to his standard the
desperate men who are too numerous in Mexico, and who saw
in the revolt an opportunity of living by contributions wrung
from the people. They have met the fate which they de-
served. A few of their chiefs yet seem to hold out, but their
principal leader, whose military fame and prowess were their
boast and their great reliance, has disappeared ; and whether
he be dead or concealed in some hiding-place in Mexico, or
has run away, nobody knows.

Of course, Mexico cannot prosper until these disturbances
cease, without a probability of their being renewed. Capital
will not flow into Mexico without some assurance that it shall
be secure, and that its earnings shall not be wrested from the
hands of the owner. Skilled laborers will not seek employment

in Mexico unless they can be sure of keeping the accumulations of their wages. Ten years of perfect quiet would make an immense difference in the condition of the country. Capital would enter from other regions, and bring with it the skilled and energetic labor that is wanted. Railways would be constructed and safely guarded; highways would be opened; the waters that fall on the mountains would be gathered in great reservoirs on the declivities, and in winter led in rivulets over the fertile valleys which for half the year are now beds of dust, and would keep them, through all the dry season, green and overspread with perpetual harvests. The only difficulty which I see in the way of these enterprises is a certain jealousy of foreigners, which influences, to some extent, not the government, but the mass of the people. At one time since the independence of Mexico was declared, the expulsion of all foreigners from the republic was decreed, and, in obedience to the fierce demand of the populace, they were all driven out. That feeling has since been greatly moderated, but it is not yet wholly extinct. I asked an intelligent member of the Mexican Congress how it was that, instead of submitting quietly to the result of an election, as we here submit, even when it is pretty manifest that the successful party has used unfair means, his countrymen so often resort to the sword, as if the question of fairness could be settled by cutting each others' throats. "It is in our blood," he answered; "it is owing to the impatience of our temperament. The cure must be to invite emigration from countries like yours, where the popular vote decides the matter, and the beaten party takes its revenge by obtaining the majority at the next election." The remedy is a sure one, but there is this difficulty in applying it, that the emigrants will not arrive until the evil shall be already cured and the country in a state of perfect quiet.

Yet there are changes going on in Mexico as great as would be this of quietly submitting to an election without an immediate revolt. I once heard Mr. Peter Cooper, the New York philanthropist, relate an incident which happened some years since, while his brother was residing for a few months in the city of Mexico. A procession passed through the streets bearing the Host, or consecrated wafer, probably to some rich person. All the people in the street kneeled save an American who kept a little shoe-shop and happened to be standing at its door. One of the crowd struck at him to make him kneel, on which he retreated into his shop. This so enraged the people in the street that several rushed after him into the shop, and one of them, with a dagger, gave him a mortal wound. The American consul was informed of the murder without delay, and he applied to the proper authorities, requiring them to bring the offender to justice. He was told that nothing could be done, for such was the temper of the populace that, if any steps were taken to punish the guilty man, the house of his victim would undoubtedly be pulled down and its inmates torn in pieces. Such was Mexico not long since. This savage fanaticism has had its day. Now the Host is not permitted to be openly carried through the streets. Protestant worship is held in churches with doors opening upon the public way, and the worshippers are not molested.

I have heard of a method taken to put an end to these demonstrations of reverence for the Host in the streets which is more remarkable for its ingenuity than its decorum. After the laws of reform had required the Host to be carried only in a close carriage, the priests made the driver lay aside his hat while he passed slowly on his way. The populace were given to understand that when they saw a carriage slowly driven by a man without a hat, it contained the consecrated wafer, and, of course, the real presence. Accordingly, all kneeled as they had been wont to do when the Host was borne openly by the priests. One day a carriage was seen to pass, driven with great deliberation by a solemn-looking coachman without a hat, through one of the principal streets. The foot-passengers on the right and left all kneeled in worship. At a place where the crowd was most numerous the carriage stopped, and two women, notoriously of the most degraded and shameless class, got out of it, to the great confusion of the worshippers. This, I was told, put an end to the adoration of the Host in the public streets, and nobody is likely hereafter to be murdered for declining to show it the accustomed reverence.

Other changes have been made in the customs of the country. There is scarce any public entertainment so well adapted to encourage and cherish a spirit of cruelty in a people as the bull-fights of Spain. When I came to Vera Cruz I heard something said about the *Plaza de Toros.* "Where are your bull-fights held?" I innocently asked. "They are held no longer," I was answered. "They are forbidden by law." Here are two important steps taken in civilization—the extinction of a fierce religious fanaticism, and the suppression of one of the most cruel of public spectacles known to modern times. Who shall say that the country which has made these advances may not yet accustom itself to submit quietly to the arbitrament of the ballot, as a lesson learned from a long series of bloody experiences?

There is one peculiarity in the political constitution of Mexico which must be done away, or it will prove a serious obstacle to her prosperity. Spain left, as an unhappy legacy to the republic, the practice of requiring duties to be paid at the frontiers of the different provinces on merchandise conveyed from one of them to another. The several states which comprise the republic are now accustomed in this way to raise the revenue which each state requires, and there seems to be little disposition to renounce the system. According to the doctrine of the protectionists, this should result in making each state the richer by taxing heavily the products of its sister states. It is felt, however, as a cruel burden upon the industry and internal trade of the country, and it must be thrown off before the republic can fully avail itself of its own rich and numerous resources.

MEXICO, MARCH 11th: One of the curiosities of Mexico is the *Peñon Nuevo,* or New Crag, a rocky eminence close to the

Lake of Tezcoco, which I visited the other morning.  It is a great volcanic rock of no very remote origin, from the summit of which you have a noble view of the plain of Mexico, of its mountain barriers, and the city, and the broad lakes.  The crest of the rock leans to the south, and there overhangs its base, looking as if, when the huge billow of molten lava was spouted into the air, the wind had swayed it from the perpendicular, and it had cooled and stiffened as it was about to fall, forming several caverns on the side opposite to the wind.  In these chambers of the rock live two or three Indian families and their dogs.  The wild-looking inmates, with their children, came about us, as we peeped into these strange abodes, and wanted money.  The women were cooking fish, caught in the lake close at hand.  I went to the lake, and on my way passed a warm spring smoking from the ground; the internal fires which caused the eruption of the lava are smouldering yet.  The water of the lake is salt, though not intensely so, and the neighboring soil is so impregnated with salt that the Indians extract from it a dark-colored salt by passing water through it.  Not far from the *Peñon* are some half-ruinous buildings enclosing a hot spring, to which invalids resort, and an old church, in the shadow of which some of them have found a grave.

We returned to town over the extensive low grounds, now dry, but elevated only two or three feet above the level of the lake, and therefore sure to be laid under water when the copious summer rains, falling on the sides of the mountains, are gathered in the great basin of the Mexican valley.  We breakfasted at the Tivoli Gardens, to which we were taken by the American consul, Dr. Skelton.  This is a favorite resort of the Mexicans, and often the place of their public banquets.  For this purpose there are broad galleries open to the air, but under a roof, while for small parties there are little summer-houses beneath the shade of great trees.  Rivulets of water keep up a perpetual verdure; there is a turf always green, and flowers always in bloom.  For the recreation of visitors, there are three or four bowling-alleys.

It was a holiday, and we went to the Véga, a public drive just without the city, beside the canal which connects the salt lake of Tezcoco with the fresh-water lake of Chalco. This time we found the ground sufficiently watered to keep the dust in its place, and all the finest equipages in Mexico were out, with many of humbler pretensions, passing and repassing each other as they drove backward and forward. Sometimes the equipage was a neat carriage drawn by a pair of mules, the handsomest creatures of their kind that I ever saw, with a spirited look which they certainly do not inherit from the parent donkey. Mingled among these were horsemen with their handsome barbs, their massive, glittering stirrups and spurs and showy saddles, their slashed pantaloons, their gay *sarapes* of many colors, and their broad-brimmed white hats, with ornaments of silver. The Mexicans ride well and gracefully, and sit their horses in such a manner that the rider seems a part of the animal. On the canal, which bordered this public drive, flat-boats, some of them quite large, were passing, filled with people from the Indian villages south of the city : women with chaplets of flowers on their heads, and young people dancing, with a slow, swaying motion—for there was no capering—to the light sound of some musical instrument as their boat slid along the water. By the canal, and under the trees which bordered it, sat people who seemed to enjoy the spectacle of the showy equipages, and still more showy cavaliers on horseback, quite as much as those who sat in the carriages. On the opposite side of the Véga were people grouped about the houses of entertainment under the trees, some of whom were amusing themselves with swings. As the sun touched the horizon the carriages turned homeward, the foot-passengers trooped toward the town, and the flat-boats disappeared from the canals.

The next day, in company with Mr. Porter Bliss, the American Secretary of Legation, we explored the canal. Going to the Paseo de la Véga, we took one of the boats, with two men carrying poles to push it forward and guide its course, and soon came to the narrow fields enclosed by canals which are called the *chinampas*, and are all that remains of the floating gardens spoken of in Mexican history. They are as fast at the present time as any of the meadows in the valley of Mexico. Here are cultivated all the garden vegetables of temperate climates—every root that comes upon the dinner-table, and a great variety of fruits. The peach and almond were now in full bloom, and the fruit of the apricot was, as the gardeners say, already set. The brown cultivators of these gardens were busy in places with a sort of long-handled ladle, scooping up the water from the canals and flinging it upon the thirsty little islands. We passed the Indian town of Santa Anita to another named Ixtacaleo, where we landed. There an artesian well had been sunk, where the cool water of the brightest transparency gushes up with force from the ground, filling a spacious tank, and then running off into the canal. An old church was near, with graves by its side, only one or two of which had any monumental stone. The rest were dusty hillocks, the newest of which had little crosses made of reed planted at the head. We returned to the town of Santa Anita, where the Indian cooks gave us a breakfast of choco-late, which here in Mexico is excellently well prepared, eggs, and *frijoles*, or beans, together with a roast chicken. But the most palatable dish—so I thought—was that which they call *tamales*, made of the meal of Indian-corn baked in the husks of the ear. The Indians often eat them seasoned with red pepper, *enchilados*, as their phrase is, but a single trial of the *tamales* prepared in this manner set my mouth on fire and satisfied me.

While the Indian women were preparing our breakfast we looked about us. The place which we were in was evidently a great resort on holidays, for here were counters for dispens-ing *pulque* and other beverages, on the walls of which were drawings rudely executed by Aztec artists, accompanied by ill-spelled inscriptions, mostly in rhyme, by the village poets. I could not help comparing this simple breakfast, furnished by the coarse cookery of these Indian villagers, with one at which I was present a few days before, at Tacubaya, on the gentle declivities which overlook the city from the west. A Scottish merchant invited a large party, including several ladies, to breakfast on the Barron estate, a fine country seat, kept in the most scrupulous order, although no one ventures to live there, or even to pass the night, on account of the frequent robberies which are committed in the neighborhood. The founder of the Barron family was from Ireland, and is said to have made his immense wealth by trade, not without the suspicion of having benefited the community in the way approved by Jeremy Bentham—that is to say, by redressing the rigors of a tyrannical system of revenue laws. However this may be, the mansion of the place is a palace, and the grounds—with their shady walks, and fragrant, blossoming thickets, and smooth lawns, and groups of trees laden with tropical fruits, and little streams traversing the ever-verdant groves, and sheets of water reflecting beds of roses in bloom— are as beautiful as any one can imagine. We were on the spot at eleven o'clock, and the breakfast was to begin not far from that time; but one or two of the guests, the most distinguished, were late in arriving, and we did not sit down till nearly one. But the breakfast—if I were to describe it, I could hardly do better than to borrow the words of Milton in "Paradise Regained," in which he gives the bill of fare provided by the Tempter in the wilderness. It was too sumptuous and exquisite to be soon over; and when we rose from the table the rain, a most unusual circumstance at this season of the year, was beating on the roof. Ere long, however, the clouds dispersed, the air was the clearer for the shower, and the volcano of Popocatepetl, which in the winter is generally concealed from sight by the haze, showed its white summit in the bright sunshine of mid-heaven. Then there were the grounds to look at again, and the bowling-alley to visit, where the ladies distinguished themselves by their address in knocking down the pins, and thus the short space between the breakfast and the hour of sunset was passed. Suddenly toward sunset we saw the attendants busy in packing up the plate and china in order to take them back to the city, and we all got into our carriages again, to return from a breakfast which might be almost said to have taken up the whole day.

In the afternoon we visited the Museum of Antiquities, to which the Minister of Justice, Señor Alcarras, was kind enough to accompany us. The samples of ancient Aztec pottery, the hideous idols, the implements and ornaments of stone, and the sharp blades of obsidian, or volcanic glass, which before the Spanish conquest were used as knives, are curious, but the description of them would be tiresome; only engravings can give anything like an accurate idea of them. Under the same roof is a cabinet of natural history, which seemed to me well arranged. I should here mention an earlier visit to the Mexican Academy of Arts. Here is an ample collection of casts from the antique, much larger than I expected to see; here are also a great number of Mexican pictures, centuries old, of quaint designs, yet not without talent; but of the works of eminent European painters, by the example of which the pupil might be guided in his art, there are very few. I saw, however, recent pictures by native artists, which bespeak the possession of a decided talent for the art. Among them was a picture of Dante and Virgil looking over a precipice into the fiery gulf prepared for the wicked, by Raphael Flores. Other pictures of merit were " Cimabue, in Company with Giotto," by Obregon; " The Sacrifice of Isaac," by Santiago Rabull; " Ishmael," by Pablo Valdez; " San Carlos Borromeo Distributing Alms," by Salome Piña, and a " Christ," by Ramon Sagrado. There were also some creditable samples of Mexican statuary, among which I saw a statue, yet in plaster, of San Carlos Borromeo and a child. Of Mexican engravings I saw no example. The artist here finds two obstacles in the way of his success. In the first place, there are few good pictures from which he can obtain an idea of his art in its highest forms of excellence. In the second place—and perhaps I ought to have put this first—there are few persons here who buy pictures. I was told of native artists, who had given proofs of no little talent, that they had been obliged to take to making shoes.

The art of music is cultivated with some zeal. There is a philharmonic society here, and I attended one of its concerts, as an honorary member newly installed. The piano was played with a skilful execution, and a choral melody was sung by several young girls in white. They sang with a precision which showed, I thought, careful training and accurate musical perception; but there was something sharp and stridulous in their voices. A few evenings since I heard, at an evening party, Señorita Peratta, famed for the sweetness of her voice. "The Mexicans," said a gentleman who was present, "are proud of Peratta, and with reason. She sings well; but she did not succeed in Paris. Her very plain face and ungraceful action carried the day against the voice, and she returned to Mexico."

But what of the literature of Mexico? Of that, as I know but little yet, I can say but little. But Mexico has her men of science, her eloquent orators, her eminent antiquaries, her historians, her successful novelists, and her poets, who, I am told, are numerous, so easily does the melodious language spoken here run into verse. All who have obtained distinction in this way are gathered into an association called the Geographical and Statistical Society—a very narrow appellation for one which embraces so wide a circle of notabilities.

I was present the other day at one of the meetings of this society, at which several persons were admitted as members, of whom I had the honor to be one. It was held in the *Mineria*, or School of Mines, one of the finest buildings in Mexico, stately and spacious, with airy galleries surrounding an inner square, and with ample rooms for its cabinets of minerals and its fossil animal remains, which had a somewhat meagre appearance in so extensive a receptacle. The members assembled in a large hall capable of holding several thousand people;

the *Ministro de Fomento*, an officer of the government who an-
swers to our Secretary of the Interior, presided, and honored
the occasion with an animated speech. By his side sat a
gentleman, evidently of the pure Aztec race, who, I was told,
generally presided at the meetings of the society ; it was Señor
Ramirez, the vice-president. At a desk in front of the presi-
dent sat Señor Altamirano, the first secretary, who bore
equally manifest tokens of Aztec descent. Many of these de-
scendants of the people subdued by Cortes are men of culti-
vated minds and engaging manners. The greater part of the
works of art in the galleries of which I have spoken are from
their hands.

I was curious to see the *Monte Pio*, a national institution
for lending money on pledges of personal property, and, ac-
cordingly, Mr. Bliss conducted us thither. It occupies what
was once the palace of Cortes, looking upon the cathedral
square, and built, it is said, on the very spot where stood the
royal dwelling of Montezuma. Cortes must have brought
over from Spain his artisans to hew and lay the stones of this
massive structure, which has furnished a pattern for all the
mansions of the wealthy residents of Mexico which have been
built since.

I found the great building filled, from the ground-floor to
the roof, with articles pawned by persons in need. The lower
part, under the galleries, was crowded with every kind of
carriage, from the heavy family coach to the light gig, and
with every movable that could be sold for money. In another
part of the building, in a well-secured apartment, and kept in
drawers safely locked, are jewels of every kind—diamonds,
rubies, pearls, sapphires, and the like, in the shape of wreaths
for the brow, necklaces, bracelets, ear-drops, and every kind of
ornament worn by women. Elsewhere I saw garments of
various kinds, from the most costly silks and shawls to the
plainest chintzes and coarsest handkerchiefs. All these things
are appraised at their just value, from which the interest for
six months is deducted and the remainder paid to the owner.

At the end of six months the objects pawned are sold by auction, and if they bring more than the original valuation, the owner receives the difference. It is worth remarking that the institution is managed with perfect integrity—at least in such a manner that there is no complaint of unfairness or wrong. I could not help thinking, with shame, of the extent to which some of our own savings banks, established under pretence of aiding the poorer class, have swindled those who gave them their confidence, and was obliged to own to myself that Mexico, in this respect, was more honest than New York.

VERA CRUZ, MARCH 20th: I left Mexico by rail on the morning of the 13th of March, regretting that my plans did not allow me to give more time to a place so interesting in many respects—the history of which is so full of remarkable incidents, the people of which have so many quaint peculairities, and the physical geography of which is so different from that of any country which I had ever seen. Several of the acquaintances whom we had made at Mexico kindly came to see us off at the station.

Soon after issuing from the city, we passed, at a considerable distance from us on the right, a small village of mud cabins, to which a fellow-passenger directed our attention. "There lives," he said, "a peculiar tribe of people, of the most degraded and beastly habits. There are no marriages among them, and their practices are free love in its grossest form. Incest of the most revolting kind is common, and there is the utmost confusion of kindred."

One of the cars attached to the train on which we travelled was full of armed men, so that we regarded ourselves as secure against any attack from those who rob travellers in the name of what they call the revolution. At one of the stations where we stopped we found an intrenchment and breastworks thrown up to defend the trains, while they stopped, against robbers coming upon them from the hills that lay to the north of the track.

Soon after leaving the capital we were among the fields of

*maguey*, the plant with stiff, thick, dark-green leaves, from which the common drink of the country, called *pulque*, is drawn. On each side we saw them stretching away over the champaign country to the bare hills that enclose it. Near at hand the broad spaces, left for other crops, between the rows were visible to the eye, but at a distance the rows seemed to run together, and the earth was completely hidden, for leagues around, under what seemed to the sight a close mass of dark-green leaves. This plant, after several years' cultivation and growth, suddenly sends up a thick, vigorous stem. Into this the sap of the plant, a milky juice, flows rapidly, pushing it upward to the height of some fifteen feet, when its summit puts forth horizontal branches hung with flowers. If left to itself, it there perfects its seeds, and then the plant perishes. But the Mexican, while the sap is rushing upward, cuts off the stem at its base, and there scoops out a sort of basin among the leaves near the root. Into this the sap intended for the stem—the Mexicans call it the milk, from its color—flows in great abundance, and, with the help of a tube at the mouth of an Aztec laborer, is drawn out by suction. This, when fermented, is the *pulque*, the ordinary drink of the country, and by distillation yields a spirit like whiskey. To one who at this season casts his eyes over the country it would almost seem as if there was nothing but the *maguey* cultivated, so few are the other crops at this time of the year, and such is the great breadth of the region occupied by this plant. The railways also attest the extent of this traffic. The freight-trains drag huge cars loaded with it in barrels, and also in skins, the primitive method of keeping wine in Spain. At the railway stations were piles of barrels and huge heaps of skins filled with *pulque* waiting their turn to be transported to market. " This *pulque*," said a Mexican gentleman to me, " this *pulque* and the spirit drawn from it are the bane of our country. It is drunk immoderately, and our people, when full of *pulque*, are good for nothing. We must contrive to wean them from its use if we mean that our country shall advance in civilization."

Of course, here is an ample field for the apostles of temperance. I was amused by hearing a young Englishman, lately arrived, whom we saw at Fortin, say very innocently that he had fallen in with some Indians who had been drinking a kind of sour wine—meaning their *pulque.*. It disagreed with them, he said, and made them sick.

The train arrived at Puebla a little before two o'clock in the afternoon, and we hired a carriage to take us to the pyramid of Cholula, in the neighborhood. We had been told in Mexico that this excursion would not be quite safe without an escort, but at Puebla they laughed at this apprehension, and we determined to go. So we went by one of these rough, neglected Mexican roads, through brown pasture-grounds, and russet fallows, and fields of *maguey*, and, crossing a little river overhung with trees in full leaf, came at length to the decayed little town of Cholula. Here is a conical hill, apparently of dark-colored earth, two hundred feet high. Examine it, and you see that it is composed of tiers of sun-dried brick, with many fragments of pottery and small, rough stones, and here and there a horizontal line of a whitish mortar—all evidently built up from the level plain. On its broad sides grew shrubs and trees, and in one or two places the ground had been terraced and cultivated. At the top is a broad, level space where the Aztecs once worshipped, but now a church is standing— an old building, but undergoing repairs, which, I was told, were done by subscription, the government neither building nor repairing any more churches. The interior of the building was in good taste and really beautiful. From the summit we had an extensive view—the little town of Cholula, immediately below, once swarming with inhabitants, but now scarcely more than a hamlet, yet with half a dozen churches; green fields artificially watered, roads crossing each other, bordered with rows of the dark-green *maguey*, the spires of Puebla in the distance, and that circle of mountains which everywhere embraces these upland plains. Near this pyramid is a smaller one, on the top of which we found small Aztec knife-blades of obsidian or volcanic glass; and yet another, the sloping parts of which had been cut down and carried away, leaving the sides completely perpendicular, and, as I judged, almost forty feet high.

Returning to Puebla, I waited on General Alatorre, to whom I had a letter from the Minister of War, Señor Balcárcel, procured for me by the kindness of Señor Romero, requiring him to furnish me with an escort to Orizaba. I found a handsome man of a fine military presence, who asked me if it was necessary that I should set out next day. "It is necessary," I answered, "in order to arrive seasonably at Vera Cruz." "Then," said he, "I must send a messenger to some distance for the cavalry you will want."

The escort was ready to proceed with us the next morning —thirteen men, good riders, all well mounted, and armed with carbines. There were four of our party; we had taken a diligence as far as Orizaba for ourselves only, and we were about to set out, when two gentlemen from Guadalajara, who were about to proceed first to the United States and then to England, asked leave to take seats with us. We gave our consent, and had no reason to regret it. They were courteous, intelligent men, and no smokers, one of them about thirty-two years of age, and the other a little more than ten years younger. They were lawyers going abroad to make themselves acquainted with the jurisprudence of our own country and that of England. Both had some knowledge of English; the memory of the elder one was well stored with passages from Milton's "Paradise Lost," and he repeated them with an accent which the residence of a few months among those who speak our language can hardly fail to improve.

We were joined by another diligence, containing a Mexican family, and traversed again those arid plains encircled by mountains, our armed escort trotting faithfully by our side. We met with no enemy save the dust rising from roads where the earth, by the constant passing of heavy vehicles, had been ground into powder, from which we protected our eyes and nostrils by gauze veils. Before the day ended, our escort had stopped and had been relieved by another of the same number. But instead of caps, our new protectors wore broad-brimmed white hats, and leathern pantaloons instead of woollen ones. Another night at San Agustin de Palmar and another day on the dusty, uneven road to the heights of Aculcingo, upon reaching which our escort was again changed. Let me say here that there will be no occasion for any further complaints of this road after the present year has closed. On the 31st of December the railway from Mexico to Vera Cruz is to be finished, and the journey between the cities will be made in a single day.

# II.

# OCCASIONAL ADDRESSES.

# LOUIS KOSSUTH.*

LET me ask you to imagine that the contest in which the
United States asserted their independence of Great Britain
had closed in disaster and defeat; that our armies, through
treason and a league of tyrants against us, had been broken
and scattered; that the great men who led them, and who
swayed our councils—our Washington, our Franklin, the ven-
erable President of the American Congress, and their illustri-
ous associates—had been driven forth as exiles.  If there had

---

* Although the newspapers of the day fell into the habit of calling Mr. Bryant
" the old man eloquent," he was not an orator in the strictest sense of the term.  He
wanted the passion and enthusiasm that are necessary to the orator.  But, by perse-
verance and hard work in overcoming his native shyness, he had gradually acquired
an easy and pleasant way of addressing public assemblages, and toward the latter
part of his life was in great demand as a public speaker.  " Few occasions," as Dr.
George Ripley said in the " Tribune," "were considered complete without his pres-
ence.  He was always," Dr. Ripley continues, " the honored guest of the evening,
and the moment in which he was to be called upon to speak was awaited with eager
expectation that never ended in disappointment.  He was singularly happy in seizing
the tone of the company, no matter what were the circumstances or the occasion ;
his remarks were not only pertinent, but eminently felicitous ; with no pretensions to
artificial eloquence, he was always impressive, often pathetic, and sometimes quietly
humorous, with a zest and pungency that touched the feelings of the audience to the
quick.  On more important public occasions, when the principal speech of the day
was assigned to him, he discharged the trust with a tranquil dignity of manner, a
serene self-possession, and an amplitude of knowledge and illustration that invaria-
bly won the admiration of the spectators.  His last address of this kind, delivered,

existed at that day, in any part of the civilized world, a pow-
erful republic, with institutions resting on the same founda-
tions of liberty which our own countrymen sought to estab-
lish, would there have been in that republic any hospitality

---

on the day of his fatal attack, at the unveiling of the bust of Mazzini in Central
Park, was a masterpiece of descriptive oratory, unsurpassed by any of his previous ef-
forts for a similar purpose. Never was there a more just or feeling tribute to the Italian
patriot. Seldom has been presented a more discriminating analysis of a great politi-
cal career, or a finer portraiture of the admirable qualities of a noble and heroic per-
sonage."

Mr. Bryant usually wrote at length what he desired to say, and repeated it from
memory ; but sometimes he spoke from the impulse of the moment, and on such oc-
casions generally with more animation and earnestness of manner than was custom-
ary with him in his prepared addresses. But whether he spoke with deliberation or
extemporaneously, his remarks were sure to contain some wise observation, some
scrap of learning, some agreeable historical reminiscence, some stroke of humor, or
some felicity of phrase, which rendered them worthy of note. For this reason the
editor has appended to his more careful performances several little public addresses,
or after-dinner talks, which, unimportant in themselves, may be of considerable
interest to many readers, either as recalling memorable and pleasant unions, or as
expressive of the thoughts and sentiments of one who, by his early, various, and
useful labors, was regarded not only as the pioneer but as the patriarch of our poetic
literature.

One of the first, if not the first, of Mr. Bryant's attempts in this line was an
address as president of the banquet given by the Press of New York to Louis Kos-
suth, December 9, 1851. While he was in Europe, during the time of the Hungarian
War, he had closely followed the course of the illustrious patriot, and afterwards was
among the first of our citizens to welcome the exile to our shores. His admiration of
the man was confirmed by their brief personal intercourse ; and, indeed, it was im-
possible for any one to come in contact with Kossuth without being impressed not
only by his extraordinary talent and eloquence, but by his amiability, earnestness,
and patriotism. It was evident, however, at the same time, that Kossuth, through
the fervor of his convictions and his imaginative exuberance, was living in something
of an ideal realm. He was by no means deficient in practical skill ; he discovered,
by an almost intuitive glance, the strong or the weak side of any question presented
to his decision, and exerted a personal magnetism, which enabled him to control
many persons of every class whom he wished to influence ; but the poetical element,
discernible in his conduct as in his sentiments, which fascinated popular feeling,
was apt to produce in hard-minded practical statesmen and managers no little dis-
trust. The very qualities of enthusiasm and hope, which attached the people to him
and his cause, estranged others less susceptible, in spite of the wonderful fascinations
of his addresses, which all acknowledged.—ED.

too cordial, any sympathy too deep, any zeal for their glorious
but unfortunate cause too fervent or too active to be shown
toward these illustrious fugitives? Gentlemen, the case I
have supposed is before you. The Washingtons, the Frank-
lins of Hungary, her sages, her legislators, her warriors, ex-
pelled by a far worse tyranny than was ever endured here, are
wanderers in foreign lands. Some of them are within our
own borders; one of them sits with his companions as our
guest to-night, and we must measure the duty we owe them
by the same standard which we would have had history apply
if our ancestors had met with a fate like theirs.

I have compared the exiled Hungarians to the great men
of our own history. Difficulty, my brethren, is the nurse of
greatness—a harsh nurse, who roughly rocks her foster-chil-
dren into strength and athletic proportions. The mind, grap-
pling with great aims and wrestling with mighty impediments,
grows by a certain necessity to their stature. Scarce any-
thing so convinces me of the capacity of the human intellect
for indefinite expansion in the different stages of its being as
this power of enlarging itself to the height and compass of
surrounding emergencies. These men have been trained to
greatness by a quicker and surer method than a peaceful
country and a tranquil period can know.

But it is not merely, or even principally, for their personal
qualities that we honor them; we honor them for the cause
in which they so gloriously failed. Great issues hung upon
that cause, and great interests of mankind were crushed by its
downfall. I was on the continent of Europe when the treason
of Görgey laid Hungary bound at the feet of the Czar. Eu-
rope was at that time in the midst of the reaction; the ebb
tide was rushing violently back, sweeping all that the friends
of freedom had planned into the black bosom of the deep. In
France the liberty of the press was extinct; Paris was in a
state of siege; the soldiery of that republic had just quenched
in blood the freedom of Rome; Austria had suppressed liberty
in northern Italy; absolutism was restored in Prussia; along

the Rhine and its tributaries, and in the towns and villages of Würtemberg and Bavaria, troops, withdrawn from the barracks and garrisons, filled the streets, and kept the inhabitants quiet with the bayonet at their breasts. Hungary at that moment alone upheld—and upheld with a firm hand and dauntless heart—the blazing torch of liberty. To Hungary were turned up the eyes, to Hungary clung the hopes, of all who did not despair of the freedom of Europe.

I recollect that, while the armies of Russia were moving, like the tempest from the north, upon the Hungarian host, the progress of events was watched with the deepest solicitude by the people of Germany. I was at that time in Munich, the splendid capital of Bavaria. The Bavarians seemed for the time to have put off their usual character, and scrambled for the daily prints, wet from the press, with such eagerness that I almost thought myself in America. The news of the catastrophe at last arrived; Görgey had betrayed the cause of Hungary and yielded to the demands of the Russians. Immediately a funeral gloom settled, like a noon-day darkness, upon the city. I heard the muttered exclamations of the people, "It is all over; the last hope of European liberty is gone."

Russia did not misjudge. If she had allowed Hungary to become independent and free, the reaction in favor of absolutism had been incomplete : there would have been one perilous example of successful resistance to despotism ; in one corner of Europe a flame would have been kept alive at which the other nations might have rekindled among themselves the light of liberty. Hungary was subdued ; but does any one who hears me believe that the present state of things in Europe will last? The despots themselves scarcely believe it; they rule in constant fear, and, made cruel by their fears, are heaping chain upon chain around the limbs of their subjects.

They are hastening the event they dread. Every added shackle galls into a more fiery impatience those who are condemned to wear it. I look with mingled hope and horror to the day—the hope, my brethren, predominates—a day bloodier, perhaps, than we have seen since the wars of Napoleon—when the exasperated nations shall snap their chains and start to their feet. It may well be that Hungary—made less patient of the yoke by the remembrance of her own many and glorious struggles for independence, and better fitted than other nations, by the peculiar structure of her institutions, for founding the liberty of her citizens on a rational basis—will take the lead. In that glorious and hazardous enterprise, in that hour of her sore need and peril, I hope she will be cheered and strengthened with aid from this side the Atlantic.

And you, our guest—fearless, eloquent, large of heart and of mind, whose one thought is the salvation of oppressed Hungary, unfortunate but undiscouraged, struck down in the battle of liberty, but great in defeat, and gathering strength for triumphs to come—receive the assurance at our hands that in this great attempt of man to repossess himself of the rights which God gave him, though the strife be waged under a distant belt of longitude, and with the mightiest despotisms of the world, the Press of America will take part—*will* take, do I say?—already takes part with you and your countrymen.

Enough of this. I will detain you from the accents to which I know you are impatient to listen only just long enough to pronounce the toast of the evening: LOUIS KOSSUTH.

# OUR NATIVE FRUITS AND FLOWERS.*

THE last exhibition of this Society was held in what was formerly called the season of roses and strawberries, the earliest and most delicious fruit of the year, and the most beautiful and most agreeably fragrant of flowers. Twenty-three hundred years ago—I believe it was nearer twenty-four hundred —the Greek poet Anacreon called the rose the Queen of Flowers. Since his time the botanist and the florist have explored every nook of the globe, wherever, in the hottest or coldest climates, the green blood flows in vegetable veins—wherever buds swell and blossoms open—and have brought home, to embellish our conservatories and gardens, every flower distinguished by beauty of form or tint, delicacy of texture or grateful perfume—flowers worthy of Paradise, to use a phrase of Milton—yet, among them all, the rose has not found a peer. She has never been dethroned, and is still the sovereign of the flowers.

In Anacreon's time and long after, down to the time when Moore, the translator of Anacreon, composed his song, entitled "The Last Rose of Summer," there was an especial season of roses. One flush of bloom came over the rose-trees, and then the delicate leaves were strewn withered on the ground ; the fruit appeared in its stead, and there were no more roses for

---

* An address delivered before the New York Horticultural Society at the exhibition of September 26, 1856.

that year; the summer must pass into autumn, the autumn into winter, and even the spring must approach its close before roses were again gathered in our gardens. But it is no longer so, as your tables this day bear witness. See what horticulture has done; how it has prolonged the gentle reign of this Queen of Flowers! The florist comes, he takes the roses of warmer climates, which are unaccustomed to our seasons, he crosses them with the hardier growth of our northern gardens, and obtains plants which endure our winters in the open air, and bloom continually from the beginning of June to the setting in of the winter frosts. There is now no last rose of summer—summer goes out in a cloud of roses; they spring up under the departing footsteps of autumn. Some poet speaks ironically of roses in December; what he meant as an extravagance has become the literal truth. I have gathered roses in my garden on Long Island on the twentieth of December; last year I broke them from their stems on the tenth. It is curious to see the plant go on putting forth its flowers and rearing its clusters of buds as if without any presentiment of approaching winter, till, in the midst of its bloom, it is surprised by a frost nipping all its young and tender shoots at once, like a sudden failure overtaking one of our men of commerce in the midst of his many projects.

With the strawberry the horticulturist has wrought nearly equal wonders. If we were in France now, your tables would show that there is a second season of strawberries. There the gardener finds means to delay the production of fruit at the usual period. When the summer heats are overpast, and a temperature like that of June returns, he encourages the blossoms to open and the fruit to mature, and in September and October the markets of Paris are fragrant with strawberries, an abundant and cheap dessert, even for humble tables.

These, my friends, are the triumphs of the art you cultivate, but it has yet to achieve peculiar triumphs in our own country. Of the cultivated vegetable productions which we inherit from the Old World, we have yet to produce or procure varieties suited to our soil and climate, we have yet to introduce new fruits and flowers from foreign countries, and we have yet to improve and draw forth into new and desirable varieties such as are the indigenous growth of our soil. On each of these points I shall say a few words, though not, I hope, so many as to weary you.

In our country the peach-tree perishes by a sort of marasmus while the tree is yet in the promise of its growth. Two or three years' bearings are all that we can expect from it, and it then becomes sickly and dies prematurely, or is torn from the ground as worthless; and, if a new supply is desired, other trees must be planted in another spot. We call our peaches the best in the world, and with good reason, but this is the fate of the tree. There is a remedy, if we could but discover it. On Long Island in the hedge-rows, or among heaps of stones, in neglected spots never turned by the spade or torn by the plough, you may see peach-trees, self-planted, which flourish in full vigor, with leaves of the darkest and glossiest green, bearing fruit every year, and surviving generation after generation of their brethren of the gardens. In the soil and situation of these places exist the qualities which are necessary to the health of the peach-tree. What are they? Can the practical gardener determine? Can the chemist? The question is worthy of long and most careful research.

The peach-tree is said to have come originally from Persia; the botanists recognize that country as its birthplace, and give it the name of *persica*. But it is more than probable that it had a remoter and more Eastern origin, since in China it has been cultivated from time immemorial. From China comes the flat peach, a remarkable production, with the stone on one side and the fleshy part of the peach on the other. There must have existed a long and intimate familiarity between the gardener and the peach-tree before it yielded to his whims, and gave its fruit so strange a shape to gratify them. Are there no healthy and enduring varieties of the peach to be procured from China out of which other healthy varieties may be bred ?   Has the Chinese horticulturist, in the practice of thousands of years, discovered no method of preventing the disease by which the tree with us perishes at the very period when it should be most vigorous and productive?

The apricot in our country, blooming at an early season, suffers by the spring frosts, which cause its fruit to drop in the germ, and often render the tree barren.   In the East, its native country, it is cultivated over an immense variety of latitudes.   Damascus lies among orchards of the apricot, lofty trees like those of the forest, with dark, stately stems and spreading branches; and I have scarce ever seen a more beautiful sight than the banks of the Barada, a river of Anti-Lebanon, in its green, narrow valley, overhung, in the month of March, with apricot-trees in bloom, vieing in height with the poplars among which they stood.   Yet, far to the north of Damascus, far to the north of the vale of Barada, groves of this tree clothe the cool declivities of the Caucasus; and they grow on the mountains of northern China, in a climate of fierce and sudden vicissitudes of heat and cold.   Our varieties of the apricot may have been procured from too southern a latitude or from a climate of very great uniformity.   It is hardly possible that prolific varieties, suited to the most inconstant climate, should not be found somewhere in Asia, to the western half of which the fruit of the apricot, in a dried state, is what the prune is to France and Germany.

I will leave this point here, which might be further illustrated by numerous examples, particularly by the cherry, of which many of the varieties most prized in Europe become worthless, under the warm and showery skies of our June, by decaying the instant they ripen; and by the plum, which in some districts, where the tree flourishes with uncommon vigor, loses all its fruit by the stings of an insect pest called the circulio.   I proceed to speak of the vegetable productions of other countries which we might advantageously introduce into our own.   Eastern Asia, situated, like these Atlantic States, on the eastern coast of a large continent, and possessing, like them, a climate subject to great extremes of heat and cold, is the region to which we must look for the most important contributions of this kind. Whatever, among the growths of the vegetable kingdom, will bear the hard winter of that region, and at the same time requires the heat of its summer to insure its perfection, will, of course, flourish here in the same latitudes as there. Japan and northern China are now opened to our commerce, and we may freely transfer all that is worth so long a conveyance to our fields and gardens. The Dutch and English florists have already adopted many of their flowering plants: the camellia of southern Japan is one of the fairest ornaments of our conservatories; Japan lilies and China roses bloom in our gardens; the Japan quince and Chinese pear embellish our shrubberies; but for fruits and esculents, as yet, we owe them little.

Although the Chinese make no wine, they have excellent table grapes; the French missionary, Huc, commends them highly; and a gentleman, long a resident in southern China, once informed me that the finest come to Canton from about the 37th degree of north latitude. It is a variety of the common grape of the Old World; but, whatever may be its quality, it is of course a variety certain to flourish here as well as in the kindred climate of China. The European vine—at least the varieties of it which are cultivated in Europe—cannot, it seems to be agreed on all hands, be naturalized here so as to escape the mildew on its fruit, when it grows in the open air. We should immediately make the experiment of adopting the Chinese varieties in its place. The lamps by which the dwellings and streets of China are lighted at night are fed with oil pressed from the fruit of a tree which grows all over the country. The chasers of the whale on our coast every year pursue their game into more remote seas, and every year bring back diminished cargoes of oil. Ere long it may be well to bethink ourselves of resorting to the vegetable oils used by the Chinese, and of procuring a supply by the same means. The evergreens of China, if introduced here, where the stock of hardy evergreens is small, would form a most desirable ornament of the grounds about our dwellings. Among these is a kind of palm, of the genus *chamærops*, which endures an intense degree of cold, and makes a singular appearance, bearing on its tropical-looking leaves, in the winter season, loads of snow. Here are large opportunities for inquiry and experiment, and one office of societies like yours in this country will, I am convinced, at no distant day, be to send a horticultural mission to eastern Asia.

The last topic on which I propose to touch would open, if I chose to expand it, a vast field of speculation and conjecture. If we had only our native fruits to cultivate; if we had but the crab-apple of our forests and the wild plum of our thickets from which to form our orchards; if we had only the aboriginal flowers of our woods and fields to domesticate in our gardens—what haste should we make to mellow the harsh juices of the fruits and to heighten and vary the beauty of the flowers! We neglect what is native, because we have the vegetable productions of the Old World already improved to our hands. Yet many of these were as little promising, when the gardener first tried his art upon them, as the crude fruits of our woodlands. The pear-tree in the woods of Poland and on the dry, elevated plains of Russia, where it grows wild, is horrid with thorns, and produces a small fruit of the austerest and most ungrateful flavor. Under culture, it lays aside its thorns, and becomes the parent of an infinitely varied family of fruits, filled with ambrosial juices for the refreshment of almost every month in the year. I have somewhere read the assertion that the grape of Europe and the East was, even in its original state, a fruit of excellent quality. I think this is a mistake. I believe that I have twice seen that grape lapsed to its primitive condition. Some years since, while travelling from Rome to Naples, on the Via Labiana, the diligence broke down; the passengers were detained several hours while it was repairing, and I took the opportunity to explore the surrounding country. I climbed a hill where, on one side of the way, was a vineyard, with grapes white and purple, just ripe, and almost bursting with their saccharine juices; while on the other side was an unfenced pasture-ground, half overgrown with bushes, on which the wild vines clambered, apparently self-sown. I tried the grapes on both sides of the way; the cultivated sorts were of the high flavor and intense sweetness common to the grapes of Italy; the fruit of the wild vine was small, of the size of our pigeon-grape, with large seeds, a thick skin, and meagre juices. In the same journey I had an opportunity to make a similar comparison in another place, and became convinced that the European grape, in its wild or primitive state, is not remarkable for any particular excellence.

In the improvement of our own native fruits we have done something; the Virginia strawberry is the parent of a numerous family called the Scarlets; the blackberry has given birth to the Lawton variety; the grape of our woods is the parent of the Isabella and the Catawba; and our wild gooseberry has been improved into the Houghton. Beyond this I think we have hardly gone. Of our flowers, we can, I believe, only boast to have domesticated and made double the Michigan rose. There is yet an ample field for experiment, with every hope of success. The American grape naturally runs into varieties of different sizes, colors, degrees of sweetness, and seasons of maturity. The richness of our woods in regard to these varieties is yet far from being exhausted. I remember, when a youth, while wandering in the woodlands of the western part of Massachusetts, where the wild vines trailed from tree to tree, I found a grape of very peculiar characteristics— of an amber color, an oval shape, a thin, slightly astringent skin like that of the European grape, and flesh of a brittle firmness, somewhat like that of the Frontignan. I am satisfied that varieties may yet be obtained from the American grape of an excellence of which we have now hardly any idea. The American plum exists in a great number of varieties of different size, color, and flavor; yet nothing has been done to improve it, by seedlings carefully produced and selected. I see nothing to prevent it from passing, under skilful treatment, into as many pleasant varieties as the domestic plum, for which, as naturalists tell us, we are indebted to Syria. At this season the papaw, sometimes called the custard-apple, a name expressive of its qualities, is ripening under its dark-green leaves in the thickets of the West. It is a fruit which, like the fresh fig, is pronounced, by many whose palates are unaccustomed to it, to be insipid; but, like the fig, it is muci-laginous and nutritive. Transplanted to our gardens and made prolific—which may, perhaps, be a difficult, but, I sup-pose, not an impossible task—it would, I doubt not, become a popular and very desirable fruit. It is wonderful with what facility—what certainty, I had almost said—Nature complies with the wishes of the assiduous cultivator; and how, after persevering solicitation, she supplies the quality of which he is in search. I have now finished what I intended, very briefly, to say on a very important subject, which deserves to be treated both more at large and more intelligently than I am able to do it.

The earliest occupation of man, we are told—his task in a state of innocence—was to tend and dress the garden in which his Maker placed him. I cannot say that as men addict them-selves to the same pursuit they are raised nearer to the state of innocence; but this I will say, that few pursuits so agree-ably interest without ever disturbing the mind, and that he who gives himself to it sets up one barrier more against evil thoughts and unhallowed wishes. The love of plants is a natural and wholesome instinct. Through that, perhaps, quite as much as through any other tendency of our natures, the sense of beauty, the grateful perception of harmony of color and of grace, and fair proportion of shape, enter the mind and wean it from grosser and more sensual tastes. The Quakers, who hesitate to cultivate some of the fine arts, indulge their love of beauty, without scruple or restraint, in rearing flowers and embellishing their grounds. I never read description of natural scenery, nor expressions of delight at the beauty of vegetable products, more enthusiastic than those in the travels of old Bartram, the Quaker naturalist, recording his wanderings in Florida. The garden of the two Bartrams, father and son, near Philadelphia, filled with the plants and trees gathered on their journeys, still remains the pride and ornament of the city.

You, my friends, who are the members of the Horticultural Society, are engaged in a good work—the work of cherishing the relations of acquaintanceship and affection, too apt to be overlooked and forgotten in a city life, with the vegetable world in the midst of which God placed us, and on which he made us so essentially dependent. So far as you occupy your minds with these natural and simple tastes, you keep yourselves unperverted by the world, and preserve in sight a reminiscence of the fair original garden.

# MUSIC IN THE PUBLIC SCHOOLS.*

MANY persons entertain doubts in regard to the expediency of making music a branch of the education acquired in our common schools. Until these doubts are removed, we shall miss what is most desirable—the hearty and efficient co-operation of those who entertain them. There are a few considerations in favor of the affirmative side of this question which, I think, can hardly be too strongly urged.

It is admitted, by those who have thought much on the subject, that the people of our country allow themselves too little relaxation from business and its cares. If this be so— and for my part I think there is no doubt of it—they will find in the cultivation of music a recreation of the most innocent and unobjectionable kind. The effect of music is to soothe, to tranquillize; a series of sweet sounds, skilfully modulated, occupies the attention agreeably and without fatigue; it refreshes us like rest. I recollect a remarkable passage in Milton's " Paradise Lost," expressive of his idea of the power of music. He describes a group of fallen angels endeavoring to divert their thoughts from the misery to which they had reduced themselves, and says:

> " —the harmony
> Suspended hell; and took with ravishment
> The audience."

---

* An address delivered at the close of a series of lectures by Richard Storrs Willis, December 29, 1856.

Milton was not only the greatest epic poet who has lived since Homer, but he was a school-master, and devised for his pupils a plan of education in which the fatigues of study were wisely interspersed by intervals of music.

Many persons relax from labor and care by the use of narcotics. Music is a better resource. A tune is certainly better than a cigar. Others, for want of some more attractive employment, addict themselves to the pleasures of the table. Music is certainly better than conviviality. In this respect the cultivation of music comes in aid of health.

In another respect vocal music—which is likely to be the kind of music principally taught in the common schools—promotes the health of the body. If you observe the physical conformation of those who are accustomed to sing in public, you will perceive that they are remarkable for a full development of the chest. This is in part, no doubt, the gift of nature, for breadth and depth of the chest give power and fulness of voice; but in part it is the effect of practice, and the chest is opened and expanded by the exercise of singing. I have no question, for my part, that complaints of the lungs would be less frequent than now if vocal music were universally cultivated. It is an undisputed truth that those organs of the body which are most habitually exercised are preserved in the soundest and healthiest state.

Not only health, but morals, are promoted by the cultivation of music. It is a safeguard not only against sickly and unwholesome habits, as I have shown, but against immoral ones also. If we provide innocent amusements, we lessen the temptation to seek out vicious indulgences. Refined pleasures, like music, stand in the way of grosser tastes. If we fill up our leisure innocently, we crowd out vices, almost by mechanical pressure; we leave no room for them.

It is no trivial accomplishment to speak our language in pleasing tones and with a clear articulation. Our countrymen are accused of speaking English in a slip-shod manner, and a nasal and rather shrill tone of voice. If vocal music be properly taught, the pupil is made to avoid these faults, and to combine the smoothest and most agreeable sounds with the most absolutely distinct articulation of the words. On this point the gentleman to whom we have just listened has dwelt with a force to which I can add nothing. Yet I may be allowed to say that they who have been trained to avoid disagreeable tones and an imperfect and slovenly articulation in singing, will see their deformity in reading and conversation, and will be very apt to avoid them there also.

In making music a branch of common education, we give a new attraction to our common schools. Music is not merely a study, it is an entertainment; wherever there is music there is a throng of listeners. We complain that our common schools are not attended as they ought to be. What is to be done? Shall we compel the attendance of children? Rather let us, if we can, so order things that children shall attend voluntarily—shall be eager to crowd to the schools; and for this purpose nothing can be more effectual, it seems to me, than the art to which the ancients ascribed such power that, according to the fables of their poets, it drew the very stones of the earth from their beds and piled them in a wall around the city of Thebes.

It should be considered, moreover, that music in schools is useful as an incentive to study. After a weary hour of poring over books, with perhaps some discouragement on the part of the learner, if not despair at the hardness of his task, a song puts him in a more cheerful and hopeful mood; the play of the lungs freshens the circulation of the blood, and he sits down again to his task in better spirits and with an invigorated mind. Almost all occupations are cheered and lightened by music. I remember once being in a tobacco manufactory in Virginia where the work was performed by slaves who enlivened their tasks with outbursts of psalmody. "We encourage their singing," said one of the proprietors; "they work the better for it." Sailors pull more vigorously at the rope for their "Yo heave ho!" which is a kind of song. I have heard the vine-dressers in Tuscany, on the hill-sides, responding to each other in songs, with which the whole region resounded, and which turned their hard day's work into a pastime.

If music be so important an art, it is important that it should be well taught. It is a sensible maxim that whatever is worth doing at all is worth doing well. Suitable teachers of music for the common schools, as we have heard from our friend, are exceedingly difficult to be found ; persons who, along with a competent knowledge, a willingness, to teach the mere rudiments of the art, and an acquaintance with the best methods of imparting them, possess a pure and unexceptionable taste. The only certain method of procuring a supply of such teachers certainly seems to be the one pointed out by the lecturer —that of training them for instruction at the normal schools. Such is now the rage for making accomplished pianists of all our young ladies that a class of teachers has been raised up whose merit I do not doubt, but who are altogether too ambitious for the common schools. We need a class for a humble but more useful ministration—teachers of home music, the importance of which has been so well set forth. It costs no more to be taught music well than to be taught it ill, but the difference to the pupil is everything.

I speak as one unlearned in the science of music, and am glad that I have the good fortune to agree in so many points with one so thoroughly versed in its principles and so conversant with its practical details as our lecturer. There is a numerous class—the majority of my countrymen—who in this respect are much like myself. They have a perception of the beauty of sweet sounds artfully modulated, and of time in music; they perceive the disagreeableness of a discord, but they do not understand complicated harmonies; they do not perceive niceties to which better instructed or more sensitive organs are acutely alive; they take no delight in difficulties overcome, for of these difficulties they have a very imperfect conception, and they are somewhat bewildered in listening to compositions which justly pass for prodigies of art. They have a partiality for the human voice, as the most expressive instrument of music which they are acquainted with, and they desire that the sentiment of the air to which they listen should be interpreted to their minds by intelligible words. But that it is not the words alone which interest them is proved by the fact that they listen with pleasure to commonplace words when they are united to music. For my part, I find that the music transfigures the words, invests them with a sort of supernatural splendor, making them call up deeper emotions and conveying more vivid images. The class of whom I am speaking require for their enjoyment of music a certain simplicity—certain aids which bring it down to their level. And yet, on that level, not only taste, but art and genius—if we are to judge music by the same rules which we apply to the other fine arts—may find an ample field for their exercise. Some of the finest productions of literature are those which are written with the greatest simplicity, and address themselves to the greatest number of minds. I suppose, therefore, that I may conclude what I have to say with an acknowledgment to the lecturer, in behalf of that large class to which I belong, for having so well stated our wants, and so clearly pointed out, in his admirable vindication of home music, the means of providing for them.

# THE NEWSPAPER PRESS.*

NEW ENGLAND was the parent of the American press, and at a time like this, when the sons of New England take account of her institutions and sum up what she has done for the continent on which we dwell, the press may be fitly remembered. It is now more than a century and a half— it is one hundred and fifty-four years and some months— since Bartholomew Green, a native of Cambridge, in Massachusetts, and the son of Samuel Green, the first printer of New England, issued the first American newspaper—a little sheet entitled the "Boston News-Letter." If that patriarch of the American press were now permitted to observe what is passing in the country which he inhabited in life, what vast consequences would he see as the fruits of that small beginning! what a mighty array of his successors would pass under his eye!—conductors of the press by myriads, some of whom are throwing off their blanket-sheets by thousands on the spot where his journal, scarcely exceeding a hand-breadth in dimensions, printed its hundreds.

Of this Mr. Green we are told that he was a deacon—a deacon of the Old South Church, of Boston; that he was

---

* Mr. Bryant, because of his prominence as a journalist, was frequently called upon to respond to toasts to the press; and from his many remarks on the subject a few are here reproduced.

"known and esteemed as a humble and exemplary Christian —one who had much of that primitive Christianity in him which has always been the glory of New England." Such were the words in which his character was spoken of at the time of his death, in 1733. It was added that he was of "a meek and peaceable spirit," cautious "not to preach anything offensive, light, or hurtful." A deacon the father of American journalism—and such a deacon! Among those who are not already acquainted with these facts there are few, I suppose, who would have suspected the American press of quite so saintly an origin. And yet, when we consider the extreme meekness of the conductors of our press at the present day, their utter unwillingness to return railing for railing, and their resolute habit of rendering good for evil [applause]; when we consider their earnest, passionate love of peace, and their sensitive aversion to mischief, we shall be almost tempted to believe that the entire race of them keep the example of the worthy Deacon Green constantly before their minds, and strive with all their might to imitate that venerable father of the American press. [Great laughter and applause.] I hope to be pardoned for paying the newspaper press this compliment, since, if it were not done by one of the profession, I fear it might not be done at all.

It was at a little later period that New England gave the world the greatest printer that the world ever saw—the man who, with the same hand that set up the types for "Poor Richard's Almanac," drew the lightning from the clouds, and assisted in penning the articles of the noble Constitution under which we live.

But the press is nothing without readers—without readers it cannot come into existence; without readers it is at once annihilated. It is only to the intelligent and instructed eye that the press has a voice; withdraw that, and the press is dumb forever; the grave, with all its silence, is more eloquent. And to what or to whom does the press owe its readers? To New England more than to any other part of the country. Wherever you find New Englanders and their descendants you find readers; wherever the New Englander goes he takes the newspaper with him or it follows him. School-masters, tutors, professors, teachers of every class, go forth from New England and raise up multitudes of readers. In their case the old mythological fable of him who sowed dragons' teeth in the furrows of the earth and there sprung up ranks of armed men, has its counterpart. The school-master scatters abroad the seeds of knowledge, and there springs up a mighty host of friends and supporters of the press. In one of the agricultural poems of Virgil he describes the husbandman directing the waters of a stream from its ancient channel along a parched hill-side, tracing a path in which they follow him, spreading verdure and fertility. It is thus that the school-master, wherever he goes, marks out new channels for the abundant and fertilizing streams of the press, which flow where he has passed, diffusing knowledge and intelligence. If I should close what I have to say by a toast, I would give you "The Pioneer and Benefactor of the American Press, the New England School-master." *

.    .    .    .    .    .    .    .

I THANK this company, in the name of the journalists, for the compliment just paid to their profession. I do not intend now to pronounce a eulogy on journalism. I can do that in my own journal at any time, but I wish to say a word or two by way of illustrating the convenience of a daily journal to some who are not journalists. You, Mr. President, and other gentlemen who have been heard and applauded this evening, have apparently spoken to a small company of guests in this dining-room. It is not so. Through the journals you have been speaking to thousands, perhaps to millions, and in a few hours those applauses will have been echoed over all the country. The busy agents of the press have taken down the utterances of your lips; while you are asleep the record will be on

---

* From a speech at the annual dinner of the New England Society of New York, December 22, 1858.

its way in a thousand different directions, and with early light will be laid at thousands of doors.

Let us go back to the time when there was no printing-press and, of course, no journals. When Cicero, in ancient Rome, launched his fiery invectives against Catiline, and delivered his grand defence of the poet Archius, small indeed must have been the circle of those who had any conception of his eloquence. But let us suppose that,, by some inscrutable means, a communication could have been established between the world of that day and the world of modern times, and that an accomplished reporter of our daily press and one of Hoe's steam printing-presses could have been quietly smuggled into the Rome of Cicero's time. We will suppose the stenographer silently to take down in his manuscript those noble examples of ancient eloquence as they were uttered; we will suppose the steam press to perform its office ; we will suppose the reporter early next morning to visit the orator with copies of his oration. He might say to him : "Mr. Cicero "— for your genuine journalist is ever courteous—"Mr. Cicero, here is your yesterday's speech. You suppose that the manuscript in one of the pockets of your toga is the only copy of it in existence, but here you see are several others. Here are your exordium, your arguments, your illustrations, your peroration; and not only those, but here are all your figures of speech, your exclamations, your rounded sentences, your well-chosen words, every one as they fell from your eloquent lips, with notes of the applauses of the audience in their proper places. The boys are already hawking it in the streets; men are reading it in the wine-shops; the patricians are conning it at their breakfast-tables; groups of plebeians are assembled in the forum, where one reads it aloud for the benefit of the rest. To-morrow they will have it at Parthenope and Baiæ, and in the northern cities of Italy, and it will soon be read in our colonies in Gaul, in Spain, and in Africa. Read it for yourself!" What would Cicero have said to such a phenomenon, or, rather, what would he have thought, for we may suppose

amazement to take away the power of speech? What could
he have thought save that here was the interposition of some
divinity—Apollo or Minerva—working a miracle to astonish
mankind, and confound those who disbelieved in the gods?

But the press, important as is its office, is but the servant
of the human intellect, and its ministry is for good or for evil,
according to the character of those who direct it. The press is
a mill which grinds all that is put into its hopper. Fill the hop-
per with poisoned grain and it will grind it to meal, but there
is death in the bread. How shall we be sure to feed these mas-
sive and ever-humming mill-stones with only the product of
wholesome harvests, the purest and finest wheat, unmingled
with the seeds of any noxious weed? We must claim the
aid of institutions of education, like that whose glories we this
evening celebrate, to diffuse among the community—both those
who write for the press and those who read—the exact knowl-
edge, the habits of careful thought, the high aims, the gener-
ous motives, the principles of justice and benevolence, which
alone can give dignity and usefulness to the newspaper press,
and make it a benefit and blessing to the world. So you per-
ceive that, although I begin with journalism, I end, as befits
the theme and the occasion, with Harvard.*

   .     .     .     .     .     .     .     .

I AM aware, fully aware, of the shortcomings of the press,
to call them by a mild name. Among journalists there is the
same variety of character as among men of other vocations.
There are men of sturdy and resolute honesty, and there are
others who are simply rogues. There are enlightened men
among them, and there are men who are deplorably ignorant.
There are men of wavering and unsettled opinions on the one
hand, and men of impracticable and pigheaded obstinacy on
the other. There are men of brilliant literary talents, and
others whom, for want of a more polite designation, I should
call stupid; there are fearless men, and men easily frightened.

---

* From remarks at a meeting of the New York Harvard Club, February 22, 1871.

When they speak to the public, they speak in character; the journals which they conduct partake in a great degree of the mental and moral qualities of their conductors. But, on the whole, I boldly maintain that, as a class, the journalists of this country are wiser and more virtuous than our legislators. It was the press which ably and persistently exposed the villanies of the set of men called the city ring—authors of a series of the most enormous frauds known to history—an exposure nobly and effectually followed up by Mr. Tilden, now Governor of the State. When a set of spies and informers had organized a system of extortion, of which our merchants were the victims, called the moiety system, the effect of which was to deliver over to these robbers our most honorable merchants, to be pillaged without mercy or remorse, it was the press that interfered, and, by dint of loud and incessant remonstrance, forced Congress to repeal the odious laws which gave these men the power to plunder. It is the journals which at this moment sustain Governor Tilden in his endeavors to strip the cheating canal contractors of their disguises and make them disgorge their spoil. If the Legislature of this State fails to screen the delinquents, it is because of the unanimity with which the press sustains the Governor's policy of a remorseless investigation and a rigid exaction of responsibility. Looking at these facts, who would not feel a certain satisfaction at belonging to a class so useful?

But I must make some abatement from this commendation. I must say how much greater would be the service which the press would render the country if it would only interfere with the same energy in the case of our revenue laws and our finances. Under the bad system which we have adopted, our merchant-flag is banished from the main ocean; in distant ports, where our stars and stripes were once a familiar sight, they are seen no more; our industry in a thousand branches is smitten with lethargy, and swoons and dies in villages where lately it was in healthful activity; our circulating medium is debased, and the world points at us in scorn as at a nation of immense resources, a growing population, and the richest gold mines in the world, yet refusing to perform its promise to pay its bills of credit. If the press of our country had the necessary intelligence, zeal, and courage, it might force Congress to reform the disgraceful state of things, repair our disordered finances, and restore our destroyed commerce.

I acknowledge the remissness of our journalists in this respect, but I am comforted by the hope that it will not be always so. Truth will prevail in its own good time, and right will triumph at last. Meantime, I would not advise any of those who hear me to drop an honestly and healthily conducted journal because of disagreeing with it on some single question, though it seems to them important. For, depend upon it, the time will arrive when, some other measure or doctrine coming up, you and the discarded journal, if it be of the character I have supposed, will be found side by side contending for the same great principle. Rather let me counsel you to deal with it after the manner suggested by Henry Clay when apologizing to an assembly of his constituents for supporting some unpopular measure. Clay knew how to speak to the hunters of Kentucky. "What," asked the orator, " would you do if your faithful and familiar rifle, which you had carried for years, and which always brought down the game it was aimed at, had for once missed fire? Would you throw it aside in anger, to be used no more? What would you do?" "What?" answered a voice from the crowd, "what would we do? Why, pick the flint and try it again." *

---

* From remarks at a dinner of the New York Chamber of Commerce, 1873.

# FREDERICK SCHILLER.*

IT might seem a presumptuous, if not an absurd, proceeding for an American to speak of the literary character of Schiller in the presence of Germans, who are familiar with all that he has written to a degree which cannot be expected of us, and by whom the spirit of his writings, to the minutest particular, must be far more easily, and, we may therefore suppose, should be more thoroughly apprehended. Yet let me be allowed to say that the name of Schiller, more than that of any other poet of his country, and for the very reason that he was a great tragic poet, belongs not to the literature of his country alone, but to the literature of the world. The Germans themselves have taught us this truth in relation to the tragic poets. In no part of the world is our Shakespeare more devoutly studied than in Germany; nowhere are his writings made the subject of profounder criticism, and the German versions of his dramas are absolute marvels of skilful translation.

We may therefore well say to the countrymen of Schiller: " Schiller is yours, but he is ours also. It was your country that gave him birth, but the people of all nations have made him their countryman by adoption. The influences of his genius have long since overflowed the limits within which his

---

* From an address delivered at the Cooper Institute on the occasion of the Schiller Festival, November 11, 1859.

mother tongue is spoken, and have colored the dramatic litera-
ture of the whole world.    In some shape or other, with abate-
ments, doubtless, from their original splendor and beauty, but
still glorious and still powerful over the minds of men, his
dramas have become the common property of mankind.    His
personages walk our stage, and, in the familiar speech of
our firesides, utter the sentiments which he puts into their
mouths.    We tremble alternately with fear and hope ; we are
moved to tears of admiration, we are melted to tears of pity ;
it is Schiller who touches the master chord to which our hearts
answer.    He compels us to a painful sympathy with his Rob-
ber Chief ; he makes us parties to the grand conspiracy of
Fiesco, and willing lieges of Fiesco's gentle consort Leonora ;
we sorrow with him for the young, magnanimous, generous,
unfortunate Don Carlos, and grieve scarcely less for the guile-
less and angelic Elizabeth ; he dazzles us with the splendid
ambition and awes us with the majestic fall of Wallenstein ;
he forces us to weep for Mary Stuart and for the Maid of Or-
leans ; he thrills us with wonder and delight at the glorious
and successful revolt of William Tell.    Suffer us, then, to take
part in the honors you pay to his memory, to shower the vio-
lets of spring upon his sepulchre, and twine it with the leaves
of plants that wither not in the frost of winter."

We of this country, too, must honor Schiller as the poet of
freedom.    He was one of those who could agree with Cow-
per in saying that, if he could worship aught visible to the
human eye or shaped by the human fancy, he would rear an
altar to Liberty, and bring to it, at the beginning and close of
every day, his offering of praise.    Schiller began to write
when our country was warring with Great Britain for its
independence, and his genius attained the maturity of its
strength just as we had made peace with our powerful adver-
sary and stood upon the earth a full-grown nation.    It was
then that the poet was composing his noble drama of " Don
Carlos," in which the Marquis of Posa is introduced as laying
down to the tyrant, Philip of Spain, the great law of freedom.

In the drama of the "Robbers," written in Schiller's youth, we are sensible of a fiery, vehement, destructive impatience with society, on account of the abuses which it permits; an enthusiasm of reform, almost without plan or object; but in his works composed afterward we find the true philosophy of reform calmly and clearly stated. The Marquis of Posa, in an interview with Philip, tells him, at the peril of his life, truths which he never heard before; exhorts him to lay the foundations of his power in the happiness and affections of his people, by observing the democratic precept that no tie should fetter the citizen save respect for the rights of his brethren, as perfect and as sacred as his own, and prophesies the approaching advent of freedom, which, unfortunately, we are looking for still—that universal spring which should yet make young the nations of the earth.

Yet was Schiller no mad innovator. He saw that society required to be pruned, but did not desire that it should be uprooted—he would have it reformed, not laid waste. What was ancient and characteristic in its usages and ordinances, and therefore endeared to many, he would, where it was possible, improve and adapt to the present wants of mankind. I remember a passage in which his respect for those devices of form and usage, by which the men of a past age sought to curb and restrain the arbitrary power of their rulers, is beautifully illustrated. I quote it from the magnificent translation of "Wallenstein" made by Coleridge. Let me say here that I know of no English translation of a poem of any length which, a few passages excepted, so perfectly reproduces the original as this, and that, if the same hand had given us in our language the other dramas of this author, we should have had an English Schiller, worthy to be placed by the side of the German. "My son," says Octavio Piccolomini, addressing the youthful warrior Max,

> "My son, of those old narrow ordinances
> Let us not hold too lightly. They are weights
> Of priceless value, which oppressed mankind

> Tied to the volatile will of the oppressor.
> For always formidable was the league
> And partnership of free power with free will."

And then, remarking that what slays and destroys goes directly to its mark, like the thunderbolt and the cannon-ball, shattering everything that lies in their way, he claims a beneficent circuitousness for those ancient ordinances which make so much of the machinery of society.

> " My son, the road the human being travels,
> That on which Blessing comes and goes, doth follow
> The river's path, the valley's playful windings,
> Curves round the cornfield and the hill of vines,
> Honoring the holy bounds of property,
> And thus, secure, though late, leads to its end."

Schiller perceived the great truth that old laws, if not watched, slide readily into abuses, and knew that constant revision and renovation are the necessary conditions of free political society ; but he would have the revision made without forgetting that the men of the present day are of the same blood with those who lived before them. He would have the new garments fitted to the figure that must wear them, such as nature and circumstances have made it, even to its disproportions. He would have the old pass into the new by gradations which should avoid violence, and its concomitants, confusion and misery.

The last great dramatic work of Schiller—and whether it be not the grandest production of his genius I leave to others to judge—is founded on the most remarkable and beneficent political revolution which, previous to our own, the world had seen—an event the glory of which belongs solely to the Teutonic race—that ancient vindication of the great right of nationality and independent government, the revolt of Switzerland against the domination of Austria, which gave birth to a republic now venerable with the antiquity of five hundred years. He took a silent page from history, and, animating the personages of whom it speaks with the fiery life of his own spirit, and endowing them with his own superhuman elo- quence, he formed it into a living protest against foreign do- minion which yet rings throughout the world. Wherever there are generous hearts, wherever there are men who hold in reverence the rights of their fellow-men, wherever the love of country and the love of mankind coexist, Schiller's drama of " William Tell " stirs the blood like the sound of a trumpet.

It is not my purpose to dwell on the eminent literary quali- ties which make so large a part of the greatness of Schiller, and which have been more ably set forth by others than they can be by me. It is not for me to analyze his excellences as a dramatic poet; I will not speak of his beautiful and flowing lyrics, the despair of translators; I will say nothing of his noble histories, written like his dramas, for all mankind—for it was his maxim that he who wrote for one nation only pro- posed to himself a poor and narrow aim. These topics would require more time than you could give me, and I should shrink with dismay from a task of such extent and magnitude. Let me close with observing that there is yet one other respect in which, as a member of the great world of letters, Schiller is entitled to the veneration of all mankind.

He was an earnest seeker after truth ; a man whose moral nature revolted at every form of deceit; a noble example of what his countrymen mean when they claim the virtue of sin- cerity for the German race. He held with Akenside that '

> "—Truth and Good are one,
> And Beauty dwells in them " ;

that on the ascertainment and diffusion of truth the welfare of mankind largely depends, and that only mischief and misery can spring from delusions and prejudices, however enshrined in the respect of the world and made venerable by the lapse of years. The office of him who labored in the field of letters, he thought, was to make mankind better and happier by illus-

trating and enforcing the relations and duties of justice, benefi-
cence, and brotherhood, by which men are bound to each
other; and he never forgot this in anything which he wrote.
Immortal honor to him whose vast powers were employed to
so worthy a purpose, and may the next hundredth anniversary
of his birth be celebrated with even a warmer enthusiasm
than this!

# JOHN WINTHROP.

TEN years after the landing of our forefathers on the Plymouth Rock there came to the New World one of the noblest men whom England ever produced, John Winthrop, the first Governor of Massachusetts, a man in whom met all the virtues of the grand old Puritan stock to which he belonged, with few of their faults. While he lived in England he had settled in his mind the principles of a large and enlightened toleration of all religious persuasions, and, if he severed from these principles after coming to America, it was owing to the force of public opinion, the madness of the times, a sort of frenzy of which there are not wanting examples even in our day, which, seizing upon a whole people, hurries along in the same course the moderate, rational, and humane, almost equally with the fierce, passionate, and relentless. In the later years of his life, however, he seems to have recurred to his earlier convictions, for we are told that he lamented the severities which had been practiced against heretics, and wished that gentler methods had been used.

But it was not this to which I wished to direct your attention. I would present him to you as one wise beyond his time in that wisdom which public men, under the discipline of

* From a speech at the annual dinner of the New England Society of New York, December 22, 1860.

the press, have learned from the experience of modern times —as one who was both too magnanimous and too far-sighted to obstruct in any degree the fresh discussion of the merits of his administration.    Chief magistrate as he was, invested with large powers, and possessing great influence, he took no notice of the attacks on his public conduct, instituted no prosecutions, formed no schemes of vengeance, laid up no malice.    He lived down calumny ; he rejected false accusations by disinterested services and a masterly silence.

There is a class of journalists—I am glad they are not numerous—who delight in nothing so much as in finding a public man so sensitive as to notice their assaults.    The more frequently and the more at large he answers, the better are they satisfied ; it gives them occupation, it furnishes them with amusement, it adds to their importance.    There were none of this tribe in the days of Governor Winthrop, but I doubt whether the public men of that day gained anything by this exemption.    The tongue then performed the office which types perform now, and a saucy letter, copies of which were handed about, answered the purpose of a modern newspaper. Winthrop was the object of both modes of detraction, but he preserved throughout the same calm forbearance.    He seemed, says Cotton Mather in his biography of this great man, to have no other language than that of Theodosius : " If any man speak evil of the Governor, if it be through lightness it is to be contemned ; if it be through madness it is to be pitied ; if it be through injury it is to be remitted."    He then proceeds to relate that a member of the court, by which is meant the legislative body of the province—the people of Massachusetts call their Legislature the General Court yet—once wrote him a very sharp letter, an abusive letter it would probably be called in modern language.    Winthrop read it and returned it to the messenger.    " Take it back," said he ; "I am unwilling to keep so great a matter of provocation by me."    Afterward came a season of scarcity of provisions, and the writer of the letter sent to Winthrop desiring that he would sell him some of his cattle. "Accept what I send you," was Winthrop's answer, "as a token of my good-will." "Sir," replied the gentleman, "the overcoming of yourself hath overcome me," and he afterward stood his friend.

Such was the greatness of mind shown by one who bore a most important part in laying the foundation of that noble commonwealth of which many whom I see at this board are natives. He saw the true policy of a political administration for more than a century and a half before it was discerned by the government of the mother country, for you will remember that it was within the present century that the prosecuting officers of the British government cast into prison James Montgomery, gentlest of poets, for having published a little paragraph in which he intimated a modest disapproval of something done by persons high in place. But, if Governor Winthrop anticipated in one respect the wisdom of later times, there is yet another respect in which the virtue of men at the present day comes far short of his. "He sometimes," says Cotton Mather, "made his private purse the public's, not by sucking into it, but by squeezing out of it; and, when the Treasury had nothing in it, defrayed the public charges with his own means." It is not often that the private purses of public men are now depleted in this way, and the rumor goes that many of them are filled by the process of suction to which Winthrop's biographer alludes.

There is an anecdote related of Governor Winthrop which illustrates equally his kindness of heart and his wit. If any of you have heard or read it before, as may well be the case, I beg you to forget that little circumstance and endeavor to be as much entertained by it as if it were entirely new. It was winter. Somebody told the Governor that a man in his neighborhood stole wood from his pile. "Does he so?" said Winthrop, in seeming anger. "Send him to me; I warrant I will cure him of stealing my wood." The man came. "Friend," said Winthrop, "this is a severe winter, and I doubt you are ill-provided with wood. Supply yourself, I pray you, from my pile till the cold season be over." And then he merrily asked his friends, says Mather, who understood and enjoyed a joke, whether he had not effectually cured the man of stealing his wood.

Let me refer to another incident in this great man's life. Between the colonies of Plymouth and Massachusetts Bay lay a broad tract of original forest, but the settlements were increasing rapidly, and Winthrop early saw the importance of united counsels and a good correspondence between the two provinces. Mather compares them to two floating bottles, with the motto: "If we strike against each other we are dashed to pieces." Winthrop, in the year 1632, made a journey on foot—in company with his friend and pastor, the eccentric John Wilson—through what his biographer calls a howling wilderness, by which I suppose is meant a region infested with wild beasts and savages. The pedestrian embassy was received with honor ; a consultation was held, and Winthrop had the satisfaction of establishing between the two colonies friendly relations, which lasted till they were finally united in one. Here was the seminal principle of our American Union —the embryo which afterward grew into our great league of States. Then was laid the corner-stone of that noble structure, on the pillars of which rash hands are now laid. Undying honor to the memory of such a man, and of his noble example thousands of imitators.

# A BIRTHDAY ADDRESS.*

I THANK you, Mr. President, for the kind words you have uttered, and I thank this good-natured company for having listened to them with so many tokens of assent and approbation. I must suppose, however, that most of this approbation was bestowed upon the orator rather than upon his subject. He who has brought to the writing of our national history a genius equal to the vastness of the subject has, of course, more than talent enough for humbler tastes. I wonder not, therefore, that he should be applauded this evening for the skill he has shown in embellishing a barren topic.

I am congratulated on having completed my seventieth year. Is there nothing ambiguous, Mr. President, in such a compliment? To be congratulated on one's senility! To be congratulated on having reached that stage of life when the bodily and mental powers pass into decline and decay! Lear is made by Shakespeare to say:

> " Age is unnecessary."

And a later poet, Dr. Johnson, expressed the same idea in one of his sonorous lines:

> " Superfluous lags the veteran on the stage."

---

* Delivered in the rooms of the Century Club, in reply to one of George Bancroft, Esq., on the occasion of Mr. Bryant's seventieth birthday, November 3, 1864.

You have not forgotten, Mr. President, the old Greek saying:

"Whom the gods love die young "—

nor the passage in Shakespeare :

—"Oh, sir, the good die first,
And they, whose hearts are dry as summer dust,
Burn to the socket."

Much has been said of the wisdom of Old Age. Old Age is wise, I grant, for itself, but not wise for the community. It is wise in declining new enterprises, for it has not the power nor the time to execute them; wise in shrinking from difficulty, for it has not the strength to overcome it; wise in avoiding danger, for it lacks the faculty of ready and swift action, by which dangers are parried and converted into advantages. But this is not wisdom for mankind at large, by whom new enterprises must be undertaken, dangers met, and difficulties surmounted. What a world would this be if it were made up of old men!—generation succeeding to generation of hoary ancients who had but half a dozen years, or perhaps half that time, to live! What new work of good would be attempted! What existing abuse or evil corrected! What strange subjects would such a world afford for the pencils of our artists—groups of superannuated graybeards basking in the sun through the long days of spring, or huddling like sheep in warm corners in the winter time; houses with the timbers dropping apart; cities in ruins; roads unwrought and impassable; weedy gardens and fields with the surface feebly scratched to put in a scanty harvest; feeble old men climbing into crazy wagons, perhaps to be run away with, or mounting horses, if they mounted them at all, in terror of being hurled from their backs like a stone from a sling! Well it is that in this world of ours the old men are but a very small minority.

Ah, Mr. President, if we could but stop this rushing tide of time that bears us so swiftly onward and make it flow toward its source; if we could cause the shadow to turn back on the dial-plate! I see before me many excellent friends of mine worthy to live a thousand years, on whose countenances years have set their seal, marking them with the lines of thought and care, and causing their temples to glisten with the frosts of life's autumn. If to any one of these could be restored his glorious prime, his golden youth, with its hyacinthine locks, its smooth, unwrinkled brow, its fresh and rounded cheek, its pearly and perfect teeth, its lustrous eyes, its light and agile step, its frame full of energy, its exulting spirits, its high hopes, its generous impulses—and add all these to the experience and fixed principles of mature age, I am sure, Mr. President, that I should start at once to my feet and propose that, in commemoration of such a marvel and by way of congratulating our friend who was its subject, we should hold such a festivity as the Century has never seen nor will ever see again. Eloquence should bring its highest tribute, and Art its fairest decorations, to grace the festival; the most skilful musicians should be here with all manner of instruments of music, ancient and modern ; we would have sackbut and trumpet and shawm, and damsels with dulcimers, and a modern band three times as large as the one that now plays on that balcony. But why dwell on such a vain dream, since it is only by passing through the dark valley of the shadow of death that man can reach his second youth?

I have read, in descriptions of the Old World, of the families of princes and barons coming out of their castles to be present at some rustic festivity, such as a wedding of one of their peasantry. I am reminded of this custom by the presence of many literary persons of eminence in these rooms, and I thank them for this act of benevolence. Yet I miss among them several whom I wished rather than ventured to hope that I should meet on this occasion. I miss my old friend Dana, who gave so grandly the story of " The Buccaneer " in his solemn verses. I miss Pierpont, venerable in years, yet vigorous in mind and body, and with an undimmed fancy ; and him whose pages are wet with the tears of maidens who read the story of

" Evangeline "; and the author of " Fanny "and the " Croakers,"
no less renowned for the fiery spirit which animates his " Marco
Bozzaris "; and him to whose wit we owe the " Biglow Papers,"
who has made a lowly flower of the wayside as classical as the
rose of Anacreon; and the Quaker poet whose verses, Quaker
as he is, stir the blood like the voice of a trumpet calling to
battle; and the poetess of Hartford, whose beautiful lyrics are
in a million hands; and others whose names, were they to oc-
cur to me here as in my study, I might accompany with the
mention of some characteristic merit.  But here is he whose
aërial verse has raised the little insect of our fields, the humble-
bee, making its murmuring journey from flower to flower, to
a dignity equal to that of Pindar's eagle; here is the "Autocrat
of the Breakfast Table," author of that most spirited of naval
lyrics, beginning with the line :

> "Aye, tear her tattered ensign down ! "

Here, too, is the poet who told in pathetic verse the story of
Jephtha's daughter; and here are others, worthy compeers of
those I have mentioned, yet greatly my juniors, in the bright-
ness of whose rising fame I am like one who has carried a
lantern in the night, and who perceives that its beams are no
longer visible in the glory which the morning pours around
him.  To them, and to all members of the Century, allow me,
Mr. President, to offer the wish that they may live longer
than I have done in health of body and mind and in the same
contentment and serenity of spirit which has fallen to my lot.
I must not overlook the ladies who have deigned to honor
these rooms with their presence.  If I knew where, amid
myrtle bowers and flowers that never wither, gushed from the
ground the fountain of perpetual youth so long vainly sought
by the first Spanish adventurers on the North American con-
tinent, I would offer to the lips of every one of them a beaker
of its fresh and sparkling waters, and bid them drink unfading
bloom.  But, since that is not to be, I will wish what perhaps
is as well, and what some would think better : that the same

kindness of heart which has prompted them to come hither to-night may lend a beauty to every action of their future lives. And to the Century Club itself—the dear old Century Club— to whose members I owe both the honors and the embarrassments of this occasion—to that association, fortunate in having possessed two such presidents as the distinguished historian who now occupies the chair, and the eminent and accomplished scholar and admirable writer who preceded him, I offer the wish that it may endure, not only for the term of years signified by its name—not for one century only, but for ten centuries—so that hereafter, perhaps, its members may discuss the question whether its name should not be changed to that of the Club of a Thousand Years, and that these may be centuries of peace and prosperity, from which its members may look back to this period of bloody strife as to a frightful dream soon chased away by the beams of a glorious morning.

# THE ACADEMY OF DESIGN.*

I CONGRATULATE the Academy of Design and all the friends of art on the event of this day. After forty years of wandering, the Academy has at length a fixed habitation. Ever since the year 1825, when the Drawing Association was formed, the germ, the embryo, out of which arose in the following year this Academy with its present name and organization, the tribes of art may be said to have dwelt in tents. The close of this nomadic stage in their history is marked by rearing this temple to art—built after a pattern of mediæval architecture, yet with an historical congruity to the purpose it will serve, since it was for the adornment of buildings not dissimilar in style that the art of modern painting put forth its early efforts, and advanced to that stage of perfection which gave us the great colorists of the Venetian school.

I congratulate you all, therefore, on the completion of a building, not one stone of which from the foundation to the roof was laid, and not one beam or rafter framed into its place, for any other purpose than the glory of art.

A little while since, I was here, and admired the spacious halls and saloons, with their lofty ceilings, and the pure light admitted only from the zenith, bringing with it no tinge of color from surrounding objects. Since that time art has en-

---

* An address delivered at the opening of the new building of the Academy of Design, April 28, 1865.

tered with the works of the pencil and the chisel, covering the bare walls and occupying the floors with imitations of nature which we view this evening with wonder and delight—the spring, the summer, the autumn, the winter of our brilliant climate disputing the palm of splendor; the blaze of the tropics and the cold light of icebergs brought into a New York saloon; Italian skies glowing beside them; the wild grandeur of our own Rocky Mountains confronting the majestic scenery of Switzerland; manly faces and the eyes of fair woman and fresh-cheeked children looking down upon us; scenes from the domestic fireside; glimpses of camp life and the tumult of war, drawn from our own civil strife; and on pedestals among the crowd of spectators the works of the statuary, busts that seem to think, and groups which are tragedies and comedies in miniature.

When I look around upon these productions of the genius of our countrymen and compare them with what we produced forty years since, I cannot help imagining to myself what must have been the astonishment of a New Yorker of that day could he have been transported to a spectacle like this from one of the meagre exhibitions of the old and now forgotten Academy of the Fine Arts, made up mostly of pictures which had appeared on its walls from year to year till they palled upon the eye.

Scarcely less would have been the surprise of one of the founders of this Academy, if he could have been assured that within forty years from that time there would be freely contributed by the residents of this city the means of erecting a gallery for the display of works of art, vying in spaciousness and beauty of arrangement with the proud repositories of art in Europe. I did not myself believe that this could be done till I was told that the necessary funds were nearly collected. What! said I to myself; are we to expect in this great seat of commerce, where everything is estimated according to the value set against it in the price-current, that men will contribute their thousands to the erection of a grand building in which young artists are to bring their works before the public eye, and recommend themselves to the public favor? A few I know would cheerfully give, the many I thought would withhold. I was mistaken. I underrated not the liberality of the New York public, for I had ample evidence of that in what shortly before it had so generously done for the relief of Kansas, but I underrated its taste and its respect for art. This sumptuous building, these wide and lofty halls, are the rebuke —the mute yet magnificent rebuke—of my incredulity. Was ever injurious misgiving shown in a more noble manner to be groundless?

Yet, while we look back to the state of art in this country at the time when the Academy was founded, let us not deem lightly of the merit of its founders. That was by no means a low condition of things which produced such men. Of those who have since passed to another life, Cole was then in the early dawn of his fame; Inman was painting those graceful portraits which we yet behold with admiration; and Ingham those elaborate female forms and faces which, now that time has ripened and mellowed his tints and softened and shadowed what was hard in his finish, remain our prized memorials of the beauty of a generation then in its prime. Of Cole, I vividly remember the interest with which his works were at that time regarded. It was like the interest awakened by some great discovery. Here, we said, is a young man who does not paint nature at second hand, or with any apparent remembrance of the copies of her made by others. Here is the physiognomy of our own woods and fields; here are the tinges of our own atmosphere; here is American nature and the feeling it awakens. You have only to look at his pictures to see that they represent the features of no region but that in which we dwell.

Concerning Inman, let me relate a single anecdote. The poet Wordsworth, whose portrait he had painted, said to me: "I have often seen the process of painting, but I never saw the pencil handled with such precision and apparent mastery as by Inman. There was no hesitation, no delay in putting any of his touches upon the canvas; he placed them at once where he meant to place them, and they were the very touches he wanted."

Inman was a rapid painter, but Ingham was an artist of a different school. He finished his portraits with infinite diligence and frequent and careful cor rections. In personal character he was a man of instant and almost impetuous decision; but, in painting, he reached the beauty at which he aimed by gradual and cautious approaches, slowly shaping his first shadowy and indefinite forms to symmetry and expression. Some of the pictures of Inman, painted in his rapid manner, are already blackened by time; those of Ingham I think will be more prized a few years hence than in his life-time. One of his most beautiful was painted just before his death—a female head, with a fine, spiritual expression, as if the bright eyes were looking directly into heaven.

Let me not, however, neglect to speak of Dunlap, the oldest member of the Academy at the time when it was founded, and the historian of the " Arts of Design " in our country. We cannot call him eminent either as a writer or as an artist, but he did much by his large historical paintings, exhibited by his pupils all over the country, to give our people an idea of what a picture ought to be, and to awaken in them a taste for art. Very much younger than this amiable man was Frederick Agate, carried off in the midst of his early promise by a consumption contracted in the zealous pursuit of his studies. I remember him as more interesting than entertaining, serious, somewhat reserved, slow of speech, choosing for his pencil such melancholy subjects as the "Dead Mother and her Child," cast by the waves on a sea-beach, and Ugolino, whose story is so pathetically told by Dante, perishing with his children of hunger in the Tower of Famine. " I like such subjects," he once said to me. Perhaps some dim presentiment of his own early departure already darkened his imagination with its shadow.

At present I believe that only three out of the twenty-five artists who founded the Academy are now living—Morse, its first president, to whom the cause of art in this country owes so large a debt; Durand, his successor, then an engraver, whose landscapes, full of sunshine and peace, are reflections of the kindly serenity of his own nature; and Cummings, the treasurer of this institution from the beginning, who has turned from the production of his beautiful miniatures to the task of teaching the art he practiced so long and well, and who has just laid before us a welcome gift, the history of the Academy for the forty years which now close. Late may arrive the hour which gathers these honored survivors to their associates.

Meantime an important change has taken place in regard to the social position of those who make the fine arts their profession. Forty years since, their occupation was not regarded as it is now. The majority of fashionable people, I believe, or, if not the majority, very many of them, would almost as soon have thought of asking a hod-carrier to their entertainments as a painter. But now I find the artists courted and caressed by that very class. Eminent artists have become lions of the *salon;* the artists' receptions are thronged with what the newspapers call the beauty and fashion of the metropolis; the artists' studios are frequented by distinguished men and elegant women; and the young artist has more invitations to mingle in society than it is perhaps good for him to accept. It is pleasant to know that art is thus honored, but I am not quite sure that the change is in every respect for the advantage of the artist, and I hope that none of my young friends of the brush or the chisel will allow themselves to be spoiled by it.

I have spoken hitherto of the past, comparing it with the present, but I cannot conclude without a word concerning the future. I am confident in the expectation that a day of great glory for art in this country is at hand—a day of which we now behold the morning—coincident with the signal overthrow of a mighty and fearful conspiracy against our national existence, and with the near prospect of returning peace. The temperament of our people and the influence of our climate are, I think, highly favorable to the cultivation of the fine arts. Some quality in the air of our part of the world, which I do not pretend otherwise to define, promotes, unless I am greatly mistaken, the activity of those faculties which conspire to make the great painter and sculptor. The phrenological philosopher Combe used to call ours a stimulating climate, and he was right in so far as it tends to generate that poetic exhilaration to which the creations of art owe their birth. An English painter, who had lived many years in this country, and who had just returned to it after a long visit to his native land, said to me: " I had hardly been in Boston twenty-four hours, after landing on the American shore, when I wanted to go out into the streets and shout—so greatly were my spirits raised by merely breathing your air." Another English artist, a sculptor, said to me on a fine October morning, when the atmosphere was full of life and spirit, the soft white clouds drifting before a pleasant wind through a deep-blue sky : " I cannot express how much I am exhilarated by your climate. I think it one of the best in the world for a young man, and one of the worst for an old man."

I quote only foreign authorities, for I know how easy it is in such matters to deceive ourselves. But I have no doubt for my part that, in the temperament formed by our diversified climate, the perceptive faculties are peculiarly awake and active, drinking in the sights and sounds of Nature with a deeper delight than in climates of a more uniform character, and that the power of invention is quickened by the same causes to the same activity and energy. These varying aspects of our skies, imposing alike in their splendor and their gloom, these grand alternations of our seasons, these majestic vicissitudes, passing from polar cold to tropical heat and from tropical heat to polar cold, with the phenomena of each fierce extreme, were not given us in vain. The genius nurtured under their influences has in the department of art commanded the admiration of the hemisphere from which our race was transplanted to this. The works of our great painters have been seen with delighted surprise in the Old World; the masterpieces of American sculpture have divided the praise of mankind with the productions of the most eminent statuaries of modern times. Let us hope that the opening of this edifice, consecrated to art, will mark our entrance upon a new stage of progress, even higher and nobler than we have yet attained.

# MEXICO AND MAXIMILIAN.*

IN giving out the third toast of the evening, allow me to introduce it by a few words. We are come together to do honor to a gentleman who, for several years past, has repre-sented among us a sister republic, with an ability worthy of a great cause, and a fortitude and constancy of purpose equal to his ability. There is nothing, my friends, which more surely commands the respect of mankind, and, let me say, there are few things which more deserve it, than a brave perseverance in a righteous cause. Of men distinguished by this virtue, history makes up her roll of heroes, and the church her noble army of martyrs. It is most fitting that when such a man has stood firmly by the cause of his country and of liberty through the years of their greatest adversity and peril, never faltering in his fidelity, never allowing himself to be disheart-ened by reverses, but resolutely trusting in the final success of the right, until at last he saw it gloriously triumphant—most fitting is it that we should gather around him to congratulate him that his constancy is at last rewarded, that the tyrannical usurpation against which he has so steadily protested has been foiled and overthrown, and the liberties which the kings of the earth stood up to destroy have been nobly vindicated. Such

---

* From remarks at the dinner given to Mr. Romero, the minister from Mexico, October 3, 1867, at which Mr. Bryant presided.

is the man who is now our guest; and such, in brief, is the history of the cause in which he distinguished himself. We who have all along given that cause our sympathies, and have looked for its triumph as certain to follow the suppression of the rebellion in our own country, offer him the expression of our sincere rejoicing at the defeat of this attempt to engraft European absolutism upon the institutions of our continent, and the tribute of our praise for the foresight of his, which, beholding the sunshine beyond the tempest, and discerning the sure connection between the cause of Mexico and that of the United States, looked with unwavering confidence for the triumph of both. The tyranny which the slave-holding class strove to set up in a part of our country has taken its place among the older abortive conspiracies against the welfare of the human race, and the despotism which a great military power of the Old World sought to enthrone in Mexico has been dragged after it in its fall, and now lies with it in the pit. While we congratulate our friend on this happy consummation, we should no less congratulate the people of Mexico on having shown, by their obstinate resistance to the imposition of a foreign yoke, and the gallant stand they have made for their independence, that they possess qualities of character for which the world has hitherto given them small credit, and have earned for themselves an honorable name in history.

There is one act of the American patriots for which they have been greatly maligned, and in defence of which our guest has thought proper at one time to speak. I mean the execution of the pseudo-Emperor of Mexico. With regard to the policy of that act, I admit that different views may be fairly entertained. I am aware also that there are those who would have had Maximilian spared, out of a tender regard for human life, and the feeling which causes a generous nature to shrink from making a victim of an enemy whom we have completely and helplessly in our power. With such I might decline any controversy. But it is not by any such transcendental and

unusual standard that the act is to be judged. Its moral qual-
ity is to be estimated according to the ideas of justice which
prevail throughout civilized countries, and which doom to
death him who takes the life of his fellow-man with malice
aforethought. Maximilian, at a time when his prospects
seemed to him brightest, issued a decree to the effect that
whoever was taken in arms, opposing his unprovoked in-
vasion of their country, should be tried by a military com-
mission and shot, and this decree was pitilessly executed in
a multitude of instances. The bitter cup which he had
forced the innocent to taste has been returned to his own
guilty lips. Who that knows this fact can deny that Maxi-
milian deserved death as richly as the ruffian who enters
your dwelling at midnight and shoots down the domestic
who attempts its defence?

Let it not be said that he was excusable because he had a
principle more guilty than himself and more deserving of the
death of a felon—the Emperor of France. Napoleon bribed
him by the offer of a crown to break into Mexico upon his er-
rand of robbery and bloodshed. He was Napoleon's hired
assassin, and I believe that is the utmost that can be said for
him. When, therefore, a peer of Great Britain and a Prime
Minister of the British Empire rises in his place and, speaking
of the execution of Maximilian, pronounces it a murder, I can
find no palliation for so gross an affront to truth save that it
was spoken in shameful ignorance of the facts of history. No,
my friend, with all my regard for human life, I find it difficult
to answer the argument of those who urge that so flagrant an
offence against the rights of nations as was committed by
Maximilian, and such a series of bloody crimes as attended his
impious enterprise, deserved something more than that their
perpetrator should be dismissed to ease and luxury within the
walls of a palace, to be pitied for the rest of his life as a
brave though unfortunate man, instead of being shunned as an
audacious criminal, but that, on the contrary, he should be
subjected to some signal punishment, which should serve as a

lesson to future invaders of unoffending republics, and teach the monarchs of the Old World to respect the liberties of the New.\*

---

\* This was no after-thought of the speaker—for several years before, in his journal of January 28, 1864, he had written in the same line, though not anticipating the precise end, under the heading of "What the Archduke Maximilian must expect."

"While the Austrian Archduke Maximilian is getting ready to embark for Mexico, in order to take possession of the government which the Emperor of France has offered him, it may be well to consider what is his chance of being allowed to possess it in peace. If the Archduke has any friends about him who understand the restless character of the people of the United States, and the impossibility of excluding them as settlers from a contiguous country like Mexico—with vast tracts of unoccupied land, yet possessing a rich soil, an inviting climate, and immense mineral resources—they might give him some advice which would make him consider whether the crown now offered him is not likely to be a crown of thorns. Of course, the government which the Archduke Maximilian will seek to establish in Mexico will be modelled after the Austrian pattern of absolute, rigid, relentless despotism. He cannot and will not trust the native Mexicans. An Austrian cabinet must be imported from Vienna ; Austrian officers will command the standing army ; the people will be kept quiet by Austrian bayonets ; and dungeons with Austrian keepers, after the manner of those at Olmutz and Spielberg, will be prepared for the reception of those who venture to criticise the new order of things, or are even suspected of desiring its downfall. Of course, such a government will be hated—hated because of its severity ; hated because it is administered by foreigners. Let such a government lay its hand upon a resident from the United States in one of the northern provinces of Mexico, who, unable to forget the habits of a freeman in his new abode, ventures to speak freely of the acts of the Austrian ruler : the sympathies of our people would be instantly kindled in his favor, and, if but a movement of sedition should appear among the Mexicans, thousands of our countrymen would soon show themselves on the other side of our southwestern frontier, ready to inflame the sedition into a formidable insurrection. We will suppose that our Government should do nothing to favor any such revolt, and even that it shall earnestly seek to restrain our citizens from taking part in it. The disposition of the Government will have no effect upon the popular feeling. The attempt to prevent our people from taking part in a rising of the Mexicans for such a cause would be as idle as to endeavor to dam the current of a stream with a net. The government of Maximilian might remonstrate, our own Government might do its best to satisfy the Austrian, but the rush of our countrymen to the scene of strife, over the long frontier of northern Mexico, would go on as steadily as the stream of the Rio Grande toward the ocean. It might, in the end, be difficult for our Government to maintain anything like a neutral attitude in a cause like this. Severities practiced on American residents in Mexico might call for energetic remonstrances on our part, to which the government of that country might not think that it could safely listen, and then the popular feeling might compel our executive to draw the sword. A war thus begun could have but one result: the occupation and conquest of the northern provinces of Mexico—and we might see the new empire dwindling to a mere principality.

But the case we have supposed implies that the present resistance of the Mexicans to the usurpation of Maximilian shall first have been subdued. That is not likely to happen soon. The friends of the liberal government there understand very well the state of our war; they foresee already the approaching submission of the rebels, and will, by every effort they can make, prolong their own war till ours is over. Then they expect to see their own army largely augmented by trained soldiers from ours. Thousands of adventurers, inured to a military life, not yet weary of it, and ambitious of entering a new field of distinction, will flock to Mexico to fight another battle for liberty. Already in our army there are men who look confidently to that event, and do not mean to abandon the profession of arms with the return of peace while such an opportunity invites them to continue in it. The victors of Chattanooga will not fear to measure swords with the invaders of Mexico. But there is yet another class who will have nothing but their swords left, the leaders in the rebellion, and such of their followers as will be withheld by pride and disdain from taking the oath of allegiance to the federal Government, coupled with the conditions on which a pardon is offered—such men, for example, as Magruder and the Texas rangers. These men—such of them as have served in Texas, at least—will be apt to espouse the cause of their neighbors the Mexicans, whom they know, and in whose fate they will naturally be interested, and thus it may happen that the American loyalist and the American rebel will fight side by side in the war for Mexican independence.

It seems, therefore, almost certain that the Archduke Maximilian, in accepting the crown of Mexico, has received the gift of a weary and disastrous war, with, perhaps, an inglorious termination. The security from interference by the United States, on which he depends, whatever course our Government may think proper to take, is a fallacious one. It often happens in thunder-storms that, after the clouds driven by the west wind have left the sky clear overhead, the roll of the thunder is yet heard below the eastern horizon. So it may be with the tempest of war, the sound of which now fills our land: after peace has returned to our shores, its tumult may perhaps be heard and its lightnings seen to glimmer from the distant fields of Mexico.

# FREEDOM OF EXCHANGE.*

AN honor like this requires from me a particular acknowledgment, which yet I hardly know how to make in fitting terms. Conferred as it is by men whom I so much value and respect, and who possess in so high a degree the esteem of their fellow-citizens, I cannot but feel that it would amply reward services infinitely greater than I can pretend to have rendered to any cause. What I have done in applying the principles of human liberty to the exchange of property between man and man and between nation and nation, has been very easy to do. It was simply to listen to my own convictions without any attempt to reason them away, and to follow whithersoever they might lead me. In this manner I have been saved a good deal of trouble, some perplexity and bewilderment, some waste of ingenuity, if I had any to waste, and perhaps no little remorse.

Another circumstance has made my task easy. I had only to walk in a path smoothed and lighted by some of the best thinkers of the age—impartial, unprejudiced men, who had no object in view but the simple discovery of truth. It was not difficult to walk in such a path. Grand and noble intellects held their torches over it, and I could not well step astray with such guidance. Besides, I had only to follow in the way which the world is going. The tendency of enlightened pub-

* Speech at a dinner given to Mr. Bryant, in New York, January 30, 1868.

lic opinion in all countries is toward the freedom of trade. There is no difficulty in swimming with the current. I saw that the navigation was safe, and let my boat float with the stream, while others laboriously tried to stem it or lay moored to the shore wondering which way they ought to go. We shall have them all with us yet, Mr. Chairman, a merry fleet of all manner of craft, bound on the same easy voyage.*

Another circumstance which has made the task of free-trade more easy is the involuntary admissions which the protectionists make of the fallacy of their system. A capitalist in New England, owning cotton or woolen mills, however great his attachment to the protective system, has no idea of employing any part of his capital in raising wheat in the fields close to his mills, that he may save the expense to him and his work-people of bringing it from the distant West. He brings it from a thousand miles away, and sends back his fabrics in exchange, at the very moment that he is procuring laws to be passed which will prevent us, the consumers, from buying iron and cloth and paper from Europe, that we may, as they say, save the expense of freight. When we make a new acquisition of territory, they do not object that we are to have free-trade with the new region. On the contrary, they rejoice in a wider market. This they did when Texas was taken into the Union. They made no opposition to the acquisition of California on the ground that all revenue laws which shut out the trade of that wide region would now be repealed. When we talk of annexing Canada, they do not object that we and

---

* Mr. Bryant was among the earliest, as he was always the most persistent and hopeful, of the advocates of free-trade in the intercourse of nations. In his journal and in his speeches he never refrained from agitating the topic, beginning as far back as 1828, and not ceasing up to the last month of his life in 1878—fifty years of championship. For four of those years he was President of the Free-Trade League of New York; and, though often disappointed in his expectation of favorable legislative action, his confidence in the ultimate success of his cause never abated. The few selections from his speeches here given are made so as to avoid repetition as far as possible.

the Canadians will then be no longer independent of each other.

In this they are in the right ; in this they tacitly admit the advantage of free-trade. Whatever other objection may be made to the acquisition of new territory, the enlargement of our borders by the addition of new and extensive provinces is a great commercial and industrial advantage, because it makes the exchange of commodities between them and us perfectly free.

Yet there is a certain plausibility in what the protectionists say when they talk of home industry and a home market —a plausibility which misleads many worthy and otherwise sensible people—sensible in all other respects, and whom as men I admire and honor. There are clever men among them, who bring to their side of the question a great array of facts, many of which, however, have no real bearing upon its solution. There is a plausibility, too, in the idea that the sun makes a daily circuit around the earth, and, if there were any private interests to be promoted by maintaining it, we should have thousands believing that the earth stands still while the sun travels round it. "See for yourself," they would say. " Will you not believe the evidence of your own senses? The sun comes up in the east every day before your eyes, stands over your head at noon, and goes down in the afternoon in the west. Why, you admit the fact when you say the sun rises, the sun sets, the sun is up, the sun is down. What a fool was Galileo, what nonsense is the system of Copernicus, what trash was written by Sir Isaac Newton ! "

I remember a case in point—an anecdote which I once heard in Scotland. A writer to the signet—that is to say, an attorney—named Moll, who knew very little, except what related to the drawing up of law-papers, once heard a lecture on astronomy, in which some illustrations were given of the daily revolution of the earth on its axis. The attorney was perplexed and bewildered by this philosophy, which was so new to him, and one day, his thoughts frequently recurring to the subject, he looked up from his law-papers and said : " The young mon says the warld turns roond. It's vera extraordin-ar'. I've lived in this place sax-and-thretty years, and that grass-plot presarves the same relative poseetion to the house that it had sax-and-thretty years sin' ; and yet the young mon says the warld turns roond. It's vera extraordinar'." Here was a man who was not to be taken in by this nonsense about the earth revolving on its axis; and, if there were any real or im-aginary pecuniary advantage to be gained by denying it, Mr. Moll would have a whole army of his way of thinking, many of them far wiser and better informed in other respects than he.

Perhaps, Mr. Chairman and gentlemen, you will allow me to make use of another familiar illustration. You have heard of a man attempting to lift himself from the ground by the waistband of his pantaloons. Now, if anything were to be gained by it, a very respectable *a priori* argument might be made in favor of the possibility of the feat. One might say : " You can lift two hundred pounds ; your weight is but one hun-dred and sixty. A power of gravitation equal to one hundred and sixty pounds holds you down to the earth. You have only to apply a counteracting force a little greater than this and you will be lifted into the air. Take hold of your waistband, there-fore, with both hands and pull vigorously. If you do not lift yourself up at the first trial you must pull harder." All that might sound very plausible to one who had no experience to guide him.

This country has been persuaded to attempt the feat of lifting itself from the ground by the waistband for nearly half a century, with occasional short relaxations of the efforts, prompted by a return of common sense. When the first pull was made and was ineffectual, we were told to try another, and then another still more vigorous, and another and an-other ; and now what do we see ? The garment, of which the waistband forms a part, is torn to shreds and tatters, present-ing what Pope, alluding to a similar accident, somewhere calls a " dishonest sight," mortifying to the pride of philosophy.

It is most true that a man can be raised from the ground by the waistband; but he cannot do the feat himself—another must perform the office. The force must come from without. One strong man may raise another in this way, and be raised by him in turn. In this case there is an interchange of good offices—freedom of trade. No man, even with the strength of Samson, can go into a room by himself and endeavor to perform the feat alone, without coming forth from the undertaking in rags, his nether garment full of ghastly rents, inviting the entrance of the January wind. So no nation can enrich itself by excluding foreign commerce: the more perfect it makes the exclusion, the more certain it is to impoverish itself.

Mr. Chairman and gentlemen: There is a great law imposed upon us by the necessities of our condition as members of human society, the law of mutual succor, the interchange of benefits and advantages, the law of God and nature, commanding us to be useful to each other. It is the law of the household, it is the law of the neighborhood, it is the law of different provinces included under the same government, and well would it be for mankind if it were in an equal degree recognized as a law to be sacredly regarded by the great community of nations in their intercourse with each other. Were that law to be repealed, the social state would loose its cohesion and fall in pieces. There is not a pathway across the fields, nor a highroad, nor a guide-post at a turn of the way, nor a railway from city to city or from State to State, nor a sail upon the ocean, which is not an illustration of this law. It is proclaimed in the shriek of the locomotive. It is murmured in the ripple of waters divided by the prow of the steamer. The nation by which it is disregarded, or which endeavors to obstruct it by artificial barriers against the free intercourse of its citizens with those of other countries, revolts against the order of nature and strikes at its own prosperity.

．　　．　　．　　．　　．　　．　　．　　．

THE cause, Mr. President and gentlemen, to which this

toast refers needs no eulogy of mine. I need not endeavor to show that it is a good cause—the cause of the great mass of mankind, the cause of the few as well as of the many; of those who buy and those who sell, of those who produce and those who consume. It contemplates the advantage of the manufacturer, if he only knew it, as much as of those who purchase his wares. And there are some among the manufacturers who do know this—wise, enlightened, impartial-minded men, who do not separate even in thought their own individual well-being from the largest liberty of trade. There are such at this table. As I speak, your eyes are naturally directed to Mr. Atkinson, of Massachusetts.

But what I wish to say is that the cause is gathering strength and making progress toward an early and glorious triumph. To my mind it is clear that there never has been a time, since the Revolution in which our republic had its birth, so favorable to the general acceptance of the principles of free-trade as the present. This is owing to various causes.

Until lately there were strong party prejudices arrayed against our cause. The great Whig party, intelligent and powerful, adopted in its day the delusion of protection. With party spirit it is impossible to reason. Those who made a point, as most men do, of following the lead of their party were not to be convinced. That hindrance to the spread of enlightened opinions on this subject is now removed. No man is now withheld by mere party considerations from listening candidly to the arguments for commercial freedom. Be he Republican or be he Democrat, he finds men in his own party who take the boldest ground for revenue reform, and who set him a worthy example.

There were formerly men of great talent and influence in political life, with a train of devoted followers, who gave all the aid of their eloquence and the weight of their character to the policy of restrictions on trade for the benefit of the mill-owners. Henry Clay, a man of chivalrous and generous nature, of fascinating manners and great powers of persuasion, gave a name to this policy, of which he was the champion, and called it the American system. Webster, at one time the able advocate of free-trade, went over to the same side with all the fame of his great talents. These were Whigs, but the eminent statesmen of the Democratic party in the North, such as Van Buren and Silas Wright, never called themselves friends of free-trade, and I doubt whether they ever took the pains to master the question. Thus an immense personal influence, aside from all considerations of interest, was exerted in favor of the policy of protection. That state of things no longer exists. The public men who have succeeded to the opinions of these great leaders have not succeeded to their standing in the public estimation nor to their power over public opinion. A generation is rising up who never knew Henry Clay, and who will not adopt his errors merely because they were his.

Another reason for the speedy triumph of free-trade doctrines is that the restrictive policy has been tried and found mischievous. The drug has been given to the patient in what the doctors call herculean doses, and the patient is frightfully nauseated. Under the present tariff our shipping, once the glory of the nation, has disappeared from the high seas. Under the malignant effect of the same policy, various branches of industry, once flourishing, have been annihilated. The same cause has made all the necessaries of life dear. The laboring man and the journeyman mechanic, once living comfortably, and the farmer, once prosperous, find themselves at their wits' end to provide for their families, and ask with astonishment what is the cause. It is our office to inform them.

And this brings me to another reason for saying that the cause of free-trade is sure to win a speedy triumph. Hitherto it has been only the partisans of protection that have combined for the support of their opinions. They have given themselves the full benefit of the maxim, "In union there is strength." It is now our policy to associate for the defence of the masses against the monopolists. And this we have done. We have established the Free-Trade League of the city of New York, and other leagues with the same object have been founded in other cities. We have circulated tracts, we have sent forth missionaries, able and eloquent men, to expound the principles of a wise economy as applied to the laws regulating our intercourse with foreign nations. Wherever they have gone they have carried knowledge and conviction, and to this cause a large part of our success in the late elections is no doubt owing. I see here a gentleman who, with a disinterested activity and a generous zeal, devotes his whole time to the work of making these means efficacious in forming public opinion. When I mention the name of Mahlon Sands, I do it that you may applaud him with the heartiness he deserves. I see, also, a gentleman with a military title, who, as a gallant volunteer, has won in these fields laurels that will require no watering to remain green. Need I mention the name of Brinkerhoff? The Free-Trade League has done much, but, if its revenues had been ten times as great—which they deserve to be, and I hope will yet become—it would have done ten times the good it has accomplished.

Mr. President and gentlemen : He who framed the universe gave to different regions of the globe different climates, yielding different productions for the use of man. He peopled them with different races of mankind, varying from each other in their aptitudes for the useful and ornamental arts of life. He gave them the skill to invent and construct rapid modes of conveyance across the land and across the deep from latitude to latitude, from realm to realm, and from continent to continent, and said to them : "Impart to each other what you can best produce ;" in other words, "to communicate, forget not" —words which you will find in an ancient book belonging to the sacred literature of Palestine. Such was the order He established, the order of nature, and by His help, and through the instrumentality of the Free-Trade League and its sister associations, and by means of a good understanding with all who think as we do, we will attack and overthrow, and trample to fragments, and utterly destroy, all the institutions and inventions of man which have for their object to obstruct and thwart the natural workings of this beneficent system of Providence. Let me, therefore, if the courtesy of the president will so far allow me, propose as a toast the Free-Trade League of the City of New York, and its sister leagues in other cities. I propose that we do honor to the toast with three cheers and a tiger.*

.    .    .    .    .    .    .    .

I HAVE little to say to this large and most respectful assemblage, save to urge upon their attention the claims which my younger friends who are most active in the cause of revenue reform have upon their sympathy, their respect, and their zealous co-operation.

I know them to be actuated by the purest motives of public spirit. They give their thoughts and their exertions to the cause of this important reform, with all the generous ardor and noble enthusiasm of their time of life. They are deeply convinced that liberal and friendly regulations respecting the trade between one region of the earth and the others, putting the least restraint that may be upon the exchange of benefits between man and man, are dictated by the soundest policy, and the highest regard to the general good. To this conviction they add what is important to give them courage and perseverance—the sanguine hope that they shall succeed in bringing their countrymen, the large majority at least, to their way of thinking as soon as they have the means of forming an impartial judgment. In this hope I fully agree with them. I believe the days of what the mill-owners call protection are numbered, and that they are few. I believe that the delusive doctrine that a village may make itself richer by refusing to trade with a neighboring village, a country with an adjoining country,

---

* Remarks at the Free-Trade Dinner at Delmonico's, in New York, on the 28th of November, 1870. Mr. Bryant was called upon to answer the toast " The Cause of Free-Trade."

a state with a state—as, for example, New Jersey with New York, or a people under one government with another, as the United States with Canada or with the countries of Europe—is assuredly destined, so far as this country is concerned, soon to perish ahd be swept away, along with the other old rubbish of false opinions which have wrought mischief in the world for a time, as exploded and cast aside.

When that time shall arrive, and we shall be delivered from the yoke of the monopolists, which is now so heavy on our necks, great and well-deserved will be the praise awarded to the men at whose instance and procurement this meeting has been called. They will have the credit of boldly attacking the conspiracy of monopolists, the drilled phalanx of protection, at the time when monopoly was most pampered, over-grown and formidable, and putting it to death by a speedier process than natural decay.

Mr. President, there is not a mail which comes to the office of the "Evening Post" which does not bring some testimony to the efficacy of the means used by the young men of this city to enlighten public opinion in regard to the mischiefs of protection. A year since, or thereabouts, there were hardly half a dozen newspapers in the country that discussed the revenue question in the interest of liberty and the people. Now you may count them by scores, perhaps I should say by hundreds. Where they formerly spoke with caution and vaguely, they now speak with boldness and decision. A year since, a meeting held in favor of revenue reform was a strange and rare thing. Now there are no meetings called for a public object which are so numerous. A year ago it was difficult to find a member of Congress who would publicly say that he doubted the policy and wisdom of protective duties. Since that time the members have been at home, among their constituents, who have listened to lecturers sent from this city, and read tracts issued here. Many of them have gone back to Washington with their impressions of what the people desire considerably modified. In short, there has been a great and striking change; not great enough, perhaps, to allow us to expect any truly liberal measure from Congress at its present session, but great enough to encourage still more strenuous exertions.

Mr. President, we must follow up with vigor the advantage we have gained, and when the people speak, Congress must and shall give way.

I remember that, when in the time of the famous corn-law agitation in England, an agitation for cheap bread—and our agitation is for cheap iron, cheap fuel, and cheap clothing—I heard Cobden, Bright, and Fox discuss the question of free-trade in corn before an immense assemblage crowded into Drury Lane Theatre. Fox insisted that the only method to move the British Ministry with Peel at its head was to move the people. He quoted the old rhyme:

> "When the wind blows, then the mill goes;
> When the wind drops, then the mill stops."

And he parodied it thus:

> "When the League blows, then the Peel goes;
> When the League stops, then the Peel drops."

The League followed his advice and blew vigorously, and Peel brought in a bill to repeal the restrictions on the trade in breadstuffs, and England had cheap bread.

Mr. President, we must get up a spanking breeze from the right quarter in this country, and we may be sure that Congress will obey its impulse, and we shall again have cheap iron, cheap fuel, and cheap clothing. During the late civil war, public opinion went sadly back on the question of protection; while we had a worse tariff of duties than had ever before been inflicted on the country, yet we did not dare to quarrel with it, inasmuch as we had more important controversies on hand.

It went back then, but it is recovering its healthy tone, and now, since the question of protection is made the grave question of the day, it is coming right.*

---

* From a speech at a public meeting of the New York Free-Trade League.

.    .    .    .    .    .    .    .

I AM glad to see this concourse. It is a worthy occasion which has called us together : the cause of the great mass of our population, the cause of human liberty, the cause of national prosperity, the cause of the useful arts, the cause of peace and good-will between nation and nation. All these are implied in the freedom of exchanges. We talk of free labor, but what is free labor if we are not permitted a free exchange of the fruits of our labor ? One man comes to another and says to him, " You shall work only when and where I direct you." That is naked slavery ; it is justly detested, and we get rid of it as soon as we can ; but, under our present commercial system, a set of men come to us and say, " Well, you have got the products of your labor in a shape proper for sending them to market ; now you shall only sell them where we direct, and for prices which we dictate, and, if you want goods for them, you shall take the goods of us, and at our prices." That is the sum and substance of the protective system, the plain English, the long and short, the proper interpretation of the laws which the protectionists have caused to be enacted for us to live under.

How much better is that system than the one which denies us leave to work where and when we please ? The same principle of despotism is the root of both ; they are both shoots from the same baleful stock.

But they who are guilty of this usurpation of our rights tell us, when we complain that we are hired to grumble, that we are paid in British gold. My friends, were you paid to come hither to-night ? Have you British gold in your pockets ? Did you take your wages at the door when you entered, or are you to be paid when you go out ? A working-man complains that, under the present tariff, the necessaries of life have become so dear that he is at his wits' end to subsist. "Ah," is the answer, "you have been receiving British gold." An old man who thought that he had laid by something to subsist on complains that, within a few years past, prices under our system of direct and indirect taxation have become so high that he is starving. British gold, British gold, say the protectionists for want of a better answer. Now I bring no railing accusation against those who make this charge. I might retort by saying that those who have imposed upon the country a system which has destroyed our shipping interest, and made American products too dear to be exported—a condition of things greatly to the advantage of the British trade—are far more likely to be corrupted by British gold than any other class of men in this country, but I do not say that. They are doubtless sincere in their attachment to what they call the principle of protection. It is a very easy thing to persuade ourselves that what seems to be for our private interest is also good for the community at large. I will say, further, that there are men who have fallen into this delusion of the protective policy whom I esteem and honor, and whom I hope yet to see converted from their error. But let us put this charge of being hired by British gold to an easy test.

You may have before you on this platform to-night an enlightened Massachusetts manufacturer who always speaks ably and nobly in defence of freedom and trade, with large knowledge, and powerful logic. He is one of the mill-owners who do not wish to separate their fortunes from those of the rest of his countrymen; he is satisfied with profits which he can make without oppressing his fellow-men. Is that man a receiver of British gold? Let me tell these calumniators that not all the profits of all the mills in Great Britain, whether moved by steam or by water, whether sending out tissues of wool or cotton, or pigs and bars of metal, were these profits laid at his feet in ignots of gold, or in gold coined into sovereigns, could bribe him to say what is not his honest thought, or to be false to the convictions of his conscience.

The other day Henry Ward Beecher addressed the people of Brooklyn at a free-trade meeting. We all remember how proud we were of this man when, during our civil war, he went to England in order to enlighten the people of that country in regard to the nature of the great struggle which we were making to preserve the Union. He went, fearless, imperturbable, eloquent, master of his subject, took John Bull by the beard, tamed one noisy mob after another, and made them listen to the brave and true words he uttered. You all remember that there was no praise which we were not then willing to bestow upon his courage, his self-possession, his disinterested defence of his country. Was he then a receiver of British gold for thus boldly speaking in behalf of his country? Just as much as he is a receiver of British gold for speaking in favor of those who are crushed to the earth by our false commercial system.

Within a few days since, William Lloyd Garrison addressed a Boston audience in favor of the freedom of exchanges. You all know the character of William Lloyd Garrison. A man who gave the labors of his life to a war against slavery, and who expended in it all that he possessed. When at last the negro race was emancipated, he was penniless. To him might be applied the noble line of Thompson:

"In pure majestic poverty revered."

Is that man a receiver of British gold? Not all the gold dug from the mines of California and those of the Ural Mountains, though to these were added all the diamonds found in Brazil and all the pearls gathered by divers on the floor of the ocean in the regions of the East, could tempt that man to espouse a cause which did not seem to him absolutely just. All the kingdoms of the world have not wealth enough to buy that man.

In 1832 Henry Clay, then a Senator of the United States, and till then a zealous protectionist, rose in his seat to oppose a pure free-trade measure. Mr. Littell, now editor of the "Living Age"—and long may he continue so—a life-long friend of free-trade, framed a bill proposing gradually to abolish every trace of protection in our revenue laws, and reduce every existing duty within the space of ten years to twenty per cent on the value of the commodities imported. Mr. Clay saw that the moment was come to abandon the protective system, and he nobly abandoned it, adopted the project of Mr. Littell, and it was carried by his influence through both Houses of Congress. Subsequently, after several years, he defended the bill, and denied that diminishing the duties had injured the prosperity of the country.

I honor Mr. Clay for his magnanimity in proposing that free-trade measure more than for any other act of his public life. He had to make a painful sacrifice of the pride of opinion, to renounce old prejudices, to disappoint attached friends, to admit practically that the protective system was not the proper policy for our country. He made all these sacrifices, these renunciations, these admissions cheerfully and like an honest man. Was Henry Clay paid by British gold? Will the detractors to whom I have referred say as much, and offer such an insult to his memory? Is there any man audacious enough to bespatter his monument with the dirt thrown so freely at us? The time has come to follow his example. The protective system will be a cause of bitter dissension in this country as long as it is allowed to exist. Its essential element is injustice, partiality, monopoly, unequal legislation, and it cannot last. It makes dear provisions, dear garments, dear household utensils and farming implements, dear fuel, dear houses, and high rents. It lies heavily upon us after we get into our graves, for the very wood of which our coffins are made is burdened with the lumber duty.*

---

* Mr. Bryant's address at a mass-meeting at Cooper Institute, March 24, 1874.

# THE ELECTRIC TELEGRAPH.*

I SPEAK, Mr. President, in behalf of the press. To the press the electric telegraph is an invention of immense value. Charles Lamb, in one of his papers, remarks that a piece of news, which when it left Botany Bay was true to the letter, often becomes a lie before it reaches England. It is the advantage of the telegraph that it gives you the news before circumstances have had time to alter it. The press is enabled to lay it fresh before the reader. It comes to him like a steak hot from the gridiron, instead of being cooled and made flavorless by a slow journey from a distant kitchen. A battle is fought three thousand miles away, and we have the news while they are taking the wounded to the hospital. A great orator rises in the British Parliament, and we read his words almost before the cheers of his friends have ceased. An earthquake shakes San Francisco, and we have the news before the people who have rushed into the street have returned to their houses. I am afraid that the columns of the daily newspapers would now seem flat, dull, and stale to the readers were it not for the communications of the telegraph.

But, while the telegraph does that for the press, the press in some sort returns the obligation. Were it not for the press, the telegram, being repeated from mouth to mouth, would, from the moment of its arrival, begin to lose something of its

* Remarks at a dinner given to Samuel Breese Morse, December 29, 1868.

authenticity. Every rumor propagated orally at last becomes false. Mr. President, you are familiar with the personification of Rumor by the poets of antiquity—at first of dwarfish size, and rapidly enlarging in bulk till her feet sweep the earth and her head is among the clouds. The press puts Rumor into a strait-jacket, swaddles her from head to foot, and so restrains her growth. It transcribes the messages of the telegraph in their very words, and thus prevents them from being magnified or mutilated into lies. It protects the reputation of the telegraph for veracity. You know, Mr. President, what a printer's devil is. It is the messenger who brings to the printer his copy—that is to say, matter which is to be put into type. Some petulant, impatient author, I suppose, who was negligent in furnishing the required copy, must have given him that name; although he is so useful that he is entitled to be called the printer's angel, the original word for angel and messenger being the same. Our illustrious guest, Mr. President, has taken portions of the great electric mass, which in its concentrated form becomes the thunderbolt; he has drawn it into slender threads, and every one of these becomes in his hands an obedient messenger—a printer's devil, carrying with the speed of a sunbeam volumes of copy to the typesetter.

In the " Treatise on Bathos," Pope quotes, as a sample of absurdity not to be surpassed, a passage from some play, I think one of Nat. Lee's, expressing the modest wish of a lover:

"Ye gods, annihilate both space and time,
And make two lovers happy."

But see what changes a century brings forth. What was then an absurdity, what was arrant nonsense, is now the statement of a naked fact. Our guest has annihilated both space and time in the transmission of intelligence. The breadth of the Atlantic, with all its waves, is as nothing; and, in sending a message from Europe to this continent, the time, as computed by the clock, is some six hours less than nothing.

There is one view of this great invention of the electric telegraph which impresses me with awe. Beside us at this board, along with the illustrious man whom we are met to honor, and whose name will go down to the latest generations of civilized man, sits the gentleman to whose clear-sighted perseverance and to whose energy—an energy which knew no discouragement, no weariness, no pause—we owe it that the telegraph has been laid which connects the Old World with the New through the Atlantic Ocean. My imagination goes down to the chambers of the middle sea, to those vast depths where repose the mystic wire on beds of coral, among forests of tangle, or on the bottom of the dim blue gulfs strewn with the bones of whales and sharks, skeletons of drowned men, and ribs and masts of foundered barks, laden with wedges of gold never to be coined, and pipes of the choicest vintages of earth never to be tasted. Through these watery solitudes, among the fountains of the great deep, the abode of perpetual silence, never visited by living human presence and beyond the sight of human eye, there are gliding to and fro, by night and by day, in light and in darkness, in calm and in tempest, currents of human thought borne by the electric pulse which obeys the bidding of man. That slender wire thrills with the hopes and fears of nations; it vibrates to every emotion that can be awakened by any event affecting the welfare of the human race. A volume of contemporary history passes every hour of the day from one continent to the other. An operator on the continent of Europe gently touches the keys of an instrument in his quiet room, a message is shot with the swiftness of light through the abysses of the sea, and before his hand is lifted from the machine the story of revolts and revolutions, of monarchs dethroned and new dynasties set up in their place, of battles and conquests and treaties of peace, of great statesmen fallen in death, lights of the world gone out and new luminaries glimmering on the horizon, is written down in another quiet room on the other side of the globe.

Mr. President, I see in the circumstances which I have

enumerated a new proof of the superiority of mind to matter, of the independent existence of that part of our nature which we call the spirit, when it can thus subdue, enslave, and educate the subtilest, the most active, and in certain of its manifestations the most intractable and terrible, of the elements, making it in our hands the vehicle of thought, and compelling it to speak every language of the civilized world. I infer the capacity of the spirit for a separate state of being, its indestructible essence and its noble destiny, and I thank the great discoverer whom we have assembled to honor for this confirmation of my faith.

# THE METROPOLITAN ART MUSEUM.*

We are assembled to consider the subject of founding in this city a Museum of Art, a repository of the productions of artists of every class, which shall be in some measure worthy of this great metropolis and of the wide empire of which New York is the commercial centre. I understand that no rivalry with any other project is contemplated, no competition, save with similar institutions in other countries, and then only such modest competition as a museum in its infancy may aspire to hold with those which were founded centuries ago, and are enriched with the additions made by the munificence of successive generations. No precise method of reaching this result has been determined on, but the object of the present meeting is to awaken the public, so far as our proceedings can influence the general mind, to the importance of taking early and effectual measures for founding such a museum as I have described.

Our city is the third great city of the civilized world. Our Republic has already taken its place among the great powers of the earth: it is great in extent, great in population, great in the activity and enterprise of her people. It is the richest nation in the world, if paying off an enormous national debt with a rapidity unexampled in history be any

---

* An address delivered at a meeting in the Union Club House, November, 23, 1869.

proof of riches; the richest in the world, if contented submission to heavy taxation be a sign of wealth; the richest in the world, if quietly to allow itself to be annually plundered of immense sums by men who seek public stations for their individual profit be a token of public prosperity. My friends, if a tenth part of what is every year stolen from us in this way, in the city where we live, under pretence of the public service, and poured profusely into the coffers of political rogues, were expended on a Museum of Art, we might have, deposited in spacious and stately buildings, collections, formed of works left by the world's greatest artists, which would be the pride of our country. We might have an annual revenue which would bring to the Museum every stray statue and picture of merit for which there should be no ready sale to individuals, every smaller collection in the country which its owner could no longer conveniently keep, every noble work by the artists of former ages, which, by any casualty, after long remaining on the walls of some ancient building, should be again thrown upon the world.

But what have we done—numerous as our people are, and so rich as to be contentedly cheated and plundered—what have we done toward founding such a repository? We have hardly made a step toward it. Yet beyond the sea there is the little kingdom of Saxony, with an area even less than that of Massachusetts, and a population but little larger, possessing a Museum of the Fine Arts, marvellously rich, which no man who visits the continent of Europe is willing to own that he has not seen. There is Spain, a third-rate power of Europe and poor besides, with a Museum of Fine Arts at her capital, the opulence and extent of which absolutely bewilder the visitor. I will not speak of France or of England, conquering nations, which have gathered their treasures of art in part from regions overrun by their armies; nor yet of Italy, the fortunate inheritor of so many glorious productions of her own artists. But there are Holland and Belgium, kingdoms almost too small to be heeded by the greater powers of Europe in the consultations which decide the destinies of nations, and these little kingdoms have their public collections of art, the resort of admiring visitors from all parts of the civilized world.

But in our country, when the owner of a private gallery of art desires to leave his treasures where they can be seen by the public, he looks in vain for any institution to which he can send them. A public-spirited çitizen desires to employ a favorite artist upon some great historical picture ; there are no walls on which it can hang in public sight. A large collection of works of art, made at great cost and with great pains, gathered perhaps during a lifetime, is for sale in Europe. We may find here men willing to contribute to purchase it, but, if it should be brought to our country, there is no edifice here to give it hospitality.

In 1857, during a visit to Spain, I found in Madrid a rich private collection of pictures, made by Medraza, an aged painter, during a long life, and at a period when frequent social and political changes in that country dismantled many palaces of the old nobility of the works of art which adorned them. In that collection were many pictures by the illustrious elder artists of Italy, Spain, and Holland. The whole might have been bought for half its value, but, if it had been brought over to our country, we had no gallery to hold it. The same year I stood before the famous Campana collection of marbles at Rome, which was then waiting for a purchaser—a noble collection, busts and statues of the ancient philosophers, orators, and poets, the majestic forms of Roman senators, the deities of ancient mythology,

" The fair humanities of old religion,"

but, if they had been purchased by our countrymen and landed here, we should have been obliged to leave them in boxes, just as they were packed.

Moreover, we require an extensive public gallery to contain the greater works of our own painters and sculptors. The American soil is prolific of artists. The fine arts blossom not only in the populous regions of our country, but even in its solitary places. Go where you will, into whatever museum of art in the Old World, you find there artists from the New, contemplating or copying the masterpieces of art which they contain. Our artists swarm in Italy. When I was last at Rome, two years since, I found the number of American artists residing there as two to one compared with those from the British Isles. But there are beginners among us who have not the means of resorting to distant countries for that instruction in art which is derived from carefully studying works of acknowledged excellence. For these a gallery is needed at home, which shall vie with those abroad, if not in the multitude, yet in the merit, of the works it contains.

Yet, further, it is unfortunate for our artists, our painters especially, that they too often find their genius cramped by the narrow space in which it is constrained to exert itself. It is like a bird in a cage, which can take short flights only from one perch to another, and longs to stretch its wings in an ampler atmosphere. Producing works for private dwellings, our painters are for the most part obliged to confine themselves to cabinet pictures, and have little opportunity for that larger treatment of important subjects which a greater breadth of canvas would allow them, and by which the higher and nobler triumphs of their art have been achieved.

There is yet another view of the subject, and a most important one. When I consider, my friends, the prospect which opens before this great mart of the western world, I am moved by feelings which I feel it somewhat difficult clearly to define. The growth of our city is already wonderfully rapid; it is every day spreading itself into the surrounding region and overwhelming it like an inundation. Now that our great railway has been laid from the Atlantic to the Pacific, eastern Asia and western Europe will shake hands over our Republic. New York will be the mart from which Europe will receive a

large proportion of the products of China, and will become
not a centre of commerce only for the New World, but for
that region which is to Europe the most remote part of the
Old. A new impulse will be given to the growth of our city,
which I cannot contemplate without an emotion akin to dis-
may. Men will flock in greater numbers than ever before to
plant themselves on a spot so favorable to the exchange of
commodities between distant regions; and here will be an ag-
gregation of human life, a concentration of all that ennobles
and all that degrades humanity, on a scale which the imagi-
nation cannot venture to measure. To great cities resort not
only all that is eminent in talent, all that is splendid in genius,
and all that is active in philanthropy, but also all that is most
dexterous in villany and all that is most foul in guilt. It is in
the labyrinths of such mighty and crowded populations that
crime finds its safest lurking-places; it is there that vice
spreads its most seductive and fatal snares, and sin is pampered,
and festers and spreads its contagion in the greatest security.

My friends, it is important that we should encounter the
temptations to vice in this great and too rapidly growing capi-
tal by attractive entertainments of an innocent and improving
character. We have libraries and reading-rooms, and this is
well; we have also spacious halls for musical entertainments,
and that also is well; but there are times when we do not
care to read and are satiated with listening to sweet sounds,
and when we more willingly contemplate works of art. It is
the business of the true philanthropist to find means of grati-
fying this preference. We must be beforehand with vice in
our arrangements for all that gives grace and cheerfulness to
society. The influence of works of art is wholesome, enno-
bling, instructive. Besides the cultivation of the sense of
beauty—in other words, the perception of order, symmetry,
proportion of parts, which is of near kindred to the moral
sentiments—the intelligent contemplation of a great gallery of
works of art is a lesson in history, a lesson in biography, a les-
son in the antiquities of different countries. Half our knowl-

edge of the customs and modes of life among the ancient Greeks and Romans is derived from the remains of ancient art.

Let it be remembered to the honor of art that, if it has ever been perverted to the purposes of vice, it has only been at the bidding of some corrupt court, or at the desire of some opulent and powerful voluptuary whose word was law. When intended for the general eye, no such stain rests on the works of art. Let me close with an anecdote of the influence of a well-known work. I was once speaking to the poet Rogers in commendation of the painting of Ary Scheffer, entitled " Christ the Consoler." " I have an engraving of it," he answered, " hanging at my bedside, where it meets my eye every morning." The aged poet, over whom already impended the shadow that shrouds the entrance to the next world, found his morning meditations guided by that work to the Founder of our religion.

# TRANSLATORS OF HOMER.*

To a toast made up of quotations from the Greek and Latin poets I suppose that I may reply in the vernacular, which all who are present, I hope, understand, even when spoken as imperfectly as I speak it.

That passable verses may be written by one who knows neither Greek nor Latin I suppose will be allowed. The very greatest of modern poets, Shakespeare, was said by the learned Ben Jonson to have "small Latin and less Greek." Nay, I suppose that a very moderate knowledge of Greek might suffice even for translating Homer. Pope, the most popular of his translators, is thought to have had but a very slender stock of Greek. I go still further, and assert that one very good translation of the Iliad was made without knowing a word of the Greek original. The eminent Italian poet, Vincenzo Monti, author of the grand tragedy of "Aristodemo," translated the Iliad into excellent blank verse without any knowledge of Greek. An epigram was made to be inscribed under his portrait in these words:

> " Questi è Vincenzo Monti, Cavaliero,
> Gran traduttor de' traduttor 'd 'Omero,"

---

* From a speech to the Williams College Alumni, February 22, 1870.
VOL. II.—18

which, if you please, may be thus translated :

> "This knight is Vincenzo Monti,
>    An author highly rated,
>    By whom the translators of Homer
>    So cleverly were translated."

So you see, Mr. President, and you gentlemen who pre-pared this toast, and you learned directors of the studies of colleges, that Homer *can* be translated without knowing even the Greek alphabet.

Let me call the attention of the company for a moment to the great marvel of the origin of the Homeric poems, at a pe-riod before letters were of general use in Greece, save, per-haps, in public inscriptions. His poems, when produced, could not have been committed to manuscript. We find nowhere in them any mention of the art of the scribe, of the pen or the papyrus, of the stylus or the tablet, of the graving-tool or the inscribed rock, of the painted or the chiselled alphabet, or any other even remote hint of a written literature, though every other art of life then known helped to furnish forth the afflu-ent imagery of his poems. He lived while all history was oral tradition. His poems—for I hold to one Homer as I hold to one sun in the firmament—were engraved on his own iron memory and that of the minstrels who inherited and repeated his poems in public assemblies. Yet in that remote and im-perfectly civilized age, while all the literature that existed was in men's heads and on their tongues, there was produced a work which, in all time since and for twenty-seven hundred years, has commanded the admiration of mankind, has occu-pied whole troops of commentators, has been regarded as the model and unsurpassable pattern of poetic excellence, has been studied in all nations by scholars in the original Greek and read with avidity in every cultivated language in numerous translations, has been imitated by poets innumerable, and bor-rowed from as an inexhaustible treasure-house of poetic thought and imagery, and is now as much admired in what we call the noon-day blaze of civilization as it was in its glimmering dawn.

It has occurred to me that the fame of the venerable Greek bard, in its progress through the centuries, may be compared with our own great midland river. The waters of our Mississippi—which fall in the remote Northwest from the clouds in unrecorded showers, which gush from unnoticed springs in nooks unknown to the geographer, and are gathered into rivulets without a name, meeting in one majestic torrent—pour themselves into the main ocean through many broad mouths, and, forming a part of it, are carried by its current to the ends of the earth. They move in the Gulf Stream; they beat on the cliffs of Europe; they sweep at one time round Cape Horn, and at another round the Cape of Storms; they join company in one distant part of the globe with the waters of the Amazon, and in another with the waters of the Congo; they are carried into the Arctic Sea; they ripple on the beaches of the Spice Islands within the tropics, and on shores overshadowed by palm-groves; they dash against the icy coasts near the southern pole; they drift into the secret caverns of the great deep, the dim abodes assigned by Homer to the venerable Oceanus and the ancient Tethys, the primal father and mother of all the gods of Olympus and the Underworld.

So wide-extended, so universal, so all-pervading—notwithstanding the rude and remote antiquity in the shadows of which it had its birth—is the fame of Homer; it knows no limit of latitude, or race, or language; in its mighty progress it is bounded only by the barriers of barbarism; nor will it cease to enlarge the sphere of its dominion while civilization extends itself on the earth from land to land and clime to clime.

# THE MERCANTILE LIBRARY.*

I ESTEEM myself fortunate in being able to congratulate the Mercantile Library Association upon having arrived at its fiftieth anniversary. Forty-five years ago, when I came to live in New York, it was in its early infancy. The public-spirited gentlemen by whom it was founded, I remember, expected much from it in the future. They hoped, and the hope was not vain, that it would greatly aid in forming the minds of the younger part of the mercantile class to liberal tastes and to generous views of their duty to their country and to mankind, and that it would be in some measure a safeguard against the temptations which beset young men in a populous city. Those who then sat by its cradle, if they survive, are now aged men; those whose birth was coeval with its origin are men of mature age, who have passed the zenith of life; the books which were collected in its first years, to form the beginning of what is now a flourishing library, belong to the literature of a past generation. Yet, in founding this institution, the men of that day left a noble legacy to future times. While other institutions have risen and fallen, it has continued to grow and to extend its beneficial influences with the growth of our city; not, indeed, in the same proportion, but steadily and with a sure advance, till now its prosperity and duration seem almost

---

* An address delivered on the fiftieth anniversary of the founding of the New York Mercantile Library, November 9, 1870.

beyond the reach of accident. I learn that there is no library in the country which increases so fast as that which belongs to this association, and that within the last ten years it has more than doubled the number of its volumes. If it proceeds at this rate it will eventually have a library which will command the admiration of the world and become the pride of our country.

In the years yet to come, far in the depths of the future, the young men who search among the old books of the library will say to each other: "See with what reading our ancestors entertained themselves many centuries since, and how the language has changed since that time! We can laugh yet at the humor of Irving, in spite of the antiquated diction. What a fiery spirit animates the quaint sentences of the old novelist Cooper! In these verses of Longfellow we still perceive the sweetness of the numbers and the pathos of the thoughts, and wonder not that the maidens of that distant age wept over the pages of 'Evangeline.' Here," they will add, "are the scientific works of that distant age. Clever men were these ancestors of ours; diligent inquirers, fortunate discoverers of scientific truth, but how far in its attainment below the height which we have since reached!"

What I have just now imagined supposes our flourishing library to escape destruction by war and by casual fires. Ah, my friends, never may the fate of unhappy Strasburg be ours! to lie for weeks under a hail-storm of iron and a rain of fire, showered from the engines of destruction, which Milton properly makes the guilty invention of the sinning angels, and doomed to see her library, rich with the priceless treasures of past centuries, suddenly turned to ashes. But, whatever may be the fate of our library, the association itself is not so easily destroyed. If the library perish, the same spirit which founded it first will restore it so far as a restoration is possible. The association, I venture to predict, will subsist till this great mart of commerce shall be a mart no longer; till the mercantile class shall have disappeared from the spot where it stands, and New York shall have dwindled to a fishing town.

But will this ever be? Will our great city share the fate of Tyre and Sidon, whose merchants were princes, and which are now but Arab villages, with a few caïques and here and there a felucca moored in their clear but shallow waters, choked with the ruins of palaces? Will she become like Carthage, once mistress of flourishing colonies, but now a desert; like Corinth, once the seat of a vast commerce—opulent, luxurious, magnificent Corinth—now a mere cluster of houses overlooked by a dismantled and mouldering citadel? *

Or, to come down to later times, will this city decay like Amsterdam, the mother of New York, and once the centre of the world's commerce? or like Genoa, surnamed the proud, and Venice, once the mistress of the Adriatic, cities which, after having successively wielded the commerce of the East, and made Italian the language of commerce in all the ports of the Levant, have long since ceased to hold a place among the great marts of the world?

I answer that none of these cities had the same firm and durable basis of commercial prosperity as our New York. It was their enterprise in opening channels of trade; it was their conquests and colonies which gave them their temporary prosperity. They had no broad, well-peopled region around them, under the same government with themselves, whose superabundant products it was their office to exchange with other countries. Their prosperity was built on narrow foundations, and it fell. Our circumstances are different. Here is a republic of vast extent, stretching from the sea which bathes the western coast of Europe to that which washes the eastern shore of Asia—a region of fertile plains, rich valleys, noble forests, mountains big with mines, water-courses whose sands are gold, mighty rivers, railways going forth from our great cities to every point of the compass, and covering an immense

---

* See the incomplete lines entitled "Corinth," in "Biography," vol. ii, p. 363

territory with their intersections, and not a hinderance to commerce between city and city or between sea and sea, or on our great rivers, or on the borders of the States forming our confederation. This mighty region, alive with an energetic population, is flanked with seaports through which the products sent by us to other countries *must* pass, and through which the merchandise sent us in exchange *must* be received. They are therefore an indispensable part of our national economy. Their prosperity is necessary, inevitable, and will endure while our political organization remains as it now is.

But, if it should come to pass that this fortunate order of things is broken up; if this great Republic should fall to pieces and become divided into a group of independent commonwealths, each animated by a narrow jealousy of the others; and if an illiberal legislation should obstruct the channels of trade now so fortunately open over all our vast territory—there are none of our great marts of exchange for whose future prosperity I could answer. Some would fall into a slow decay, some pass into a rapid decline; some would become like Ascalon on the coast of Palestine, once a harbor crowded with shipping, but, when I saw it, a desolate spot, where the sea-sand had drifted upon the foundations of temples and palaces, invaded the harvest-fields, and, moving .before the wind, had entered the olive-groves and piled itself among them to the tops of the trees.

Our security from such unhappy results will, in a good degree, lie in such institutions as this, and in other means of a like character, the object of which is to diffuse knowledge, to open men's eyes to their true interests, and accustom them to large and generous views of the relation of communities to each other and to the world at large. For this reason let us hope for the permanent and increasing prosperity of the Mercantile Library Association.

# ITALIAN UNITY.*

WE are assembled to celebrate a new and signal triumph of liberty and constitutional government—not a victory obtained by one religious denomination over another, but the successful assertion of rights which are the natural inheritance of every man born into the world—rights of which no man can divest himself, and which no possible form of government should be allowed to deny its subjects. A great nation, the Italian nation, while yet acknowledging allegiance to the Latin church, has been moved to strike the fetters of civil and religious thraldom from the inhabitants of the most interesting city of the world in the midst of their exulting acclamations. We are assembled to re-echo those acclamations.

The government which has just been overthrown in Rome denied to those who had the misfortune to be its subjects every one of the liberties which are the pride and glory of our own country—liberty of the press, liberty of speech, liberty of worship, liberty of assembling. It was an iron despotism, which, to the scandal of the Christian church, insisted on persecution as a duty, set the example of persecution to other Catholic countries, and, wherever it could make itself obeyed, maintained the obligation of repressing heresy by the law. of force.

---

* An address delivered at a popular meeting in the Academy of Music, New York, January, 1871.

Take a single example of the manner in which the govern-
ment was administered. An American lady, an acquaintance
of mine, a resident in Rome for several years, was summoned
one morning to appear before the police of that city. She
went, accompanied by the American consul.

"You are charged," said the police magistrate, " with hav-
ing sent money to Florence, to be employed in founding a
Protestant orphan asylum. What do you say?"

" I did send money for that purpose," was the lady's an-
swer. " I did not ask for it; it was brought to me by some
ladies, who requested me to forward it to Florence, and I did
so; and I take the liberty to say that it is no affair of yours."

" Of that you are not to judge," replied the magistrate.
" See that you never repeat the offence."

Such was the government which, to the great joy of the
Roman people and the satisfaction of the friends of liberty
everywhere, has been overthrown. Was it worthy—I put
this question to this assembly—was such a government worthy
to subsist even for an hour?

And yet there are those who protest against this change
—American citizens, and excellent people among them, who
lend their names to a public remonstrance against admitting
the people of Rome to the liberties which we enjoy. My
friends, is there a single one of these liberties which is not
as dear to you as the light of day and the free air of heaven?
The liberty of public worship—would you give it up without a
mortal struggle? The liberty of discussing openly, in conver-
sation or by means of the press, in books or in newspapers,
every question which interests the welfare of our race—a lib-
erty of which the poor Romans were not allowed even the
shadow—this and the liberty of assembling as we now assem-
ble in vast throngs, thousands upon thousands, to give an ex-
pression of public opinion the significance of which cannot be
mistaken—are not these as dear to you as the crimson current
that warms your hearts, and are they not worthy to be de-
fended at the risk of your lives? How is it, then, that any citi-

zen of our own country, in the enjoyment of these blessings, and prizing them as he must, can protest against their being conferred upon the Roman people—a people nobly endowed by nature, and worthy of a better lot than the slavery they have endured for so many generations?

What sort of Protestantism is this? Protestantism in its worst form of misapplication. I should as soon think of protesting against the glorious light of the sun, of protesting against admitting the sweet air of the outer world into a dungeon full of noisome damps and stifling exhalations. I should as soon think of remonstrating with Providence against the return of spring, with its verdure and flowers and promise of harvests, after a long and dreary winter. Is it possible that those of our countrymen who lend their names to condemn this act of justice to the Roman people are aware of what they do?

My friends, I respect profound religious convictions wherever I meet them. I honor a good life wherever I see it, and I find men of saintly lives in every religious denomination. But, when I hear it affirmed that there is a natural alliance between despotism and Christianity, that the necessary prop and support of religion is the law of force, and that the Christian church should be so organized that its head shall be an absolute temporal monarch, surrounded by a population compelled to be his slaves, I must say to those who make this assertion, whatever be their personal worth, that their doctrine dishonors Christianity, that it brings scandal upon religion, and blasphemes the holy and gracious memory of the Saviour of the world.

It is now nearly two centuries and a half since Roger Williams established in Rhode Island a commonwealth on the basis of strict religious equality. That was a little light shining upon the world from a distance, and slow has been the progress of the nations in taking that commonwealth for an example. Yet, though slow, the progress of religious liberty has been constant; the day of its triumph has arrived; to-night we celebrate its crowning conquest. It was but a little while since that Austria thrust out the priesthood from that partnership in the political power which it had held for centuries. It is not many years since that at Malaga, in Spain, when a heretic died, his corpse was conveyed to the sea-beach, amid the hootings of the populace, and, that the soil of Spain might not be polluted by his remains, it was buried in the sand at low-water mark, where the waves sometimes uncovered it and swept it out to sea to become the prey of sharks. Now the heretic may erect a temple and pay worship in any part of Spain. Not long since there was no part of Italy in which any worship save that of the Latin church was permitted. Now we 'owe to an eminent Italian statesmen the glorious maxim, "A free church in a free state," and we behold the religious conscience set free from its fetters even in the Eternal City. With the aid of popular education it will remain so forever.

When I think of these changes I am reminded of that grand allegory in one of the Hebrew prophets, in which we read of a stone cut out of the quarry without hands, smiting a gigantic image with a head of gold and legs of iron, and breaking it to pieces, which became like the chaff of the summer threshing-floors, to be carried away by the wind, while the stone that smote the image grew to be a great mountain and filled the whole earth. Thus has the principle of religious liberty, a stone cut out of the quarry without hands—an inspiration of the Most High—smitten the grim tyranny that held the religious conscience in subjection to the law of force, and broken it into fragments, while it is rapidly expanding itself to fill the civilized world. Let us hope that the rubbish left by the demolition of this foul idol, made small as the chaff of the summer threshing-floors and dispersed by the breath of public opinion, may never be gathered up again and reconstituted, even in the mildest form it ever wore, while the globe on which we tread shall endure.

# SAMUEL F. B. MORSE.*

THERE are two lines in the poem of Dr. Johnson's on the
"Vanity of Human Wishes" which have passed into a proverb:

> "See nations slowly wise and meanly just,
> To buried merit raise the tardy bust."

It is our good fortune to escape the censure implied in
these lines. We come together on the occasion of raising a
statue, not to buried but to living merit—to a great discoverer
who yet sits among us, a witness of honors which are but the
first-fruits of that ample harvest which his memory will gather
in the long train of seasons yet to come. Yet we cannot con-
gratulate ourselves on having set an example of alacrity in
this manifestation of the public gratitude. If our illustrious
friend, to whom we now gladly pay these honors, had not
lived beyond the common age of man, we should have sorrow-
fully laid them on his grave. In what I am about to say, I
shall not attempt to relate the history of the electric tele-
graph, or discuss the claims of our friend to be acknowledged
as its inventor. I took up the other day one of the forty-six
volumes of the great biographical dictionary compiled by
French authors, and immediately after the name of Samuel
Finley Breese Morse I read the words "inventor of the electric

---

* Address delivered on the unveiling of the statue of Samuel Finley Breese Morse,
June 10, 1871.

telegraph." I am satisfied with this ascription. It is made by a nation which, having no claims of its own to the invention, is naturally impartial. The words I have given may be taken as an expression of the deliberate judgment of the world, and I should regard it as a waste of your time and mine to occupy the few minutes allotted to me in demonstrating its truth. As to the history of this invention, it is that of most great discoveries. Coldly and doubtingly received at first, its author compelled to struggle with difficulties, to encounter neglect, to contend with rivals, it has gradually gained the public favor till at length it is adopted throughout the civilized world.

It now lacks but a few years of half a century since I became acquainted with the man whom this invention has made so famous in all countries. He was then an artist, devoted to a profession in which he might have attained a high rank had he not, fortunately for his country and the world, left it for a pursuit in which he has risen to a more peculiar eminence. Even then, in the art of painting, his tendency to mechanical invention was conspicuous. His mind, as I remember, was strongly impelled to analyze the processes of his art—to give them a certain scientific precision, to reduce them to fixed rules, to refer effects to clearly defined causes, so as to put it in the power of the artist to produce them at pleasure and with certainty, instead of blindly groping for them, and, in the end, owing them to some happy accident, or some instinctive effort, of which he could give no account. The mind of Morse was an organizing mind. He showed this in a remarkable manner when he brought together the artists of New York, then a little band of mostly young men, whose profession was far from being honored as it now is, reconciled the disagreements which he found existing among them, and founded an association, to be managed solely by themselves—the Academy of the Arts of Design—which has since grown to such noble dimensions, and which has given to the artists a consideration in the community far higher than was before conceded to

them.   This ingenuity in organization, this power of combin-
ing the causes which produce given effects into a system and
making them act together to a common end, was not long
afterward to be exemplified in a very remarkable manner.

The voyage made by Mr. Morse from Havre to New York,
on board the packet-ship Sully, in the year 1832, marks an im-
portant era in the history of inventions.   In a casual conversa-
tion with some of the passengers concerning certain experi-
ments which showed the identity of magnetism and electricity,
the idea struck his mind that in a gentle and steady current of
the electric fluid there was a source of regular, continued, and
rapid motions, which might be applied to a machine for con-
veying messages from place to place, and inscribing them on
a tablet at their place of destination.   We can fancy the in-
ventor, full of this thought, as he paced the deck of the Sully,
or lay in his berth, revolving in his mind the mechanical con-
trivances by which this was to be effected, until the whole
process had taken a definite shape in his imagination, and he
saw before him all the countries of the civilized world inter-
sected with lines of his electric wire, bearing messages to and
fro with the speed of light.

I have already said that this invention met with a tardy
welcome.   It was not till three years after this—that is to say,
in 1835—that Morse found means to demonstrate to the public
its practicability by a telegraph constructed on an economical
scale, and set up at the New York University, which recorded
messages at their place of destination.   The public, however,
still seemed indifferent; there was none of the loud applause,
none of that enthusiastic reception which it now seems natural
should attend the birth of so brilliant a discovery.   The invent-
or, however, saw farther than we all, and, I think, never lost
courage.   Yet I remember that some three or four years after
this he said to me, with some despondency : " Wheatstone, in
England, and Steinheil, in Bavaria, who have their electric
telegraphs, are afforded the means of bringing forward their
methods, while to my invention, of earlier date than theirs, my

country seems to show no favor." He persevered, however, and the doubts of those who hesitated were finally dispelled in 1844 by the establishment of a telegraph on his plan between Washington and Baltimore. France and other countries on the European continent soon adopted his invention, and vied with each other in rewarding him with honors. The indifference of his countrymen, which he could not but acutely feel, gave place to pride in his growing fame, and to-day we express our admiration for his genius and our gratitude for the benefit he has conferred upon the world by erecting this statue, which has just been unveiled to the public.

It may be said, I know, that the civilized world is already full of memorials which speak the merit of our friend, and the grandeur and utility of his invention. Every telegraphic station is such a memorial; every message sent from one of these stations to another may be counted among the honors paid to his name. Every telegraphic wire strung from post to post, as it hums in the wind, murmurs his eulogy. Every sheaf of wires laid down in the deep sea, occupying the bottom of soundless abysses, to which human sight has never penetrated, and carrying the electric pulse, charged with the burden of human thought, from continent to continent, from the Old World to the New, is a testimonial to his greatness. Nor are these wanting in the solitudes of the land. Telegraphic lines crossing the breadth of our continent, climbing hills, descending into valleys, threading mountain passes, silently proclaim the great discovery and its author to the uninhabited desert. Even now there are plans for putting a girdle of telegraphic stations around the globe, which in all probability will never be disused, and will convey a knowledge of his claims on the gratitude of mankind to millions who will never see the statue erected to-day. Thus the latin inscription in the Church of St. Paul's, in London, referring to Sir Christopher Wren, its architect, "If you would behold his monument, look around you," may be applied in a far more comprehensive sense to our friend, since the great globe itself has become his monument. All this may be said and all this would be undeniably true, but our natural instincts are not thus satisfied. It is not the name of a benefactor merely, it is the person that we cherish ; and we require, whenever it is possible, the visible presentment of his face and form to aid us in keeping the idea of his worth before our minds. Who would willingly dispense with the image of Washington as we have it in painting and sculpture, and consent that it should be removed from the walls of our dwellings and from all public places, and that the calm countenance and majestic presence with which we associate so many virtues should disappear and be utterly and forever forgotten? Who will deny that, by means of these resemblances of his person, we are the more frequently reminded of the reverence we owe to his memory? So in the present instance we are not willing that our idea of Morse should be reduced to a mere abstraction. We are so constituted that we insist upon seeing the form of that brow beneath which an active, restless, creative brain devised the mechanism that was to subdue the most wayward of the elements to the service of man and make it his obedient messenger. We require to see the eye that glittered with a thousand lofty hopes when the great discovery was made, and the lips that curled with a smile of triumph when it became certain that the lightning of the clouds would become tractable to the most delicate touch. We demand to see the hand which first strung the wire by whose means the slender currents of the electric fluid were taught the alphabet of every living language—the hand which pointed them to the spot where they were to inscribe and leave their messages. All this we have in the statue which has this day been unveiled to the eager gaze of the public, and in which the artist has so skilfully and faithfully fulfilled his task as to satisfy those who are the hardest to please, the most intimate friends of the original. But long may it be, my friends—very long— before any such resemblance of our illustrious friend shall be needed, by those who have the advantage of his acquaintance, to refresh the image of his form and bearing as it exists in their minds. Long may we keep with us what is better than the statue—the noble original; long may it remain among us in a healthful and serene old age; late, very late, may He who gave the mind to which we owe the grand discovery to-day commemorated recall it to His more immediate presence, that it may be employed in a higher sphere and in a still more beneficial activity.

# NEGOTIATION VS. WAR.*

WHEN the press is toasted on an occasion like this, it is natural to suppose that the toast particularly refers to that department of the press which deals immediately with the events and questions of the day, and gives expression to the opinions prevailing at the time. For that department of the press I rise to answer.

One of the most important of these events, embracing the adjustment of some of the most earnestly agitated questions of the time, is the Treaty of Washington, in framing which several of the distinguished persons who sit at the board have borne a part. So far as the press of this country is concerned, I believe I may answer for it that, as a general thing, it will faithfully express the public satisfaction with what they have done. While two of the greatest nations of the civilized world have been engaged in mutual slaughter, bringing upon each other the miseries and sufferings of one of the bloodiest wars of modern times, two other great nations, Great Britain and our Republic, at variance upon some important points, have deputed their trusted agents to settle these differences, to restore a somewhat interrupted friendship, and to leave no cause of dispute which by any possibility could occasion a

---

* Remarks made at the dinner given to the High Commissioners who negotiated the Treaty of Washington, New York, May, 1871.

war. This has been done with wisdom and moderation, and a sincere desire to meet every reasonable expectation that could be entertained in either country. History will give the treaty they framed a place on its pages as a settlement alike just and honorable to both parties. The press of this country, I am sure, will in this agree with history, nor can I believe that a different judgment will be expressed by that of Britain.

When we review the history of the past twelvemonth we cannot fail to be struck with the contrast between the triumphs of war and this triumph of peace. The new empire of Germany has wrested from France and added to its territory two important provinces bordering upon the Rhine; but at what a cost of her best blood, at what a sacrifice of the flower of her population, and with what a sad certainty of the lasting hate of the nation from which these provinces have been severed! On the other hand, her adversary, proud and high-spirited France, has been thrust down into the very pit of humiliation; not only dismembered and weakened, but wasted, smitten with famine, and covered with ruins—the cemeteries of her populous towns, long under the bombs of the German armies, choked with the graves of helpless women and innocent children. As if these horrors were not enough, the people of her magnificent metropolis, when the war with Germany was scarce ended, have risen in revolt against the government of the country and engaged in a murderous civil contest. Ah, Mr. President, if, instead of the news which we now receive through the sheaf of telegraphic wires laid by your enterprise—news of the destruction of the Vendôme Column and other monuments with which the arts have illustrated the history of France—the press could record that the popular fury had turned upon the fortifications of Paris, which make it a vast prison-house and have been the cause of such terrible suffering! Happy would it have been for that country if, at the very moment that the third Napoleon was dethroned, the populace had flung itself on these fatal ramparts with shouts, and levelled them to the ground, as the walls of Geneva were not long since levelled, leaving not one stone upon another! Happy would it have been if that grim circle had been transformed to a park with grassy eminences and sheltered hollows and bowery plantations of trees, where children might sport and lovers walk and friends saunter, and the weary artisan rest and be refreshed with the sweet air and with listening to the breezes among the leaves and the song of birds!

In those triumphs of war to which I have referred, both parties are the losers. In the triumph of peace which we celebrate to-day, both parties are the gainers. The possibility of war between them for causes already existing is done away; rival interests are conciliated, doubtful rights are defined, and the two nations are put each in its own path to prosperity, beyond danger of collision with the other. Mr. President and gentlemen, may their friendly relations be perpetual.

# GERMAN LITERATURE.*

THE toast which has just been given (to the literature of Germany) opens a vast field for remark. I shall hardly venture to enter it; I shall merely peep over its hedge, and so refrain from inflicting upon the patience of this company a tenth part of the tediousness for which the toast gives an opportunity. A most affluent literature is that of Germany; rich in every one of its departments, and great in the influence which it has exerted upon the literature of other countries. I well remember the time—it was in my early youth, almost in my childhood—when a very serious alarm was manifested lest the literature of our own language should become distempered and spoiled by the contagion which threatened it from Germany. The German mind had then just shaken itself free from the fetters of a cold and slavish imitation of French models, and the German authors boldly set up for themselves. Schiller's tragedy of " The Robbers," of which Campbell, in a poem of that day, speaks with so much enthusiasm, had been represented on the English stage, and the blood of large audiences was frozen in their veins. Young maidens were weeping in their closets over Goethe's " Sorrows of Werther." An inferior genius, Kotzebue, had littered a numerous brood of sentimental comedies, which had

---

* Remarks at a dinner given to Baron Gerolt, German ambassador, May 17, 1871.

taken possession of our stage. In narratives and ballads the German authors had made a daring use of the supernatural, in which they were followed, with some exaggeration, by the English author Lewis, in his " Monk," his " Castle Spectre," and "Tales of Wonder." The German metaphysicians had laid before the world a mass of speculations in philosophy of a subtiler nature than had ever before claimed the attention of the world. The German rationalists, learned and persevering, were questioning without reserve a multitude of points of belief which had hitherto been held with undoubting reverence. All these symptoms created a certain uneasiness and anxiety for the final result, as I remember, both in England and here, and called forth a good deal not only of criticism but of ridicule.

But this anxiety gradually wore away. Schiller and Goethe produced nobler works, grew to be great men, and took their exalted stations in the temple of fame. Kotzebue in due time was forgotten. The ballads of Schiller and Goethe and Bürger were found to be among the most exquisite things of their kind ever written. Our metaphysicians welcomed the impulse which they received from those of Germany, and walked with delight in the dim mazes of the new fields which they opened. If the rationalists in theology found their weapons of attack in German authors, there were German authors on the other side who supplied as largely the weapons of defence. The Germans were acknowledged as the most profound inquirers into ancient history, the most acute and erudite philologists, and in classical literature to have no rivals. The poets of our own language who introduced a new era of poetical literature— Wordsworth and Coleridge, Southey and Scott—drank deeply at the German fountains.

Great poets, pre-eminent in their class, like Goethe and Schiller, may be compared, in the universality of their reception by mankind, to the main ocean, which connects with each other all the shores of the earth—its continents and its brood of islands—holding them all in its mighty embrace. Over it passes the commerce of the world, the beneficent exchange of commodities between nation and nation. Its ports run up into every land; it receives the water of a thousand rivers, the cold streams of northern latitudes, the warm floods of the tropics, tributes from the Alps and the Andes, from the Rocky Mountains and the Mountains of the Moon. The icebergs of the Pole drift over it to dissolve in the waters of the Gulf Stream. On its surface the swift steamers are shooting from land to land, and deep in its bosom lies the electric wire of Morse, which conveys with the speed of light, from zone to zone, tidings of peace and war, of the deliberations of senates and the edicts of monarchs, of empires overthrown and empires founded, and of the fate of ancient hierarchies in their struggle with the youthful spirit of the age.

Like this in their connection with the people of all countries are the poets who stand at the head of their class. Schiller has somewhere said that the poet is a citizen of the world. The greater ones are certainly and emphatically so. Their works speak to the human heart everywhere; their voice is heard from age to age; their fame is the common property of mankind; their writings are among the ties that bind the tribes of men in a common brotherhood. How many have studied English that they may read Shakespeare in the original! How many have learned German that they may enjoy the writings of Goethe! How decidedly have the plays of Schiller, naturalized in all countries, communicated their own character to the dramatic literature of the age! Into how many languages have the dramas of Shakespeare been translated, and how many times into the same language? The Germans have translated him the most perfectly of all. How many attempts have been made to transfuse the poetry of Goethe into the words and phrases of our own tongue, and make the poet of Weimar speak English! One such has just been made, with signal success, by an eminent poet of our republic, who, in translating the grandest of all extravaganzas, "Faust," has even adventured upon the second part, and admirably acquitted himself there, having found his way to daylight out of that mysterious labyrinth. Another American had previously translated with skill and spirit the first part, and both are proud to be the interpreters of Goethe to their countrymen. With two such splendid illustrations of my remarks, furnished by these authors, I could not more fortunately conclude.

# DARWIN'S THEORY.*

It is a good while since the remark was made by an English wit that he did not like to look at monkeys, they seemed to him so much like poor relations. What was regarded at that time as a clever jest has since been taken by an eminent naturalist as the basis of an extensive system which professes to account for the origin of the human species. According to this system, man is an improved monkey, and the lowest form of animal life is found in a minute animated cell. A number of these cells come casually together and form a dab of jelly fixed on a crag in the ocean. They somehow become arranged in a sort of symmetry; they gradually acquire organs; they rise to the dignity of oysters and mussels; the weak are weeded out by a principle of natural selection; others rise higher and higher in the scale of being; they become quadrupeds; they crawl out upon the land; they waddle on the shore in shape of seals; they build houses as beavers; they climb trees as squirrels; their talons and paws become hands furnished with fingers, and we have the monkey; the monkey acquires the faculty of speech, and matures into a man. It is the old theory of Monboddo propounded a hundred years ago, but spread over a larger surface and set forth with new illustrations.

But allowing all that Darwin says of the consanguinity

---

* Remarks at Williams College Alumni Dinner, December 28, 1871.

of man and of the inferior animals, admitting that we are of the same flesh and blood as the baboon and the rat, where does he find his proof that we are improving instead of degenerating? He claims that man is an improved monkey; how does he know that the monkey is not a degenerate man, a decayed branch of the human family, fallen away from the high rank he once held, and haunted by a dim sentiment of his lost dignity, as we may infer from his melancholy aspect? Improvement, Mr. President and gentlemen, implies effort: it is up-hill work; degeneracy is easy: it asks only neglect, indolence, inaction. How often do the descendants of illustrious men become the most stupid of the human race! How many are there, each of whom we may call

"The tenth transmitter of a foolish face!"

—a line of Savage, the best he ever wrote, worth all his other verses put together—

"The tenth transmitter of a foolish face"—

and that face growing more and more foolish from generation to generation. I might instance the Bourbon family, lately reigning in Spain and Naples. I might instance the royal family of Austria. There is a whole nation, millions upon millions—our Chinese neighbors—of whom the better opinion is that they have been going backward in civilization from century to century. Perhaps they wear the pigtail as an emblem of what they are all coming to some thousands of years hence. How, then, can Mr. Darwin insist that if we admit the near kindred of man to the inferior animals we must believe that our progress has been upward, and that the nobler animals are the progeny of the inferior? Is not the contrary the more probable? Is it not more likely that the more easy downward road has been taken, that the lower animals are derived from some degenerate branch of the human race, and that, if we do not labor to keep the rank we hold, our race may be frittered away into the meaner tribes of animals, and finally into animalculæ? Then may our Tweeds become the progenitors of those skulking thieves of the western wilds, the prairie-wolves, or swim stagnant pools in the shape of horse-leeches; our astute lawyers may be represented by foxes, our great architects by colonies of beavers, our poets by clouds of mosquitoes, famished and musical; our doctors of divinity—I say it with all respect for the cloth—by swarms of the mantis, or praying insect, always in the attitude of devotion. If we hold to Darwin's theory—as I do not—how are we to know that the vast multitudes of men and women on the earth are not the ruins, so to speak, of some nobler species, with more elevated and perfect faculties, mental, physical, and moral, but now extinct?

Let me say, then, to those who believe in the relationship of the animal tribes, that it behooves them to avoid the danger which I have pointed out by giving a generous support to those institutions of wholesome learning, like Williams College, designed to hold us back from the threatened degeneracy of which there are fearful protents abroad—portents of moral degeneracy at least. Let them move before we begin to squeak like bats or gibber like apes; before that mark of the brute, the tail, has sprouted, or, at least, while it is in the tender germ, the mere bud, giving but a faint and distinct promise of what it may become when the owner shall coil its extremity around the horizontal branch of a tree and swing himself by it from one trunk of the forest to another. If any one here be conscious of but a friendly leaning to the monkey theory, let him contribute liberally to the fund for putting up a building where the students of Williams College can be cheaply boarded; if the taint have struck deeper, let him found a scholarship; if he have fully embraced the theory, let him, at any sacrifice, found a professorship, and then, although his theory may be wrong, his practice in this instance will be worthy of universal commendation.

# MUNICIPAL REFORM.*

I AM glad, my fellow-citizens, to see that this occasion has
brought so many of you together. It is not for any narrow
party purpose that we are assembled; it is not that we may
consult how to advance the interests of a popular favorite and
his associates; it is not to pull down his rival and the set of
men by whom his rival is supported. It is by a higher and
nobler motive that you are animated, one in which all honest
men necessarily concur—the wish to secure to the State, and
to all the smaller communities of which the State is made up,
the benefits of a just, honest, economical, and, in all respects,
wise administration of public affairs. You could hardly come
together for a more worthy purpose.

It seems an idle remark, because it is perfectly obvious,
that the great mass of the people have no interest in being
badly governed, but that, on the contrary, their interest lies in
committing their public affairs to men who will manage them
honestly and frugally. It is the great mass who suffer when
rapacious and knavish men obtain authority and power. The
robbers are the few; the robbed are the many. If the many
would only come to a mutual understanding and act together,
the robbers would never obtain public office, or, if by accident
they obtained it, would be thrust out the first opportunity. In

---

* An address delivered at a meeting held in the Cooper Institute, September 23,
1872.

these matters concert of action is everything, and the rogues know it. As long as the opposition to their designs is divided into many little minorities, they laugh at it. High-handed villany takes its adversaries, one after another, by the throat, and strangles them in detail. An army scattered is an army defeated. It has passed into a proverb that in union there is strength; it is just as true that in division there is weakness, and there are none who know this better than the knaves who enrich themselves by plundering the public.

The material world abounds with instances of the power obtained by the combination of forces. I came a few days since from a rural neighborhood which a few weeks before had been visited by a shower of rain more copious and violent than any living person remembered. In two hours the roads leading down the hills were ploughed by it into deep channels for the torrents, and rendered impassable; bridges were swept away; huge stones were rolled down before the waters; and beds of soil, sand, gravel, pebbles, and fragments of rock were borne along from field to field and found new owners. Yet this sudden flood was composed of single drops of rain, each one of which, as it reached the earth, had not force enough to displace the smallest pebble. It was combination, it was concert of action, it was organization, that gave them their fearful power. The drops were gathered into rills, the rills into streams, the streams into torrents. By union they became terrible; by union they were made irresistible; and all that man could do was to look on till their work was done.

Just as irresistible, and just as sure to accomplish their work, will be the men whose interest it is that public affairs shall be frugally and wisely administered, if they can only be brought to combine with one purpose and one system of action. To promote this end we are assembled this evening. Let me not be told that if we keep one set of rogues out of office another will be sure to have their place. That is the moral of an old fable of Æsop, but the moral is a false one. You remember the ingenious parable: A fox among the reeds of a stream was tormented by gnats. A swallow, I think it was, saw his distress, and offered to drive them away. "Do not," said the fox, "for, if you drive these away, a hungrier swarm will come in their place and drain my veins of their last drop of blood." But, my friends, all that I infer from this fable is that official corruption is more than two thousand years old, at least. The lesson which this fable seems to inculcate— that they who plunder the public should not be molested in their guilty work—is absurd. There are in the community men whom you know to be absolutely honest, men of proved integrity, and all that you have to do is to agree upon such men as your candidates for office, and the public interest is safe. Let me relate for your encouragement what has already been done in this city.

It was about forty years ago—when many who now do me the honor of listening to me were in their cradles, but I will not be certain as to the year—that the people of this city of New York were very much dissatisfied with their Common Council, which was then composed of a single board, the Aldermen. Some of the Aldermen had grown rich while in office. They knew sooner than other persons where new streets were to be laid out, and they purchased lands contiguous to those streets, which they afterward sold at a large advance. One of the Aldermen owned a country seat at the northern extremity of the Third Avenue, and through his influence a great deal of money was expended upon that thoroughfare, making it as hard as a rock, and so smooth and even that, as I heard a gentleman say at the time, there was not on its whole surface a hollow deep enough to hold a pint of water. These now seem small offences, which, compared with the crimes of Tweed and his set, almost whiten into perfect innocence ; yet the people of that day were discontented, and declared that they wanted men in office who thought only of the public good. So we all went to work and elected a Common Council of honest men, in spite of Æsop and his fable. Let me name some of them : There was Stephen Allen, the very impersonation of downright honesty. There was Myndert Van Schaick, wholly incorruptible and devoted to the public interest. There was Dr. McNevin, too much taken up with science to think of making money. There was Dr. Augustine Smith, who brought to the tasks of his office large knowledge and an integrity beyond question. There were other men in the Common Council worthy by their character to be the associates of these, and there was no complaint of corruption or malversation of any sort in our municipal affairs. We were all proud of our Common Council. It was an honor to belong to such a body of men. I doubt whether the affairs of any municipality since the time of the elder Cato have ever been administered by men so virtuous and intelligent as those to whom I have referred. It was only by slow gradations, and after many years, that our municipal affairs lapsed into that frightful state from which we are now seeking effectually to reclaim them.

This, fellow-citizens, was what we did forty years ago, and something like this, if by the blessing of God we can act heartily and vigorously in concert, we may do now.

# LITERARY MISSIONARIES.*

It is my office this evening to introduce to this audience, which I am glad to see so numerous, a native of the British Islands, a kinsman of ours by race, whose comments on a great work of the greatest poet of modern times we have not only come to hear, but whose own character and genius we are assembled to honor. For, greatly as we admire his genius, we no less admire the noble purposes in which it has employed itself. In one of his poems Walter Scott has said that Dryden "profaned his God-given strength." The countryman of Scott who addresses us to-night has hallowed his God-given strength by putting it under the direction of the most generous aims— by using it in the grand endeavor to make his fellow-men better and happier. It is not as the mere contributor to our entertainment that we admire him; we reverence him as a benefactor of mankind.

When I think of the eminent persons who of late have visited our continent from the British Islands, with the view of addressing our public assemblies, my mind is carried forward to a state of things which in future years will be almost certain to result from the relations borne to each other by the different regions in which our language is spoken. In the early times of Greece, at the very birth of Greek literature, when

---

* From remarks at a lecture of George MacDonald on "Hamlet," introducing the lecturer, New York, 1872.

that remarkable people, the Greek race, were scattered in cities on almost every coast of the Mediterranean and on all its isles, they acknowledged the bond of a common language, and regarded each other as brethren.   Before the use of letters had become common, a tribe of minstrels had arisen, who journeyed by land and sea, from coast to coast, from isle to isle, wherever the Hellenic stock had planted its colonies, and sang the traditions of the past, delighting vast multitudes with recitals of wonderful adventure, and examples of heroism, and love of country.   These were the lecturers of those early days. Something like this, although on a vaster scale, is beginning to result from the wide dispersion of that branch of the human family the language of whose firesides is English.   As the different communities, which they have planted on different continents and islands, in different belts of latitude, and under different constellations, become great and populous and advance in civilization, their eminent men—their expounders of the laws of universal nature, their reconcilers of apparently discordant truths, their teachers of human duty, their inquirers into the traditions of the past—will go forth to stand before vast audiences, in regions distant by a whole hemisphere from that in which they themselves were trained, and speak to hushed thousands concerning subjects to which they have given the study of their lives.   Then will the native of Vancouver's Island address the assembled men and women of Australia, and the chemist of Nova Scotia will perform his brilliant experiments  before audiences at the Cape of Good Hope. The people of these regions will demand the corporeal presence of those whose renown fills the circle of the  globe, and, by the aid of even more rapid  means of communication  than we now enjoy, the call will be obeyed.

# SHAKESPEARE.*

In a part of this republic, which within a few years has been added to our Union, lying between the Rocky Mountains and the western sea, are yet standing a few groves of a peculiar kind of tree, prodigious in height and bulk, and seemingly produced by nature to show mankind to what size a tree can attain in a favorable soil and a congenial climate, with no enemy to lay the axe to its root. The earth, in its most fertile spots, in its oldest forests, and under its mildest skies, has nothing like them—no stems of such vast dimensions, no summits towering so high and casting their shadows so far, putting forth their new leaves and ripening their seed-vessels in the region of the clouds. The traveller who enters these mighty groves almost expects to see some huge son of Anak stalking in the broad alleys between their gigantic trunks, or some mammoth or mastodon browsing on the lower branches.

So it is with those great minds which the Maker of all sometimes sends upon the earth and among mankind, as if to show us of what vast enlargement the faculties of the human intellect are capable, if but rarely in this stage of our being, yet at least in that which follows the present life, when the imperfections and infirmities of the material frame, which is now the dwelling of the spirit, shall neither clog its motions

---

* From an address on the unveiling of Shakespeare's statue in the Central Park, May 22, 1872.

nor keep back its growth. Such a great mind was that of Shakespeare. An imagination so creative, a reason so vigorous, a wisdom so clear and comprehensive, taking views of life and character and duty so broad and just and true, a spirit so fiery and at the same time so gentle, such acuteness of observation and such power of presenting to other minds what is observed—such a combination of qualities seems to afford us, as we contemplate it, a glimpse of what, in certain respects, the immortal part of man shall be when every cause that dims its vision, or weakens its energy, or fetters its activity, or checks its expansion shall be wholly done away, and that subtiler essence shall be left to the full and free exercise of the powers with which God endowed it.

It has occurred to me, in thinking what I should say at this time, that the writings of Shakespeare contained proofs that, if he had but given his attention to the work of preparing for usefulness and distinction in other pursuits than that in which he acquired his fame, he might have achieved in some of them a renown almost equal to that which attends his dramatic writings. The dramatic poet, who puts into the mouths of personages whom he would represent as great beyond the common stature of greatness words and sentiments corresponding to their exalted character, must, in order to do this, possess an intellectual character somewhat like theirs, must in some sort partake of their greatness. I wonder not, therefore, that some, who have insisted that Shakespeare did not write the plays attributed to him, should, in searching for the true author, have fixed upon Lord Bacon, finding in them passages which may be plausibly referred to the father of modern philosophy and the most profound jurist of his age. I do not accept their theory, but I say to myself, when I read what they have quoted from his writings in support of it: "What a giant among philosophers was lost in this dramatic poet! what an able jurist and legislator allowed the faculties which would have made him such to slumber while he employed himself in writing for the stage!"

So, when I read the passages gathered from his plays to show that Shakespeare anticipated Harvey in his knowledge of the circulation of the blood in its channels through the animal frame, my reflection is that here was an embryo physiologist, endowed beyond his fellow-men with an instinctive perception of the interior mechanism of the human body, and the power of detecting its subtile workings, hidden from man for so many ages from the birth of our species. Not the less, nay, perhaps still more remarkable, was the insight of Shakespeare into the different, even the most subtile, forms of mental distemperature, an insight shown in his portraiture of the madness of Hamlet, that of Ophelia, and that of King Lear—all how distinctly drawn, yet each how diverse from the others! What a physician might he not have made to an insane asylum! How tenderly and how wisely might he not have ministered to the mind diseased—he who so shrewdly traced its wanderings and was so touched with a feeling of its infirmities! How gently might he not have led it away from its illusions and guided it back to sanity!

Moreover, if Shakespeare had worn the clerical gown, what a preacher of righteousness he would have become, and how admirably and impressively he would have enforced the lessons of human life!—he who put into the mouth of Cardinal Wolsey the pathetic words:

> " Had I but served my God with half the zeal
> I served my king, he would not in mine age
> Have left me naked to mine enemies."

I am sure that, if those who deny to Shakespeare the credit of writing his own dramas had thought of ascribing them to the judicious Hooker or to the pious Bishop Andrews instead of to Lord Bacon, they might have made a specious show of proof by carefully culled extracts from his writings. Nay, if Jeremy Taylor, whose prose is so full of poetry, had not been born a generation too late, I would engage, in the same way, to put a plausible face on the theory that the plays of Shakespeare, except, perhaps, some passages wickedly interpolated, were composed by the eloquent and devout author of "Holy Living and Dying."

The fame of our great dramatist fills the civilized world. Among the poets he is what the cataract of Niagara is among waterfalls. As those who cannot take the journey to Niagara, that they may behold its vast breadth of green waters plunging from the lofty precipice into the abyss below, content themselves with such an idea of its majesty and beauty as they can obtain from a picture or an engraving, so those who cannot enjoy the writings of Shakespeare in the original English, read him in translations, which have the effect of looking at a magnificent landscape through a morning mist. All languages have their versions of Shakespeare. The most eminent men of genius in Germany have been his translators or commentators. In France they began by sneering at him with Voltaire, and they end by regarding him in a transport of wonder with Taine. He stands before them like a mighty mountain, filling with its vastness half the heavens, its head in an eternally serene atmosphere, while on its sides burrow the fox and the marmot, and tangled thickets obstruct the steps of the climber. The French critic, while amazed at the grandeur and variety of its forms, cannot help suffering his attention to wander to the ant-heaps and mole-holes scattered on its broad flanks.

To the great chorus of admiration which rises from all civilized nations we this day add our voices as we erect to the memory of Shakespeare, in a land distant from that of his birth, yet echoing through its vast extent with the accents of his mother-tongue, the effigy of his bodily form and features. Those who profess to read in the aspect of the individual the qualities of his intellectual and moral character, have always delighted to trace in the face, of which we this day unveil an image to the public gaze, the manifest signs of his greatness. Read what Lavater wrote a hundred years since, and you shall see that he discovers in this noble countenance a promise of

all that the critic finds in his writings. Come down to the
phrenologists of the present day, and they tell you of the visi-
ble indications of his boundless invention, his universal sympa-
thy, his lofty idealism, his wit, his humor, his imagination, and
every other faculty that conspired to produce his matchless
works.

This counterfeit presentment of the outward form of Shake-
speare we offer to-day to the public of New York as an orna-
ment of the beautiful pleasure-ground in which they take so
just a pride. It has been cast in bronze, a material indestructi-
ble by time, in the hope that perchance it may last as long as
his writings. It is nobly executed by the artist, and with a
deep feeling of the greatness of his subject. One profound
regret saddens this ceremony—that our friend Hackett, who
was foremost in procuring this expression of our homage to
the memory of Shakespeare, is not with us, but sleeps with
the great author whose writings he loved and studied, and in-
terpreted both to the ear and the eye.

The spot in which this statue is placed will henceforth be
associated with numberless ideas and images called up to the
mind of the visitor by the name of Shakespeare. To all whose
imagination is easily kindled into activity it will seem forever
haunted by the personages whom he created and who live in
his dramas: the grave magician Prospero and his simple-
hearted daughter Miranda, and his dainty spirit Ariel, the
white-haired Lear and the loving Cordelia, the jealous Moor
and the gentle Desdemona, Imogen and Rosalind, and the ma-
jestic shadow of Coriolanus. Before the solitary passer-by
will rise the burly figure of the merry knight, Falstaff, and
round about this statue will flit the slight forms of Slender
and Shallow and Dogberry. To those who chance to tread
these walks by moonlight, the ghost of the royal Dane may
shape itself from the vapors of the night and again dis-
appear. But may the sound of battle never be heard here,
nor the herbage be trampled by the rude heel of the popu-
lace in its fury to disturb the fairy court of Oberon and

Titania, and scare the little people from their dances on the greensward.

To memories and associations like these we devote this spot from henceforth and forever.

．　　．　　．　　．　　．　　．　　．　　．

SHAKESPEARE, though he cannot be called an American poet, as he was not born here and never saw our continent, is yet a poet of the Americans. It will be granted that, if all the English were to migrate to some other region, and the French were to come in and occupy their place, Shakespeare could by no means be called a French poet, but would, by the justest title, belong to the race which had migrated. By parity of reasoning, if only a part of the English race migrate, they carry with them not only their language but its literature; they carry with them the poets who flourished before their migration, and who are as truly theirs as they are the poets of those who remain. Shakespeare died while the colonists of Jamestown, Virginia, were building their cabins; he died seven years before the first white child was born on the island now covered with the dwellings of this great city; he died four years before the landing of the pilgrims on the Plymouth Rock. We Americans may therefore claim an equal property in the great English poet with those who remained in the Old World—with you, Mr. President, and you, gentlemen, natives of the British Isles.

It is common to speak of the blood of the ancestor as flowing in the veins of his descendants, and the expression has a certain truth in it. The tissues of the brain, the seat of wit and of imagination, are woven of fibres lent by our progenitors. The generation which now walks the stage of the world is the reproduction, the re-entrance, in a certain sort, of the generation which has made its exit. The blood that now warms American hearts and gushes through American arteries was once—nearly three hundred years ago, when it ran in the veins of our ancestors in the Old World, and while Shakespeare was yet alive—made to tingle by his potent words. It coursed slowly or swiftly through its purple channels at the will of that great master of the passions. It was quickened and made to glow with indignation at the conduct of Lear's ungrateful daughters; it curdled and was chilled at the sight of the ghost of the royal Dane, and of the sleep-walking murderess in "Macbeth"; it was resolved to tears at the fate of the innocent Desdemona. What American, therefore, who is willing to acknowledge that his ancestors came from the Old World, will fail to claim Shakespeare as his own poet?

It is fortunate that we have in our literature writings of such superlative excellence, so universally read and studied, and, by the exercise of memory, so incorporated into our own minds, as the dramas of Shakespeare. They keep alive the connection between the present and the remote past, and stay the hurrying process of change in certain respects in which change is undesirable. Language is an unstable thing, and, like everything dependent on usage, tends to constant variation; but this tendency has no advantage save as it is demanded by the introduction of new ideas. There are critics who affirm that the English language reached its perfection of expressiveness and copiousness in the time of Queen Elizabeth, and whoever reads the authors of that age will see little cause to wonder at this opinion. Let us congratulate ourselves that we have such an author as Shakespeare, so admired, so loved, to protect our noble language against the capricious innovations of those who read only the authors of yesterday, and that, by dwelling upon what he wrote, the speech of the master minds of his age continues familiar to our ears. There is yet another advantage—that, by tending to preserve the identity of language in regions remote from each other where English is spoken, it keeps alive the remembrance of kindred and brotherhood, and multiplies the pledges of amity and peace between the nations.*

---

\* From a speech made at the annual dinner of the St. George's Society, April 23, 1870.

THE toast is Shakespeare; and what a host of recollections is called up by that name—associations connected not only with the marvellous works which Shakespeare has left us, but with the great men who lived in his time! For that age produced in England men of towering intellect. There were giants in those days—Bacon, the prince of philosophers; Sir Walter Raleigh, eminent as a navigator, a commander, and an author; Sir Philip Sidney, of whom Hallam has said that he was the first writer of good prose in our language; Sir Thomas Moore, great in jurisprudence; Spenser, illustrious in poetry—a host of eminent divines and a galaxy of dramatic authors such as England has not seen since.

Naturalists tell us that in the acorn lie folded and wrapped up the embryos of thousands, nay, millions, of trees, every acorn being a possible tree, with a sturdy stem and wide-spreading branches, and the power of indefinite multiplication, by means of successive harvests of acorns trom year to year. So that in the little cup and ball which you hold in your hand you grasp the mighty forests of future years, tall and wide enough to cover the earth, majestic groves of such extent as to clothe every mountain-side, darken every valley, embower every river, and overhang every sea-coast. So it is with the generation which produced Shakespeare, glorious Shakespeare, master of the passions, with uncontrolled dominion over hope and fear, pity and terror, and endowed from above with a double portion of the creative power. In his time we were all in Europe—all of us; the millions who now inhabit our swarming cities, dig in our rich mines, till our broad valleys, navigate our great rivers and lakes, or, to come nearer, build our public edifices, paint our pictures, and spin our verses—all wrapped up in that generation of the Old World which laughed the first laugh at Falstaff's wit, and shed the first tears drawn from men's eyes by the fate of Desdemona. Who, then, shall deny to us born in this hemisphere a share in the glory of those who claim Shakespeare as their country-man?

I have sometimes fancied what would become of Shake-speare and his renown in case the Darwinian theory of the origin of races should hold good, which I by no means ad-mit, and, through the process of evolution and the survival of the fittest, a race of beings should arise on the earth, while man is yet upon it, as much superior to man as man is supe-rior to the monkey. Then will happen what was imagined by Pope and expressed by him in these well-known lines:

> "Superior beings, when, of late, they saw
> A mortal man unfolding nature's law,
> Admired such wisdom in an earthly shape,
> And showed a Newton as we show an ape."

Suppose that a genius like Shakespeare should at that time remain on the earth—a man endowed with like eminent gifts of mind—what will the superior race of those days do with a creature as much below them in the scale of intellect as a very intelligent monkey is below the race of human kind? This specimen of humanity in its perfection would, of course, be led about by a chain and made to exhibit himself—perform his tricks, they would probably phrase it—for the entertainment of those whose captive and drudge he would be. We might then imagine them to say to him: "Come, Shakespeare, let us have Hamlet's soliloquy," or something to that effect. "Very fine for a beast!" would they exclaim who witnessed the ex-hibition; "very clever indeed!" And then a scene from the "Merry Wives of Windsor," or its equivalent; and, after the spectators were weary of the sport, the captive would be led off to be fed or to sleep in his kennel.

But in the mean time, while we are waiting for this consum-mation, while the parts or particles which by force of natural selection are getting ready to form themselves into the more perfect race of future times, let us continue to delight in

Shakespeare as we have him—the poet eminent beyond all other poets, and not likely to be surpassed while the human race retains its present rank on the earth, and man is still what another poet has called him—" Lord of the fowl and the brute." *

---

* From a later speech before the St. George's Society.

# SIR WALTER SCOTT.*

THE Scottish residents of this city, whose public spirit and reverence for genius have moved them to present to the people of New York the statue of their countryman which has just now been unveiled to the public gaze, have honored me with a request that I should so far take part in these ceremonies as to speak a few words concerning the great poet and novelist, of whose renown they are so justly proud.

As I look round on this assembly I perceive few persons of my own age—few who can remember, as I can, the rising and setting of this brilliant luminary of modern literature. I well recollect the time when Scott, then thirty-four years of age, gave to the world his " Lay of the Last Minstrel," the first of his works which awakened the enthusiastic admiration that afterward attended all he wrote. In that poem the spirit of the old Scottish ballads—the most beautiful of their class—lived again. In it we had all their fire, their rapid narrative, their unlabored graces, their pathos, animating a story to which he had given a certain epic breadth and unity. We read with scarcely less delight his poem of " Marmion," and soon afterward the youths and maidens of our country hung with rapture over the pages of his " Lady of the Lake." I need not enumerate his other poems, but this I will say of them

---

* An address on the unveiling of the statue of Sir Walter Scott, in Central Park, November 4, 1872.

all, that no other metrical narratives in our language seem to me to possess an equal power of enchaining the attention of the reader, and carrying him on from incident to incident with such entire freedom from weariness. These works, printed in cheap editions, were dispersed all over our country; they found their way to almost every fireside, and their popularity raised up, both here and in Great Britain, a multitude of imitators now forgotten.

This power over the mind of the reader was soon to be exemplified in a more remarkable manner, and when, at the age of forty-three, Scott gave to the world, without any indication of its authorship, his romance of "Waverley," all perceived that a new era in the literature of fiction had begun. "Here," they said, "is a genius of a new order. What wealth of materials, what free mastery in moulding them into shape, what invention, humor, pathos, vivid portraiture of character—nothing overcharged or exaggerated, yet all distinct, spirited, and lifelike! Are we not," they asked, "to have other works by the same hand?"

The desire thus expressed was soon gratified. The expected romances came forth with a rapidity which amazed their readers. Some, it is true, ascribed them to Scott as the only man who could write them. "It cannot be," said others; "Scott is occupied with writing histories and poems, and editing work after work which require great labor and research; he has no time for writing romances like these." So he went on, throwing off these remarkable works as if the writing of them had been but a pastime, and fairly bombarding the world with romances from his mysterious covert. It was like what in the neighborhood of this city we see on a fine evening of the Fourth of July, when rocket after rocket rises from the distant horizon and bursts in the air, throwing off to right and left jets of flame and fireballs of every brilliant hue, yet whose are the hands that launch them we know not. So we read and wondered, and lost ourselves in conjectures as to the author who ministered to our delight; and, when at length, at a public dinner in the year 1827, Scott avowed himself to be the sole author of the " Waverley Novels," the interest which we felt at this disclosure was hardly less than that with which we heard of the issue of the great battle of Waterloo.

I have seen a design by some artist in which Scott is shown surrounded by the personages whom in his poems and romances he called into being. They formed a vast crowd, face beyond face, each with its characteristic expression—a multitude so great that it reminded me of the throng—the cloud I may call it—of cherubim which in certain pictures on the walls of European churches surround the Virgin Mother. For forty years has Scott lain in his grave, and now his countrymen place in this park an image of the noble brow, so fortunately copied by the artist, beneath which the personages of his imagination grew into being. Shall we say *grew*, as if they sprang up spontaneously in his mind, like plants from a fruitful soil, while his fingers guided the pen that noted down their words and recorded their acts? Or should we imagine the faculties of his mind to have busied themselves at his bidding in the chambers of that active brain, and gradually to have moulded the characters of his wonderful fictions to their perfect form? At all events, let us say that He who breathed the breath of life into the frame of which a copy is before us, imparted with that breath a portion of his own creative power.

And now, as the statue of Scott is set up in this beautiful park, which a few years since possessed no human associations historical or poetic connected with its shades, its lawns, its rocks, and its waters, these grounds become peopled with new memories. Henceforth the silent earth at this spot will be eloquent of old traditions, the airs that stir the branches of the trees will whisper of feats of chivalry to the visitor. All that vast crowd of ideal personages created by the imagination of Scott will enter with his sculptured effigy and remain—Fergus and Flora MacIvor, Meg Merrilies and Dirk Hatteraik, the Antiquary and his Sister, and Edie Ochiltree, Rob Roy and

Helen Macgregor, and Baillie Jarvie and Dandie Dinmont, and Diana Vernon and Old Mortality—but the night would be upon us before I could go through the muster-roll of this great army. They will pass in endless procession around the statue of him in whose prolific brain they had their birth, until the language which we speak shall perish, and the spot on which we stand shall be again a woodland wilderness.

# ROBERT BURNS.*

THIS evening the memory of Burns will be celebrated as it never was before. His fame, from the time when he first appeared before the world as a poet, has been growing and brightening, as the morning brightens into the perfect day. There never was a time when his merits were so freely acknowledged as now; when the common consent of the literary world placed him so high, or spoke his praises with so little intermixture of disparagement; when the anniversary of his birth could have awakened so general and fervent an enthusiasm.

If we could imagine a human being endowed with the power of making himself, through the medium of his senses, a witness of whatever is passing on the face of the globe, what a series of festivities, what successive manifestations of the love and admiration which all who speak our language bear

---

* Mr. Bryant was almost invariably a guest at the annual festivals of the Burns Club, of New York, and was quite as invariably called upon to say a word in honor of the national poet. He once gave as a reason for attending these festivals the fact that he had Scotch blood in his veins. " Some hundred and fifty years since," he said, " there came from Scotland to this country a young man of the name of Keith, educated at Marechal College, Aberdeen, who for more than fifty years was pastor of a New England church, dying at a good old age, and leaving many descendants. Him I claim as an ancestor of my family ; but this is a slender foundation on which to build a title to be heard in response to a toast in honor of the prince of Scottish poets. It is much as if the keeper of an apple-stall in the street should think, with a capital of ten dollars saved by his vocation, to set up as an importer of cargoes of fruit from the West Indies.

" From distinguished literary men of that country to whom I was not personally

to the great Scottish poet, would present themselves to his observation, accompanying the shadow of this night in its cir- cuit round the earth ! Some twelve hours before this time he would have heard the praises of Burns sung on the banks of the Ganges—the music flowing out of the open windows on the soft evening air of that region and mingling with the murmurs of the sacred river. A little later, he might have heard the same sounds from the mouth of the Euphrates ; later still, from the southern extremity of Africa, under constella- tions strange to our eyes—the stars of the southern hemi- sphere—and almost at the same moment from the rocky shores of the Ionian Islands. Next they would have been heard from the orange-groves of Malta, and from the winter colony of English and Americans on the banks of the Tiber. Then, in its turn, the Seine takes up the strain ; and what a chorus rises from the British Isles—from every ocean-mart and river and mountain-side, with a distant response from the rocks of Gib- raltar ! Last, in the Old World, on its westernmost verge, the observer whom I have imagined would have heard the voice of song and of gladness from the coasts of Liberia and Sierra Leone, among a race constitutionally and passionately fond of music, and to which we have given our language and litera- ture.

In the New World, frozen Newfoundland has already led in

---

known I have received particular kindness. Many years since, various kind mes- sages were conveyed to me from the poet Thomas Campbell. When, more than thirty years since, a volume of my verses was published here, it came into the hands of Professor John Wilson, who did it the honor to notice it at great length in ' Blackwood's Magazine,' with liberal extracts, accompanied with comments of so eu- logistic a character that I am almost ashamed to refer to them. Nor should I fail to mention that the residents in this country of Scottish birth have, during our late fear- ful Civil War, stood firmly and unflinchingly by the Union and the Constitution, aided manfully in putting down the rebellion, and resolutely discountenanced the wicked doctrine of secession, which would make an anarchy of the best government. Still less can I forget that some of the most distinguished commanders in the war bear Scottish names, and that the great general whose mind conceived the series of mili- tary operations by which the rebellion was suppressed, and whose skill carried them into successful operation, was of Scotch descent."

the festival of this night ; and next, those who dwell where the St. Lawrence holds an icy mirror to the stars ; thence it has passed to the hills and valleys of New England ; and now it is our turn, on the lordly Hudson. The Schuylkill will follow, the Potomac, the rivers of the Carolinas ; the majestic St. John's, drawing his dark, deep waters from the Everglades ; the borders of our mighty lakes, the beautiful Ohio, the great Mississippi, with its fountains gushing under fields of snow, and its mouth among flowers that fear not the frost.    Then will our festival, in its westward course, cross the Rocky Mountains and gather in joyous assemblies those who pasture their herds on the Columbia and those who dig for gold on the Sacramento.

By a still longer interval, it will pass to Australia, lying in her distant solitude of waters, and now glowing with the heats of midsummer, where, I feel, the zealous countrymen of Burns will find the short night of the season too short for their festivities.    And thus will this commemoration pursue the sunset round the globe, and follow the journey of the evening star till that gentle planet shines on the waters of China.

Well has our great poet deserved this universal commemoration—for who has written like him ?  What poem descriptive of rural manners and virtues, rural life in its simplicity and dignity—yet without a single false outline or touch of false coloring—clings to our memories and lives in our bosoms like his " Cotter's Saturday Night"?  What humorous narrative in verse can be compared with his " Tam o' Shanter"?  From the fall of Adam to his time, I believe, there was nothing written in the vein of his " Mountain Daisy "; others have caught his spirit from that poem, but who among them all has excelled him?  Of all the convivial songs I have ever seen in any language, there is none so overflowing with the spirit of mirth, so joyous, so contagious, as his song of " Willie brewed a Peck o' Maut."  What love-songs are sweeter and tenderer than those of Burns?  What song addresses itself so movingly to our love of old friends and our pleasant recollections of old

days as his "Auld Lang Syne," or to the domestic affections
so powerfully as his "John Anderson"?

You heard yesterday, my friends, and will hear again to-
night, better things said of the genius of Burns than I can say.
That will be your gain and mine. But there is one observation
which, if I have not already tried your patience too far, I
would ask your leave to make. If Burns was thus great
among poets, it was not because he stood higher than they by
any pre-eminence of a creative and fertile imagination. Origi-
nal, affluent, and active his imagination certainly was, and it
was always kept under the guidance of a masculine and vigor-
ous understanding; but it is the feeling which lives in his
poems that gives them their supreme mastery over the minds
of men.

Burns was thus great because, whatever may have been
the errors of his after-life, when he came from the hand that
formed him—I say it with the profoundest reverence—God
breathed into him, in larger measure than into other men, the
spirit of that love which constitutes his own essence, and made
him more than other men—a living soul. Burns was made
by the greatness of his sympathies—sympathies acute and deli-
cate, yet large, comprehensive, boundless. They were warm-
est and strongest toward those of his own kind, yet they over-
flowed upon all sentient beings—upon the animals in his stall;
upon the "wee, sleekit, cowerin', timorous beastie" dislodged
from her autumnal covert; upon the hare wounded by the
sportsman; upon the very field-flower, overturned by his share
and crushed among the stubble. And in all this we feel that
there is nothing strained or exaggerated, nothing affected or
put on, nothing childish or silly, but that all is true, genuine,
healthy, manly, noble; we honor, we venerate the poet while
we read; we take the expression of these sympathies to our
hearts and fold it in our memory forever.*

.   .   .   .   .   .   .   .

---

* From an address at the Burns' Centennial, January 25, 1859.

VERY fitly indeed is the term genius, in its highest meaning, applied to the literary character of the great poet of Scotland. To him was given, in large measure,

" The vision and the faculty divine ! "

He possessed, in as high degree, I think, as ever man possessed, the power of which Coleridge speaks in defining the term genius, the power to combine the child's sense of wonder and novelty with appearances which the experience of years had rendered familiar. The commonest objects, incidents of the slightest apparent significance, were taken up by him and given back to us, transfigured and glorified by the thoughts which he had connected with them, and which he had expressed in verse that will endure as long as our language. It is as if a magician had scooped up a handful of gravel from the trodden highway and shown it, in his palm, transformed to grains of glittering gold and precious stones resplendent with an inward light.

I admit that in his songs Burns was a disciple of those who composed the old Scottish songs and ballads, and whose names have perished while their verses are immortal. A breath of fire from the times in which they lived touched the inflammable material in his bosom, and it was instantly in a blaze. He wrote songs in their manner, with all their simplicity and sweetness, and yet in excellence went beyond them.

But there are other productions of his for which he found no pattern in our literature. I find none for his " Tam o' Shanter," the very pearl of comic poems. It is written in the same measure as Butler's " Hudibras," but what a difference ! a difference owing simply to this, that Butler was a man of wit and Burns a man of genius. Butler is prolific in droll conceits; he hammers them out one after another and flings them down in clusters, but he is infinitely tiresome, and we yawn over his pages. However resolute we are to read on, our jaws will expand in spite of ourselves. Burns has all that

Butler has, but he has also all that Butler lacks—rapid action, narrative interest, joyous gayety, imagination, apt touches of character, and free and flowing numbers. These make the poem original and place it beyond imitation.

When, in reading the poems of Burns, we come to that beginning with the line,

"Wee, modest, crimson-tipped flower,"

occasioned by uprooting a daisy with the share of the plough which he guided across the field; and when we reach the beautiful companion-piece to this, beginning with the words,

"Wee, sleekit, cowerin', timorous beastie,"

and ask ourselves where Burns found the prototype of these charming poems, we are obliged to confess that he found them not in all our literature. We have had others since in the like vein, but it was Burns who showed us how to write them. Both of them are testimonies to the largeness of his sympathies —sympathies which extended to every form of life between the caverns of the earth and the stars of the sky, which comprehended the lowliest flower of the field and the humblest animal that burrows in the earth, as well as the nobler forms of existence. The hand that penned the verses of which I have just spoken wrote down the pathetic lines, "To Mary in Heaven."

An old Roman poet was the author of the often-quoted saying, "I am a man, and there is nothing human that does not interest me." A noble sentiment; but Burns in his poems gave it a wider application, and showed that there was nothing in the great universe, the dwelling of the human race, that did not interest him. He perceived in every form of animal or of vegetable life, whether it moves on the earth, or winnows the air, or swims the waters, or fixes its roots in the soil, some relation to the fortunes of human beings. He saw by what harmonies, unperceived by the common mind, they were allied to human destiny, and as he spoke of them he invested them, to our apprehension, with that radiant newness which we may conceive them to have worn in the sight of the first man when he opened his eyes on the fresh creation around him. Such is the genius of Burns.*

*        *        *        *        *

ONE circumstance alone is enough to stamp Burns as a man of the highest order of genius. He took a local dialect and made it classical, gave it a character of great universality. I am not ignorant of what the poets who had lived before Burns did for the dialect of Scotland, nor what has been done since by Walter Scott, whose works are read by everybody, and will be read for ages to come. But the poets of the Scottish dialect before Burns never attained that general and popular perusal which his works have acquired, and it was the good fortune of Scott that he wrote after Burns had made that dialect familiar to all classes of English readers.

It was Burns who taught us all to love the Scottish dialect—its graceful diminutives, its rich store of comic expressions, its homely but intensely significant phrases of pathos and tenderness, which go to the heart. Within his lifetime—and his life was not a long one—his poems were read wherever the English language is spoken : on the banks of the Hudson, of the Ashley and the Santee, of the Mississippi, of the St. Lawrence, of the Ganges, as well as on the banks of the Tweed and the Thames. It is owing to Burns that the natives of Scotland have it in their power to say that to him who has not some knowledge of the Scottish dialect and some relish for its significance there is one chamber of the common treasury of our literature—a chamber filled with gems and jewels—to which he has not the key.

*        *        *        *        *

Burns it was, as I have said before, who made the Scottish dialect classical wherever our language is known. The ut-

---

* From a speech at the Burns Dinner, January 25, 1876.

terances of his genius, in going forth to the ends of the earth, have carried with them the dialect in which his finest things were written. Before the time of Burns there was a long period in which the poets of Great Britain "looked at nature through the spectacles of books"—a period during which, as remarked by Wordsworth, scarce a single new image from nature found its way into their verses. They contented themselves with ringing the changes on those which the authors before them had made familiar. Then arose a Scottish poet, James Thompson, who flung these spectacles to the ground, crushing them under his remorseless heel, and, looking at nature with his own unassisted and clear sighted eyes, crowded his poem of the seasons with images as new, fresh, and bright as Nature herself. He it was who, in the time of Pope, when the poetry in vogue was the poetry of the drawing-room, started boldly away from the common track, and, to the wonder and delight of his readers, gave them the poetry of the woods and fields, and, in part of his poem, the poetry of the household. It was a literary revolution effected by a Scottish poet; but he did not venture to employ the Scottish dialect.

It was reserved for Burns to do this in such a manner as to give the Scottish dialect a place in the general literature of our language. It was he who struck the grand master-note of Scottish song, making it heard in almost every latitude of the globe, and calling forth an answering reverberation from far-distant regions. Many of those who sit at this table have doubtless heard the report of a cannon discharged among the Highlands that overlook the Hudson, our own "exulting and abounding river." The sound has scarcely left the cannon's mouth before it is re-echoed by one of the majestic mountains —Dunderberg, perhaps—on whose summit the clouds rest and the lightnings are born. Cro' Nest rolls it back from his dark precipices and ancient forests. Then some headland more remote receives it, and from its cliffs flings it back to the listener. The sound travels swiftly on, and a response

comes from height after height, until it passes away among
the hills and shores which lie beyond the sight.

.        .        .        .        .        .        .        .

In these times of great and rapid changes in the political
and social world it is a relief to be able to sometimes fix our
attention, as we do to-night, on things which have a certain
character of permanency.  For this is a period of mighty and
sudden, and even of bloody changes, such as the world has
rarely seen — powerful empires overthrown; new empires
founded; monarchs, lately the dread of the civilized world, now
dethroned and scorned; statesmen, on whom seemed to depend
the fate of nations, assassinated; fair and flourishing regions
wasted by war and given over to famine; populous cities be-
leaguered and made heaps of ruins. The spirit of change now
abroad respects neither the old nor the new, spares neither the
strong nor the defenceless, but sets its foot on crowns and
tiaras, on sceptres and croziers, on usages and institutions of
yesterday, and those of a thousand years, and crushes them
alike without remorse.

In the midst of these convulsions, following close upon
a great, sudden, and even violent change in our own insti-
tution, we are met to celebrate, not the birth of any of the
renowned statesmen who lead in making these changes or in
resisting them, nor any of the generals who command the
mighty armies of invasion or the hosts embattled for defence,
but the advent of a lowly peasant, in a humble cottage in a
secluded district of Scotland, among hills and dales and brooks
and pasture-grounds, who wrote verses and passed to a prema-
ture grave.  Yet what he wrote will dwell, as it now dwells,
in the hearts of thousands hereafter, when the names of those
who figure in the revolutions of our day shall be but dimly
remembered.  "The Cotter's Saturday Night" will be re-
peated, and "Auld Lang Syne" will be sung, by those who, if
they ever think of the Third Napoleon, will perhaps ask what
was the name of that foolish and wicked tyrant who long ago,
in 1870, madly plunged France into a war which blotted her

fields with pools of blood and laid her cities in ashes. For Burns took the themes of his verse from the common events of life—the common joys and sorrows of men and women; he took what was said and felt at the fireside, the words and phrases of the household; he took the most familiar images and breathed into them all a life and soul such as nobody but himself could give them, and made them a part of the literature which endures from age to age.*

---

* From a speech at the Burns Anniversary, January 25, 1871.

# THE PRINCETON LIBRARY.*

IN rising to address a public assembly in this pleasant town of Princeton, allow me to say that there is something in the solid and venerable aspect of the place, in its historical associations as the scene of one of the most important battles of our Revolution, and for a time the seat of the Continental Congress, and in the recollection that a president of its noble institution of learning was one of the leaders in that Revolution, and that from these learned shades have gone forth more statesmen than from any other college, to shape the polity of our Republic and direct its workings—not to speak of the illustrious men whom it has trained up for other walks of life —in all these there is something which inspires a kind of awe, and I naturally dread to encounter the grave judgment of those whom I see before me. But, inasmuch as I do not mean, fortunately for myself and those who hear me, to hold the audience long, the dread will soon be over.

Before I congratulate the public and all the friends of good learning—and this includes, of course, the friends of the College of New Jersey—on the opening of this beautiful building as the College Library, let me congratulate the gentleman to whose liberality we are indebted for it, and for the provision

---

* An address spoken at Princeton, New Jersey, June 24, 1873, on the opening of the new building for the College Library.

made for the gradual enlargement of the collection of books which it is to contain. He is one, I am happy to say, who prizes the uses of wealth beyond its possession; and, instead of clinging to it while life lasts, and only then directing how it shall be disposed of when he can possess it no longer, he forces it to go from his hands upon an errand of beneficence. He has his reward in seeing how worthily thus far it has performed the office on which he sent it forth.

I read the other day, in a book published in 1839, that the library of New Jersey College then consisted of eight thousand volumes. At present, with the aid of the benefactions of Mr. Green, to whom I have just referred, I am informed that the number will exceed a hundred thousand—a number equal to that of several of the public libraries of Europe which have long been famous—while provision is made for its future increase from year to year. If in the next half century its increase should be in the same proportion, it will take its place among libraries of the first class in the Old World—the accumulations of many centuries. It is well that the library should keep pace in its growth with the institution to which it belongs. Under the present wise and fortunate administration of the college, the course of study prescribed to the students has been greatly enlarged; new branches of learning and science have been added; new professorships have been created, fellowships endowed, and prizes proposed to reward the diligence of the students. A library amply stored has become more important than ever, for with a wider sphere of study there must be wider and deeper research.

To form an adequate idea of the value of books, it is only necessary to suppose a state of things which should cause their sudden destruction. I do not recollect that any author into whose works I have looked has ever taken the trouble to imagine and describe the condition to which the immediate annihilation of books and manuscripts would reduce the human race. It may be said that such an event is altogether impossible. Nay, not so—improbable, I grant—improbable, if you please, to the utmost limit of improbability—but still possible. Let us suppose the white ant—the insect pest which in South America devours and destroys books and manuscripts with such fearful voracity that, as Humboldt avers, they have not left in an extensive district a single manuscript a hundred years old—to become unexpectedly numerous in all civilized countries. Let us suppose it to multiply as strangely as the sugar-ant in the West India island of Grenada, when, coming from nobody knew where, it invaded the plantations in vast armies, forming dams across the streams with their drowned bodies, over which the living ones crossed to the opposite bank, devouring everything before them which had animal or vegetable life, desolating the fields and gardens, and threatening to drive the human race from Grenada, until, in 1780, the beneficent interposition of a terrific storm of wind and rain annihilated the vast mass of insect life and delivered the island. Imagine the white ant, produced in like numbers, by means as mysterious, invading the haunts of men everywhere, creeping into our libraries and publication offices, and consuming every printed page and every manuscript, and everything on which the pen or the press can leave its trace. Into what confusion and dismay would society at once be thrown! The reader of the daily gazette from that moment would find himself ignorant of what was going on in the world, and would long in vain to learn what had happened since yesterday. In the crowded city he would find himself a hermit. The reader for entertainment would miss his accustomed refreshment; the inquirer after knowledge would find no path open to his researches; the daily reader of Scripture would look about him in vain for the sacred volume. The tribunals would be forced to grope their way without statutes or lawbooks; the advocate would have no precedents on which to found his arguments save those which he might possibly remember or invent for the occasion. All the records of the past, all the lessons of history, all the discoveries of science, all the conclusions of philosophy, all that the poets have woven

into song, all that has been written down of moral and relig-
ious truth, would be lost, and be as if they had never been,
save such portions of these priceless treasures as might be re-
tained in that treacherous repository, the human memory ; and
how soon, by the process of oral transmission, might that por-
tion become changed and corrupted and encumbered with spu-
rious additions ! In the places of worship, half-remembered
litanies would be stammered, half-forgotten hymns given out
in halting metre and sung to tunes imperfectly recollected, and
mutilated passages of Holy Writ repeated to unedified con-
gregations.

In such a state of things we should become deeply sensi-
ble of our immense obligations to the past. For it is to the
past that we owe what we are, both in body and mind. The
past ages have moulded the age in which we live to the shape
it now wears; but for the past, man would be helplessly in a
savage state. Every advance in civilization, every shining ex-
ample of active virtue, every wise or sacred precept of human
conduct, every triumph of art and skill, everything, in short,
that stores the mind with wisdom, or instructs the hand, or en-
lightens the conscience, is of the past, and books are the reposi-
tories in which they are laid up for the use of mankind from
generation to generation. Destroy the volumes in which they
are contained, and you blot out the past ages, with all that
they have done for us, and the human race would drift hope-
lessly into barbarism.

And now we stand under a roof dedicated to the great
minds of the past—the temple of a thousand venerable memo-
ries. The illustrious ones who have passed the gates of death
before us may have left their material part in graves marked
by some known memorial, or their dust may be scattered to
the winds, but here is what the earth still possesses of their
higher nature. Here are their words, still animated by the
living soul, and here is the record of their glorious example.
It matters not where their bones are laid while we have among
us, in the volumes which this structure will contain from cen-

tury to century, this remnant of the immortal spirit. May
none enter among them without an emotion of reverence ; may
none who come to hold converse in these alcoves with the
mighty minds of other years fail to recognize with gratitude
the providence which, through the invention of letters, has en-
abled those whom God endowed with eminent gifts of intellect
to speak to their fellow-men of all succeeding time, and has
thus in part repealed the doom of death.

# FRANKLIN AS POET.*

THE illustrious printer and journalist whose birth we this evening commemorate is often spoken of with praise as an acute observer of nature and of men, as a philosopher, as an inventor, as an able negotiator, as a statesman. But in this latter respect, the capacity of statesman, he has not received all the praise which is his due. For he saw, as it seems to me, farther into the true province and office of a free government, and the duties of its legislators, than any man of his time. He saw and pointed out the folly of governing too much. He saw that it is not the business of a government to do what can be done by individuals. He saw that what the Government had to do was to restrain its citizens from invading each other's rights, and compel them to respect each other's freedom. He therefore condemned the corn laws—the laws against the importation of grain—a hundred years before the people of Great Britain became convinced of their folly and repealed them. He held also that it was not the policy of a state to put any limitations on paper credit—in other words, he was for free banking, believing that the intermeddling of the Government with that branch of commercial business could only lead to mischief. Franklin saw also the wisdom and humanity of mitigating the calamities of war by allowing trading

---

* From a speech at the celebration of Franklin's birthday by the New York Typographical Society, January 17, 1874.

vessels to pass and repass unmolested on the high seas in time of war, and, before he returned from Europe in 1785, he negotiated a treaty with Prussia which contained an article against privateering. Thus he anticipated by more than half a century the proposition which our Government has since made to Great Britain.

Franklin is not often spoken of as a witty man, but his wit was as remarkable as his statesmanship. I think that he would have had as much wit as Swift or as Voltaire if he had but cultivated this talent. Only his clear, practical good sense predominated, and he never showed himself in the capacity of a humorist save when some practical purpose was to be effected by it. Only twenty-four days before his death he composed the amusing parody of a speech delivered on the floor of Congress by Mr. Jackson in defence of slavery—a parody which evidently suggested to Sidney Smith the famous conservative oration of Noodle. I took up lately a French biographical account of Franklin, and there I found a list of some of the proverbs coined by him, and added to the common stock. Among these was one illustrating the difficulty which those who are in extreme poverty find in keeping to the strict line of rectitude. "It is hard," said Franklin, "to make an empty bag stand upright." "The Petition of the Left Hand" and the dialogue between Franklin and the Gout are examples of his wit, which was all of the genuine sort. I suppose he never made a pun in his life, because he could see no use for it.

If I should say that Franklin was also a poet, this assembly, I suppose, would smile. Yet the poetic element was not wanting in his mental constitution, though he did not write verses, at least but rarely. You remember his tract written on seeing a fly crawl out from a glass of Madeira wine just drawn from the cask, where it had been immersed, perhaps, for years. That was a fine poetic thought which he wrought out from that circumstance, of being himself preserved in a state of suspended animation by some such means for a century or two, and being then recalled to life and the world and shown the mighty changes which had taken place in the interval in the aspect of things and the state of society—a new and strange world in place of the one which he inhabited. But the most remarkable example of his possession of the poetic faculty was given when, in the year 1787, he sat in the convention which framed the Federal Constitution. As the convention finished its labors, the sun, emerging from a cloud, poured a flood of radiance into the hall where the assembly was held. You know that the ancients made the god of the sun, Phœbus Apollo, the god of poetry also, and the source of poetic inspiration. The aged philosopher, then in his eighty-second year, caught the inspiration, and, in a few well-chosen words, accepted and proclaimed the omen. I cannot give the precise words, because I have not been able lately to find the record of them, but they were in substance these: " Thus," he said, " are the clouds that lowered over our Republic in its infancy destined to pass away. Thus will the smile of Heaven be vouchsafed to our completed labors, and the sunshine of prosperity rest on our country!" My friends, may his words, in all the coming time, prove as prophetic as they are poetical.*

---

* This incident is reported by Madison in his debates on the Federal Constitution ; and it would have given additional point to Mr. Bryant's illustration if he had remembered the precise words of the reporter. " While the last members were signing, Dr. Franklin, looking toward the President's chair, at the back of which a *rising sun* happened to be painted, observed to a few members near him that painters had found it difficult to distinguish, in their art, a rising from a setting sun. ' I have,' said he, ' often and often, in the course of the session and the vicissitudes of my hopes and fears as to its issue, looked at that behind the President without being able to tell whether it was rising or setting ; but now, at this hour, we have the happiness to know that it is a rising, not a setting sun.' "—ED.

# NATIONAL HONESTY.*

I AM glad to see in this concourse a proof of the interest with which the public of New York regard the object of this meeting. For it is a most important question that we are now to consider—the question whether our Government is to go any deeper into the ignominy of a false financial policy—the policy of palming upon the country a currency of dishonored notes as a measure of value.

You remember the circumstances under which this policy was resolved upon. It was excused only as a war measure. Its advocates said in so many words : "We adopt it only under the pressure of necessity ; we shall discard it as soon as the country is again at peace. We here solemnly pledge ourselves to pay, at the earliest possible period, in coin, the notes which we now make a lawful tender." There were many who remonstrated against this step at the time, and I was among the number. We urged that there was no necessity for it. We urged that those who had cheerfully sent their sons to the war would even more willingly lend the Government the credit it required ; that those who willingly shed their blood would even more readily part with the necessary means to carry on the war, and that nothing more was needed for this than for the Government to issue certificates of stock for small amounts, which the people were ready to take up as fast as issued. We

* Address at a mass-meeting held in Cooper Institute, March 25, 1874.

urged that the artificial plethora caused by issuing paper-money not to be redeemed with coin would stimulate specu-lation; that the fever of speculation would be followed by a collapse and a panic; and that, in spite of all pledges, there would then be a clamor for new and larger issues of paper.

Well, the irredeemable paper was issued, the era of mad speculation came and passed; the era of panic arrived, and now we hear the predicted clamor for more issues of lying promises from the government presses. If they are sanc-tioned by Congress, and have the effect which they are in-tended to have, they will revive speculation, they will lead to another collapse of credit, another era of commercial ruin, and the stagnation of trade. This is simply repeating the les-sons of history. If this be not so, the annals of the world are a fable and experience a cheat. Against a measure fraught with such consequences we are assembled to protest.

Will you hear an anecdote illustrative of this topic? It was some forty years ago that a tall, thin gentleman, in a long great-coat and a cap, stalked into the Mechanics' Bank in this city. He leisurely took from his pocket-book a five-dollar note of the bank, and, laying it before the teller, requested its payment. The teller said : " We do not pay our notes." The tall, thin man—who it appeared was John Randolph—put on his spectacles and read the note in a high-keyed voice. " ' The president and directors of the Mechanics' Bank promise to pay the bearer five dollars, value received.' There, I want the five dollars which you promise to pay." " But we do not pay," re-joined the teller; " the banks have suspended payment." " Oh, *stopped* payment! Then let me tell you what to do. Take the sledge-hammer out of the hand that hangs over your door, and in its place put a razor."

My friends, if Congress should be moved by this clamor to disgrace the country by issuing more notes the condition of whose existence is to be dishonored, may we not take a hint from this anecdote? What business will the king of birds— the eagle, whose flight is above that of all other fowls of the air—have on an escutcheon which this policy will disgrace in the eyes of the world? Let his image then be blotted out; obliterate also the stars of heaven; efface the stripes of morning light which should be the promise of a day of glory and honor, and, instead of those emblems, let the limner draw on the broad sheet the image of a razor, huge enough to be wielded by the Giant Despair—a gentleman with whom, if this demand for more paper-money be granted, we are destined to scrape a closer acquaintance than we have enjoyed yet—and on the enormous blade let the words be inscribed, in staring letters, " Warranted to shave"; and let the two supporters of this majestic implement—the two razor-bearers— be ——— of Indiana and ——— of Pennsylvania; or, perhaps, ——— of Massachusetts, may sustain the charge alone.

# GOETHE.*

WE whom this occasion has brought together are assembled
for a purpose which, in order to its perfect fulfilment, looks to
future years and to generations yet unborn. We are to erect
to the greatest literary genius of Germany a bust which, placed
in our Central Park, may fix the gaze of those who frequent
its walks and repose in its shades so long as this great mart of
commerce shall remain the abode of civilized man. It is our
fate, my friends, to pass away like shadows. I look around
me on this concourse and see only those whom the lapse of
time is bearing onward to the close of life. The light of the
soul will soon pass from the brightest eye here; the firmest
health will give way; the strongest muscles will become pow-
erless and be resolved into dust. The mind recoils from the

---

* An address delivered at the Centennial Festival given by the Goethe Club, of
New York, in honor of Goethe, August 27, 1875. On the day on which the festival
was held, Mr. Bryant's journal, the " Evening Post," spoke of the occasion in this
wise :

"In that charming little book, 'Goethe and Mendelssohn,' there are recorded,
among the musician's reminiscences, Goethe's remarks upon that great period in
the history of German literature—the year 1775. This year Goethe called the spring
of the epoch which succeeded, and he said (it was upon the occasion of a visit of
Mendelssohn to him in 1830) that no man lived who could remember it and describe
it as he could. 'Yes,' said Goethe, 'that time was like the spring, when every-
thing is bursting into life and one tree stands bare while another is already in
full leaf.' Therefore, in seeking for some proper centennial celebration of Goethe's
career, no better date could be fixed upon than that time which was fullest of the

idea of an extinguished consciousness, and, in its impatience at the universal tendency to decay and dissolution, calls on the arts to perpetuate the outward semblance of those who have been admired or beloved for their talents or their virtues and their influence on society. At our bidding, the sculptor comes and copies, in lasting marble or imperishable bronze, the faces and forms of those whose death has saddened the nations. To this material under his hands he gives the expression of the soul and fixes it there forever. This is one of the modes in which the human species manifests its longing for immortality, its strong desire to escape from the fate which is sure to overtake the bodily frame.

We obey this instinct to-day in the proceedings which are to end in erecting a bust to John Wolfgang Goethe.

It is said by his biographers that in his youth Goethe planned a migration to America. His imagination was captivated by the idea of a life passed with one whom he loved in the sylvan solitudes and flowery, natural meadows of our continent. He had become enamored of a young woman named Lilli, and thought to transplant this blossom of his native land to the virgin soil of America, to bloom under our brighter skies. That purpose was short-lived, like a similar one entertained a quarter of a century later by Coleridge and Southey; it was a poet's dream, and soon faded away. But now, after the lapse of a hundred years since it was formed, we make it, in part at least, a reality. We welcome the great German

---

brilliant future; Goethe appears to men as perhaps the finest type of a superb and successful Apollo among the famous characters of history. Nature and fortune combined to produce in him one of those bright, enviable beings whom men love to contemplate, because seeing in them the completion and perfection of their own inadequate and imperfect selves. In no one thing was fortune kinder to him than in the happy conjunction of his own youth with the dawn of the new time, and no scene could be fixed upon more suggestive and significant, more replete with thought and picture, more full of food for mind and fancy, than the quaint little town of Weimar as it lay in the sun a hundred years ago. How marvellous the change! How striking the contrast between the world as it seemed to that little group of enthusiasts and that which we behold to-day!"

poet to our western hemisphere, to our youthful republic, to this populous mart, to the spacious and beautiful pleasure-ground which is one of its chief ornaments, and invite him to grace it with his majestic presence while the world shall stand. If he had come to the United States at the time when his youthful imagination formed the plan of which I have spoken, he would have found the American continent still in great part a wilderness, with a few tracts of cultivation along its Atlantic borders enclosed in a vast forest, where the savage warrior, armed with bow and tomahawk, still hovered on the skirts of the settlements. But now we celebrate his coming to a mighty empire, to a population almost as large as that of all the region in the Old World inhabited by those who speak the German language, to valleys where the songs of the Teuton are sung, and where his own ballads are recited and his trage-dies read in thousands of families which have migrated from his own fatherland, and where his mystic drama of "Faust" has found a translator worthy of the original, an interpreter of its meaning to those who speak the language of Milton and Shakespeare.* We bring from a distant land his image, that it may be placed where thousands in a day, who throng to our Central Park to be refreshed by its sweet air and pleasant shades, shall become familiar with his features and learn to see in them the tokens of a mighty intellect and a calm spirit.

We shall place his bust in the same grounds with the bust of Schiller, with whom in his lifetime he maintained a cordial friendship, and kept up a correspondence dictated by mutual regard and kindness. For Goethe, my friends, was not of that class who regard praise bestowed upon a rival as so much detracted from their own merits. No satirist could say of him what Pope said of Addison when, after speaking of his talents and endowments, he added how lamentable it would be

> "Should such a man, too fond to rule alone,
> Bear, like the Turk, no brother near the throne,

---

* Bayard Taylor.

View him with scornful yet with jealous eyes,
And hate for arts that caused himself to rise."

There has been a literary feud in Germany between the
admirers of Schiller and those of Goethe, each party claiming
for its favorite the palm of superior greatness; but there was
no hostility between those eminent men while they lived.
Goethe was himself too great and of too serene a tempera-
ment to allow himself to be made unhappy by competition in
any walk of literature. If no other reason existed for honor-
ing his memory, it should be remembered, to his praise, that
he was superior to the selfishness and littleness of repining at
the fair fame of another. He looked with a generous tolerance
upon rivalry, deeming the field of letters a common inheri-
tance, where every one was entitled to the harvest which he
had the strength to reap. It may be that in the consciousness
of his great powers he felt that he had no rival to fear; but
even this implies soundness of judgment, and a certain sense
of justice and greatness of soul which disdained to claim a
monopoly of praise.

If such was Goethe's estimate of his own powers, it is not
for me to say that he was mistaken. The large majority of
critical voices has placed him at the head of German litera-
ture. An imagination so affluent and creative, such wealth of
knowledge, such acute observation of nature, such insight into
men's characters and motives, rarely exist together; and these,
presided over by a taste which, in guiding, never fettered the
sallies of his imagination, form the literary character of Goethe.
He has been praised for his many-sidedness, and the commenda-
tion is just. He was master not only of many modes of poetic
invention, but of several sciences. He, as well as Milton—that
high and sacred name—is an example to show how knowledge
may become the handmaid of poetry, and how a poet of the
higher class fuses, by the fire of his imagination, the stores of
erudition at his command into a mass bearing the stamp and
seal of his own genius, and ready to be shaped into any form

that he may please to give it, and how his invention is stimulated rather than encumbered by the large abundance of his materials.

It is far from my intentions to enter, at this time, upon an analysis of the literary character of Goethe. It would weary those who have the patience to hear me if I were to repeat what others have better said, and, certainly, I am not disposed unnecessarily to delay the more acceptable entertainments of the evening. A hundred years—and it is somewhat more than a hundred years since his first work was published—have fixed his rank among the great poets of the world. It is true that, on account of the difficulties which attend the task of translating poetry, the reputation of an eminent poet must be somewhat national rather than universal, and his genius must be most perfectly apprehended in the country where his language is spoken. Notwithstanding this, we find Goethe, by general consent, placed among those whose genius is the common possession of the nations, and whose fame is bounded only by the limits of the civilized world. I remember a remark of the poet Halleck—that when a writer of verse begins to be quoted, from that moment he is famous. It is a still surer sign, perhaps, of the extent of his fame, when he begins to be made the subject of commentary. I saw it remarked the other day in a literary periodical that the writer had found in a catalogue of the Heidelberg University one hundred and twelve volumes of commentaries on the poem of "Faust," and all of them in the German tongue. I may venture to say that these are but a part of what has become a special branch of German literature, and, mere rubbish as some of them must be, they attest the power of that poem over the minds of its readers— a poem in which Goethe laid the reins loose upon his imagination, and allowed it to range without restraint. Few are the works produced, since books began to be written, which have given birth to such a brood of expositions. A strange attraction has kept men hanging over its pages and prying into its inner meaning. Only the great poem of Dante occurs to me as vieing with it in the number and voluminousness of its commentaries. But the secret force which draws the attention of readers to the poem of "Faust" cannot make them unmindful of the merits of his other writings—his noble tragedies, full of the results of his power of observing and delineating character; his works of 'fiction, possessing in no small degree the attractiveness which belongs to his "Faust"; his writings on science and his exquisite ballads, composed with a perfection of grace and skill beyond which it seems impossible to go. Goethe was a master of expression; the noble German language as it flowed from his pen took its fairest and most perfect form, and became a transparent vehicle of the thought. No author of the purest age of Greek literature surpassed him in grace. For, after all, the style is a part of the thought, and a bad style is a distortion of the thought.

In this country of free institutions we cannot, perhaps, make Goethe our model in politics. It is urged against him, not without a show of reason, that, possessing a power over public opinion which would have given effect to his slightest remonstrance against absolute government, he yet acquiesced in its wrongs, and consented to become one of those who profited by them. Those who take an unfriendly view of his character complain that he did not care to make men happier so long as his own condition was fortunate and agreeable, nor, better, so long as their moral condition, whatever it might be, ministered to his convenience. He did not admit the truth of this accusation, but claimed that he had labored, during a long life, in overcoming pernicious prejudices and narrow views among his countrymen, in elevating the intellect and purifying the taste of the community, and that his real offence was that he would have nothing to do with party politics. I do not care on this occasion to discuss the question whether this was a satisfactory answer, and willingly draw a veil over the circumstances which might lead to an unfavorable conclusion.* Yet may we not say for Goethe that there is one ami-

---

* Although Mr. Bryant was a member of the Goethe Club, punctual in his attendance at its meetings, where he listened with delight to the many able papers read by

able quality of his character, which he might not have retained had he taken upon himself the troublesome office of a political reformer? I mean the quiet of a contented spirit, which makes the best of surrounding conditions, and converts them, as far as may be, into the means of happiness.

But if Goethe was not a reformer in politics he was a reformer in literature. In that province he did not shrink from innovation. In his very first published works, written before his taste was matured—in " Götz of the Iron Hand " and in "The Sorrows of Werther "—he broke away from the prevalent imitation of French models, and from the cold classicism which was its result, and took his own road to fame. This originality, this courageous self-reliance, marked all his subsequent writings throughout his long literary career.

My friends, the bust of Goethe, of which I have spoken, is already landed on our shores, and will soon be unveiled to the public gaze. A place for it will yet be found in our Central Park, where it is to stand for centuries—possibly as long as ships shall enter from the main ocean between the fair islands that enclose our beautiful harbor. We shall place this bust of Goethe among a noble company—with the statue of Shakespeare, the greatest name in all literature ; with that of Scott, who translated " Götz of the Iron Hand," and who learned from Goethe to weave the traditions of his own country into recitals of romantic adventure ; with that of his countryman Humboldt, to whom the mechanism of the universe was as familiar as the motions of his own watch ; and with that of our own Morse, who taught us to charge the electric spark

---

its members relating to the character and genius of the great poet, it is doubtful whether he was always in sympathy with the admiration for Goethe's character they sometimes expressed. He could not have said, as Heine writes in one of his letters : "As for Goethe and myself, we are at bottom two heterogeneous and consequently repulsive natures. Goethe was essentially a man of this world, for whom the easy enjoyment of life was the sovereign thing, who at times had felt life in the idea and been able to express it in his poetry, but who had never seized hold of it profoundly, and still less really lived it." But it is to be observed that Mr. Bryant, while extolling the genius, treads cautiously when he approaches the man.

with messages from distant lands, and to prepare for it a path across broad continents and through deep waters. Other statues of those whose lives were illustrious and whose memory is cherished will be set up in the same grounds. That of our countryman, author of the impassioned lyric of "Marco Bozzaris," is even now only waiting to be cast in bronze, in order to join the band already there; but late, very late, may the time arrive when the American poet whose tribute to the memory of Goethe forms a part of the entertainments of the evening, and whose translation of "Faust" has made that poem a familiar volume in our libraries, shall be added, after death, to the number of those whose statues shall grace that beautiful pleasure-ground. As the throng of those who resort thither shall pass the sculptured forms of famous personages, may the hope to copy their example in the good which they have done, and to avoid the errors into which they have fallen, if any such are recorded against them, rise in their hearts to make them better men and women for their visit to the spot made sacred by images of the chosen ones who lived and passed away before us.

# MAZZINI.*

HISTORY, my friends, has recorded the deeds of Giuseppe Mazzini on a tablet which will endure while the annals of Italy are read. Art has been called to do her part in perpetuating his memory, and to-day a bust is unveiled which will make millions familiar with the divine image stamped on the countenance of one of the greatest men of our times.

The idea of Italian unity and liberty was the passion of Mazzini's life; it took possession of him in youth, it grew stronger as the years went on, and lost none of its power over him in his age. Nor is it at all surprising that it should have taken a strong hold on his youthful imagination. I recollect very well that when, forty-four years ago, I first entered Italy, then held down under the weight of a score of despotisms, the same idea forcibly suggested itself to my mind as I looked southward from the slopes of the mountain country. There lay a great sisterhood of provinces requiring only a confederate republican government to raise them to the rank of a great power, presenting to the world a single majestic front, and parcelling out the powers of local legislation and government among the different neighborhoods in such a manner as to educate the whole population in a knowledge of the duties

---

* Mr. Bryant appeared for the last time in public on the 29th of May, 1878. He then took part in the ceremony of unveiling the bust of Mazzini, the Italian states-man, in the Central Park, in New York, and delivered this address.

and rights of freemen.   There were the industrious Piedmon-
tese, the enterprising Genoese, among whom Mazzini was
born—a countryman of Columbus; there were the ambitious
Venetians and the Lombards, rejoicing in their fertile plains;
and there, as the imagination followed the ridge of the Apen-
nines toward the Strait of Messina, were the Tuscans, famed
in letters; the Umbrians, wearing in their aspect the tokens of
Latin descent; the Romans in their centre of arts; the gay
Neapolitans; and farther south the versatile Sicilians, over
whose valleys rolls the smoke of the most famous volcano in
the world.   As we traverse these regions in thought we rec-
ognize them all as parts of one Italy, yet each inhabited by
Italians of a different character from the rest, all speaking
Italian, but with a difference in each province; each region
cherishing its peculiar traditions, which reach back to the be-
ginning of civilization, and its peculiar usages observed for
ages.

Well might the great man whose bust we disclose at this
time to the public gaze be deeply moved by this spectacle of
his countrymen and kindred bound in the shackles of a brood
of local tyrannies which kept them apart that they might with
more ease be oppressed.   When he further considered the
many great men who had risen from time to time in Italy as
examples of the intellectual endowments of her people—states-
men, legislators, men of letters, men eminent in philosophy,
in arms, and in arts—I say that he might well claim for the
birthplace of such men the unity of its provinces to make it
great, and the liberty of its people to raise them up to the
standard of their mental endowments.   Who shall blame him
—who in this land of freedom—for demanding in behalf of
such a country a political constitution framed on the most
liberal pattern which the world has seen?

For such a constitution he planned; for that he labored;
that object he never suffered to be out of his sight.   No pro-
claimer of a new religion was ever more faithful to his mission.
Here, where we have lately closed a sanguinary but successful

war in defence of the unity of the States which form our Republic; here, where we have just broken the chains of three millions of bondmen—is, above all others, the place where a memorial of the great champion of Italian unity and liberty should be set up amid a storm of acclamation from a multitude of freemen.

Yet, earnestly as he desired these ends and struggled to attain them, the struggle was a noble and manly one; he disdained to compass these ends by base or ferocious means; he abhorred bloodshed; he detested vengeance; he spoke little of rights, but much of duties, resolving the cares of an enlightened statesmanship into matters of duty. The only warfare which he would allow, and that as a sorrowful necessity, was an open warfare waged against that brute force that violates human duty and human right. In that warfare his courage rose always equal to the occasion—a courage worthy of the generous political philosophy which he professed. For there was no trial he would not endure, no sacrifice, no labor he would not undertake, no danger he would not encounter for the sake of that dream of his youth and pursuit of his manhood, the unity and liberty of Italy.

That country is now united under one political head—save a portion arbitrarily and unjustly added to France—and to the public opinion formed in Italy by the teachings of Mazzini the union is in large measure due. Italy has now a constitutional government, the best feature of which it owes to the principles of republicanism in which Mazzini trained a whole generation of the young men of Italy, however short the present government of the country may fall of the ideal standard at which he aimed.

One great result for which he labored was the perfect freedom of religious worship. Well has he deserved the honors of posterity who, holding enforced worship to be an abomination in the sight of God, took his life in his hand and went boldly forward until the yoke of the great tyranny exercised over the religious conscience in his native country was broken. Such a hero deserves a monument in a land where the Government knows no distinction between religious denominations and leaves their worship to their consciences.

I will not say that he whose image is to-day unveiled was prudent in all his proceedings; nobody is; timidity itself is not always prudence. But, wherever he went and whatever he did, he was a power on earth. He wielded an immense influence over men's minds; he controlled a vast agency; he made himself the centre of a wide diffusion of opinions; his footsteps are seen in the track of history by those who do not always reflect by whose feet they are impressed. Such was the celerity of his movements and so sure the attachment of his followers that he was the terror of the crowned heads of Europe. Kings trembled when they heard that he had suddenly disappeared from London, and breathed more freely when they learned that he was in his grave. In proportion as he was dreaded he was maligned.

Image of the illustrious champion of civil and religious liberty, cast in enduring bronze to typify the imperishable renown of thy original, remain for ages yet to come where we place thee, in this resort of millions; remain till the day shall dawn—far distant though it may be—when the rights and duties of human brotherhood shall be acknowledged by all the races of mankind! *

---

* These were the last words uttered by Mr. Bryant in public, and almost the last that he ever spoke.

# III.

# EDITORIAL COMMENTS AND CRITICISMS.

VOL. II.—23

# ON WRITING TRAGEDY.*

THIS work appears from the title-page to be printed from a London edition, but we learn that the author is a countryman of our own. We are glad to meet with so respectable a production in this department of literature from the pen of a native writer. Indeed, we are pleased to receive any modern tragedy in the English language so well worthy of notice. Whatever may be the cause, it is certain that late attempts in that species of composition, with few exceptions, have failed. Few writers, indeed, of any note, have ventured upon it, and it must be confessed that the discouragements are many and serious. In other kinds of poetical composition the author writes for those whose minds have many habits in common with his own : he writes to the contemplative, to the learned, to those who have leisure to follow him in his reviews and to accompany him till he finishes his favorite disquisitions. But the tragic poet has not only to deal with these, but with a more vivacious and impatient race of beings ; it must be his aim to please the many as well as the few ; he can offend neither with safety. His piece may be well received in the theatre, but, if destitute of those higher qualities which should recommend it to the more polished and enlightened part of

---

* From a review of Percy's " Masque," a drama, in the " North American Review," vol. xi, p. 384. It was the design of the editor to include in this volume a copious selection from the editorial comments and criticisms of Mr. Bryant ; but he found, on approaching this division of the work, that he had already so far encroached upon the space to which he was limited that he was obliged to confine his extracts to a comparatively few, written at different periods of the author's life.

society, the multitude soon grow weary of the bauble, and it comes first to be despised, and then forgotten. On the other hand, he may frame his work according to the most judicious and sensible rules of criticism; he may introduce many fine situations and much beautiful poetry; he may produce what shall be called a pleasing composition; still he may have failed to touch those springs which move the hearts and kindle the imaginations of all, and he goes off with the cold and equivo-cal compliment of having written a good closet tragedy. It is, perhaps, more difficult, and requires intenser effort, to bring the mind to a proper state for writing tragedy than for the other kinds of poetical composition. In the latter we commune with the author; he describes to our imaginations, he appeals to our feelings in his own favorite way, and these peculiarities interest us. But the dramatic poet must put off his identity and put on the characters which he invents. He must bring before him the personages of his plot, and see their faces and hear their voices in his retirement. He must do more: he must enter into their bosoms, he must feel with their hearts, and speak with their lips. Now, it is obvious that all this demands great versatility of talent as well as a state of strong and peculiar mental excitement. It demands, too, a great sac-rifice of the self-love and vanity of authorship. Many a flight of imagination, many an elegant refinement, which the author would be glad that the world should have an opportunity to admire, but which have no special connection with the busi-ness of his play—stately phrases and pretty epithets, which suggest themselves to his mind and win upon his partiality, but which would ill suit the ease of dialogue or the language of passion—must be rigidly excluded. Everything that inter-rupts the interest, everything that destroys the scenic illusion, all that is merely fine and showy, must be retrenched without mercy. It cannot be objected that these rules would make the writer tamely and coldly correct. On the contrary, they do not forbid, they even require, that the diction and sentiment should be highly glowing and impassioned; but they still require, what is the best means of attaining to these qualities, that he should never forget his subject. With all these difficulties in their way, it is no wonder that the most celebrated English poets of our day should choose to exert their talents in those walks of poetry which leave them more at liberty to move in the free and natural current of their own feelings and fancies. It may be doubted, too, whether the general manner of most of these writers, greatly superior as we think it to the cautious and unimpassioned style which immediately preceded it, is not yet too quaint, fanciful, and over-wrought to succeed well on the stage. Be this as it may, tragedy is a noble province of poetry, demanding great powers of invention, deep knowledge of the human heart, and a strong and manly judgment; and proud would be the triumph of him who at this day should overcome its difficulties and take his place by the side of those great and ancient masters of the drama whose race seems to have passed away from among us, like that of the giants who lived before the flood. It were glorious to succeed ; it is not dishonorable, however, to have failed.

# AMERICAN SOCIETY AS A FIELD FOR FICTION.*

On more than one occasion we have already given. our opinion somewhat at large of the fertility of our country, and its history, in the materials of romance. If our reasonings needed any support from successful examples of that kind of writing, as a single fact is worth a volume of ingenious theorizing, we have had the triumph of seeing them confirmed, beyond all controversy, by the works of a popular American au-

* From a review of " Redwood," by Miss Sedgwick, in the " North American," vol. xx, p. 245.

thor, who has shown the literary world into what beautiful creations those materials may be wrought. In like manner, we look upon the specimen before us as a conclusive argument that the writers of works of fiction, of which the scene is laid in familiar and domestic life, have a rich and varied field before them in the United States. Indeed, the conviction on this subject, which till lately prevailed among us, that works of this kind, descriptive of the manners of our countrymen, could not succeed, never seemed to us to rest on a very solid foundation. It was rather a sweeping inference, drawn from the fact that no highly meritorious work of the kind had appeared, and the most satisfactory and comfortable way of accounting for this was to assert that no such could be written. But it is not always safe to predict what a writer of genius will make of a given subject. Twenty years ago, what possible conception could an English critic have had of the admirable productions of the author of " Waverley," and of the wonderful improvement his example has effected in that kind of composition? Had the idea of one of those captivating works, destined to take such strong hold on all minds, been laid before him by the future author, he would probably only have wondered at his vanity.

There is nothing paradoxical in the opinion which maintains that all civilized countries—we had almost said all countries whatever—furnish matter for copies of real life, embodied in works of fiction, which shall be of lasting and general interest. Wherever there are human nature and society there are subjects for the novelist. The passions and affections, virtue and vice, are of no country. Everywhere love comes to touch the hearts of the young, and everywhere scorn and jealousy, the obstacles of fortune and the prudence of the aged, are at hand to disturb the course of love. Everywhere there exists the greed of wealth, the lust of power, and the wish to be admired; courage braving real dangers, and cowardice shrinking from imaginary ones; friendship and hatred, and all the train of motives and impulses which affect the minds and influence the conduct of men. They not only exist everywhere, but they exist, infinitely diversified and compounded, in various degrees of suppression and restraint, or fostered into unnatural growth and activity, modified by political institutions and laws, by national religions and subdivisions of those religions, by different degrees of refinement and civilization, of poverty or of abundance, by arbitrary usages handed down from indefinite antiquity, and even by local situation and climate. Nor is there a single one of all these innumerable modifications of human character and human emotion which is not, in some degree, an object of curiosity and interest. Over all the world is human sagacity laying its plans, and chance and the malice of others are thwarting them, and fortune is raising up one man and throwing down another. In none of the places of human habitation are the accesses barred against joy or grief; the kindness of the good carries gladness into families, and the treachery of the false friend brings sorrow and ruin; in all countries are tears shed over the graves of the excellent, the brave, and the beautiful, and the oppressed breathe freer when the oppressor has gone to his account. Everywhere has Nature her features of grandeur and of beauty, and these features receive a moral expression from the remembrances of the past and the interests of the present. On her face, as on an immense theatre, the passions and pursuits of men are performing the great drama of human existence. At every moment, and in every corner of the world, these mighty and restless agents are perpetually busy, under an infinity of forms and disguises, and the great representation goes on with that majestic continuity and uninterrupted regularity which mark all the courses of nature. Who, then, will undertake to say that the hand of genius may not pencil off a few scenes acted in our vast country, and amid our large population, that shall interest and delight the world?

It is a native writer only that must and can do this. It is he that must show how the infinite diversities of human character are yet further varied by causes that exist in our own country, exhibit our peculiar modes of thinking and action and mark the effect of these upon individual fortunes and happiness. A foreigner is manifestly incompetent to the task; his observation would rest only upon the more general and obvious traits of our national character, a thousand delicate shades of manner would escape his notice, many interesting peculiarities would never come to his knowledge, and many more he would misapprehend. It is only on his native soil that the author of such works can feel himself on safe and firm ground, that he can move confidently and fearlessly, and put forth the whole strength of his powers without risk of failure. His delineations of character and action, if executed with ability, will have a raciness and freshness about them which will attest their fidelity, the secret charm which belongs to truth and nature, and without which even the finest genius cannot invest a system of adscititious and imaginary manners. It is this quality which recommends them powerfully to the sympathy and interest even of those who are unacquainted with the original from which they are drawn, and makes such pictures from such hands so delightful and captivating to the foreigner. By superadding to the novelty of the manners described the interest of a narrative, they create a sort of illusion which places him in the midst of the country where the action of the piece is going on. He beholds the scenery of a distant land, hears its inhabitants conversing about their own concerns in their own dialect, finds himself in the bosom of its families, is made the depositary of their secrets and the observer of their fortunes, and becomes an inmate of their firesides without stirring from his own. Thus it is that American novels are eagerly read in Great Britain, and novels descriptive of English and Scottish manners as eagerly read in America.

It has been objected that the habits of our countrymen are too active and practical; that they are too universally and continually engrossed by the cares and occupations of business to have leisure for that intrigue, those plottings and counter-plottings, which are necessary to give a sufficient degree of action and eventfulness to the novel of real life. It is said that we need for this purpose a class of men whose condition in life places them above the necessity of active exertion, and who are driven to the practice of intrigue because they have nothing else to do. It remains, however, to be proved that any considerable portion of this ingredient is necessary in the composition of a successful novel. To require that it should be made up of nothing better than the manœuvres of those whose only employment is to glitter at places of public resort, to follow a perpetual round of amusements, and to form plans to outshine, thwart, and vex each other, is confining the writer to a narrow and most barren circle. It is requiring an undue proportion of heartlessness, selfishness, and vice in his pictures of society. It is compelling him to go out of the wholesome atmosphere of those classes, where the passions and affections have their most salutary and natural play, and employ his observations on that where they are the most perverted, sophisticated, and corrupt.

But will it be seriously contended that he can have no other resource than the rivalries and machinations of the idle, the frivolous, and the dissolute, to keep the reader from yawning over his pictures? Will it be urged that no striking and interesting incidents can come to pass without their miserable aid? If our country be not the country of intrigue, it is at least the country of enterprise; and nowhere are the great objects that worthily interest the passions and call forth the exertions of men pursued with more devotion and perseverance. The agency of chance, too, is not confined to the shores of Europe; our countrymen have not attained a sufficient degree of certainty in their calculations to exclude it from ours. It would really seem to us that these two sources, along with that blessed quality of intrigue which even the least favorable view of our society will allow us, are abundantly fertile in interesting occurrences for all the purposes of the novelist. Besides, it should be recollected that it is not in any case the dull diary of ordinary occupations or amusements that forms the groundwork of his plot. On the contrary, it is some event, or at least a series of events, of unusual importance, standing out in strong relief from the rest of the biography of his principal characters, and to which the daily habits of their lives, whatever may be their rank or condition, are only a kind of accompaniment.

But the truth is that the distinctions of rank and the amusements of elegant idleness are but the surface of society, and only so many splendid disguises put upon the reality of things. They are trappings which the writer of real genius, the anatomist of the human heart, strips away when he would exhibit his characters as they are, and engage our interest for them as beings of our own species. He reduces them to the same great level where distinctions of rank are nothing and difference of character everything. It is here that James I and Charles II and Louis IX and Rob Roy and Jeanie Deans and Meg Merrilies are, by the author of the " Waverley Novels," made to meet. The monarch must come down from the dim elevation of his throne; he must lay aside the assumed and conventional manners of his station, and unbend and unbosom himself with his confidants before that illustrious master will condescend to describe him. In the artificial sphere in which the great move, they are only puppets and pageants, but here they are men. A narrative the scene of which is laid at the magnificent levees of princes, in the drawing-rooms of nobles, and the bright assemblies of fashion, may be a very pretty, showy sort of thing, and so may a story of the glittering dances and pranks of fairies. But we soon grow weary of all this and ask for objects of sympathy and regard; for something the recollection of which shall dwell on the heart, and to which it will love to recur; for something, in short, which is natural, the unaffected traits of strength and weakness, of the tender and the comic, all which the pride of rank either removes from observation or obliterates.

If these things have any value, we hesitate not to say that

they are to be found abundantly in the characters of our coun-
trymen, formed as they are under the influences of our free
institutions, and shooting into a large and vigorous, though
sometimes irregular, luxuriance. They exist most abundantly
in our more ancient settlements, and amid the more homo-
geneous races of our large populations, where the causes that
produce them have operated longest and with most activity.
It is there that the human mind has learned best to enjoy our
fortunate and equal institutions, and to profit by them. In
the countries of Europe the laws chain men down to the con-
dition in which they were born. This observation, of course,
is not equally true of all those countries, but, when they are
brought into comparison with ours, it is in some degree ap-
plicable to them all. Men spring up and vegetate and die
without thinking of passing from the sphere in which they
find themselves any more than the plants they cultivate think
of removing from the places where they are rooted. It is the
tendency of this rigid and melancholy destiny to contract and
stint the intellectual faculties, to prevent the development of
character and to make the subjects of it timid, irresolute, and
imbecile. With us, on the contrary, where the proudest
honors in the State and the highest deference in society are
set equally before all our citizens, a wholesome and quickening
impulse is communicated to all parts of the social system.
All are possessed with a spirit of ambition and a love of ad-
venture, an intense competition calls forth and exalts the pas-
sions and faculties of men, their characters become strongly
defined, their minds acquire a hardihood and an activity
which can be gained by no other discipline, and the com-
munity, throughout all its conditions, is full of bustle and
change and action.

Whoever will take the pains to pursue this subject a little
into its particulars will be surprised at the infinite variety of
forms of character which spring up under the institutions
of our country. Religion is admitted on all hands to be a
mighty agent in moulding the human character; and, accord-

ingly, with the perfect allowance and toleration of all religions, we see among us their innumerable and diverse influences upon the manners and temper of our people. Whatever may be his religious opinions, no one is restrained by fear of consequences from avowing them, but is left to nurse his peculiarities of doctrine into what importance he pleases. The Quaker is absolved from submission to the laws in those particulars which offend his conscience, the Moravian finds no barriers in the way of his work of proselytism and charity, the Roman Catholic is subjected to no penalty for pleasing himself with the magnificent ceremonial of his religion, and the Jew worships unmolested in his synagogue. In many parts of our country we see communities of that strange denomination, the Shakers, distinguished from their neighbors by a garb, a dialect, an architecture, a way of worship, of thinking, and of living, as different as if they were in fact of a different origin, instead of being collected from the families around them. In other parts we see small neighborhoods of the Seventh Day Baptists, retaining their simplicity of manners and quaintness of language delivered down from their fathers. Here we find the austerities of puritanism preserved to this day, there the rights and doctrines of the Church of England are shown in their effect on the manners of the people, and yet in another part of the country springs up a new and numerous sect, who wash one another's feet and profess to revive the primitive habits of the apostolic times.

It is in our country also that these differences of character, which grow naturally out of geographical situation, are least tampered with and repressed by political regulations. The adventurous and roving natives of our sea-coasts and islands are a different race of men from those who till the interior, and the hardy dwellers of our mountainous districts are not like the inhabitants of the rich plains that skirt our mighty lakes and rivers. The manners of the Northern States are said to be characterized by the keenness and importunity of their climate, and those of the Southern to partake of the softness of theirs. In our cities you will see the polished manners of the European capitals, but pass into the more quiet and unvisited parts of the country, and you will find men whom you might take for the first planters of our colonies. The descendants of the Hollanders have not forgotten the traditions of their fathers, and the legends of Germany are still recited, and the ballads of Scotland still sung, in settlements whose inhabitants derive their origin from those countries. It is hardly possible that the rapid and continual growth and improvement of our country, a circumstance wonderfully exciting to the imagination and altogether unlike anything witnessed in other countries, should not have some influence in forming our national character. At all events, it is a most fertile source of incident. It does for us in a few short years what in Europe is a work of centuries. The hardy and sagacious native of the Eastern States settles himself in the wilderness by the side of the emigrant from the British Isles; the pestilence of the marshes is braved and overcome; the bear and wolf and catamount are chased from their haunts; and then you see cornfields and roads and towns springing up as if by enchantment. In the mean time pleasant Indian villages, situated on the skirts of their hunting-grounds, with their beautiful green plats for dancing and martial exercises, are taken into the bosom of our extending population, while new States are settled and cities founded far beyond them. Thus a great deal of history is crowded into a brief space. Each little hamlet in a few seasons has more events and changes to tell of than a European village can furnish in a course of ages.

But, if the writer of fictitious history does not find all the variety he wishes in the various kinds of our population, descended, in different parts of our country, from ancestors of different nations, and yet preserving innumerable and indubitable tokens of their origin, if the freedom with which every man is suffered to take his own way in all things not affecting the peace and good order of society does not furnish him with a sufficient diversity of characters, employments, and modes of life, he has got other resources. He may bring into his plots men whose characters and manners were formed by the institutions and modes of society in the nations beyond the Atlantic, and he may describe them faithfully as things which he has observed and studied. If he is not satisfied with indigenous virtue, he may take for the model of his characters men of whom the Old World is not worthy, and whom it has cast out from its bosom. If domestic villany be not dark enough for his pictures, here are fugitives from the justice of Europe come to prowl in America. If the coxcombs of our own country are not sufficiently exquisite, affected, and absurd, here are plenty of silken fops from the capitals of foreign kingdoms. If he finds himself in need of a class of men more stupid and degraded than are to be found among the natives of the United States, here are crowds of the wretched peasantry of Great Britain and Germany, flying for refuge from intolerable suffering, in every vessel that comes to our shores. Hither, also, resort numbers of that order of men who, in foreign countries, are called the middling class, the most valuable part of the communities they leave, to enjoy a moderate affluence, where the abuses and exactions of a distempered system of government cannot reach them to degrade them to the condition of the peasantry. Our country is the asylum of the persecuted preachers of new religions and the teachers of political doctrines which Europe will not endure; a sanctuary for dethroned princes and the consorts of slain emperors. When we consider all these innumerable differences of character, native and foreign, this infinite variety of pursuits and objects, this endless diversity and change of fortunes, and behold them gathered and grouped into one vast assemblage in our own country, we shall feel little pride in the sagacity or the skill of that native author who asks for a richer or a wider field of observation.

# ON THE DRAMATIC USE OF SCRIPTURE CHARACTERS.*

THOUGH the author of "Hadad" has chosen to give his work the more general denomination of a dramatic poem, it has all the incidents and characteristics of a tragedy. It is continued through the proper number of acts, is written with a sufficient regard to dramatic unity, and is furnished with a reasonable number and variety of characters. It has a regular plot and catastrophe, and the personages are all finally disposed of according to the fairest rules of poetical justice. Perhaps, however, the author was prevented from calling it a tragedy by supposing that the nature of the subject, and the introduction of supernatural agents into the plot, would exclude it from the stage. Let it be a dramatic poem, then, since the author chooses to call it so—at all events, we are ready to acknowledge that it is a very good one.

The story of this drama is founded on the rebellion of Absalom. This is a very interesting event in the annals of the Jewish nation, and the actors in it were some of the most important personages of Scripture history. How far subjects drawn from the sacred writings are proper for narrative or dramatic poetry is a question about which there has been much discussion. It has been urged, among other objections to this use of such subjects, that it is a sort of unhallowed mingling of fiction with the pure truth of the sacred records, the tendency of which is to impair our reverence for the history of our religion, and our respect for the lessons which that history was intended to inculcate. We must say, however, that, with all proper deference for these scruples, we cannot help thinking them entirely unnecessary.

The human persons mentioned in sacred history must be

---

* From a review of "Hadad," by James A. Hillhouse. New York Review, 1825.

considered as actual human beings, subject to the common passions and infirmities of our race, and, for the most part, to the ordinary influences of good and ill fortune. It cannot surely be impious to suppose that what we are told of them in Scripture is not the whole of this history. We are not forbidden to dwell on what we may conceive to be their emotions in the various passages of their lives which are recorded, nor to fancy the particulars of those events which are related only in general terms, nor even to imagine them engaged in adventures of which no account has come down to us. So long as this is done in such a manner as to correspond with what is related of their characters and actions in Holy Writ, we cannot see that anything is done to offend the most delicate conscience. We cannot see that it has the least tendency to weaken the impression produced upon us by the narratives of Scripture; on the contrary, it seems to us that, leading the mind to dwell upon them more intently, it will naturally deepen and confirm it. This field ought at least to be as free to the poet as to the pulpit orator. Nobody thinks of passing a censure upon the latter when, suffering his imagination to kindle and his heart to become warm with his subject, he expatiates upon the fraternal affection of Joseph, or amplifies the filial devotion of Ruth.

It is obvious that the form in which the poem is cast can make no difference with the principle in this case. It is immaterial whether it be dramatic or narrative, as long as it is not made the subject of scenic representation; for no greater liberty is taken with Scripture history in the one case than in the other.

We are aware, however, that it may be further said that the natural effect of these subjects upon the mind of the writer is not such as to ensure the free and happy exertion of his powers. The habitual reverence with which we regard them awes and represses the imagination. The dread of taking improper liberties with his subject, and the fear of offending the scruples of others, act as shackles upon the invention of the writer; and, amid all these influences, there is danger that he will rest in common places, and that his work will be tame and spiritless. There is great difficulty, also, in awakening in the mind of the reader a strong interest in the characters and fortunes of the personages upon whom the action of the piece depends. This is a consequence of the extraordinary dispensation of which they were the subjects. There is something in the idea of mortals, taken into so intimate a relation with the Divine Being, which rebukes and repels earthly sympathy.

These are difficulties — serious difficulties; but they are not insurmountable. They render the work of the poet arduous — not impossible. The imagination may still soar high, and the invention act vigorously, in the permitted direction; and that sympathy which we are slow to yield may still be wrung from us by the truth and force with which his scenes and situations are brought home to our hearts. The great epic of Milton was written in defiance of the highest degree of these difficulties, yet it is the noblest poem in our language; nor is his " Paradise Regained " unworthy to be the last work of so great a man. His " Samson Agonistes," full of grand sentiments and strains of high philosophy, seems to owe its want of dramatic interest, not to any inherent defect in the subject, but to the cold model of the Grecian tragedy after which it was composed. Cowley appears to have discontinued the writing of his " Davideis " because it was not worth finishing; but neither would it have been had the subject been taken from profane history. In our time, Byron, in his dramatic poems founded on subjects taken from the Scriptures, has emancipated himself, as might be expected, even from the most salutary of those restraints which their sacredness imposes on the mind. Along with many interesting situations, and much impassioned sentiment, they contain no small proportion of indecency and blasphemy. This impiety, however, is by no means the consequence of his choice of subjects; his choice of subjects only renders his impiety the more palpable and revolting.   Moore, in his "Loves of the Angels," is apparently too little in earnest to be deeply interesting; he dallies too idly with his subject, and his pretty amatory language has an unnatural sound in the mouths of celestials.   In the instance of Montgomery, however, it should seem that a sacred subject has imparted, to a genius of no great original power and unwonted spring and vigor, a deeper pathos and a finer play of imagination.   His "World before the Flood" we think altogether the best of his larger poems.   The sacred dramas of Milman are admitted to be superior to anything else that he has written.   They certainly possess great tragic effect, and, though composed with little skill in the delineation of character, and overloaded with ambitious ornament, are yet much sought after, and read with interest and pleasure. It is owing, we suspect, to some other cause than the chilling influence of such subjects upon the powers of the writers, or their want of attraction over the minds of readers, that the "Exodiad of Cumberland" is forgotten, that the "Conquest of Canaan" reposes in the dust of the bookseller's shelves, and that the sacred dramas of Miss Hannah More have found little favor in the eyes of the light age for which they were written.

In looking over the names of those English poets who have made use of the materials furnished by the sacred writings, it will appear that, generally speaking, wherever great powers of mind have been brought to work, their exertion has been attended with success; and that those who have written bad poems owe their failure quite as much to the want of talent as to the unfortunate choice of a subject.   Thus we have something better than mere theory to guide us in this discussion.   The very history of our literature proves that these materials may be converted to the purposes of poetry, and that although, perhaps, not the most attractive in their nature, nor the best adapted to the favorable execution of ordinary talents, they are yet capable of being turned to good account in the hands of a master.

# THE CHARACTER OF SHERIDAN.*

IT would be almost impossible, we should think, for the dullest author to make a dull book of Sheridan's life, provided he had used what the lawyers call ordinary diligence in collecting the materials. The mixture of good and bad qualities in his character, the romantic adventures of his early youth, his wit, his conviviality, the very irregularity of his private habits, his public life, his eloquence, his parliamentary dexterity, his intimacy not only with the first literary, but with the most eminent political men of his time, and with those whose greatness lay only in their titles, as ciphers derive a value from their position, his connection with the theatre, and the many eccentric adventures with which it must have thrown him into contact; in short, the constant existence of this man in the midst of society, in all its various modes and classes, must have afforded a rich and various mine of anecdote, such as the lives of few men offer. With a little less tenderness to the reputation of Mr. Sheridan, and a little more fondness for gossiping, it is quite clear to us that Mr. Moore might have made a much more entertaining book, as well as have presented us with a more faithful view of Mr. Sheridan's character.

We are not disposed, however, to complain of the way in which he has chosen to execute his undertaking, nor to blame him for the oblivion in which he is willing to leave the infirmities of his friend. He has given us a graver book than we should expect from one wit writing the life of another; but very interesting withal, and quite sensible, as well as quite characteristic of the vivacity and activity of the writer's mind.

One excellence in Mr. Moore's work is that, with all its tenderness to the blemishes of Sheridan's character, and all the ideal coloring which he spread over it, there is still enough

---

* From a review of Moore's " Life of Sheridan," " New York Review," 1826.

of truth in his delineation to enable us to distinguish pretty clearly both the good and the evil ingredients of which it was compounded.   At this distance from the country in which he flourished, we can consider his character almost as impartially as if we were not his contemporaries; and, with the materials furnished by Mr. Moore, it is not difficult to estimate it fairly.   It was the misfortune of Sheridan that his animal nature, if we may so speak, had so much the mastery over his intellectual.   He not only loved pleasure with a more impetuous fondness, but suffered less from the excessive pursuit of it than most men.   The strength of his constitution, the possession of high health, the excitability of his feelings, and his fine flow of animal spirits, all either seconded the temptations of the siren, or secured him from the immediate penalties which so often follow her gifts.   In proportion to his love of pleasure was his hatred of labor.   No man loves labor for its own sake—at least not until long habit has made it necessary—but some seem originally to dread and hate it more vehemently than others.   It is almost impossible to imagine anybody more unwilling to look this severe step-mother of greatness and virtue in the face than was Sheridan.   This disposition showed itself while he was yet a school-boy, and seems to have lost no strength in his maturer years.   He never had, he never would have, any regular pursuit, for neither his connection with the theatre nor his parliamentary career deserve this name.   He avoided all periodical industry; it was a principle of his conduct to delay everything to the last possible moment; and his whole life seems to have been a series of experiments to escape, or at least to put off to another day, that greatest of evils—labor.   Yet he was capable, in a high degree, of intellectual exertion; and the instances in which he submitted himself to it are so many successful experiments of the force of his genius.   His political career was marked by the same unpersevering character as his private life.   He was ambitious, but his was not that deep-seated ambition which broods long over its plans, and follows and watches them, year after year, with unexhausted patience. If a single blow could prostrate the party he opposed, Sheridan was the man to strike it—and with great force; but it was not for him to assail it with attacks, continually repeated, till it was overthrown. After a powerful effort, he would turn again to his pleasures and dissipations until they palled upon him, or until the entreaties of friendship, or some sudden excitement of feeling, recalled him to the warfare. That such a man should, notwithstanding, have exerted himself so far as to produce those celebrated comedies and speeches which were the admiration of his age, may be easily accounted for on these views of his character. His indolence was not of that dreamy kind which delights in visions of its own creation ; no man was less imaginative than Sheridan. It is true that there are some attempts at fancy in his writings, but they do not seem to be the natural effusions of his mind. They were evidently written for display, and consist of broken images laboriously brought together. Indeed, it would probably have been fortunate for him had he delighted more in reveries of the imagination, for it is the tendency of these to make us look with a kind of dissatisfaction on the world about us; but it was the error and the danger of Sheridan that he loved that world, and its splendors and its pleasures, quite too well. He was not disposed to search for imaginary enjoyments, but to possess himself greedily and immoderately of those within his reach. He was the creature of society; its light and changing excitements were the food of his mind ; and to dazzle and astonish it was a pleasure which he enjoyed with the highest zest. This is the secret of those irregular and brief, but for the time vigorous, sallies of industry. Everything with him was planned for effect; his comedies, his operas, his speeches, are all brilliant, showy, and taking. His more elaborate efforts, however, were stimulated by the additional motive of necessity. "The Rivals" and "The Duenna" were written when he was forced to think of doing something for a livelihood, and the "School for Scandal" at the same period. All his exertions respected some immediate advantage. He loved to shine, but thought not of laying up fame for future ages; just as he loved the enjoyments of wealth, but chose not to perplex himself for its accumulation and preservation. It was characteristic of Sheridan ·that he was too economical of labor even to labor in vain. All the quips and jests and smart things which came into his head he treasured up for the convivial meeting or the floor of Parliament. He came fresh from his stolen studies, on subjects of which he was before ignorant, to make a splendid speech about them before the vividness of his new impressions had faded from his mind. Among the few papers left behind him, it would seem, from the extracts given us by Mr. Moore, that there was nothing on which much study had been expended, nor which was in itself capable of being made valuable.

Sheridan was a man of quick but not deep feelings; of sudden but not lasting excitements. He was not one of those who suffer a single passion to influence the whole course of their lives. Even the desire to dazzle by his wit, great as was its power over him, was not always awake, for we are told that he would sometimes remain silent for hours in company, too lazy to invent a smart saying for the occasion, but idly waiting for the opportunity to apply some brilliant witticism already in his memory. His writings themselves show that he never dwelt long enough on any particular feeling to analyze it; the few attempts at sentimentalism they contain are excessively false and affected; their excellence lies wholly in a different way. His romantic love for the beautiful, amiable, and accomplished woman who became his wife, though his biographer would have us believe that it continued unabated to the end of her life, seems to have operated on his mind only at intervals, for it is hinted in this very book that it was not steady enough to secure his fidelity. Her death, and that of her little daughter, who soon followed her, deeply as they affected him at the time, threw no cloud over his after-life. His griefs might have been violent, but they were certainly brief, and he quickly forgot them when he came to look again at the sunny side of things. Even his political disappointments do not seem in the least to have soured his temper, or abated his readiness to adopt new hopes and new expedients. Indeed, it seems not improbable, from some appearances of pliancy in his political character, that, had not his daily habits enfeebled the vigor of his mind and shortened a life which great robustness of constitution seemed to have marked out for a late old age, he might have long continued a favorite with the present sovereign of England.

Some of the excellences of Sheridan's character were such as could not easily suffer by this disposition to indolence and pleasure. That a man possessing an abundant flow of agreeable animal sensations, determined to make a matter of enjoyment of everything, and to avoid everything in the shape of care, should have possessed likewise an engaging good nature, is by no means extraordinary. That he who had no solitary pleasures, but whose happiness was in some way connected with that of those about him, should be obliging, generous, and humane, is almost a natural consequence. The man who lives only among and by his friends is naturally led to study the art of making friendships. Nor is the frankness and openness of Sheridan's disposition any less in harmony with the rest of his character. It is not among men of his temperament that we are to look for the habit of dissimulation, for concealed designs, and the weaving and carrying on of frauds and artifices. The labor and perplexity of falsehood were with him sufficient objection, had no other existed, to the practice of it. The anxious and persevering necessity to provide against detection he left to those who were more steadily diligent than himself. Had the practice of deceit been as easy as that of integrity, we are not sure that Sheridan would not have fallen into it, induced by the prospect of immediate and present advantages which it always holds out—for it seems that he had not sufficient firmness of principle to resist the temptations of many other vices.

## BONAPARTE'S CORSICAN TRAITS.*

THE name of Corsica is associated in the minds of most men, not with that of its great hero and patriot Paoli, but with that of a Bonaparte ; and it would be a curious study to examine how far the peculiar character of its inhabitants is to be traced in that of Napoleon, and how far the state of society in which he was born and passed his boyish years may be presumed to have moulded the mind of him of whom Europe so long stood in fear.  In addition to what was already known of the inhabitants of Corsica, the work before us contains many curious particulars, which might be used for this purpose.

The barbarism and ignorance into which the Corsicans are sunk are beyond those of almost any European nation.  Even the Russian, notwithstanding he is flogged, if we may believe Dr. Clarke, every hour in the day, is his superior in point of civilization ; he lives in a more comfortable dwelling, and cultivates his fields with far greater skill.  We have heard somewhat of the degeneracy and degradation of modern Greeks, but they are a polished and enlightened people compared with the Corsicans.  A colony of Mainotes, who were planted on this island many years ago by the Genoese, and of whom the remains are now settled in Ajaccio, excited the wonder and jealousy of the natives by building commodious houses, cultivating gardens, planting fine vineyards, possessing thriving flocks and herds, and living in every respect in a style of comfort new to the Corsicans.

(The reviewer adds several pages descriptive of Corsican life, and then continues :)

. . . . It was this singular and oppressed race of men that, in our time, has given to Europe an emperor whose reign did

---

* From a review of Robert Benson's " Sketches of Corsica." " New York Review," 1826.

more to change the condition of that continent than any politi-
cal event which has happened since the irruption of the north-
ern nations. It shook and overthrew the old Gothic institu-
tions, and brought back, in some degree, the state of things
that existed before them. The days of the Lower Empire
seemed to have returned, not only in the rapidity with which
the kingdoms of Europe changed masters, but in the humble
origin of those who were raised to sit upon their thrones, and
of those chiefs and warriors who stood around them and up-
held them. The parallel to the history of that period is to be
found in those times when a Dacian herdsman, and after him
a Thracian soldier, were invested with the imperial purple.
Yet, if the world must have a master, Corsica was not un-
worthy to give it one. The rude island was in many respects
a fitting nurse of those qualities which lead to the summit of
military glory. It would indeed be hardly possible for a set-
tled state of society, a state of submission to the laws, and of
personal security, to form a proper temperament for pushing
one's fortune to such a height as Napoleon carried his; still
less could we expect to see it spring up in the enervating at-
mosphere of courts. That constant presence of mind, that
cool and quick speculation on emergencies which startled and
took away the power of reflection from other men, and that
incredible promptitude of expedients which he possessed,
could nowhere be so perfectly acquired as in a country where
personal danger is a thing of course, where it besets every
man from his childhood, where it lurks about his dwelling
and lies in ambush in his path, and where his vigilance is al-
ways awake and his sagacity always in exercise to avert it
or to encounter it. These qualities were what such a man as
Napoleon needed most, and these are, in a greater or less de-
gree, common to every Corsican peasant. When they had re-
ceived a direction in Napoleon's mind by the severities of a
military education, when he had been taught to become as per-
severing as he was ardent, when he had added a knowledge of
the science of war, as practiced in Europe, to those military

dispositions of mind acquired in a school of which the rest of Europe knew nothing, his advantage over other men was immense. It was probably that contempt of the female sex belonging to the Corsican people that prevented Bonaparte, with an Italian warmth of constitution and no great disposition to regulate his amours by any strict notions of morals, from becoming, like too many other monarchs, the slave of women. He boasted, with truth, that he never suffered them to gain an ascendancy over him, or to cause him to withdraw his eyes for a moment from his projects of ambition. Had he been the founder of a new religion instead of a mighty empire, he would probably have assigned to them no higher importance in his system than did Mohammed. His lofty and far-reaching ambition was only Corsican pride, operating in a wider and grander sphere. The florid but emphatic and effectual eloquence with which he animated his soldiers in the battle was equally characteristic of the race to which he belonged. Add to all this the Corsican disregard of law and defiance of authority, and you have a man disposed to acknowledge no superior, fitted to dare and to do all that is possible to military skill and strength to overthrow established governments and to rule the world.

It is somewhat singular that Napoleon should never have distinguished his native island by any particular marks of his favor, and that he should have done nothing to improve the condition of a part of his dominions which needed improvement the most. In early life he had joined the party who wished to keep the inhabitants under the yoke of the French, who had bought them of Genoa, and whom they hated ; and afterward, when he ascended the throne of France, he seemed to have forgotten them. He could talk in his exile at St. Helena of the affection he still felt toward the country of his birth, of the sublimity of its scenery, the fragrance of its air, the hospitality and high spirit of its inhabitants, and the happy days of his youth spent in wandering among its mountains and making himself an inmate of its cottages. He could wish, too, that, at his abdication in 1814, he had reserved to himself, as he might have done, this neglected country. Corsica, however, owed him nothing in his lifetime, and at his death she received no share of the plunder of Europe. The Corsicans do not look upon contempt for the country of one's birth as a slight offence; and, while the name of Paoli is pronounced among them only with veneration, no honors are paid to the memory of Bonaparte.

---

# EFFECT OF CLIMATE ON AGE.*

NOTWITHSTANDING the complaints made of our variable climate, there is no doubt that it has its advantages and its beauties. We have sometimes the frosts of a Siberian winter, and sometimes the continued heats of a West India summer; but we have days of the most delicious temperature, the clearest and bluest skies, the brightest sunshine, and the most inspiring airs. We have the word of an artist—who lived years in Italy, and who has as fine an eye for nature as ever looked upon her works—that he has seen as glorious evenings here as ever flushed the skies of that picturesque country; not so many of them, perhaps, but still to the full as beautiful. The praise which has been bestowed so lavishly on the beauty of the skies of Italy comes from those who were nurtured under the pale climate of England. Jefferson, it will be remembered, was glad to escape from the moist and clouded skies of Paris to the drier atmosphere and sunnier skies of Virginia. A distinguished and intelligent Hollander, who had resided in France, Switzerland, and England, and who reached his eightieth year in this country, always maintained that we have one of the best climates in the world. He was desirous

---

* From the " Evening Post," March 1, 1832.

of living in his native country, but, being subject to asthmatic
affection, found the fogs of that country too dense for his
lungs.   We have heard him rail, in good-set terms, at the
famed climate of Montpelier, for its easterly winds and raw,
damp atmosphere.   The towns of England do not experience
the intense cold during winter that we do, but they are wrapt
in almost perpetual fogs and wet with drizzling rains that
scarcely cease.   We have before us at this moment a letter
from Dr. Burgess, of Leicestershire, to the editor of the " Lon-
don Courier," in which he is laboring to prove that the cholera
will not be so fatal in the climate of England as it has been
on the Continent, and among other reasons he mentions "the
*quick succession and vicissitudes* of dry and wet—the utmost pre-
valence of the former scarcely ever continuing long enough
to induce disease from that cause alone, and the long duration
of the latter being timely succeeded by genial and favorable
alternations."   This is an equivocal compliment either to the
beauty or steadiness of the climate of England.   There is a
prevailing notion that the period of decay in the human con-
stitution arrives earlier here than in the mother country, and
that the duration of human life is shorter in consequence of
the climate.   Let us see how this is.   Dr. Kitchener dates the
commencement of the decline of the physical faculties at the
age of forty-two.   Crabbe, in one of his tales, puts it four
years later :

> " Six years had past, and forty ere the six,
>    When time began to play his usual tricks."

And then he goes on, in his fine manner, to describe the circum-
stances which mark the abatement of bodily activity and the
growing disinclination to exertion belonging to that time of
life.   We leave it to be decided by the experience of our
countrymen whether the period of decline in the animal
powers arrives earlier than this; whether in this country
men begin to feel the approaches of age before forty-six.
We believe not.   An Englishman of fifty may have as fair

and fresh a complexion as an American at thirty; but this is the mere effect of a moist and shaded sky. We are a more spare and meagre race than the English—and, indeed, than most of the nations of Europe. Artists will tell you that the difference between Americans and the natives of Europe in the fleshy parts of the human frame is astonishing. The tendency to corpulency there is much greater than with us, and is distinguishable even in the hands, which with us are lean and bony, and with the Europeans plumper and fatter. This is no advantage, but it keeps the skin smooth and prevents the approach of wrinkles, which are looked upon as one of the signs of old age.

We remember once hearing an ingenious medical friend remark that the difference between people who grow old in England and those who grow old in this country is that the former bloat up and the latter dry up. Old age among us is less unwieldy. We can point to many a man,

> " adust and thin,
> In a dun night-gown of his own loose skin,"

who yet preserves all the vigor of mind and activity of body which distinguished his greener years. The same man in the climate of England would have been more round and rosy, with better teeth, perhaps, for they decay in this country sooner than there, with fewer wrinkles, but, after all, no younger in constitution and no farther from the close of life. There are no such prodigies of corpulence among us as Louis XVIII, who was obliged to be rolled in a go-cart, being too unwieldy to walk, and who finally burst with obesity. There are no cases like that of George IV, who perished, as was said, from a collection of fat about the heart, which prevented it from performing its functions. Whatever be the cause of the difference in the human frame on the two continents, whatever it be that makes our countrymen taller and more spare than the Europeans, whether it arises from the violent alternation of cold and heat, or from a difference in the electric state of the atmosphere, it is enough that it has no effect to shorten life. The same difference has been remarked in some kinds of animals; the climate is said to elongate their forms; and there are not wanting those who think they have observed it also in trees and plants. It is a physical variety, but not an unhealthy one, and is produced by causes equally friendly to the existence of the human species. It has been stated that of the population of London only *one in forty* arrives at the age of seventy. We have before us the bills of mortality for the city of New York for five years, commencing with 1826, from which it appears that the average number of deaths of persons over seventy years of age is *one in twenty-seven.*

As respects the moral effect of our climate, there is nothing to complain of. The inhabitants of lands blessed with a soft and equable temperature are apt to be voluptuous; the people of less genial regions have made the greatest advances in civilization, and carried the arts and sciences to their highest perfection. Labor is never loved for its own sake; men require severe necessity, or some desire, to sting them into activity. Our climate, while it presents many of the beautiful phenomena of those which are reckoned the finest, is yet (for the truth must be acknowledged) variable, capricious, and severe, and exacts more ingenuity and foresight in guarding against the extremes to which it is subject than almost any other.

---

# ABOLITION· RIOTS.*

A MEETING of the people of Cincinnati have proclaimed the right of silencing the expression of unpopular opinions by violence. We refer our readers to the proceedings of an anti-

---

* From the " Evening Post," August 8, 1836.

abolition meeting lately held in that city. They will be found in another part of this paper.

The Cincinnati meeting, in the concluding resolution offered by Wilson N. Brown and adopted with the rest, declare in so many words that, if they cannot put down the abolitionist press by fair means, they will do it by foul; if they cannot silence it by remonstrance, they will silence it by violence; if they cannot persuade it to desist, they will stir up mobs against it, inflame them to madness, and turn their brutal rage against the dwellings, the property, the persons, the lives of the wretched abolitionists and their families. In announcing that they will put them down by force all this is included. Fire, robbery, and bloodshed are the common excesses of an enraged mob. There is no extreme of cruelty and destruction to which, in the drunkenness and delirium of its fury, it may not proceed. The commotions of the elements can as easily be appeased by appeals to the quality of mercy as these commotions of the human mind; the whirlwind and the lightning might as well be expected to pause and turn aside to spare the helpless and innocent as an infuriated multitude.

If the abolitionists *must* be put down, and if the community are of that opinion, there is no necessity of violence to effect the object. The community have the power in their own hands; the majority may make a law declaring the discussion of slavery in a certain manner to be a crime, and imposing penalties. The law may then be put in force against the offenders, and their mouths may be gagged in due form and with all the solemnities of justice.

What is the reason this is not done? The answer is ready. The community are for leaving the liberty of the press untrammelled; there is not a committee that can be raised in any of the State legislatures north of the Potomac who will report in favor of imposing penalties on those who declaim against slavery; there is not a legislature who would sanction such a report; and there is not a single free State the people of which would sustain a legislature in so doing. These are facts, and the advocates of mob-law know them to be so.

Who are the men that issue this invitation to silence the press by violence? Who but an insolent, brawling minority, a few noisy fanatics, who claim that their own opinions shall be the measure of freedom for the rest of the community, and who undertake to overawe a vast, pacific majority by threats of wanton outrage and plunder? These men are for erecting an oligarchy of their own and riding rough-shod over the people and the people's rights. They claim a right to repeal the laws established by the majority in favor of the freedom of the press. They make new laws of their own, to which they require that the rest of the community shall submit, and, in case of a refusal, they threaten to execute them by the ministry of a mob. There is no tyranny or oppression exercised in any part of the world more absolute or more frightful than that which they would establish. So far as we are concerned, we are determined that this despotism shall neither be submitted to nor encouraged. In whatever form it makes its appearance, we shall raise our voice against it. We are resolved that the subject of slavery shall be as it ever has been—as free a subject of discussion and argument and declamation as the difference between whiggism and democracy, or the difference between the Armenians and the Calvinists. If the press chooses to be silent on the subject, it shall be the silence of perfect free-will, and not the silence of fear. We hold that this combination of the few to govern the many by the terror of illegal violence is as wicked and indefensible as a conspiracy to rob on the highway. We hold it to be the duty of good citizens to protest against it whenever and wherever it shows itself, and to resist it, if necessary, to the death.

# FUNERAL OF AARON BURR.*

THE remains of Aaron Burr were on Friday committed to the earth at Princeton, New Jersey, beside the graves of President Edwards and President Burr, his father and grandfather. It was natural enough that the relatives of this man should wish to perform his obsequies with decency and propriety, but we protest against the puffery of which he is made the object in the public prints, the effect of which is to confound all moral distinctions. When we read of " admiration for his greatness," " respect for his memory," and " condolence for his loss," we are tempted to ask ourselves if the community have ceased to discriminate between the good and bad actions of men. The truth is, nobody is to be condoled with for his loss; no respect is entertained for the memory of one so profligate in private and public life ; and, though Colonel Burr was a man of acute and active mind, he did not rise to the measure of intellectual greatness, as he certainly was at a deplorable distance from moral greatness. We would willingly have passed by this subject in silence, but these remarks have been forced from us by what we must regard as a shameful prostitution of the voice of the press.

Some of the public prints are indulging in anticipations of the publication of a posthumous record of Colonel Burr's political and personal adventures, prepared under his direction for the press ; and they are essaying to awaken a prurient curiosity concerning them by the intimation that they contain disclosures of things which ought never to be revealed. We have no expectation of advantage to the cause of truth or of morals from the appearance of such a work. It were better that the memory of his intrigues should die with him.

---

* From the " Evening Post," September 19, 1836.

# ON USURY LAWS.*

THE fact that the usury laws, arbitrary, unjust, and oppressive as they are, and unsupported by a single substantial reason, should have been suffered to exist to the present time, can only be accounted for on the ground of the general and singular ignorance which has prevailed as to the true nature and character of money. If men would but learn to look upon the medium of exchange, not as a mere sign of value, but as value itself, as a commodity governed by precisely the same laws which affect other kinds of property, the absurdity and tyranny of legislative interference to regulate the extent of profit which, under any circumstances, may be charged for it, would at once become apparent.

The laws do not pretend to dictate to a landlord how much rent he may charge for his house; or to a merchant what price he shall put upon his cloth; or to a mechanic at what rate he shall sell the products of his skill; or to a farmer the maximum he shall demand for his hay or grain. Yet money is but another form into which all these commodities are transmuted, and there is no reason why the owner of it shall be forbidden to ask exactly that rate of profit for the use of it which its abundance or scarcity makes it worth—no reason why the laws of supply and demand, which regulate the value of all other articles, should be suspended by legislative enactment in relation to this, and their place supplied by the clumsy substitute of feudal ignorance and worse than feudal tyranny.

The value of iron and copper and lead consists of exactly the same elements as the value of gold and silver. The labor employed in digging them, the quantity in which they are found, and the extent of their application in the useful arts, or, in other words, the relation of the demand to the supply, are

---

* From the "Evening Post," September 26, 1836.

the circumstances which fix their market price. Should some great manufacture be undertaken in which a vast additional amount of iron or copper or lead would be used, a sudden and considerable rise of price would be the inevitable consequence. Should this increased demand lead to any valuable improvement in the mining art, or to investigations which should discover new and prolific beds of ore, a corresponding fall of prices would occur. These fluctuations are continually taking place, and an attempt to prevent them by state legislation would be about as effectual as the command of the barbarian king that the ocean should not overpass a certain bound. Silver and gold, though in a less degree, are liable to precisely the same fluctuations of intrinsic value, and to seek to confine them to a fixed point is an attempt marked by equal folly.

If, then, the intrinsic value of money cannot be established by law, the value of its use is no less beyond the proper compass of legislation. Though a certain per centum is established as the rate which may be demanded for the use of money, we find, when the article is relatively abundant, that, notwithstanding the law, a much lower rate is received; and why, on the other hand, when money is scarce, should an attempt be made to prevent it from rising to its natural level?

Such attempts have always been, and always will be, worse than fruitless. They not only do not answer the ostensible object, but they accomplish the reverse. They operate, like all restrictions on trade, to the injury of the very class they are framed to protect; they oppress the borrower for the advantage of the lender; they take from the poor to give to the rich. How is this result produced? Simply by diminishing the amount of capital, which, in the shape of money, would be lent to the community at its fair value, did no restriction exist, and placing what is left in the most extortionate hands. By attaching a stigma and a penalty to the innocent act of asking for money what money is worth, when that value rises above seven per cent, the scrupulous and reputable money-lenders are driven from the market and forced to employ their funds in other modes of investment. The supply, the inadequacy of which in the first place caused the increase in the rate of usance, is thus still further diminished, and the rate of usance necessarily rises still higher. The loanable funds, too, are held only by those who do not scruple to tax their loans with another grievous charge as security against the penalty imposed by an unwise law; and thus our Legislature, instead of assisting the poor man, but makes his necessities the occasion of sorely augmenting his burden.

But usury laws operate most hardly in many cases, even when the general rate of money is below their arbitrary standard. There is an intrinsic and obvious difference between borrowers, which not only justifies but absolutely demands, on the part of a prudent man disposed to relieve the wants of applicants, a very different rate of interest. Two persons can hardly present themselves, in precisely equal circumstances, to solicit a loan. One man is cautious; another is rash. One is a close calculator, sober in his views, and unexcitable in his temperament; another is visionary and enthusiastic. One has tangible security to offer; another nothing but the airy one of a promise. Who shall say that to lend money to these several persons is worth in each case an equal premium?

Should a person come to us with a project which, if successful, will yield an immense return, but, if unsuccessful, leave him wholly destitute, shall we not charge him for the risk we run in advancing his views? The advocates of usury laws may answer that we have it at our option either to take seven per cent or wholly refuse to grant the required aid. True; but suppose the project one which is calculated, if successful, to confer a vast benefit on mankind. Is it wise in the Legislature in such a case to bar the door against ingenuity, except the money-lender turns philanthropist and jeopards his property, not for a fair equivalent, but out of mere love to his fellow-man?

The community begin to answer these questions aright, and

there is ground for hope that they will ere long insist upon their legislative agents repealing the entire code of barbarous laws by which the trade in money has hitherto been fettered.

---

# MR. WEBSTER'S WIT.*

THAT men of some wit and humor have lived before the present age is not, we believe, contested. Not to speak of the Greeks and Romans, there is wit in Boccaccio, and wit in Ariosto, and wit in Casti. Witty was Rabelais, and witty was Scarron, and witty, in another way, was Paul Courier. There are things in Cervantes which will make the reader laugh in spite of himself; Molière has been known to coax a grin from the most splenetic, and some passages in Shakespeare no man can read or hear without acknowledging that they are quite droll.

These authors were very well in their time, and some of their works are passable even now. We must not speak disparagingly of what made our fathers and mothers laugh. It would be irreverent.

But the age for wit is decidedly the present age; and the wittiest man of the time, beyond all question, is Mr. Webster, the gentleman spoken of last summer as the Whig candidate for the presidency. Wit has hitherto been only in the bud— Mr. Webster is the full-blown flower; wit has till now remained in the clumsy chrysalis state—Mr. Webster is the broad-winged butterfly. We have had indeed the promise of wit, but Mr. Webster is its fulfilment and perfection.

On Tuesday evening last a brilliant festival was given at East Boston, by John W. Fenno, Esq., in honor of the recent glorious Whig victories in New York. It was held in the Maverick House, the largest hotel in the city, gorgeously

---

* From the "Evening Post," November 20, 1837.

illuminated for the occasion. The festivity is duly chronicled in the columns of the " Boston Centinel." Elbridge G. Austin presided at the dinner, and at his right was placed the witty Mr. Webster. Mr. Austin gave a toast in compliment to Mr. Webster, and Mr. Webster responded. We give his speech in the words of the " Boston Centinel," cautioning our readers to look well to their diaphragms, and to hold their sides with both hands, for the drollery of this Mr. Webster is irresistible.

" Mr. Webster rose and pronounced a most eloquent and agreeable speech, which occupied the profound attention of his audience for three quarters of an hour. He touched happily on the great questions before the nation, and enlarged on the glorious results of the present and past week, and, although now and then he spoke in the most serious and impressive tones, yet at other times he was sportive and humorous to admiration, and kept the company in roars of laughter. He remarked pleasantly that at the approaching session, when he should go to Washington and call on the President, he should probably have occasion to say : ' How do you do, Mr. Van Buren ? How go the times ? What news from New York ? ' "

" The effect of this frank colloquy was irresistible ; the room was convulsed with laughter. It was all uttered with so much pleasantry and respect, and with such perfect good humor and *naiveté* of manner, that, had Mr. Van Buren himself been present, he would have forgotten his own reverses and joined heartily in the laughing all round the board. Mr. Webster then added that when he should see the Secretary of the Treasury he might have occasion to say : ' How is Mr. Woodbury ? What are the exact financial statements and plans that you propose to report for our consideration ? What do the people say of your *sub-treasury system ?* ' These words were accompanied by appropriate action, and the effect was such as may be imagined, but cannot be described."

Ah, the wag ! We are tempted to say to Mr. Webster as the negro boy said to Garrick when the great actor had stolen into the back-yard and was personating the cock-turkey for his entertainment : " Massa Webster, you make a me die wid laffin."

"How do you do, Mr. Van Buren? What news from New York? How is Mr. Woodbury? What do people say of your sub-treasury system?" Is there any mortal whose gravity is stern enough to stand anything so superlatively comic as this? Why, it would have drawn a horse laugh from the lungs of the weeping philosopher.

We take it upon us to say that there is not so irresistible a jest in the works of all the wits who ever wrote, from Lucian down to the last number of the "Pickwick Papers" by Boz.

In his true history of New York, Diedrich Knickerbocker relates the fate of a fat little Schopen who died of a burgomaster's joke. If a mere burgomaster's joke, a hundred and fifty years since, when wit was in its infancy, could do such execution, what must be the effect of the joke of so accomplished a wag as Mr. Webster? We have, however, looked carefully over the account given by the "Boston Centinel," and we find no return of the killed. How is this? Is there no concealment of the consequences of Mr. Webster's waggery?

---

# SLAM, BANG & CO.*

SHORT work is made in certain quarters with the President of the United States. Mr. Van Buren has issued his message, and the Whig journalists have answered it with the phrase "Slam, Bang & Co."

It is wonderful how much the Whigs make of the combination of these little words, Slam, Bang & Co. Those who are not in the habit of reading the journals of that party cannot imagine to what a degree they have illuminated and enlivened

---

* From the "Evening Post," December 8, 1837. At this time the Democratic party in New York numbered among its leaders gentlemen of the not euphonious names of Slamm, Bangs, and Ming, which, furnishing the opposition with a good deal of amusement, provoked this reply.—ED.

their columns by this happy invention. Slam, Bang & Co. stands them in place of wit—it stands them in place of reason —it is their resort in all emergencies—it is their answer to all arguments. With Slam, Bang & Co. they attack their enemies; with Slam, Bang & Co. they protect themselves against attacks; it is their weapon, offensive and defensive.

Pope, in his "Dunciad," speaks of certain affectors of obsolete phraseology

"Who live upon a *whilome* for a week."

But this is a trivial feat in comparison with what has been done by certain modern Whig journalists. We know one or two who have lived upon Slam, Bang & Co. for a twelvemonth. We know some who set up with Slam, Bang & Co. as their whole stock in trade, and have carried on a flourishing business of editorials on no other capital.

One of Shakespeare's clowns boasts of having invented an answer to fit every question—using always the simple phrase, O Lord, Sir. But the phrase Slam, Bang & Co. will not only answer but ask all questions; it will serve as a commentary to all texts, or a text to all commentaries; it will furnish matter for a squib of three lines, or may be beaten out into a political disquisition of two columns. Reader, if you are the conductor of a Whig newspaper, learn this mystery at once; it will save you all expense of thinking. If you wish to find fault with a public measure, or attack a public candidate, or censure a public document, or condemn a political doctrine, print the words Slam, Bang & Co., and it will answer your purpose without any further trouble. Pepper your articles well with Slam, Bang & Co., and you may be sure they will be swallowed.

Useful inventions are sometimes long in being adopted, but they are sure to make their way at last. One or two grave journals, which were slow in learning the trick of using Slam, Bang & Co., now begin to employ them with a praiseworthy diligence, and in time they may possibly be brought to utter them with as much flippancy as the inventors of the phrase.

But, after all, Slam, Bang & Co. is not the superlative degree. If you would goad your enemies with the utmost keenness of sarcasm, if you would wield the lightnings of the most brilliant wit, and crush, confound, and annihilate the Democracy with the thunders of the most potent argument, you must go a step farther and utter the magic words Slam, Bang, Ming & Co.

## NEW YORK BIRD-CATCHERS.*

In the first volume of " Hone's Table-Book " is an engraving of a London Bird-Catcher in the year 1827, and under it are printed the calls, or *jerks*, as they are technically called— the peculiar sounds and articulations of the voice by which the people of this profession allure wild birds within their reach. Our readers will perhaps be amused with a sample of these *jerks* :

> Tuck—Tuck—Fear.
> Tuck—Tuck—Fear—Ic, Ic, Ic.
> Tuck—Tuck—Fear—Ic quake-e weet.
> [This is a *finished jerk.*]
> Tolloc, Ejup, R—weet, weet, weet.
> Tolloc, Tolloc, cha—Ic, Ic, Ic.
> Lug, Lug, G—cha, cha.
> Lug, Lug—Orchee, weet.

New York has its bird-catchers as well as London. One of these goes under the name of the " Express." He has established himself at the corner of Wall and Water Streets, where he practices his jerks diligently every morning for the catching of such foolish birds as he finds in that neighborhood. Here is a sample of his jerks :

---

* From the " Evening Post," June 27, 1838.

Slam Bang—Slam Bang—Slam Bang & Co.
Slam Bang—Slam Bang—Slam Bang Ming & Co.
  [This is a *finished jerk.*]
Loco Foco, Loco Foco—Jacques, mob—Eli.
Loco Foco, Loco Foco—Eli Hart's flour store—
Flour riot, Flour riot.
Agrarians, Agrarians—Fanny Wright, Fanny Wright,
Levellers, Levellers, Levellers—Jack Cade, Jack Cade, etc., etc.

The birds allured and taken by means of these calls are chiefly of the kinds called gulls, boobies, noodles, doddrels, and geese, which do mostly affect maritime places. Plenty of lame ducks which haunt the neighborhood where the bird-catcher has established himself are also taken, being more easily made prisoners on account of their disabled state; and that fiercer fowl, that bird of prey, the kite, which delights to hover over and swoop upon his victims in the atmosphere of Wall Street, is often by these calls decoyed into the net. When caught, the birds are made to practice the jerks which we have given, until they become quite perfect in their parts, when you will hear the boobies, noodles, lame ducks, geese, kites, etc., call out "Slam Bang, Slam Bang, Jack Cade, Jack Cade," etc., all at once, with astonishing energy and correctness of accent. A friend of ours heard the words Slam, Bang, Ming & Co. pronounced by one of these birds the other day in Broadway, not far from Leonard Street, as distinctly as the bird-catcher himself could have uttered it. A great black and white bird called the "Journal of Commerce," from its coming out every morning and hovering over the shipping, was once caught, and for two or three mornings uttered the words Slam, Bang & Co. as distinctly as a human being, of which there are at present several living witnesses.

# SENSITIVENESS TO FOREIGN OPINION.*

COOPER'S last work, "Home as Found," has been fiercely attacked, in more than one quarter, for its supposed tendency to convey to the people of other countries a bad idea of our national character. Without staying to examine whether all Mr. Cooper's animadversions on American manners are perfectly just, we seize the occasion to protest against this excessive sensibility to the opinion of other nations. It is no matter what they think of us. We constitute a community large enough to form a great moral tribunal for the trial of any question which may arise among ourselves. There is no occasion for this perpetual appeal to the opinions of Europe. We are competent to apply the rules of right and wrong boldly and firmly, without asking in what light the superior judgment of the Old World may regard our decisions.

It has been said of Americans that they are vainglorious, boastful, fond of talking of the greatness and the advantages of their country, and of the excellence of their national character. They have this foible in common with other nations; but they have another habit which shows that, with all their national vanity, they are not so confident of their own greatness, or of their own capacity to estimate it properly, as their boasts would imply. They are perpetually asking, What do they think of us in Europe? How are we regarded abroad? If a foreigner publishes an account of his travels in this country, we are instantly on the alert to know what notion of our character he has communicated to his countrymen; if an American author publishes a book, we are eager to know how it is received abroad, that we may know how to judge it ourselves. So far has this humor been carried that we have seen an extract, from a third- or fourth-rate critical work in

---

* From the " Evening Post," January 11, 1839.

England, condemning some American work, copied into all our newspapers one after another, as if it determined the character of the work beyond appeal or question.

For our part, we admire and honor a fearless accuser of the faults of so thin-skinned a nation as ours, always supposing him to be sincere and well-intentioned. He may be certain that where he has sowed animadversion he will reap an abundant harvest of censure and obloquy. We will have one consolation, however, that if his book be written with ability it will be read ; that the attacks which are made upon it will draw it to the public attention ; and that it may thus do good even to those who recalcitrate most violently against it.

If every man who writes a book, instead of asking himself the question what good it will do at home, were first held to inquire what notions it conveys of Americans to persons abroad, we should pull the sinews out of our literature. There is much want of free-speaking as things stand at present, but this rule will abolish it altogether. It is bad enough to stand in fear of public opinion at home, but, if we are to superadd the fear of public opinion abroad, we submit to a double despotism. Great reformers, preachers of righteousness, eminent satirists in different ages of the world—did they, before entering on the work they were appointed to do, ask what other nations might think of their countrymen if they gave utterance to the voice of salutary reproof ?

---

## A REPLY TO ATTACKS.*

WE are sometimes inquired of why we do not oftener answer the attacks so frequently made upon the " Evening Post " in other journals. Burger, the German poet, shall answer for us :

---

* From the " Evening Post," June 7, 1839.

"A plain man," says Burger, "on a fine morning, passed in his walk the door of an ale-house. A dog, whose collar was hung round with little bells, sprung out, tinkling his bells and barking at him with the greatest fury. The plain man paid him no attention, and, without even lifting his cane at the animal, walked quietly away from the noise. The next moment a well-dressed young man passed the ale-house ; the dog was out again in an instant ; the bells tinkled and the barking was terrible. The young man was nettled, and thought to quiet the cur by stoning him ; but the dog growled furiously at every stone that was thrown, and, coming nearer, barking louder than ever, took liberties with the flap of the young fellow's coat, and finally began to snap at his legs. Half a dozen other dogs, roused by the yelping of their brother, joined in the chorus ; windows were thrown up, doors were opened on every side, the business of the neighborhood was suspended to look at the battle, and the boys clapped their hands and shouted to encourage the combatants, till the young man was ready to sink into the earth with shame."

Besides the inconveniences so well set forth by Burger, we have another reason for not indulging very deeply in these quarrels with newspapers. We must have time for better things. There are graver questions to be settled than those which are generally raised by the journalists which attack us. When we find any of their arguments worth answering, we are not backward to engage in controversy; when we find a misrepresentation which is likely to do mischief if not corrected, we correct it; but to mere scolding we are quite indifferent. It is evident that, if we were to answer every assault of this kind, we should be obliged to give up our whole time and the whole space of our columns to the answers we might make. There are two evening papers, and twice as many morning papers, in this city belonging to the Whig party ; and we have sometimes had all of them, or nearly all, in full cry upon us at once, to say nothing of the attacks made upon us by the journals we receive by the mails.

There are a few prints which would be sadly puzzled for matter out of which to concoct the excellent speculations with

which they daily edify their readers were it not for the
" Evening Post." But for the opportunity afforded them by
our journal, their facility of abuse might unfortunately be lost
for want of exercise. To such the " Evening Post " is their
stock in trade, the capital with which they carry on business.
The " New York Gazette," we believe, is one of that class.
We do not often see the paper, by reason of which we doubt-
less escape many sleepless nights ; but we have " good-natured
friends " who often insist upon telling us how cruelly we are
cut up in it. The " New York Gazette " has not been, we
believe, once alluded to, either for good or for evil, in the
" Evening Post " for two years past or more, until the other
day a Southern correspondent deprecated its defence of South-
ern rights as doing more harm than good ; yet we hear that
it rails at us daily with the eloquence of ten fish-women.

There is an honest shoemaker living on the Mergellina, at
Naples, on the right hand as you go toward Pozzuoli, whose
little dog comes out every morning and barks at Vesuvius.

Some of the prints to which we refer occasionally indulge
in personal allusions to persons concerned, or supposed to be
concerned, in the management of this paper. With such prints
it is manifest we cannot enter into controversy.

Three or four of the New York daily journals, among
which are the " Courier " and " Gazette," have adopted a style
of political writing which seems to be copied from the
speeches of Mr. Wise and his imitators. It consists of run-
ning off at the end of the quill a set of opprobrious epithets
which answer for all occasions. These words are profligacy,
hypocrisy, perjury, robbery, rascality, and other names of vices
and crimes that end in *y*—meanness, obsequiousness, perverse-
ness, and the names of all other bad qualities that end in *ness*
—corruption, degradation, assassination, and every name of
evil that ends in *tion*, with every other possible epithet of vitu-
peration, of whatever ending, are put together, like pieces of
colored glass into a kaleidoscope, and shaken up into as many
different forms as they will make. Arithmeticians can tell by

calculation into how many thousand different forms of abuse a hundred different epithets may be combined. With these presses, which turn out railing accusations to order, as a button-machine turns out buttons, it is evident that it would be folly to engage in dispute. In the words of Pope,

" We wage no war with Bedlam,"

we cannot dispute with those who never reason.

It is a great mistake in these writers to suppose that calling names without discrimination or selection is strong writing. The sing-song of abuse is as easily learned as any other sing-song. A parrot can be taught to curse and swear as easily as to say " Pretty Poll." Gresset, in his work entitled " Vert-Vert," gives the history of one of these birds who was educated in a nunnery, and who said his *Ave Maria* and his *Pater Noster* with an appearance of devotion which edified everybody. The inmates of a distant convent were desirous to see the wonderful parrot, and, accordingly, he was sent to them on board a coasting schooner. But during the voyage the bird learned other accomplishments, and on his arrival the good sisters were struck with horror on hearing him swear like a boatswain.

---

# JOHN QUINCY ADAMS.*

LEARNED, eloquent; always acute, though often wrong; ambitious, disputatious, pragmatical, unforgiving; conscientious, except when some strong prejudice or personal grudge, as is too often the case, opposes itself to his moral sense; aged, yet preserving in a late old age his intellectual faculties as vigorous as ever, perhaps even sharpened during the last ten years of his life by constant and intense exercise in quarrels

---

* From the " Evening Post," August 4, 1843.

and controversies of every kind—John Quincy Adams is one of the most extraordinary men of his country and his time. He is now enjoying, what it was never his lot to enjoy before, voluntary demonstrations of respect from his fellow-citizens of every party. He has been making a kind of tour through this State, and wherever he goes he is welcomed with a formal reception; speeches of compliment are made to him, and he makes speeches in return. At Auburn, at Utica, at Herkimer, at Little Falls, at Schenectady, and at Albany this ceremonious reception was had; at the latter place it seemed as if the whole city rose up to welcome him. We are glad of this, for Mr. Adams, when we consider his long public life, has had few of those honors fall to his share. While he was President of the United States he used to come and go with as little notice as almost any other passenger on the steamboats and stage-coaches. Yet is he a better and an honester man than some who have snuffed more of this popular incense, owing, no doubt, to their possessing certain attractive qualities of character which do not belong to Mr. Adams? People are shy of approaching one who bristles with sharp points and controversies like a porcupine. For the present there seems a disposition to forego that shyness and to do honor to one who, fifteen years ago, held the place of Chief Magistrate of our nation, who was probably the most learned man that ever administered the government, and who, in his old age, has become one of the most dreaded debaters of our national Legislature. The veteran politician wears gracefully the honors which have been so long in coming, and evidently enjoys with a high zest the demonstrations of respect which are paid him.

# THE CORN-LAW CONTROVERSY.*

A FRIEND has placed in our hands numbers of the tracts which the corn-law reformers of England circulate among the people. They are about the size and length of the religious tracts of this country, and are put up in an envelope which is stamped with neat and appropriate devices. These little publications comprise essays on all the topics involved in the corn-law controversy, sometimes in the form of dialogues, sometimes of tales, and sometimes of extracts from famous books and speeches. The arguments are so arranged as to be easily comprehended by the meanest capacities.

The friend to whom we are indebted for these is well informed on the subject, and says that a more advanced state of opinion prevails among the people of England in relation to the operation of tariffs than in this nation, generally so much more enlightened. It is a singular spectacle which is thus presented to the eyes of the civilized world. While the tendency of opinion under an aristocratic monarchy is toward the loosening of the restraints under which the labor of the people has long suffered, a large and powerful party in a nation, whose theory of government is nearly a century in advance of the world, is clamoring for their continuance and confirmation. Monarchical England is struggling to break the chains which an unwise legislation has forged for the limbs of its trade; but democratic America is urged to put on the fetters which older but less liberal nations are throwing off. The nations of Europe are seeking to extend their commercial relations, to expand the sphere of their mutual intercourse, to rivet the market for the productions of their soil and skill, while the "model republic" of the New World is urged to stick to the silly and odious policy of a semi-barbarous age.

---

* From the "Evening Post," August 24, 1843.

We look upon the attempt which is making in Great Britain to procure a revision of the tariff laws as one of the most important political movements of the age.   It is a reform that contemplates benefits whose effects would not be confined to any single nation or to any period of time.   Should it be successful, it would be the beginning of a grand and universal scheme of commercial emancipation.   Let England—that nation so extensive in her relations and so powerful in her influences—let England adopt a more liberal policy, and it would remove the only obstacles now in the way of a complete freedom of industry throughout the globe.   It is the apparent unwillingness of nations to reciprocate the advantages of mutual trade that has kept back this desirable reform so long.   The standing argument of the friends of exclusiveness —their defence under all assaults, their shelter in every emergency—has been that one nation cannot pursue a free system until all others do; or, in other words, that restriction is to be met by restriction.   It is a flimsy pretence, but, such as it is, has answered the purposes of those who have used it for many centuries.

The practice of confining trade by the invisible but potent chains of law has been a curse wherever it has prevailed.   In England, more dependent than other nations on the extent of its commercial intercourse, it may be said to have operated as a scourge.   The most terrible inflictions of natural evil, storms, famine, and pestilence have not produced an equal amount of suffering.   Indeed, it has combined the characteristics of the worst of those evils.   It has devastated, like the storm, the busy hives of industry; it has exhausted, like famine, the life and vital principle of trade; and, like the pestilence, it has "walked in the darkness and wasted at noon-day."   When we read of thousands of miserable wretches, in all the cities and towns of a great nation, huddled together like so many swine in a pen, in rags, squalor, and want; without work, bread, or hope; dragging out from day to day, by begging or the petty artifices of theft, an existence which is worthless and a burden; and when, at the same time, we see a system of laws that has carefully drawn a band of iron around every mode of human exertion, which, with lynx-eyed and omniscient vigilance, has dragged every product of industry from its retreat to become the subject of a tax—can we fail in ascribing the effect to its cause, or suppress the utterance of our indignation at a policy so heartless and destructive?

Yet this is the very policy that a certain class of politicians in this country would have us imitate. Misled by the selfish and paltry arguments of British statesmen, but unawed by the terrible experience of the British people, they would fasten upon us a system whose only recommendation, in its best form, is that it enriches a few, at the cost of the lives and happiness of many. They would assist a constrictor in wrapping his folds around us until our industry shall be completely crushed.

---

## FRIAR TUCK LEGISLATION.*

> " A famous thief was Robin Hood ;
> But Scotland had a thief as good :
> It was—it was the great Rob Roy."
> *Old Ballad.*

A SPEAKER, Mr. Thomas Gisborne, at one of the recent meetings of the Anti-Corn Law League, made a happy allusion to what he called Friar Tuck legislation. He had in his mind the story which is told in some of the old chronicles of Robin Hood and his merry foresters when they were once assembled in congress to deliberate upon the proper distribution of a pretty large amount of spoils. These legislators, persuaded by the soft and honeyed words of Friar Tuck, left him to frame a law for the proper adjustment of their claims.

---

*From the " Evening Post," April 26, 1844.

When the law was reported by the able committee which had it in charge, it became instantly evident that Friar Tuck himself would get much the largest share. Public opinion, continues the history, thereupon went against the holy man, and a league was formed to resist the iniquity of his decision.

Now, what did the good friar in the emergency? Why, he met the people boldly and openly, and said: " For whose benefit are laws made, I should like to know?" And then immediately answering his own question, lest some silly objector might give it another turn, he went on: " First for the benefit of those who make them, and afterward as it may happen." Nor did the disinterested judge stop there, but he proceeded: "Am I not the law-maker, and shall I not profit by my own law?" The story runs, we believe, that the good man next quietly pocketed his share of the booty and left his unreasonable companions to make the best of what remained.

Friar Tuck represents a class; he is a type and pattern of a large circle of imitators; his peculiar method of legislation is not obsolete. There are many persons at this day whose morality seems to be framed according to the same standard. Members of the United States Congress, for instance, who pass tariff laws to put money into their own pockets, are the legitimate descendants of Friar Tuck.

It is quite remarkable how many are the points of resemblance between this legislation of Sherwood Forest and that of the manufacturers at Washington. In the first place, the plunder to be distributed is raised from the people; in either case without their being formally consulted; in the one by high duties, in the other by the strong arm. Then the persons who take upon themselves to decide how this plunder is to be divided, like Friar Tuck, have a deep interest in the result, and generally manage to appropriate to themselves the largest share. They are the owners of manufacturing capital, and they continue to make this capital return an enormous interest. " For what benefit," they gravely ask, " are laws made?" and then answer: " First for the benefit of those who make them, and afterward as it may happen." Let us impose high duties; let us fill our pockets; let us who make the laws take all that we can get—and as to the people, the mass of laborers and consumers, why, that's as it may happen! This is virtually the reasoning of one sort of our just and disinterested legislators.

But there is one point in which the resemblance does not hold. Friar Tuck was a bold, straightforward, open-mouthed statesman, willing to proclaim his principles, and justify the consequences to which they led. His followers in Congress act upon precisely the same principles, but assign another reason. He avowed that he wished to cram his pocket; they hold up some mock pretence of public good. "Shall I not benefit by my own law?" he said, and gathered up his gains; but they gather the gain and leave the reason unsaid, or rather hypocritically resort to some more palatable reason. The advantage of consistency is on the side of Robin Hood's priest. There is a frankness in his philosophy which throws the sneaking duplicity of the legislators of the cotton-mills quite into the shade.

---

# LORD BROUGHAM'S LAST CONTRIBUTION TO SOCIAL SCIENCE.*

IT is a gross injustice that applies the name of scold to individuals of the female sex alone. There are male scolds as well as female; there are viragos in pantaloons, and bearded termagants. Fluency and volubility in abuse are never more exemplified than in the case of some public speakers. Henry A. Wise, afterward Governor of Virginia, while a member of Congress, was an instance of this sort; he was simply a shrew—a shrew never tamed except once for a few days,

---

* From the "Evening Post," October 22, 1863.

when John Quincy Adams took him in hand and administered so terrible a scathing that the Virginia member was as quiet as a lamb for nearly a week afterward. On the other side of the Atlantic they have a venerable termagant in plaid pantaloons whom they call Lord Brougham.

The very physiognomy of Lord Brougham proclaims his character. There is a sort of portable stopper for claret-bottles and decanters containing different kinds of wine, fashioned at the top into a resemblance of the human head, often grotesque. A likeness of Lord Brougham would figure very appositely as the top of a stopper for a vinegar-cruet. Sourness and dissatisfaction are written in every line of his face. One can hardly believe that in the veins which supply the facial muscles there circulates any fluid milder than acetic acid. Lavater, in his physiognomical works, talks of the "eloquent mouth," the " eloquent lip," in certain of the faces of which he gives an engraved outline. The mouth of Brougham suggests to the physiognomist the idea of fluent speech, but, instead of dropping honey, as was said of Nestor in the " Iliad," you at once see that it drops only mingled gall and vinegar.

This personage has taken occasion to heap the grossest abuse upon Americans in the speech delivered by him on the seventh of October, when he opened the annual session of the Association for the Promotion of Social Science. This precious contribution to the cause of social science we copy from the London "Morning Herald " into another part of this sheet. According to him, the Americans are the "slaves of a national vanity without example and without bounds—a vanity leading to many crimes, and to that disregard of truth which is the root of all offences." In short, the Americans, in his judgment, are a nation of liars. They lie to the world, they lie to each other, they lie to themselves. They coin falsehoods concerning the war, converting defeats into victories, by way of deceiving Europe and keeping up their own spirits ; and not only concerning the events of war, but concerning " everything else—the measures of the Government and the acts of foreign nations; the truth they will never hear." Their nation "magnifies itself and despises the rest of mankind." Its people "thirst for blood"; they are "not content with the destruction of half a million lives, but vain of the slaughter." They "exult in wholesale bloodshed." "Instead of feeling shame at cruel scenes, which modern ages have seen nothing to equal, they actually glory in them," etc., etc. This is but a part of the flood of foul accusations and abusive epithets which he pours upon the American character.

We need not take the pains to refute these calumnies. Those who have observed the course of events in this country with a moderate degree of impartiality are aware how groundless they are; those who have not, will probably never see what we write. One part of the speech of Lord Brougham is remarkable enough; he vehemently condemns the orderly behavior of the people of the United States under the extraordinary measures to which the Government has been forced to have recourse for the suppression of the rebellion. Their "submission," he says, "to every caprice of tyranny has been universal and habitual, never interrupted by a single act of resistance to the most flagrant infractions of personal freedom." What he would desire, therefore, is a rising at the North against the Government, one civil war within another, the civil authorities set at defiance, and the social order of the free States broken up, in order that the seceding States might easily triumph.

One of the charges made against us in this respect is that the proclamation emancipating the slaves was "designed to promote slave insurrection." It almost exceeds the limit of charitable construction to suppose that any person with Lord Brougham's opportunities of information could say this without knowing it to be false.

There is much said of the perfect preservation of Lord Brougham's mental faculties at the advanced age which he has reached. One talent the aged peer certainly retains in great perfection, perhaps even in an improved state — the facility of abuse. It sometimes happens, in the last stage of human life, that some single faculty of the mind starts into preternatural activity, predominating over all the others and exhibiting itself at their expense. We suppose this to be the case with Lord Brougham, who, always more or less a scold, has become pre-eminently so within a few years past, and now finds a cheap and convenient indulgence of this propensity in railing at the United States.

----

## THE UTILITY OF TREES.*

WHILE Congress is occupied with the disposition of the public lands, it has been suggested, by persons who can think of something else besides railroads, that it will be an act of provident wisdom to reserve considerable tracts of forest in different parts of the country, as the public domain, with a view of preventing the destruction of trees which is so rapidly proceeding, and which may yet lead to inconvenient consequences. One of the objections to any such measure as this is the difficulty of protecting the forests from depredation. What is the public domain is regarded in most parts of our country as, in a certain sense, common property, from which any man may take what he has occasion for. In order to prevent the trees from being felled and the public property wasted, a body of foresters to watch it and keep out trespassers must be retained in the pay of the Government.

We do not propose here to discuss the merits of any such plan, but we would refer our readers to the extracts we have made in another part of this paper from Dr. Piper's work on

----

* From the " Evening Post," June 20, 1865.

the " Trees of America," as opening a very important subject for their consideration. We are fully persuaded, for our part, that scarce anything is more prejudicial to the fertility of a country, or has a worse effect on its climate, than the thoughtless practice of denuding it of trees. The effect is to open the region to the winds which parch the surface and dwarf the vegetation, to cause the springs to dry up, and turn the watercourses into torrents in the rainy season and dusty channels in summer and autumn. If the public could but be thoroughly convinced of this truth, it might, perhaps, be unnecessary for the Government to give itself any concern about the matter in the disposition of the public lands. We should see the highways skirted by double rows of trees, long lines of plantation following the courses of the railroads, belts of forest-trees planted to break the force of the winds and shelter the tender crops and the orchards which bear fruit.

Travellers see in the Orkney and Shetland Isles a remarkable example of the unfavorable effect of the winds on vegetation, and the kindly influence of shelter. There, within the high garden-walls, shrubs and trees grow and flourish till their summits reach the top of the wall, and beyond that they do not rise. Strong winds sweep almost constantly over the surface of the islands and prevent the growth of any vegetable production except those which flower and perfect their fruit near the surface. Within the enclosures of these stone fences, where the wind is excluded, or in hollows which form a natural screen, the vegetation is often juicy and luxuriant. Of the effect of the destruction of forests in drying up a country the Old World affords many remarkable instances. The poets and historians of antiquity speak of mighty forests which are now shadowless wastes, and of streams that flow no longer. Addison thus laments the disappearance of rivers and brooks celebrated in ancient times :

" Sometimes, misguided by the tuneful throng,
   I look for streams immortalized in song

> ˙ That lost in silence and oblivion lie ;
> Dumb are their fountains, and their channels dry,
> Yet run forever, by the Muses' skill,
> And, in the smooth description, murmur still."

The streams of Attica, now a bare and treeless region, are for the most part but mere water-courses, in which the rains pass off to the sea, and disappoint those who form their ideas of them from the ancient writers.

The rivers of Spain are for the most part only channels for the winter rains. The Guadalquivir, which some poet calls "a mighty river," enters the sea at Malaga without water enough to cover the loose black stones that pave its bed. The Holy Land now often misses "the latter rain," or receives it but sparingly ; and the brook Kedron is a long, dry ravine, passing off to the eastward from Jerusalem to descend between perpendicular walls beside the monastery of Mar Saba to the valley of the Jordan and the Dead Sea. Mr. Marsh, in his very instructive book entitled "Man and Nature," has collected a vast number of instances showing how, in the Old World, the destruction of the forests has been followed by a general aridity of the country which they formerly overshadowed.

Whether there are any examples of frequent rains restored to a country by planting groves and orchards we can not say : but we remember, when travelling at the West thirty-three years since, to have met with a gentleman from Kentucky who spoke of an instance within his knowledge in which a perennial stream had made its appearance where at the early settlement of the region there was none. Kentucky, when its first colonists planted themselves within its limits, was a region in which extensive prairies, burnt over every year by the Indians, predominated.

More than forty years since a poet of our country, referring to the effect of stripping the soil of its trees, put these lines into the mouth of one of the aboriginal inhabitants :

" Before these fields were shorn and tilled,
　　Full to the brim our rivers flowed ;
　The melody of waters filled
　　The fresh and boundless wood ;
　And torrents dashed and rivulets played,
　And fountains spurted in the shade.

" Those grateful sounds are heard no more ;
　　The springs are silent in the sun ;
　The rivers, by the blackened shore,
　　With lessening currents run.
　The realm our tribes are crushed to get
　May be a barren desert yet."

In all woodlands nature has made provision for retaining the moisture of rains long in the ground. The earth under the trees is covered with a thick carpeting of fallen leaves, which absorb the power and prevent the water from passing immediately into the streams and hurrying to the sea. Part of the moisture thus confined under the fallen leaves, and shielded from evaporation by sun and wind, finds its way slowly into the veins of the earth, rises in springs, and runs off in rivulets; part is gradually drawn up by the rootlets of the trees and given off to the air from the leaves, to form the vapors, which are afterward condensed into showers. We fear that this statement of the process is somewhat commonplace, but we make it here because, though obvious enough, it is too little in the minds of those whose interest it concerns to notice it. Thus it is that forests protect a country against drought, and keep its streams constantly flowing and its wells constantly full  Cut down the trees, and the moisture of the showers passes rapidly off from the surface and hastens to lakes and to ocean.

# A RETROSPECTIVE GLANCE.*

It is our purpose to present, within a moderate compass, a view of changes, political and social, occurring within our Republic, which have an interest for every nation in the civilized world, and the history of which could not be fully written until now.  In the two centuries and a half of our existence as an offshoot of the great European stock a mighty drama has been put upon the stage of our continent, which, after a series of fierce contentions and subtile intrigues, closed in a bloody catastrophe, with a result favorable to liberty and human rights and to the fair fame of the Republic.  Within that time the institution of slavery, springing up from small and almost unnoticed beginnings, grew to be a gigantic power, claiming and exercising dominion over the confederacy, and at last, when it failed in causing itself to be recognized as a national institution and saw the signs of a decline in its political supremacy, declaring the Union of the States dissolved, encountering the free States in a sanguinary five years' war, and bringing upon itself overthrow and utter destruction.

We stand, therefore, at a point in our annals where the whole duration of slavery in our country from the beginning to the end lies before us as on a chart; and certainly no history of our Republic can now be regarded as complete which should fail to carry the reader through the various stages of its existence, from its silent and stealthy origin to the stormy period in which the world saw its death-struggle, and recognized in its fall the sentence of eternal justice.  It is instructive to observe how, in its earlier years, slavery was admitted, by the most eminent men of those parts of the country where it had taken the deepest root, to be a great wrong; and how,

---

* From the Preface to "A Popular History of the United States.  By William Cullen Bryant and Sidney Howard Gay."  New York, Charles Scribner's Sons, 1878.

afterward, when the power and influence of the slave-holding class were at their height, it was boldly defended as a beneficent and just institution, the basis of the most perfect social state known to the world—so powerfully and surely do personal interests pervert the moral judgments of mankind. The controversy assumed a deeper interest as the years went on. On the side of slavery stood forth men singularly fitted to be its champions; able, plausible, trained to public life; men of large personal influence, and a fierce determination of will nourished by the despotism exercised on their plantations over their bondmen. On the other side was a class equally able and no less determined; enthusiasts for liberty; as courageous as their adversaries were imperious; restlessly aggressive; ready to become martyrs, and from time to time attesting their sincerity by yielding up their lives. So fierce was the quarrel, and so general was the inclination, even in the free States, to take part with the slave-owners, that the name of Abolitionist was used as a term of reproach and scorn; and to point out a man as worthy of wearing it was in some places the same thing as to recommend him to the attentions of the mob. Yet, even while this was a name of opprobrium, the hostility to slavery was gathering strength under a new form. The friends of slavery demanded that the authority of the master over his bondman should be recognized in all the territory belonging to the Union not yet formed into States—in short, that the jurisdiction of the Republic, wherever established, should carry with it the law of slavery. A party was immediately formed to resist the application of this doctrine, and, after a long and vehement contest, elected its candidate President of the United States. Meantime, the rapid settlement of our Pacific coast by a purely free population, in consequence of the opening of the gold mines, showed the friends of slavery that they were to be hereafter in a minority, the power of which would diminish with every successive year. They instantly took the resolution to revolt against the Union, declared it thenceforth dissolved, and rushed into a war, in which their defeat carried with it the fall of slavery. It fell, dragging down with it thousands of private fortunes, and leaving some of the fairest portions of the region whence it issued its decrees ravaged and desolate, and others, for a time, given over to a confusion little short of anarchy.

Writers who record the fortunes of nations have most generally and wisely stopped at a modest distance from the time in which they wrote, for this reason among others, that the narrative could not be given with the necessary degree of impartiality, on account of controversies not yet ended and prejudices which have not had time to subside. But in the case of American slavery the difficulty of speaking impartially, both of the events which form its history and of the characters of its champions and adversaries, is far less now than it ever was before. Slavery has become a thing of the past; the dispute as to its rights under our Constitution is closed forever. The class of active and vigilant politicians who, a few years since, were ever on the watch for some opportunity of promoting its interests by legislation, is now as if it had never been; slavery is no longer either denounced or defended from the pulpits; the division of political journals into friends and enemies of slavery exists no longer, and, when a candidate for office is presented for the suffrages of his fellow-citizens, it is no longer asked, "What does he think of the slavery question?" So far, indeed, does this fierce contest seem already removed into the domain of the past, and separated from the questions and interests of the present moment, that when a person is pointed out as having been a distinguished abolitionist he is looked at with somewhat of the same historical interest as if it had been said, "There goes one who fought so bravely at Lundy's Lane"; or, "There is one who commanded a company of riflemen at the battle of New Orleans." The champions of slavery on one side—able men and skilled in the expedients of party warfare, and in many instances uncorrupt and pure in personal character—and the champions of the slave on the other, fearless and ready for the martyrdom which they sometimes suffered, their faculties exalted by a sense of danger—can now, as they and their acts pass in review before the historian, be judged with a degree of calmness belonging to a new era of our political existence.

But the great conclusion is still to be drawn that the existence of slavery in our Repulic was at utter variance with the free institutions which we made our boast; and that it could not be preserved in the vast growth which it had attained without altering in a great degree their nature and communicating to them its own despotic character. Where half the population is in bondage to the other half there is a constant danger that the subject race will rise against their masters, who naturally look to repression and terror as their means of defence. The later history of slavery in our country is full of examples to show this—severe laws against sedition in the slave States, an enforced silence on the subject of human liberty, an expurgated popular literature, and visitors to the slave States chased back by mobs across the frontier which they had imprudently crossed. It is remarkable that, not very long before the civil war, certain of the Southern journals began to maintain, in elaborate leading articles, that the time had arrived for considering whether the entire laboring class, of whatever color, should not be made the serfs of the landowners and others of the more opulent members of society.

A history like this would have been incomplete and fragmentary had it failed to record the final fate as well as the rise and growth of an institution wielding so vast an influence both in society and politics, with champions so able and resolute, organized with such skill, occupying so wide and fertile a domain, and rooted there with such firmness as to be regarded by the friends of human liberty with a feeling scarcely short of despair. To have broken off the narrative before reaching the catastrophe would have been like rising from the spectacle of a drama at the end of the fourth act. Few episodes in the world's history have been so complete in themselves as this of American slavery. Few have brought into activity such mighty agencies, or occupied so vast a theatre, or been closed, although amid fearful carnage, yet in a manner so satisfactory to the sense of natural justice.

Here is the place to speak of another important conclusion to be drawn from the result of our late civil war. It has proved the strength of our political system. When the slave States first revolted, it was wonderful with what unanimity the people of the Old World, even those who wished well to the Northern States, adopted the conclusion that the Union could endure no longer, and that the bond once broken could never be reunited. Those powers which had regarded the United States as a somewhat uncomfortable neighbor, rapidly becoming too strong to be reasonable in its dealings with the monarchies of Europe, fully believed that thereafter there would exist on the North American continent two rival commonwealths of the same origin, yet so diverse from each other in their institutions as to be involved in frequent disagreements, and thus to prove effectual checks upon each other, relieving the European powers from the danger of aggression in this quarter. It was sometimes said by Englishmen who thought that they were speaking in the interest of humanity: "All the interest we feel in your quarrel is this, that you should go to pieces as quickly and with as little bloodshed as possible." The steps taken by Great Britain and France were in accord with the expectation of which I have spoken; Britain instantly declaring the slave States a belligerent power — a virtual acknowledgment of their independence—and France posting a dependent prince in Mexico with the view of intervening in that quarter as soon as it might appear politic to do so. Till the close of our civil war the armed cohorts of France hung like a thunder-cloud over our southwestern border, but the hour never came when the signal might be given for the grim mass to move northward.

The period of time at which the nation inhabiting the domain of our Republic came into being is so recent that we may trace its growth with as much distinctness as if we were

the contemporaries of its birth. The records of its early exist-
ence have been preserved as those of no other nation have
been which has risen to any importance in the annals of the
world. To the guidance of these the historian may trust
himself securely, with no danger of losing his way among
the uncertain shadows of tradition. It is with a feeling of
wonder that he sees colonies, planted in different parts of the
North American continent so remote from each other, under
such different circumstances, and so entirely without concert
on the part of the adventurers who led them thither, united at
last in a political fabric of such strength and solidity. The
columns of the great edifice were separately laid in the wil-
derness, amid savage tribes, by men who apparently had no
thought of their future relation to each other; but, as they
rose from the earth, it seemed as if a guiding intelligence had
planned them in such a manner that in due time they might
be adjusted to each other in a single structure. Those who
at the outbreak of our civil war administered the govern-
ments of Europe had, it is certain, little confidence in the
stability and duration of a political fabric so framed. It was
loosely and fortuitously put together, they thought, of ele-
ments discordant in themselves, whose imperfect cohesion a
shock like that of the southern revolt would destroy forever.

It survived that shock, however, and, in part at least, for
the very reason of its peculiar structure. It survived it be-
cause every man in the free States felt that he was a part of
the government; because in our system of decentralized
power a part of it was lodged in his person. He felt that he
was challenged when the Federal Government was defied, and
that he was robbed when the rebels took possession of the
forts of the Federal Government and its munitions of war.
The quarrel became his personal concern, and the entire people
of the North rose as one man to breast and beat back this bold
attack upon a system of polity, which every man of them was
moved to defend by the feeling which would move him to de-
fend his fireside. Perhaps out of this fortuitous planting of

our continent in scattered and independent settlements has arisen the strongest form of government, so far as respects cohesion and self-maintenance, that the world has seen.  Certainly the experience of the last few years, beginning with the civil war, gives plausibility to this idea.

All the consequences of that war have not been equally fortunate with this.  It may be admitted that, in some instances, the influence of a military life on the young men who thronged to our camps was salutary, in bringing out the better qualities of their character and moulding it to a more manly pattern, by overcoming the love of ease and accustoming the soldier to endure suffering and brave danger for the common cause. Yet it is certain that in other men it encouraged brutal instincts which had been held in check by the restraints of a peaceful order of things; that it made them careless of inflicting pain and indifferent to the taking of life.  Accordingly, after the close of the war, crimes of violence became fearfully numerous, men more often carried about deadly weapons, quarrels more often led to homicide, robberies accompanied by assassination were much more frequent, and acts of housebreaking were perpetrated with greater audacity.  It would seem invidious to say that these crimes were most frequent in the region which had been the seat of the war; but it is certain that there the peace was often deplorably disturbed by quarrels between the white race and the colored, which led to bloodshed.  Thus the state of society left by the war may be fairly put to the account of the great error committed in allowing slavery to have a place among our institutions.

But, while men were watching with alarm these offences against the public peace, it was discovered, with no little surprise, that crimes of fraud had become as numerous, and were equally traceable to the war as their cause.  So many opportunities had presented themselves of making easy bargains with the agents of the Government, and so many chances of cheating the Government offered themselves in the haste and confusion with which most transactions of this kind were accomplished, that hundreds of persons, of whom little was known save that they had become suddenly rich, flaunted in all the spendor of exorbitant wealth, and exercised the influence which wealth commands. The encouragement which their success and the mystery with which it was accompanied gave to dishonest dealings was felt throughout the community, and the evil became fearfully contagious. The city of New York was a principal seat of these enormities. In that busy metropolis men are so earnestly occupied with their private affairs, so absorbed in the competitions of business, that it is not easy to fix the attention of the greater proportion, even of the most intelligent, upon matters of public and general interest as long as the chances of individual success are left open. But the boundless waste of those who had possession of the public funds, the sudden increase of the city debt, and the enormous taxation to which the citizens were subjected, at length alarmed the entire community; the tax-payers consulted together; they called in the aid of the most sagacious and resolute men, who with great pains tracked the offenders through all their doublings and laid their practices bare to the public eye. The infamy of those who were concerned in these enormities followed their exposure.

I have already spoken of the contagious nature of these examples of corruption. The determination to effect a reform and drag the offenders to justice, when once awakened, spread with equal rapidity. It is remarkable how, immediately after the exposure of the enormous knaveries committed in New York, the daily journals were filled with accounts of lesser villanies in less considerable places. It seemed for a while as if peculation had been taken up by a large class as a profession, so numerous were the instances of detection. The public vigilance was directed against every person in a pecuniary trust; some who had never before been suspected found themselves suddenly in the custody of the law, and others, fearing that their turn might soon come, prudently ran away. There never has been a time when it was so dangerous for a public man to make a slip in his accounts. Investigation became the order of the day, and a considerable part of the contents of every daily paper consisted of the proceedings of committees formed for examining into the accounts of men who held pecuniary trusts. At first sight, it seemed as if the world had suddenly grown worse; on a second reflection, it was clear that it was growing better. A process of purgation was going on; dishonest men were stripped of the power of doing further mischief and branded with disgrace, and men of whom better hopes were entertained put in their places. The narrative of these iniquities could not properly stop short of the punishment which overtook the offenders, and which, while it makes the lesson of their otherwise worthless lives instructive, vindicates to some extent the character of the nation at large.

In reviewing the history of the last hundred years there is one question which stands out in special prominence: the policy of encouraging domestic manufactures by high duties on goods imported from other countries. It was recommended in the early years of our Republic by Hamilton, whose authority had great weight with a large class of his fellow-citizens; and afterward, under the the name of the American System, was made the battle-cry of a great party under a no less popular leader, Henry Clay. But, after a struggle of many years, during part of which the protective system seemed to have become thoroughly incorporated into our revenue laws, a tendency to freedom of trade began to assert itself. The tariff of duties on imported commodities became from time to time weeded of the provisions which favored particular manufactures, and, although still wanting in simplicity of proceeding, and far more expensive in its execution than it should have been, was in the main liberal, and not unsatisfactory to all parties. The manufacturers had ceased from the struggle for special duties, and seemed content with those which were laid merely for the sake of revenue. The question of protection was no longer a matter of controversy.

But the war revived the old quarrel, and left it a legacy to the years which are yet to come. When the Southern members at the beginning of the war withdrew from Congress, there were found, among those whom they left in their seats, a majority who had been educated in the Henry Clay school of politics, and were therefore attached to the protective system. In laying taxes to supply the necessities of the Treasury, they enacted a tariff of duties more rigidly restrictive and of more general application than the country had ever before known. This opened again the whole controversy. The struggle of forty years, which had ended as we have already related, is revived under circumstances which strongly imply that we have the same ground to go over again. The manufacturers are not likely to give up without a struggle what they believe so essential to their prosperity, and the friends of free trade, proverbially tenacious of their purposes, are not likely to be satisfied while there is left in the texture of our revenue laws a single thread of protection which their ingenuity can detect or their skill can draw out.

The history of our Republic shows that a nation does not always profit by its own experience, even though it be of an impressive nature. Our Government began the first century of its existence with a resort to paper money, and closed it with repeating the expedient. In the first of these instances slips of paper with a peculiar stamp were made to pass as money by the authority of Congress, and were known by the name of Continental money, which soon became a term of opprobrium. The history of this currency is a sad one—a history of creditors defrauded, families reduced from competence to poverty, and ragged and hunger-bitten soldiers who were paid their wages in bits of paper scarcely worth more than the coarse material on which their nominal value was stamped. The more of this Continental money was issued, the lower it sank in value. The whole land was filled with discontent, and the leaders of the Revolution were in the utmost perplexity. The injustice inflicted and the distress occasioned by this policy are not merely recorded in our annals; there are many persons yet living who have heard of them in their youth at the fire-sides of their fathers.

Eighty years afterward, in the midst of our late civil war, when the necessity of raising money for the daily expenses of maintaining and moving our large armies from place to place upon the vast theatre of our war began to press somewhat severely upon our Government, the question was again raised whether the government notes should not be made a legal tender in the payment of debts, and the Treasury relieved from the necessity of providing for their redemption in coin. The Secretary of the Treasury applied to some of the most eminent bankers and men of business, English and American, for their opinions. Certain of the wisest of these vehemently dissuaded him from a resort to paper money. They pointed to the dis-asters which experience had shown to have invariably attended the measure, and urged him to trust to the loyalty of the coun-try, of which he had seen such gratifying proofs already given, for obtaining the necessary supplies of money for the war. This could be done by issuing debentures payable at a some-what distant date, and for such moderate sums as persons of moderate means could conveniently take. At all events, they urged that the expedient of resorting to paper money should be postponed till every other was tried and the necessity for it became imminent and unavoidable. These wise counsels were not followed. Others had given their opinion that a resort to paper money was unavoidable, and, after some hesitation, it was resolved to take the step immediately. The moment that the project was brought before Congress it found eager cham-pions, both on the floor of the two chambers and in the lob-bies; for, whenever a measure is proposed which involves a change of nominal values, there spring up in unexpected quar-ters hundreds of patriotic persons to assist in hurrying it through Congress. The Government was relieved of the obli-gation of paying its notes; but a solemn pledge was given that they should be paid at the earliest practicable moment. While the war lasted, we went on making issue after issue of these notes, with no provision for their payment. Meantime, the prices of every commodity rose, and with them the expenses of the war—and speculation flourished.

For eight years after the war no approach had been made toward the fulfilment of the solemn pledge of which I have spoken, although in that time many millions of the national debt had been paid off in our depreciated currency. So vast was the mass of promises to pay, and so small the accumulations of gold within the reach of the Government, that not one of those who within that period administered the Treasury Department ventured to propose any plan for returning to specie payments, but, averting his eyes from the difficulty, allowed our finances to drift toward an uncertain future. Then came the panic of 1873, which swept so many large banking and commercial houses to their ruin. Immediately a loud call was heard for a new issue of paper money from those who fancied that they saw in the measure a remedy for their own pecuniary embarrassments. The question was hotly debated in Congress; a majority of both Houses was found to be in its favor; the pledge which bound the country to return to specie payments was scouted, as given in ignorance of the true interests of the country; and a bill was passed adding, as President Grant observed in his message, a hundred millions to our depreciated currency. Fortunately for the country, he sent back the bill with his objections, and it failed to become a law; else the mischiefs and disasters of the days of Continental money might have returned upon us, with a violence proportioned to the growth which our commercial interests had in the meantime attained.

It is not likely that this question will again be raised in our day, and the bitter experience which we have had of the mischiefs of paper money in these two instances will remain as a warning to the coming times; though who shall say with any confidence that the warning will be duly heeded? But there is another controversy bequeathed to us by the late civil war, which will probably lead to acrimonious and protracted disputes, and perhaps be made, to some extent, the basis of party divisions.   Of that I would now speak.

Before the war the boundaries of the powers assigned to the national Government, and those which remained with the several States, were pretty sharply defined by usage, and attempts were but rarely made to go beyond them.   The leaders of opinion in the Southern States deemed it necessary, to the security and permanence of slavery, that any encroachment of the national Government on the rights reserved to the States should be resisted to the utmost; and it must be admitted that, although many of them pushed the claim of State sovereignty to an absurd extent, they did good service in keeping the eyes of the people fixed upon that limit beyond which, under our Constitution, the national Government has neither function nor power.   When the civil war broke out it was apparent that the majority of those who remained in Congress had not been trained to be scrupulous on this point. One of their early measures—the creation of a system of national banks—would, twenty years before, have been regarded by a majority of the people of the United States as a direct violation of the Constitution.   Other measures were adopted in the course of the war for which it was impossible to find any authority in the Constitution, and of which the sole justification was military necessity.   As compared with the state of opinion which prevailed before the war, it is manifest that a certain indifference to the distinction between the Federal power and that of the States has been creeping into our politics.   Schemes for accumulating power in the Government at Washington by making it the owner of our railways, for administering telegraphic communication by Federal agency, for cutting canals between river and river, and for an extensive system of national education with a central bureau at Washington—show this tendency.   These and kindred projects will most certainly give ample occasion for protracted disputes on the floor of Congress and in the daily press.   On one hand will be urged, and plausibly, the public convenience; and on the other the danger lest our government of nicely balanced powers should degenerate into a mere form, and the proper functions of the States be absorbed into the central authority —a fate like that predicted by some astronomers for our solar system, when the orbs that revolve about the sun, describing narrower and narrower circles, shall fall into the central luminary, to be incorporated with it forever.

In looking over this vast array of important questions settled, and of new ones just arising on the field of vision, it is difficult to resist the conclusion that the historian of our Republic would perform his office but in part who should stop short of the cycle of a hundred years from the birth of our nation. In that period great interests have been disposed of and laid aside forever; with the next hundred years we have a new era with new responsibilities, which we are to meet with what wisdom we may. It is matter of rejoicing that among the latest events of this first century, and following close upon our great civil war, we are able to record a great triumph of the cause of peace and civilization in the settlement of our collateral quarrel with Great Britain—a quarrel which in other times might easily have been nursed into a war. Let us hope that this example will be followed by all the nations of the earth in their future controversies.

# INDEX.

THE END.